The Secrets for Motivating, Educating, and Lifting the Spirit of African American Males

The Secrets for Motivating, Educating, and Lifting the Spirit of African American Males

Ernest H. Johnson, Ph.D. and the Champions for Peace Mastermind Institute

iUniverse, Inc.
Bloomington

The Secrets for Motivating, Educating, and Lifting the Spirit of African
American Males

iUniverse books may be ordered through booksellers or by contacting:

iUniverse
1663 Liberty Drive
Bloomington, IN 47403
www.iuniverse.com
1-800-Authors (1-800-288-4677)

ISBN: 978-1-4620-4642-3 (sc)
ISBN: 978-1-4620-4644-7 (hc)
ISBN: 978-1-4620-4643-0 (ebk)

Printed in the United States of America

iUniverse rev. date: 11/07/2011

CONTENTS

Dedicated to the dreams of Dr. Martin Luther King, Jr., Medgar Evers determination, Malcolm's fierce wisdom, and the promises and prayers for a better world that were stirred up within us from our memory of Jerome (Jerry) Franson who laid the groundwork for our coming together at a place in the mountains called The North Carolina Center for the Advancement of Teaching (NCCAT)!

We are also thankful to Pia Forbes for her editorial assistance during the initial stages of this book. Her encouragement, insightful criticisms, and endless patience enabled us to make this a better book.

Preface

All Black boys have dreams . . . They want to believe that deep down in their souls that they have a special gift, that they can make a difference, that they can touch others in some special way, and that they can have an impact on the world. At one time in their lives, they had a vision about the life they desired. Yet, for many, those dreams have become so shrouded in the frustrations and routines of being a student in an unfriendly environment that they no longer make an effort to even think about their dreams. For far too many, the dreams have dissipated because of the persistent ways that society has conditioned (brainwashed) them to see themselves as weak, not smart, undeserving, and not capable of being anything other than a burden to society. In 1933, Dr. Carter G. Woodson proclaimed, "No people can go forward when the majority of those who should know better have chosen to go backward."[1] More than 75 years later, the education situation for Black males in America shows that less than half who start high school graduate within four years, and students in low-income, urban schools only have a 50 percent chance of having a qualified math or science teacher.[2,3] To say that it is difficult, challenging, unfair or traumatic to be a Black male in America is an understatement. The Black boy sitting in your classroom or living room is the result of over 200 years of conditioning (brainwashing) using the power of words and images to shift, shape, and change his consciousness so that he will see himself as inferior to his white peers. The magnitude of brainwashing has been so thorough that even today, as was the case over fifty years ago in a study to demonstrate children's internalization of racism, when young

Black children are given an opportunity to choose a doll that is good, smart, and the one they want to be like, they choose the white doll over the black doll.[4,5,6]

The most recent "doll test" was conducted in Harlem in 2005 by 17-year-old film student Kiri Davis of Manhattan's Urban Academy who participates in the Reel Works Teen Filmmaking program, a after-school program supported by cable network *HBO*. What is amazing is that more than a half-century after the doll test was used by psychologists Kenneth Clark and his wife Mamie Phipps Clark, to help make the case for desegregation in the landmark *Brown v. Board of Education* Supreme Court decision that outlawed segregated public schools, the results of the 2005 doll test were virtually identical.[7] In essence, the majority (fifteen of twenty-one) of black children said they would rather play with the white doll. Most said the white doll was nicer than the black doll, and nearly half of the black children said the white doll looked most like them.

It is amazing that four decades after the 'Black Is Beautiful' mantra of the 1960s and James Brown's chart-topper, 'I'm Black and I'm Proud,' some African Americans still believe that black is not beautiful. Even today, black children are bombarded and brainwashed with images every day on television screens, magazines, newspapers, websites—images that reflect self-hatred and the believe that to be black is inferior to being white. Regardless of the jobs I have held or the directions my career has taken me, my life mission has been to empower young Black males to rebuild their lives so they can restore their dreams. In addition, for some Black males, including myself at times, the work to restore dreams and ambitions has been similar to what a surgeon goes through to remove a cancerous tumor that has spread. Even though it looks like you have removed the last bit of the brainwashed thinking and beliefs, problems popup in other areas of life because of the deep nature of the emotional wounds from being brainwashed.

I will never forget the Thursday night it really hit me that I was instrumental in bringing together a group of African American male educators who were committed to working with young African American males. As we started the teleconference call, I suddenly realized that there were over twenty Black men on the telephone. At the time, my life was focused on how I was going to come up with meaningful topics for the seminars and workshops I was organizing for teachers and parents in North Carolina. I had recently moved from the busy urban life of Atlanta to a small rural college town that had few amenities. I felt frustrated and alone, but on that Thursday evening, as the men begin to talk about themselves and their work, I thought about the impact that we could have on teachers (parents, counselors, clergy, etc.) if we continued to work together. I had dreams of us working together back then, but at that time, it seemed like they would never be realized. Today, I have come to believe that all my past frustrations and challenges were actually laying the foundation for the interdependent and fruitful relationships that I have with the Black men who are members of our Champions for Peace Leadership and Mastermind Institute. I have been blessed to have many colleagues (brothers) in my life who have served as beacon lights to guide me on difficult roads. In our own way, each of us, have overcome enormous odds to reap the benefits of a solid education. We have depended on each other to remain focused and have encouraged each other to seek excellence without excuse. We understand that education is the key to success and that success is a journey not a destination. In addition, as our nation struggles to devise effective strategies to reach Black males, we are unwilling to sit on the sidelines while Black boys and their teachers (and parents) work to overcome many of the obstacles we have successfully mastered in order to live our dreams.

The Secrets for Motivating, Educating, and Lifting the Spirit of African American Males contains essays, each written by Black male educators, who resound the same truth: By cultivating a deep inner awareness, teachers and parents can stir in the minds of young Black males the desire to develop the drive and motivation necessary to create happy and fulfilling lives. This book is about what teachers, parents, mentors, and counselors can do to heal the minds of young Black males who have been brainwashed into a mindset of inferiority where they believe education will not provide value to their lives or guarantee them a better position in the larger society.

You might ask yourself, why Black males refuse to accept the educational challenges put forth by a society that prides itself on the strides it has made to provide equal opportunities for everyone. Similar to the glass ceiling many women have had to contend with, for young Black males, at one time in history, there was a window into the future that many faced when entering school. The window was solidly built, but dirty and smudged up from unfair discriminatory practices that barely provided Black children with decent books or teachers who were adequately compensated. With strong soap and water, the window could be cleaned up so that the view of Black males by their teachers was crisp. You could see Black males as vividly as you could see a smile on the face of a baby. The school was old and run-down, but the glass was clean and the windowpane was unbroken. Teachers had high expectations about what they wanted from Black males, and Black males wanted what their teachers had to offer them. No surprises and nothing was unexpected. Teachers knew that Black males had a will to learn, and they continually discovered ways to motivate them to learn more. Then, suddenly, the window cracked. A rock broke the window. Perhaps the rock struck when you were a child and still learning about the world around you and the people you could trust. Maybe the rock hit in adolescence when a Black boy disrespected you and your best friend.

Maybe you made it into college on your way to be a teacher before the window was cracked. Was it the growing awareness that you and people around you treated Black males differently? Was it the heightened anxiety you had about interacting with Black males? Was it your growing awareness that our culture typically depicts Black males as being angry and unworthy of being trusted?

Maybe you made it into adulthood before the rock crashed through the window. Was it the fear you experienced on that stormy night when a Black man suddenly appeared on that lonely highway while you were waiting with your car for the tow truck?

Maybe you made it into your career as a teacher or school counselor before the window was cracked. Was it the anxieties you experienced knowing that you had Black boys in your classroom? Was it the uncertainty you had talking to Black parents about their sons' schoolwork? Was it the end of year report showing that Black boys at your school were falling behind other students? For many of us, the rock struck as our nation was dealing with its anxieties and doubts about whether a Harvard educated African American male, Barack H. Obama, could be an effective president.

Whatever the rock's form, the result was the same—a shattered window with cracks that shot from the point of impact, creating a spider web of fragmented pieces. And suddenly, it was not easy to see Black boys. The crisp view became distorted. It was hard to see Black males through the pain and anguish they experienced or the stereotype created by a society that pretends to accept them but treats them as outcast. Educators from every corner of the US continued to look for that familiar view of Black males, but all that was left was the fragmented pieces of their futures and the anguish associated with being denied a quality education.

The moment the rock struck, the window became a reference point. From then on, there was life before the break and life after the break. Before the rock shattered the window, the view of Black males was clear. After the break, Black males were harder to see. They seemed angry, distant, unmotivated, not interested in school, and harder to understand. And now you (teachers, parents, school counselors, and clergy) aren't quite sure what you see. At times, you see a ray of hope in the battle to disarm stereotypes about the intellectual capabilities of Black males, but then you realize that being educated at Harvard, like president Obama, or any university is a remote possibility for Black males who seem unmotivated to learn and destined to dropout of school and add to the financial burden of our nation—becoming a tax eater rather than a wage earning tax payer.

Maybe these words don't describe your situation as a teacher, mentor, counselor, member of the clergy or parent. There are some people who never have to redefine or refocus their view of Black males. However, most of us are not so fortunate.

Each of the authors recognizes the immense pressure teachers are facing to close the achievement gap between Black boys and their peers. Whatever school district you look at, African American boys are at the bottom. While each chapter in this book is unique, each chapter is ultimately about what educators (and parents) can do to have empowering relationships with African American males. More than any other factor, we believe that it is the presence of caring and qualified teachers that is the most important factor in the education of African American males. But we also recognize that the level of brainwashing (mental conditioning to see themselves negatively) that Black males have experienced has been so intense that it will take a team of Black male professionals working along side of teachers and parents to have a meaningful impact.

The Secret for Motivating, Educating, and Lifting The Spirit of African American Males provides the seeds that we want to plant in the hearts of those responsible for educating Black boys so that they can uplift Black males and ease some of the suffering in the Black community and the world-at-large. While the essays in *The Secret for Motivating, Educating and Lifting The Spirit of African American Males* focus on Black males, the strategies and techniques can apply to all children who have difficulties seeing beyond the mental and emotional imprisonment of poverty, low social class, and coming from homes where education is not valued. This book is about the interconnectedness we share and the healing that will occur in our world when no children are left behind or denied their human rights to a quality education. The economic and social costs to our nation are outrageously high when a child, regardless of their ethnicity or race, drops out of school because we failed to help them discover the value of receiving a good education. When we recognize that it is our money that is paying for the high cost of dropout and juvenile delinquency, then we might be more willing to deal with the fact that these are our children. They might be from an ethnic or racial group that is different from our own and their parents might be poor and not well educated, but all of these children who are falling through the cracks in our education system belong to us.

Ernest H. Johnson, Ph.D.
Durham, North Carolina
Champions for Peace Leadership
and Mastermind Institute
www.championsforpeace.net

Editor's Introduction
Answering the Call for Help

By Ernest H. Johnson

It's a hot during the afternoon when Wanda, the mother of two boys, James, almost twelve, and Cedric fourteen, arrives home from her early morning shift at the local clothing warehouse. She gathers her mail, mostly notices for overdue bills, and quickly opens the letter from the school James attends. She is not surprised that it's another troubling letter from one of his teachers about the slow academic progress James is making in the sixth grade. She can barely stop herself from weeping as she reads that James will probably have to repeat sixth grade. Wanda worries about her youngest son's future. As she continues to read, she becomes momentarily hopeful when the teacher states, "I believe that James is more capable than his failing grades reflect." Whatever hope there was soon disappears and transforms into rage when Wanda realizes that the teacher who sent the letter is the same white woman, fresh out of college, who claims that since she took some Black history courses in college, she understands how to reach Black boys like James. Upon further reflection, she also realizes this is the same teacher James has been complaining about because she reprimands him for speaking out of turn in class while she ignores the same behavior from the white children.

Walking through the living room, Wanda angrily glances at Cedric, who is comfortably sitting on the sofa watching television and playing video games when he should be at school. Instead, he was facing his third suspension from school for fighting and mandated to start seeing a therapist before he can return to school. Cedric doesn't say much when his mother enters the room because he knows that she is angry about him missing school. Wanda doesn't say much because she is upset and has only a few minutes to change clothes before leaving for work at her second job. But once she settles into her bedroom, her silent weeping turns into a deep soulful wrenching cry, "Lord, what can I do to help my boys get a good education when the people teaching them don't know a damn thing about Black boys?" Like so many single parents, Wanda believes that God does not hear her cry for help, and she finds herself desperately worrying about the future prospects for her two sons. She feels angry with her two boys and guilty because she does not have access to the resources to teach them how to navigate through the obstacles Black boys must face.

While Wanda is attempting to get a little rest before leaving for her second job, James' teacher, Carolyn Whitlock, is sitting alone in her office at the end of a long day. She is tired, hungry, and anxiously looking through a stack of papers and preparing herself to make phone calls to the parents of some of her students. Information about James is at the top of the stack. After reviewing his academic file, she realizes that his mother has not responded to either of her letters. Looking through the file, she notices that none of his other teachers have ever taken the time to talk with or meet with Miss Wanda Harris, but all made comments about James being a potentially bright student. She too has noticed how readily James grasp concepts, even though it seems that he spends little or no time preparing his homework or doing his reading assignments. Carolyn gathers herself and has a quiet contemplative moment wherein she questions herself, "I wonder how it would feel to be a Black boy like James? Would I hate school because I am never recognized as one of the smart children? How would I feel if I had problems at home and yet my teachers still expected me to do well? How would I feel knowing that my friends would consider me a wimp if I allowed a teacher to convince me to do well in school? How would I feel coming home to a family without a father? How would I feel sitting in school knowing that getting an education might not offer me any possibilities for a life better than what I could have hustling on the streets? How would I feel, day after day after day, thinking that what I did in school did not matter, except when I did something wrong?" They are tough questions for Carolyn to answer and she contemplates how she would feel about herself after seven or eight years of failure in school, a place that was supposed to prepare you for life.

Carolyn is at a loss about how to reach James, but she knows that she has to say more to his mother than, "You need to encourage James to do better in school." And she knows that it is well past time that the two of them meet, face to face, to talk things through. Carolyn mutters to herself aloud, "Why can't I get a break and have students that are motivated to do this work and create a meaningful life for themselves?" As she starts dialing the phone number, contemplating what to say while feeling frustrated, she realizes that requesting his removal from her class, although not in his best interest, might be in the best interest of the class. She knows that sending him to the assistant principal may work temporarily or that keeping him after school could also offer some relief, but unlike many other teachers, she wants to teach him, reach him, and engage him in the pursuit of learning. "What am I to do . . . how can I help this boy if he does not seem interested in school? I've tried everything I know. I don't know how to get his attention or to make him more interested in school, but I know if I give up on him, then he might never develop an appreciation for school." The thoughts are running through her mind when a woman sounding more asleep than awake answers the phone and says, "Hello . . . hello there . . . this is Wanda, how I can help you?" After a long silence, Carolyn replies, "Hello, Miss Harris, this is Carolyn Whitlock, your son's teacher. I'm so glad that I caught you at home. We need to talk about James." After a long silence, she continues, "As you know, James is a brilliant student, one of the best in my class, but he is not doing his homework or passing his exams. I need your help, and I want you to help me find the best way to motivate James. He's smart and has potential to go to college. Is this a good time for us to talk? I would like to setup a time where we can meet, face to face, and figure out what we are going to do. I need your help."

After a long silence filled with anxieties and uncertainties, Wanda replied, "That's all you are going to say. I was waiting for you to say something bad, something about kicking him out of school for good. You mean you are calling to talk about helping my boy. If you are, then you are the first teacher to call me, and I thank the Lord for your help. I know he is a smart boy, and I don't want to see him end up like so many other Black boys. Yes, I want to help my boy. I just don't know what to do. I'm so glad you called."

This scene is typical for so many single Black mothers raising boys, and, unfortunately, most teachers will wait until the problem is more severe to make the phone call. In doing so, they increase the odds that the boy will become rebellious, disengaged, dropout, and eventually have problems finding employment and experience difficulties assuming adulthood responsibilities. Regardless of the statistics you examine, single mothers (or grandmothers or aunts) are raising most Black males. The majority of Black boys will receive the bulk of their academic instruction from white females, many of whom are fresh out of college and don't understand the psychosocial complexities associated with motivating Black boys to excel academically. Most Black males attend schools where a larger percentage of students are considered poor and too many of their teachers lack the necessary qualifications to teach certain courses. Their schools will have computers and other technology, but few students will have an opportunity to integrate technology into their lesson plans because the supply of computers is insufficient, outdated, or inoperable. The dropout rate is over fifty percent for Black boys, and a larger proportion of Black men are incarcerated or on probation or parole than other groups. The odds of a Black boy graduating from high school are less than fifty percent, and only nine out of a 100 Black boys will attend college. Of those nine who start college, only three will graduate. In essence, hard working Black mothers like Wanda know the odds are against their Black boys yet they strive to keep their sons in school and working toward goals that could provide them a way out of poverty.[1,2,3,4,5,6]

Bombarded with stories about the ill effects of the lack of positive male role models, Black mothers like Wanda feel guilty and ashamed because of their inability to prepare their sons to deal with the devastating emotional and developmental effects of being raised by a single mother. They have read articles and watched television programs about the influence of rap and Hip hop music on gang membership and violence. Black mothers, like Wanda, know all of the things society says are "wrong" about being Black and male in America, but they have not been offered many solutions for helping their sons successfully navigate through the complexities associated with acquiring the one thing, a sound education, that makes it possible for them to have a chance for a better life. To a certain extent, the challenges Black parents, most often single mothers, have raising their sons are also reflected in the difficulties teachers, most often white females, have motivating Black boys to live up to their real capabilities.

Teachers like Carolyn Whitlock know that her classes in college did not prepare her to deal with the issues like those she is facing with James and other students in her classes. She can plan lessons, outline a semester, create seemingly exciting and original approaches to most subjects, but she does not know how to reach young Black males who dare not trust another white teacher. For the most part, Black males are not troublemakers. They prefer, instead, to become invisible, rather than seek a meaningful and purposeful life at school. What is a teacher like Carolyn to do, knowing the research states that reaching a young Black male by his early teen years (middle school) is the last best chance to get him interested in school? After the early teen years, their paths are often set toward self-destructive acts, such as addiction, violence, criminal behavior, and dropping out of school.

Patience, kindness, and gentleness are among the greatest virtues a teacher can show toward her students, but sometimes Black boys believe they are signs of weakness. It takes great resolve to love someone who has been unlovable, disrespectful, and has done everything to ruin the atmosphere for learning in your classroom. It also takes great strength for a teacher to model the behavioral and emotional reactions she wants for her students when she feels hurt and disrespected.

Loving Black boys requires openheartedness and the moral courage reflected by the lifework of Dr. Martin Luther King, Jr. It requires a teacher to make a fundamental choice to act with kindness, encouragement, and charity and to reorganize her thinking and her classroom in ways that are consistent with loving all their students. Teachers like Carolyn, if they are to thrive in these changing times, will need to learn that their commitment to loving their students, including the Black males, will give them the courage and conviction to provide each of their students with the best education possible. While today's teachers may not make the enormous personal sacrifices that Dr. King made, they, too, must search their souls to discover what choosing to love all students (regardless of the race, ethnicity, poverty status, reading and math ability, or religion) will mean in their lives. I hope that they will come to the conclusion that, no matter how horrible a students' attitude may be, negativity is diminished in the light of love that radiates from their classrooms.

What is a teacher like Carolyn to do about the Black boys who believe she doesn't like them because their behavior requires her to act as disciplinarian? What is she to do about the Black boys who submit to pressures from peers that prevent them from paying attention in class? What about the ones who have to maintain such a tough imagine that they can't afford to participate in a class discussion about nonviolent approaches to handling conflict? What is a parent like Wanda to do when she feels the need to trust teachers like Carolyn, but questions whether her son's teachers have the knowledge and experience to show a Black boy how to be successful in life? Ideally, the means for answering these and other questions should be part of the continuing education process that all teachers receive, but for the most part, our system of education leaves the decision for seeking out continuing education up to the teachers. And figuring out effective ways to reach, teach, and motivate Black boys seems to be at the bottom of the list. Oftentimes, teachers are provided with the "one shot" rushed approach to professional development usually occurring at the end of a busy school day when most teachers are exhausted, hungry, frustrated, and ready to go home. Very little learning occurs under these conditions. And what little learning that does occur is often lost because the focus tends to be on the exchange of information rather than ways to implement and evaluate techniques for reaching, teaching, and motivating Black males. Consequently, teachers like Carolyn and mothers like Wanda are often left with the choice of seeking answer to their questions through friends, colleagues, books, and clergy.

This book is vastly different from most others in that it reflects the collective wisdom and advice of a group of Black male educators who are currently working directly with young Black males or providing training for teachers, parents, and counselors. While our focus is on Black males, most solutions are based on good parenting and educational practices and could also be considered in educating and lifting the spirits of young Black girls.

This book pulls together the views of Black men from different disciplinary backgrounds and perspectives to explore new ways to address an issue of national debate: the underachievement of Black males in our public schools. Similar books prepared by university professors, philosophers, cultural critics or a Black male author/educator working solo, while contributing important insights about the problems facing Black males, have neglected to address the people (teachers who are most likely white females) most involved in the raising and shaping of young Black males.

Our approach to working with educators took root at The North Carolina Center for the Advancement of Teaching (NCCAT). For over 25 years, the state of North Carolina has supported the center, which was born from the idea of North Carolina's 1983 Teacher of the Year, Jean Powell. Ms. Powell sought out opportunities to speak with legislators and the governor about her ideas for attracting and retaining the best teachers. She thought it was necessary to "provide a time and place for teachers to go, a few days of residential study, to become enthusiastic about learning again so that they could pass this enthusiasm on to their students." The North Carolina governor and legislators at the time were enthusiastic about this idea and three years later NCCAT was born.

Many of us became familiar with NCCAT after receiving a call from a man by the name of Jerome "Jerry" Franson, whom we would later learn was one of God's special messengers. For me, the call from Jerry came in 1997, and it was quite simple: He wanted me to come to the mountains of western North Carolina to do a session about how unexpressed anger contributed to poor relationships between Black males and their teachers. Once he began to describe the weeklong in-residence seminar, called *Young, Black, and Male in America (YMBA)* I experienced a sense of both relief and excitement. He insisted that my involvement would provide the "psychological glue" needed to hold together the many approaches and solutions offered for helping young Black males succeed.

To my surprise, in 1998, I found myself, like the other contributors to this book, being drawn to the mission of NCCAT and being a regular part of the team of presenters for the YBMA seminar. I joined the NCCAT faculty in 2002, after Jerry's death, and my main role has been to develop weeklong seminar experiences that help teachers overcome the barriers they face in motivating and educating African American children, particularly males. Being part of a small team of Black male presenters was quite enriching, but things took on a new perspective when I joined the NCCAT faculty. After Jerry's death, the number of Black males who were interested in helping to provide professional development training for the YBMA seminar skyrocketed. After a year or so of hearing the views of many presenters, we implemented a Thursday evening teleconference, where there can be ten to twenty-five Black male educators on the conference call. The idea for the book emerged from our teleconference calls and our need to expand our audience to include a larger number of educators, parents, mentors, and school counselors with ways to educate, motivate and lift the spirits of Black males.

Summary of Our Work at NCCAT

Since connecting with NCCAT in 1998, we have been involved with 30 in-residence seminar experiences where 660 teachers, most often white females, have received benefits from our expertise. Before we turn you loose on the chapters in this book, we want to summarize the evaluation data that was gathered from some of the educators who attended either the "Young, Black and Male in America" or the "Best Practices for Motivating African American Children" seminars conducted at NCCAT from 2003 thought 2005.[7] Participation for both seminars is limited to teams of two members from the same school—a classroom teacher and a principal, assistant principal, school counselor, or social worker. As a result, 14 percent of the participants were Principals/Assistant Principals, 35 percent were School Counselors, and 51 percent were classroom teachers. The majority of teachers were age 50 or greater (56%), while 26% were younger than 39. The majority of the participants were Caucasian (65%). Although the sample for the evaluation was small (39 educators), the demographic profile reflects the population of teachers who have attended the seminars over the past 25 years.

Questions for the study were derived from the larger NCCAT impact survey but were modified to reflect the interest areas.[7] The items were then reviewed by three faculty members to determine whether the content of the individual items were consistent with the constructs being measured.

The final questionnaire consisted of 45 items which required the educators to respond using a 5-point Likert-type scale (1-Never, 2-Hardly Ever, 3-Some of the Time, 4-Most of the Time, and 5-Always). Responses to items falling in the Never and Hardly Ever categories were combined for several of the individual items because of the low frequency that participants selected these choices. The data on the following pages represent some of the highlights of the evaluation and the responses to all questions are available upon request. Responses to items falling in the Some of the Time, Most of the Time, and Always categories were combined.

The data in Table 1 shows that, overall, the majority of educators (over 90%) indicated that the experience increased their capacity to make lessons plans more appealing to African American Males (Question #4) and that they acquired knowledge to promote self-esteem and to help Black boys feel good about themselves and their educational experiences (Question #8; Question #26; Question #30). Following the seminar experience, teachers designed strategies for motivating African American students (Question #9) and helped their peers (Question #36) develop strategies. The responses to Question #25 and Question #44 indicate that following the seminar experience, teachers felt more comfortable talking to African American students about their culture. The responses also indicate that their relationship with their African American students improved as a result of their experiences with us at NCCAT. Finally, the responses to Question #45 indicated that the teachers felt excited, energized, renewed, and more ready to teach African American males how to cope with life as a result of their NCCAT seminar experiences.

Table 1: Responses To Questions From The NCCAT Impact Survey

- Question 4: 90 percent of the teachers had acquired knowledge and skills about how to make their lesson plans more appealing to African American males.

- Question 7: 98 percent of the teachers learned how to build on students' culture in classroom instruction and activities as a result of their NCCAT seminar experience.

- Question 8: 100 percent of the teachers acquired knowledge from the seminar they use to promote high self-esteem among African American students.

- Question 9: 95 percent of the teachers designed strategies for motivating African American students based on the content of their seminar.

- Questions 25: 98 percent of the teachers reported improvements in their relationships with African American students because of the seminar experience.

- Question 26: 97 percent of the teachers acquired insights from the seminar that helped them to better motivate African American students to be interested in school.

- Question 30: 98 percent of the teachers acquired knowledge from the seminar they use to help African American students feel good about themselves.

- Question 36: 89 percent of the teachers helped their peers to design strategies for motivating African American students based on the content of their seminar.
- Question 39: 100 percent of the teachers acquired knowledge from their seminar experience to help them not to prejudge a student's performance based on cultural differences or socioeconomic status.
- Question 44: 93 percent of the teachers felt more comfortable talking to African American males about their culture as a result of the seminar.
- Question 45: 95 percent of the teachers felt excited and ready to teach African American males about how to cope with life.

We were also interested in whether the teachers had successfully implemented some of the strategies they learned about during the NCCAT seminar. The data in Table 2 shows that the majority of teachers (65%) made some changes in the "atmosphere" of the classroom because of their participation in the seminar. A large percentage (61%) also used additional books and resources written by African American scholars or used classroom and school-wide poetry writing and storytelling presentations (53%) as a way to get the attention of African American students. Whereas a smaller percentage of teachers created mentoring program (37%) or critical thinking clubs (18%), such as chess or debate, it should be noted that the majority of the educators were white females, many of them over age 50. Finally, when asked to estimate the number of African American students who benefited from their participation in the NCCAT seminars, the sample of 39 teachers indicated that, on average, 79 African American students, most of them male, benefited. Therefore, approximate 3,081 African American children derived some benefits from having their teachers attend either the "Young, Black and Male in America" or "Best Practices for Motivating African American Children" seminar. The "Young, Black and Male in American" seminar has been conducted once a year for the past sixteen years, while the Best Practices seminar has been conducted eight times. The total number of times that both seminars have been conducted is 24 with 24 teachers in attendance. In short, 576 teachers have had an opportunity to learn about strategies for motivating and educating African American males. Using our data from the pilot study, which indicated that 79 African American students benefit from the teachers participation in the NCCAT seminar experience, we estimate that over the past fifteen years, 45,504 African American students in the state of North Carolina have derived some benefit from having their teachers attend the seminars at NCCAT. While we have no way to determine the exact nature of this impact, we are actively exploring possibilities for conducting a large scale research project to uncover the full extent that teachers, mostly white females, have on the academic practices of Black males.

Table 2: Strategies Started After The NCCAT Seminar Experience
What strategies did you put in place at your school for motivating or educating African American students?

- 65 percent of the teachers changed the classroom atmosphere— knowing all students names within a few days; standing ovations for good work; eye contact; greetings; assigned African American students important roles in classroom lessons; diversity reflected through posters and pictures of current African American leaders, having African American parents and speakers in classroom, etc.
- 61 percent of the teachers acquired additional books and resources written by African Americans—made recommendation about books that should be in the school library/media center; invited African American speakers for school wide presentations.
- 53 percent of the teachers created poetry or storytelling competitions as a way to increase interest in writing and reading; stated a hip hop history club.
- 37 percent of the teachers created Mentoring Programs for African American students.
- 18 percent of the teachers created programs that focused on critical thinking skills—started a chess, debate, law or photography club for African American students; encouraged African American students to join the science club.
- 21 percent of the teachers implemented other activities like cooperative learning teams where all students have opportunities to feel included and important as a classroom leader.

How many African American students would you estimate have benefited over the past year from your NCCAT experience?

On average, the educators estimate that 79 African American students benefited from their experience. Therefore, we estimate that nearly 3,081 African American children in the state of North Carolina benefited in positive ways as a result of having 39 educators participate in either the "Young, Black and Male in America" or "Best Practices for Motivating African American Children" seminar. Given that we have provide professional development services to 660 teachers, we can then estimate that 52,140 African American children in North Carolina have received some benefit since the team of African American male educators have been assisting with the 5-day in-residence seminar conducted at The North Carolina Center for the Advancement of Teaching.

In conclusion, we believe that these data show that exposing teachers to strategies about the best ways to motivate and educate African American students has been highly effective in motivating teachers, most of whom are white females, to implement some of the strategies in their classroom and to share what they have learned with their peers. We also believe that there are two elements that made this possible: (1) teachers having an opportunity to spend an entire week, in residence, with a team of highly qualified trainers who provided the teachers with ample opportunities to learn how to implement strategies, and (2) exposing teachers to African American males who are experts in helping educators, mentors, counselors, and parents motivate African American males. The richness of this later point is reflected by the following comment from a teacher in one of the recent seminars. "I know you to told us that the week would be inspirational, emotional, and loaded with information, but having all of these sessions with Black men has changed the way I see the boys I'm going back home to teach. Spending a week like this is invaluable to teachers like me (white women) who are out of touch with young Black men . . . but having this opportunity to learn from and interact with you and the other men have given me hope and encouragement for making a real impact on the Black boys I teach. The first thing I'm doing when I get back to home is to start an afterschool mentoring and reading club. I've got to standup and become the great teacher I think that I am."

Overview Of The Book

The book is comprised of fifteen chapters, plus an epilogue, each prepared by Black male educators who have done extensive training with teachers and parents concerning the topics covered within the chapter. Our mission is to enhance educational achievement and improve the quality of life for children and young adults, and their families. We aim also to assist all educators who are interested in learning about the most effective ways to motivate, educate, enhance resiliency, empower youth to become financially literate, reduce high-risk behaviors, and lift the spirit of children and young adults. We seek to serve as a beacon of change by utilizing our diverse talents to motivate African American males to achieve academic success, make healthy lifestyle choices, and to become self-sufficient shareholders in the social, economic, and spiritual fabric of the communities in which they reside. Also, we are committed to empowering children and young adults to appreciate the value of entrepreneurship and how business and networking in the US and abroad can enhances their future.

The first chapter, "Why Focus on Black Males?" prepared by Mychal Wynn, provides an overview of the challenges Black males encounter in education, maturation, college matriculation, and in gaining employment. Despite the many task forces, state accountability standards, high school exit exams, and the No Child Left Behind legislation, Black males continue to be among the students most likely to be referred to the office, suspended from school, sent to an alternative school, placed into special education, drop out of school, incarcerated in a state or federal prison, or be the victim of a homicide. The tragic reality concerning the plight of Black males in the past two decades has changed little and shows signs that the conditions for Black males are becoming more critical.

The second chapter, "Closing The Widest and Whitest Gaps: White Female Teachers and Black Males" prepared by Ernest H. Johnson, builds on the idea that a better representation of minority and Black male teachers might help reverse the disproportionate numbers of Black males who are suspended and expelled. The likelihood, however, is low and getting lower for the possibility that Black males will attend school with a significant number of male or minority teachers. Consequently, white females will educate the majority of Black children. The chapter discusses the reasons behind the lack of minority teachers and outlines strategies used by white female teachers who have been successful in motivating Black males to pursue academic excellence. In essence, the chapter provides many useful insights for white female teachers who wish to reduce their apprehension about educating African American males.

The third chapter, "Transformational Teaching: Practices for Ensuring That No Black Boys are Left Behind" written by Tavares Stephens and William Greene, describes an educational philosophy where teachers, in addition to focusing on test scores and accountability, are encouraged to sharpen the mind and expand the soul of African American male students. This message is particularly important to beginning teachers who have entered the profession at a time where many seem to be preparing students to pass a standardized test, rather than to be successful in life. The chapter offers teachers many techniques they can use with African American males to help them understand that they have an active role in their rights to a great education.

Chapter Four, "Using Character and Culture to Close The Achievement Gap: A Special Message For Beginning Teachers" written by Chike Akua argues the point that the self-esteem and poor academic performance of African American males is rooted in their lack of knowledge and appreciation of their own culture. Brother Akua's chapter is particularly relevant for beginning teachers since many have misperceptions about how to integrate information about African American culture into their curricula.

Chapter Five, "Honoring The Culture of Black Males Through Storytelling" prepared by Obakunle Akinlana and Madafo Llyod Williams, describes the important work that African American storytellers are doing to provide African American youth with information about their identity and culture as well as to help develop a true character that reflects who they are rather than what their peers or society want them to be. The chapter describes how storytelling provides African American youth with a sense of community where they learn to know themselves through their heritage, cultural expression, art, and the educational and scientific contribution of members of the community that are passed along from one generation to the next in the form of stories. The chapter also includes a section by Ray Mapp that describes the important work he is doing to bring attention to the stories of African Americans who have made major contributions in the fields of science, technology, engineering, and mathematics (STEM).

Chapter Six, "Addicted To Success: The Secrets For Turning Academic Excellence Into A Habit" prepared by Ernest H. Johnson, Stephon Hall, and Stephen Hall describes the beliefs, attitudes, and mental habits of Black boys who are academically very successful (e.g., making As and Bs in all of their courses) despite the fact that they are considered to be a "high risk" child because of their home and family life. The information is presented so that parents, educators, counselors and mentors can use the steps derived from the investigation to help other "at risk" boys learn how to become academically successful.

Chapter Seven, "Early Exposure to Reading and Positive Male Role Models" prepared by Pryce Baldwin, Jr., discusses the power of reading and offers advice to parents and educators about the best ways to motivate Black boys to fall in love with reading. The chapter describes how mentoring programs can be used to encourage reading to help build the self-confidence of Black boys. In addition, the chapter offers insights about why it is important for schools and parents to create ways to put books into the hands of Black boys during the summer months.

Chapter Eight, "Using Poetry and Spoken-word to Motivate Black Males" written by Jerold Bryant and Phillip "Professor Pitt" Colas, describes how poetry and spoken-word is currently being used to create a better environment to foster learning science, social science, and mathematics among Black males. The chapter discusses strategies aimed at increasing comprehension, fluency, vocabulary and oral language development, as well as analyzing and synthesizing information.

Chapter Nine, "The Importance of Cultivating An Interest In Creativity Among Black Boys" prepared by Anthony Goldston and Vandorn Hinnant, shows how the arts allow Black males to use their creative process to look inside themselves for answers that may help them survive and overcome some of the pitfalls in life. The chapter describes how the arts allow Black boys to connect success experiences to their own efforts and reviews research about the impact of the arts on academic achievement. Tony and Vandorn discusses, from their personal experiences, how the arts can prevent Black boys from developing self-defeating habits that do not serve them well in school or in life.

Chapter Ten, "The Impact Of Mentoring and Critical Thinking Skills on Achievement" prepared by Tavares Stephens takes another look at the impact of mentoring on the academic development of Black males, while Chapter Eleven, "Why We Must Encourage African American Males to Become Financially Literate Entrepreneurs" discusses the advantages of involving African American males in programs that offer them an opportunity to learn about financial literacy and the power of cooperative economics by starting their own business. This chapter is organized by Winston Sharpe and comprised of information derived from all of the contributors of the book, many of whom are successful entrepreneurs.

Chapter Twelve, "The Role Of The Hip hop and Rap Culture In Motivating Black Males to Succeed" prepared by Danya Perry, Mervin "Spectac" Jenkins, Patrick "9th Wonder" Douthit, and Christopher "Dasan Ahanu" Massenburg," discusses connections between Hip hop and an earlier form of art, Jazz, that also imitated the life circumstances of youth. The chapter describes how the elements of Hip hop can be used to enhance multiple intelligences and activate different learning strategies during the instructional process.

Chapter Thirteen, "Breaking Through the Barriers to Excellence," by Kenston Griffin and Christopher Land takes a look at motivational factors that can inspire and motivate educators and parents to make changes in their own personal lives and provides an array of psychosocial tools for successfully educating/working with African American males.

Chapter Fourteen, "What Society Gains By Ignoring The Sexual Development of Black Boys" prepared by Morris Gary III, paints a startling picture of what can happen to Black males, as far as the biological and social consequence of HIV/AIDS is concerned, when educators ignore the sexual development of Black males.

Chapter Fifteen, "The Role of Resiliency in Achieving Against the Odds" prepared by Winston Sharpe, discusses resiliency as it pertains to Black males, examines how resiliency contributes to academic success, and determines the factors that hinder and enhance resiliency for Black males.

Finally, the book ends with an epilogue, "The Covenant For Motivating and Educating African American Males" that reaches across all the chapters to offer a comprehensive agenda for motivating and educating Black males.

The time has come to accept the fact that despite a handful of successful reforms, the state of education for Black males is pitiful, and getting worse. Spending on schools has more than doubled in the last three decades, but increased resources have not produced better results. Overall, the U.S. is currently 21st, 23rd, and 25th among 30 developed nations in science, reading, and math respectively. We pray that this book will serve as a beacon of change and transformation for parents, prospective teachers, current teachers, and other educators who are concerned about the best ways to motivate Black males to take off the emotional, mental, and social shackles that have made them prisoners of their own collective intellect. Whereas the essays in this book can be read sequentially or as separate pieces depending on your particular needs and interests as an educator, parent, counselor or mentor. But I sincerely hope you read the book from cover to cover, because I believe you will be transformed by the essays, all of which include concrete, step-by-step instructions on how you can grow, think, and become a different kind of "mentor and advisor" to the Black males in your life.

1

Why Focus on Black Males?

By Mychal Wynn

Every 5 seconds during the school day, a Black public school student is suspended. Every 46 seconds during the school day, a Black high school student drops out. Every minute, a Black child is arrested and a Black baby is born to an unmarried mother. Every 3 minutes, a Black child is born into poverty. Every hour, a Black baby dies. Every 4 hours, a Black child or youth under 20 dies from an accident, and every 5 hours, a Black youth is a homicide victim. Every day, a Black young person under 25 dies from HIV infection and a Black child or youth under 20 commits suicide. Marian Wright Edelman, The Children's Defense Fund[1]

African-American Males—Black Males

While the title of this book reflects the culturally appropriate term, "African-American" referring to Americans of African descent, the terminology, 'Black' will also be used throughout the text. Whether Black American, Black Caribbean, Black Bermudian, Black Canadian, or Black African, the issues confronting Black males, and their parents, wherever they live, are very similar across cultural and socioeconomic lines. These boys, young men, and men who share a cultural frame of reference, are adversely influenced by peer pressures, frequently struggle in classrooms,

1

are the students most likely to be disciplined, and are likely to matriculate through an educational system which fails to affirm their cultural contributions or connect them to their historical past.

My mother, bless her soul, when told of my plans to visit Africa, asked, "Son, why are you going to Africa?" When I told her, "Mama, Nina and I are going on a tour of Egypt and Ghana to trace our roots," she responded, "Boy, you ain't from Africa; you were born in Alabama!" However, when I saw firsthand the statues and artifacts in the Egyptian Museum in Cairo, Egypt; when I went into the pyramids, temples, and tombs in Giza and Luxor; when I journeyed along the Nile to a Nubian village; when I witnessed the monuments and statues in Abu Simbel; and when I flew by airplane across the Sahara, landing in Accra, Ghana and witnessed at the airport the thousands of Black people who looked like the Black people pictured on the walls and chiseled in stone throughout Egypt, I knew, despite thousands of miles and hundreds of years of physical and cultural separation, the Ghanaians, the Nubians, and those portrayed in the temples and tombs of Egypt were "Black like me" and I was in fact home.

African Black males, Bermudian Black males, Canadian Black males, Caribbean Black males, and Black males from Alabama face similar challenges in education, maturation, college matriculation, and, in gaining full access through the glass ceilings into the ivory towers of business in their respective countries, states, islands, and communities. Subsequently, the strategies set forth in this book, are pertinent to the raising, teaching, nurturing, and empowering of 'Black' males whether they live in the United States, Canada, Bermuda, Africa, or on one of the many islands in the Caribbean.

Addressing the Black male crisis requires first, raising the question, "What's the problem?" If there is in fact a problem, we must then raise the question, "What do we want to do about it?" In the original version of my book, *Empowering African-American Males to Succeed: A Ten-Step Approach for Parents and Teachers*, I cited the 1990 U.S. Census Bureau statistics that showed:[2,3,4,5]

> African-American males have higher unemployment rates, lower labor force participation rates, lower high school graduation and college enrollment rates, while ranking first in incarceration and homicide. The leading cause of death for African-American men between the ages of 15 and 24

is homicide, and while representing only 6 percent of the population, African-American men represent 49 percent of prison inmates. Only 4 percent of African-American males attend college, while 23 percent of those of college age are either incarcerated or on probation. While African-American children nationwide comprise approximately 17 percent of all children in public schools, they represent 41 percent of all children in special education. Of the African-American children in special education, 85 percent are African-American males. African-American males, while comprising only 8 percent of public school students, represent the largest percentage, nationally, in suspensions (37 percent).

The tragic reality concerning the plight of Black males in the decade between the 1990 and 2010 census shows that little has changed. In many categories, the 2010 census shows a worsening of the Black male condition. Despite the many task forces, state accountability standards, high school exit exams, increased NCAA student-athlete eligibility requirements, and the No Child Left Behind legislation, Black males continue to be among the students most likely to be referred to the office, suspended from school, sent to an alternative school, placed into special education, drop out of school, incarcerated in a state or federal prison, or be the victim of a homicide. Moreover, Black males are punished more severely for the same infractions as their white peers. On average, more than twice as many white male students are given the extra resources of gifted and talented programs by their schools as Black male students. Advanced Placement classes enroll only token numbers of Black male students, despite The College Board urging that schools open these classes to all who may benefit. In schools districts with selective academic classes and programs, whether they be elementary school gifted and talented programs, middle school advanced math and science classes, or high schools with college-preparatory programs or honors and AP classes, Black male are noticeably and disproportionately absent from such programs and classes.[6,7,8,9,10]

Black males suffer from a cultural disconnect in schools and classrooms. As evidenced by data contained in the National Center for Education Statistics' report, *Educational Achievement and Black-White Inequality*, there is no doubt there is a problem and something needs to be done about it.[11,12,13,14]

Discipline, Special Education, and Jail

- Black students, while representing only 17 percent of public school students, account for 32 percent of suspensions and 30 percent of expulsions. In 1999, 35 percent of all Black students in grades 7-12 had been suspended or expelled from school. The rate was 20 percent for Hispanics and 15 percent for Whites.
- Black children are labeled "mentally retarded" nearly 300 percent more than White children and only 8.4 percent of Black males are identified and enrolled in gifted and talented classes.
- Black males in their early 30s are twice as likely to have prison records (22 percent) than bachelor's degrees (12 percent) and 700 percent more likely than a White male to be sentenced to a local, state, or federal prison.
- A Black male born in today has a 29 percent chance of spending time in prison at some point in his life. The figure for Hispanic males is 16 percent, and for White males is 4 percent.
- Black males are imprisoned at a rate of 3,405 per 100,000 (3.4 percent); Hispanics at a rate of 1,231 per 100,000 (1.2 percent); and Whites at a rate of 465 per 100,000 (.465 percent).

Freeman Hrabowski, in Beating the Odds: Raising Academically Successful African American Males, notes:[15]

"By junior high school, many are working below grade level or barely passing; consequently, they see school as a place where they fail. The environment becomes even more frustrating because of problems between these students, their peers, and teachers and administrators—problems often related to behavior . . . We see that Black students are more often tracked into lower-ability groups involving general education and vocational education and, in contrast, very few Black students are placed in gifted classes. In fact, White children are twice as likely to be placed in these classes as Black children. We also know that males, in general, are more likely than females to be overrepresented in the educable mentally retarded and learning-disabled children and underrepresented in gifted and talented programs. Blacks, Hispanics, and Native Americans are underrepresented in as many as 70 percent of the gifted programs in the nation, and overrepresented in almost half of all special education programs."

High School Performance, Enrollment, and Graduation

- 13 percent of Blacks ages 16-24 have not earned a high school credential. The rate for Whites is 7 percent.
- 17.5 percent of Black students, 13.2 percent of Hispanic students, and 9.3 percent of White students in grades K-12 have been retained at least one grade.
- 70 percent of Black students will not take advanced math.
- 73 percent of Black students will not take advanced English.
- 88 percent of Black students will not take science classes as high as chemistry and physics.
- 95 percent of Black students will not take a fourth year of a foreign language.
- 98 percent of Black students will not take an AP foreign language course.
- 97 percent of Black students taking the ACT will not be considered "College Ready."
- Black students take AP exams at a rate of 53 per 1,000 students. The rate for Hispanic students is 115 per 1,000 and for Whites it is 185 per 1,000.
- The average SAT scores for Black students is 433V and 426M; for Whites it is over 22 percent higher at 529V and 531M.
- The average ACT score for Black students is 16.9; for Whites it is nearly 30 percent higher at 21.8.

Unemployment

- The unemployment rate for Blacks ages 16-19 is 25 percent.
- The unemployment rate for Blacks without a high school credential is 30 percent, 19 percent with high school but no college, 10 percent with some college but no degree, and 6 percent with a bachelor's degree.

Black men, on average, are two and one-times as likely to be unemployed as whites and Black men earn substantially lower incomes even if they have reached the middle class.[7,8,11] If the primary means for male identity in our society is, the "job" you have and the "work" that you do, then the inability of Black males to gain meaningful employment, a decent education, and a good income means that they are nothing; "invisible" men as the Black writer Ralph Ellison [16] put it. Ultimately, the lack of meaningful employment results in a "downward spiral" ending with a loss of self-respect, intense and often overwhelming feelings of hopefulness, anger and fear, and further interpersonal and economic problems for Black men and their families. While these statistics may be alarming for the general population, they have left barely any Black family untouched and place all Black males at risk.

Societal perceptions, law enforcement interactions, and peer pressures of friends, relatives, and friends of friends who are either undereducated, unemployed, in gangs, involved in criminal activity, or on parole have an immediate and far-reaching impact on the lives of current and future generations of Black males. The issue for the Black community—indeed, for America—is much more than merely closing an achievement gap; it is ensuring that future generations of Black men have jobs, function as fathers, and contribute to the health and economic well-being of their local and national community.

Opening the Kindergarten to College Pathway for Black Males

The examination of various data sources suggests that for every 100 Black males only 3 are projected to graduate from college. More generous data sources may increase this number to 5, yet even combining the most optimistic data sources (i.e., high school graduation rate, college enrollment rates, and college graduation rates) cannot project this number to be higher than 7. Due to the enormity of the social-cultural factors contributing to such a tragically abysmal college graduation rate (i.e., gangs, drugs, urban crime, lack of school readiness, lack of at-home support, lack of highly-qualified teachers in urban schools, high unemployment rates, and the likelihood of being raised in a single-parent female-headed household) most community, institutional, and even family discussions are held within a philosophical context rather than a strategic one. Such discussions,

6

which typically begin with statements such as, "I believe . . . ." "If there were more . . . ," "The only thing that we have to do . . ." and "Until we have more . . . we cannot change things." Since such discussions are unlikely to lead to systemic or sustainable strategies, the resulting outcome is invariably to purchase a "Researched-based Student Achievement Program." However, despite all of the programs that have been developed, researched, and sold to parents, schools, and school districts to increase Black male achievement, none can lay claim to have done so.

In an article that focused on cultural proficiency by Patricia Guerra and Sarah Nelson, the authors indicate that one of the most troubling aspects of preparing students for college is that educators may not be aware of how their personal beliefs are depriving students and their families of their right to decide whether to pursue going to college.[15] They go on to make the case that educators often have little knowledge of students' abilities, aspirations, or interests and that what often happens is that educators will assume that since a child is Black and not from a wealthy family, then college is not for them. This following advice is based on the questions Gurra and Nelson present in their article and the answers should help you as a parent (or teacher or school counselor) to determine whether the decision about going to college is being made for Black males and their families rather than by them.

Consider the answers to the following questions to determine whether the schools Black males are attending is helping them make college a possibility or an unsupported fantasy:

- Which students are placed in honors and advanced placement classes that offer a rigorous and challenging curriculum, and which are steered into remedial courses?
- Which students are advised to take higher-level science and math courses, and which are tracked into vocational education?
- Who are the students advised to take at least two years of a foreign language, and which are assumed to not need these courses?
- Which students are advised to join band, cheerleading, student council, and other extracurricular activities to demonstrate well-roundedness, and which are not?
- Which parents are invited to attend college night and made to feel welcome, and which do not receive the information or feel marginalized at the event?

- Which students are urged to make college visits, and which are not?
- Which students take college admissions exams such as the ACT or SAT, and which do not?
- Which students are advised to apply to a four-year university, and which to the local community college?
- Which students are encouraged to apply at prestigious institutions, and which are discouraged from doing so?
- Which students are given applications for academic scholarships, and which are informed only of student loans?
- Which students are supported in their pursuit of college admissions with encouragement, advice, and information? Which students are told, "You're not college material," "You don't have what it takes to make it in a four year college, so consider the community college," or "With your family's lack of financial resources, perhaps you should go to work and think about college at a later time"?

If the answer to the first question in each set does not include Black males, then it is highly likely that the decision about higher education is being made for Black males (and their families) rather than by Black males. While obtaining a college education might not be the best option for every Black male, a college degree can have a significant impact on the quality of life of a Black male, and all Black males (and their parents) should have the right to make this decision rather than to have it made for them.

Clearly there is no singular solution to increasing the number of Black male college graduates. If there was so, surely we would have discovered it. However, there are a number of strategies that can increase the number of Black males graduating from college. We know this to be the case because of the many pockets of success we have witnessed. With a national Black male graduation rate of less than 50 percent, we have high schools that are graduating and sending the majority of their Black males to college. We have families where every Black male has entered and graduated from college, many with advanced degrees. In addition, we know of high school bands, athletic programs, and mentoring programs that have experienced success far beyond the norm.

Following are some strategically-responsive strategies, many of which are commonsense, for opening the kindergarten to college pathway for Black males:[2,18,19,20]

1. Begin your efforts with a clear mission/vision to increase the number of Black males graduating from college. Verbally declare it, visually affirm it, and focus all strategic discussions around it.

2. Build strong relationships with the Black males within your sphere of influence and ensure that conversations around academic achievement become imbedded within the natural flow of daily discussions whether they be parent-child, coach-athletic, mentor-mentee, pastor-youth, or boy-girl.

3. Make academic achievement a top family or institutional priority. Monitor grades, test scores, and learning through family and institutional influences. Whether an athletic coach, single mother, faith-based institution, classroom teacher, or counselor, the personal and institutional focus must be on academic achievement.

4. Cultivate a household and institutional culture that recognizes, publicizes, and celebrates academic achievement. While such celebrations would clearly recognize academic grades and test scores, they should me expanded into all of the Multiple Intelligences areas that represent brain development, i.e., music, poetry, art, leadership, dance, science, and mathematics.

5. Use high expectations to drive early and ongoing academic intervention and social skill development. Again, if the mission/vision is to prepare a generation of educators, scientists, mathematicians, engineers, political leaders, entrepreneurs, attorneys, doctors, and scholars then early intervention, appropriate tutorial assistance, SAT/ACT prep, and AP course enrollment should become part of the cultural make-up of families, communities, and institutions.

It Takes A Village

Increasing Black male achievement will require a systemic and sustained collaboration between adults throughout the school community—the village.[2,19,20] In the case of our sons, their academic and social development, school and personal success, exposure and opportunities, and maturation and spiritual development have been, and continue to be, the result of the village. A diverse group of stakeholders must be included in the discussion of problems, identification of solutions, and acceptance of roles in implementing strategies:

1. Parents must be actively involved in the academic, social, spiritual, and physical development of their sons and provide a household culture built around a set of spiritual core values and academic expectations that encourage and celebrate excellence. Fathers and mothers must accept responsibility for opening communication and building relationships with the influential adults in the lives of their sons, i.e., teachers, principals, coaches, pastors, or mentors. On a regular basis, they must inquire about school, the application of something learned at school, and what their sons are "planning" to do with their lives after high school. Because many Black parents have not attended college, they may lack the knowledge, advice, contacts, and strategies for facilitating college readiness in their children. In these cases, it is absolute necessary for teachers and other school leaders to reach out to Black parents to develop strong relationships that build trust, knowledge, skills, contacts, and parents' confidence.

2. Teachers must be willing to better understand the needs of parents, learning-styles of children, and have a genuine desire to ensure frequent opportunities for Black males to be successful in their classrooms. As soon as a Black male enters high school, it is a great practice for teachers to make personal contacts with his parents to learn about their expectations and aspirations and to enter into ongoing conversations about how the school and family can work together to develop college readiness.

3. Counselors and Coaches must be willing to supplement the lack of student/family knowledge about academic planning, school success, and postsecondary preparation.

4. Administrative leadership must be willing to provide advocacy for Black males within their schools and programs and must encourage and expose students to a wide range of personal, intellectual, and creative development opportunities.

5. School-based support personnel, i.e., custodians, law enforcement personnel, front office staff, and other non-instructional and administrative personnel must be willing to assume an active role in protecting, encouraging, and nurturing Black males

throughout elementary, middle, high school, and college. One of the custodians at our older son's high school approached my wife and me one day in the corridor: "Mr. and Mrs. Wynn, you know your son thinks he has a little girlfriend. I see them standing together between every class. I'll let you know what her name is tomorrow." On another occasion, one of the cafeteria workers approached me at my son's elementary school: "Mr. Wynn, did you know Jalani doesn't eat his fruit? He throws his fruit away almost every day. Now, he does not throw his cake and cookies away. He is going to get fat and ruin his teeth if he does not eat his fruit and stop eating so many sweets. Also, did you know he buys a cupcake almost every day?"

6. Faith-based institutions must understand and serve the needs of families and support the efforts of their local schools.

Like other school children, Black males begin school interested in learning, experiencing, and engaging in the entire process of school from the classroom to the cafeteria and from the school bus to recess. However, any failure to establish effective home-school collaborations with shared beliefs, goals, and expectations will most certainly result in classroom disruptions and underachievement.

Our older son began experiencing all of the stereotypical, if not predictable, conflicts in school (clashes with classmates, challenges to the teacher's authority, and frequent off-task classroom behaviors). However, a first-grade collaboration with his classroom teacher, Mrs. Barbara Mabry, helped us to help him discover his passion for drawing and to begin to construct around him a web of protection which inspired a dream he has held on to since the first grade: he graduated as an honors student in the Math & Science and Visual & Performing Arts Magnet Program at North Springs High School in Atlanta, Georgia. In part, due to the quality of his art portfolio, he was accepted into Amherst College.

Teacher collaboration is crucial to the success of the village. Teaching and nurturing Black males through their own self-imposed obstacles and behaviors is a marathon. Parents are expected to share what they know about their son's needs, teachers share their expectations, and together they devise strategies to meet student needs. This collaboration recognizes that one young man's pace throughout the race may not be the same as other classmates—not as organized, does not process the information as quickly, is frequently out of step in preparing for tests and quizzes, requires more warm-up time for class participation, is not always prepared for class, does not always have books and required materials, frequently forgets homework, and does not always make note of project due dates. Oftentimes, males simply do not get out of the starting blocks as quickly as teachers or parents would like, or expect them to.

When our younger son, Jalani, was in the fourth grade, my wife and I had a meeting with his classroom teacher, his gifted teacher, and the school's assistant principal. On three occasions during third grade, our son had been referred to the office, twice resulting in in-school suspension. On each occasion, he was in a situation with an adult other than his classroom teacher, with whom my wife and I were collaborating. His conflicts were occurring with substitute teachers, in the cafeteria, and on the school bus.

Fourth grade was proceeding reasonably well when he was forced to serve another in-school suspension for "threatening" a little girl. He told the little girl who had demanded he get out of a chair at a computer that she wanted to use, "You'd better leave me alone. I could hurt you if I really wanted to!" At the meeting, everyone was genuinely concerned about Jalani's success. The frustration and exasperation were apparent in everyone's voices as his teacher, gifted teacher, assistant principal, and even my wife shared examples of how they had all been trying to work with Jalani to help him increase his social skills, manage his time, complete his assignments, and perform at a level at which everyone believed him to be capable. Nearing the end of the meeting, the assistant principal turned to me and asked, "Mychal, what do you think we should do?" I responded, "Nothing different; just what we are doing." This was not a sprint! This was a marathon! We were already collaborating and had put strategies into place. My wife and I shared our thoughts about our son and his needs. Some of the issues we identified were:

- Our son was having a difficult time in his gifted class. He was experiencing cultural isolation (there was only one other Black student, a girl in the entire fourth-grade gifted program).
- Our son was struggling with managing his own time. Both in the regular classroom and in his gifted classes and he needed constant reminders to complete his work.

- He was raising his voice, talking over other children in the classroom (a bad habit that was unfortunately being modeled by his older brother who was going through his own issues as a tenth-grader).
- He was generally well behaved in the classroom, but was having conflicts while under the supervision of adults other than his classroom teacher with whom he had his primary relationship.

Despite these challenges there was nothing else we needed to do. We had already ensured he was in a fourth-grade classroom that was looping. The entire class, together with the teacher, would be staying together for fifth grade. My wife and I recognized one of the challenges our son had was in establishing new relationships. His personal conflicts were occurring largely during the first half of the school year while he was getting to know other students. We also developed, via regular e-mails, between his teacher, and us, a time-management plan that helped to keep him focused on his responsibilities on a daily basis. All we needed to do was to continue what we were doing to support Jalani and to allow the marathon to continue its course.

As a result of staying with the same teacher and classmates, Jalani was quickly out of the starting blocks in fifth grade. With strong teacher and student relationships, Jalani soared academically and amazed everyone (except me) with his level of personal responsibility, his ability to remain on task, and his ability to avoid conflicts with classmates. He even appeared in his first Shakespeare production, *A Midsummer Night's Dream*, where he brought down the house with his performance as Nick Bottom. Following his performance, we received an e-mail from his teacher.

> My, what a journey this has been!!!!
>
> Teachers who know of Jalani (but have never taught him) stopped me all day long to comment on how impressed they were with his performance today. What an awesome experience it has been for me to watch the little boy who ran around the front office transform into the confident kid on stage performing one of the lead roles in *A Midsummer Night's Dream*!
>
> Jalani was basking in the stage lights and clearly joyous about being on stage and having full permission to talk,

dance, perform, and be a goofball, as well! Have you ever seen more of an advertisement for playing to an individual's learning style? Wow!!!!

I have always loved Jalani—you know I asked to have him in my class for fourth grade. This year has been fascinating for me because I have watched him grow into himself day by day. Mychal, you were right!!!!! I give you full credit—you know your kid, and you could predict the outcome of looping for Jalani—even as he was struggling with relationships last year.

Watching Jalani grow has been interesting because he seems to be developing different facets of who he is: the dedicated student alongside the kind, funny, and caring friend. He is taking responsibility for his academics while goofing off with buddies! What fun!!!!!! These are the qualities we all strive for . . . discipline when necessary for career success, and compassion and humor when it comes to family and friends. It is a pleasure to watch him be-bop down the hall with a constant smile on his face now, too. No more sour puss as sometimes found in the past.

What a job you have done—allowing Jalani to be Jalani (and listening to his constant stream of words as he is continuing to grow into himself!!) Thank you for your support, always, and letting me witness and take part in this kid's life. As teachers, we aren't supposed to have favorites, but . . . you've got two children who are completely and totally unforgettable! Favorites who will never be forgotten—for being themselves and helping me to become a better teacher.

Happy Thanksgiving!

These factors in the lives of our children provide clear evidence to support the African proverb, "It takes a village to raise a child." Solutions to closing the achievement gap and increasing Black male achievement are complex processes, comprised of many variables, requiring many strategies, and mandating collaboration between the adult stakeholders within each school community. To create the type of village which nurtures the academic achievement and social development of Black males, we must develop a willingness to objectively assess the effectiveness of how we are serving their needs and the type of relationships we are building with their families, by school setting (i.e., elementary, middle, high school, junior college, and college), and by department, program, grade level, and classroom within the school.

Can a Single Mother Raise a Son to Be a Good Man in The Village?

Many of the Black males sitting in your classroom (or homes) are not as fortunate as my sons to have two parents who are actively involved in their education. In fact, as things stand, marriage and childrearing do not appear to go together for many Black Americans. A Black child born today has only a one-in-five chance of growing up with two parents until the age of sixteen. What is also startling about this phenomenon is that out-of-wedlock births are not solely the problem of the entrenched underclass. For example, 22 percent of never-married Black women with incomes above $75,000 a year have children out of wedlock, a rate that is almost ten times higher for whites.[21]

The reasons for the shortage of Black men are numerous. We lose too many men to homicide, suicide, death from drug abuse, industrial-related deaths from jobs in "hazardous areas," AIDS, and other health problems. And then there are some who just gave-up on their families because they were too immature to have started a family in the first place. When women and children exist in a larger world ruled by men and there are no men to look up to as role models, we have the right atmosphere for high levels of anger, anxiety, depression, low self-regard, and confusion about sex role identity. So, regardless of the reasons for the shortage of Black men, the fact is that millions of Black males are being raised without a father present, and it should not come as a surprise that many survive and thrive during the passage to manhood without guidance from a father. For example, Les Brown, the highly acclaimed speaker who talks to Fortune 500 companies and conducts personal and professional seminars around the world, grew up the hard way. Born into poverty, Brown was adopted and raised by a single woman. He was labeled "educable mentally retarded" as a youth. Yet he was able to control who he became, and he speaks with great affection about his mother, his role model and the source of his wisdom and strength.[22]

Benjamin S. Carson, Sr., M.D., is another example of a successful Black man who did not allow the challenges of being raised by a single mother to hinder his childhood dream of becoming a physician. Growing up in a single parent home with dire poverty, poor grades, a horrible temper, and low self-esteem appeared to preclude the realization of that dream until his mother, with only a third-grade education, challenged her sons to strive for excellence. Young Ben persevered and today is a full professor of neurosurgery, oncology, plastic surgery, and pediatrics at the Johns Hopkins School of Medicine, and he has directed pediatric neurosurgery at the Johns Hopkins Children's Center for over a quarter of a century. He became the inaugural recipient of a professorship dedicated in his name in May, 2008. He is now the Benjamin S. Carson, Sr., M.D. and Dr. Evelyn Spiro, R.N. Professor of Pediatric Neurosurgery.

Dr. Carson holds more than 50 honorary doctorate degrees. He is a member of the Alpha Omega Alpha Honor Medical Society, the Horatio Alger Society of Distinguished Americans, and many other prestigious organizations. He sits on the board of directors of numerous organizations, including Kellogg Company, Costco Wholesale Corporation, the Academy of Achievement, and is an Emeritus Fellow of the Yale Corporation, the governing body of Yale University. He was appointed in 2004 by President George W. Bush to serve on the President's Council on Bioethics. He is a highly regarded motivational speaker who has addressed various audiences from school systems and civic groups to corporations and the President's National Prayer Breakfast.[23]

Les Brown and Ben Carson are just two of the success stories of Black boys who grew up without a father but whose strong connectedness and identity with their mother provided the catalyst and fuel for their climb to success. This is quite remarkable since most Black boys don't have a father in their lives and the situation does not seem to be getting better. Rather than ignoring, cutting off, or denying their family background and roots, both Les and Ben celebrated and fully accepted the challenges that life provided them. In doing so, they learned to be comfortable stretching the boundaries of their family roots rather than cutting them off. What they did was analogous to what people did in the good old days when a pair of new shoes fit too tightly; they were stretched by a machine to acquire a comfortable fit. In Les Brown and Ben Carson's case, the machine used to stretch them to new limits was their minds, imagination, and creativity.

This is the same machine that all Black males must use to deal successfully with the sources of frustration in their lives.

Despite the bleak circumstances for Black males, not all sons raised by single mothers have deep emotional, social, and adjustments problems that lead them to a life of crime and drugs. Literally millions of Black males have achieved great things with their lives despite the challenges they have faced. Unfortunately, the media tends to focus on those few who have gotten into trouble rather than the large majority who are doing significant things with their lives. While the presence of a "father figure" contributes strongly to how a family functions, a stable family is possible, even in the absence of a father. Many good men, including several of the contributors to this book, were raised by single mothers or grandmothers and used their intelligence and creative ingenuity to develop successful lives. In my case, I was born in rural poverty in Pike County Alabama during the year of the Montgomery Bus Boycott. At just six months of age, I was given up for adoption and raised in urban poverty on the south side of Chicago. I was a low performing student throughout elementary and middle school, but I beat the odds to survive the gangs and despair of poverty to graduate with honors from Boston's Northeastern University as my family's first college graduate.[18]

One element I have in common with Les Brown, Ben Carson and other Black males who have bet the odd is that that reading and learning was essential to our dreams. Education was the armor against poverty and racism; if you got an education, spoke well, and committed yourself to be a lifelong learner, then you could make it in anyplace in this world. You might not be able to control certain circumstances, but you can lean to control how you chose to react to your circumstances. In essence, another skill that I shared with Les Brown and Ben Carson is the ability to think critically and solve problems through a process by asking the right questions while engaging others in vital conversations that often reveals alternative ways to deal with circumstances. We were fortunate to have people in our lives that instilled in us the belief that to be successful you must think creatively, solve problems, work in groups, speak in public, and apply what you have learned in the real-world. These same skills, critical thinking and communication, are the same abilities that are important for success at every education level. They are also essential skills that an individuals needs to be an informed and active citizen in our democracy.

Education is no longer just about teaching Jamal (or Johnny or Juan) to read. It's about teaching him to think critically about what he reads, question what he reads, interpret what he reads, and relate what he reads to his own life. All students need to learn how to persevere, to respect others, to be aware of their actions, to reason and weigh evidence, and to appreciate people who are different from themselves; aspects of what Daniel Goleman calls Emotional Intelligence.[24,25,26] Students who have learned to collaborate, to think critically, and to be more confident about their own ideas also tend to make better moral judgments. Emotional intelligence (EI) refers to the ability to perceive, control, and evaluate emotions. For decades, a lot of emphasis has been put on certain aspects of intelligence such as logical reasoning, math skills, spatial skills, understanding analogies, verbal skills etc. Researchers were puzzled by the fact that while IQ could predict to a significant degree academic performance and, to some degree, professional and personal success, there was something missing in the equation. Some of those with fabulous IQ scores were doing poorly in life; one could say that they were wasting their potential by thinking, behaving and communicating in a way that hindered their chances to succeed.

One of the major missing parts in the success equation is emotional intelligence, a concept made popular by the groundbreaking book by Daniel Goleman, which is based on years of research by numerous scientists such as Peter Salovey, John Meyer, Howard Gardner, Robert Sternberg and Jack Block, just to name a few. For various reasons and thanks to a wide range of abilities, people with high emotional intelligence tend to be more successful in life than those with lower EIQ even if their classical IQ is average. Therefore, while a decent IQ might get a Black male through school, including a good college, it won't get him far without a well-developed Emotional Intelligence.

Our minds are like sponges. We soak up all types of knowledge and our brains never stop growing. If we feed our minds new information and stretch our minds by developing thoughts and ideas, our mind will grow. Moreover, whatever your dreams are, what you eventually are paid, what type of job you get, what type of opportunities you have, where you live, and where you travel will all depend of what you know, and on knowing what to do with what you know. If the main goal of education reform is to make sure that all Black males acquire the skills needed for success in the twenty-first century, then we have to motivate them to be curious and imaginative and to enjoy learning for its own sake. In addition, we

18

have to help educators rethink the meaning of "family." Any teacher who wants to make meaningful connections with African American males and their families should begin by asking who comprises a family. While a significant amount of research has been devoted to understanding the various definition of family, it can be argues that African American families are typically organized across several households and children are often not considered to be the possessions of a single, private family. This is in stark contract to the typical European American family that is organized according to a triadic family model (i.e., mother-father-child).[27, 28,29,30,31]

African American families are best understood as a network of persons related immediately, distantly, and associatively who work together to sustain themselves in spite of challenges or obstacles.[32,33] These diverse structures have contributed to the myth that African American parents and families do not care about and are not invested in their children's schooling. When educators challenge their beliefs and biases about normative family structures to include multiple generations and extended family and non-family members, then they can start to see the strengths of the student's emotional intelligence rather than to be overly focused on deficits. When educators' change their beliefs in this regard then it will be easier to see how and why a Black male raised primarily by a grandmother and a single mother could grow up to become a Harvard educated lawyer, senator, and president of the United States of America.

My final thoughts about why we must focus on Black males has to do with the economic and national security consequences of our nation having a 50 percent dropout rate for Black males and an overall dropout rate of 25 percent for all students. Approximately, one-million children dropout out of school each year, which translates to 7,000 children dropping-out per day and one child dropping-out every 26-seconds. The obvious Black-white gap in dropouts is apparent, but it is estimated that the 2009 class of dropouts (50 percent or more being children of color) will cost the nation $335 Billion in lost wages, taxes, and productivity.[34] We are becoming more and more of a minority nation. In one or two generations from now, the minority population will become the majority. Without a high school education a child in our nation, regardless of their race or ethnicity, has a poor chance for a successful life where they can provide their own children the educational foundation necessary to escape the consequences of poverty.[34]

Globalization and technology have contributed to making the value of higher education greater than ever and the price for lacking it more punishing than ever. More countries are graduating increasing numbers of young people who not only have basic technical and analytic skills but also are hungry for the middle-class lifestyle we have promoted through media around the world. In short, Black males are now in direct competition with youth from developing countries for many of what traditionally have been considered our "good middle-class white-collar" jobs. Whereas some of our students are learning skills essential for interpreting and manipulating information and data, the sheer number of students who are learning these skills in other countries and the fact that they don't demand as much money to work puts Black males at an extreme competitive disadvantage.

There was a time when children could dropout and get a job working in some factory or join the arm forces to make a living for themselves. These options do not exist for children today. Children who dropout today are condemned to a life of poverty and social failure. There are barely any jobs left for someone with only a high school diplomas, and that's only valuable today if it has truly prepared the student to go on to higher education without remediation. Clearly, having received a quality education is the only ticket to a decent career.

Jobs in the large factories have gone overseas and the arm forces has put into place new requirements for their recruits. In addition to requiring a higher level of academic aptitude to enter the arm forces, 70 percent of the young people in the 18-24 year old age group the military recruits from are being denied entry because they don't have a high school diploma or they can't pass the basic entry exam or they are obese or they can't pass the physical exam or their health is not good or they have a jail record. If we are to continue to maintain a secure nation with capable leaders in all branches of the military, then we've got to look at what we are doing to ensure that all of our children receive a quality of education so that none of our children are left behind. By omission or commission, every child attending school or dropping out of school belongs to all of us. We need to ensure that our children are prepared to be productive citizens so that our nation does not continue to suffer the economic, social, and national security problems we are encountering because we are not providing our children the best education possible.

The balance of this book will, hopefully, encourage the necessary strategic conversations of what we, as educators, policy makers, parents, mentors, mental health professionals, clergy, scholars, and concerned citizens will do in response to this national tragedy. These conversations must move beyond finger pointing and the propensity to engage in philosophical discussions and instead, focus on engaging in strategic discussions. Discussions that are focused on identifying strategies, followed by implementation of those strategies.

Whenever strategies are implemented, there must be a period of observation and data gathering. The observations that are made and data that is gathered must be used to assess our success. For years, this is precisely what coaches have done when working with Black males. They outline a plan of practice and preparation. They play, and video tape the game. They get together as a team to review, debrief, and preplan. They hold on to successful strategies, discard failed strategies, and conceptualize new strategies. This process continues, game by game, play by play, throughout the season, albeit basketball, football, or wrestling. All of this must be done with the appropriate sense of urgency, i.e., adjustments are made continually. In contrast, we typically assess Black male achievement at the beginning of the school year; utilize a constant set of curriculum and instructional methods for the entire school year; assess their achievement levels at the end of the school year (if they have not already dropped out of school or been assigned to an alternative school); analyze the results over the summer; and, despite drastic (if not predictable) underachievement levels, we make modest changes (if any) to curriculum and instruction the ensuing school year! The data is clear—what we have been doing is not working and it has not worked for a long time. Right now, what we need to do is fight for the lives of Black males. We can be respectful about the fight and use this time to examine the truth about the pitiful state of education for Black males. There is much disagreement about what kind of progress is possible and what strategies will be the most effective, but we can't sweep the issues under the rug and do nothing because it is too costly to our nation.

2

Closing The Widest and Whitest Gaps: White Female Teachers and Black Males

By Ernest H. Johnson, Stephon Hall, and Stephen Hall

The population of African American, Hispanic, and other minority teachers continues to shrink in classrooms across the country, while the African American and Hispanic student populations continue to explode. This nationwide trend began at about the same time as Brown vs. Board of Education was forcefully implemented throughout the United States.[1,2] Instead of providing students, schools, and communities with better learning environments, Brown created a situation where African American students and White women teachers shared dysfunctional relationships built on fear, guilt, ignorance, and resentment.[3,4,5] While this wasn't the original intent of Brown, the decision created educational environments where cultural illiteracy and racial contempt prevailed and dominated school policy and classroom practices. In addition, the desegregation decision resulted in a dramatic reduction of African American teachers. It's estimated that in the eleven years between 1954 and 1965, 38,000 African American teachers lost their jobs, and more than 50 percent of the African American administrators were demoted, dismissed, or dissuaded from teaching.[6,7] Moreover, many school systems infused Jim Crow tactics and educational policy to further lower the number of African American teachers, particularly those in Southern states.[8,9,10,11,12]

Because of discriminatory hiring practices, African American students saw fewer Black teachers and thus surmised that teaching was not an available profession. Consequently, African American college students who might have aspirations to teach (between 1975 and 1985, the number of Black students majoring in education declined by 66%) saw teaching, especially elementary education, as white women's work. Rather than becoming teachers, these students entered fields of business, law, medicine, and other areas, leaving a minority void in the teaching profession.[10] Despite the intent of Brown, today our schools, particularly those in urban districts, are more segregated than ever before, and we have the lowest percentage of Black teachers and few new recruits to fill the void. As the crisis of schools continues, the solution pivots on a delicate point where African American students and White female teachers are being forced to find mutual respect and develop relationships in a hostile environment in an effort to facilitate their academic, personal, financial, and social development.

Today, roughly about ten percent of the nation's teaching force is made up of minorities. Of those, only about eight percent are African American, while 30 percent or more of public school students are minorities (more in some cities than others), and the number is growing every year.[7,14,15] Some scholars claim that the teaching force in our nation is about 90 percent white females, while the students they teach will be overwhelmingly comprised of people of color, nearly 80 percent African American and Latino American in urban school districts.[14,15,16] As the gap between students of color and teachers widens, schools in every state across the country are struggling to attract and keep diverse staff members. The highest concentrations of African American and Hispanic teachers are in urban districts, but the numbers are not even close to matching student enrollments. In addition to a steady decline in the number of minority teachers, we are also experiencing a nationwide decline in the number of male teachers.

Men are clearly in demand in America's public schools as a greater focus is placed on the need to diversify the historically female-dominated profession. According to National Education Association research, just 24.9 percent of the nation's three million teachers are men, and over the last two decades, the ratio of males to females in teaching has steadily declined.[17,18] The number of male teachers now stands at a 40-year low. Furthermore, the percentage of male teachers in elementary schools has fallen regularly since 1981—that year, it reached an all-time high of 18 percent. Today, a scant 9 percent of elementary school teachers are men. Likewise, the percentage of males in secondary schools has fluctuated over the years but now stands at its lowest level (35 percent) in history. While these numbers are not as easily accessible as those for minority teachers are, it is bleak, especially in terms of African American males going into teaching. Much like their non-minority counterparts, Black males are not drawn into teaching because they don't see the teaching profession as a lucrative way to provide for their families, which lowers the prestige and social value of a career in teaching. It seems like the prevailing philosophy within education is that men go into teaching to "teach the subject," and women enter teaching to nurture and develop children. Since males tend to gravitate toward secondary teaching, this leaves a critical shortage of male teachers at the elementary level where teacher salaries are lower. In addition, given the steady rise in the numbers of children, both Black and white, who are being raised by single mothers, it is likely that some children may miss out on being exposed to the male perspective during their early years of psychosocial development.

One of the premises behind the alternative certification movement is that it can help increase the diversity of the teaching force in terms of race, gender, and real-world experience of new teachers. Overall, the research shows that roughly equal numbers of male and female alternatively certified teachers are hired across the country. This supports the premise that alternative certification programs can increase the number of male teachers. The data, however, on back males is dismal. Nearly one-third (32 percent) of entrants into teaching via alternate routes are nonwhite, compared to 11 percent of the total current teaching force. At first glance, the alternate routes seem to show an increase in the number of African American or Hispanic teachers, but keep in mind that the percentages are based on individuals who enter the teaching professional, not those who remain. The research does show that White women are on the front lines, and while it's important to recruit and retain minority teachers, it is crucial that we also focus attention on helping to educate white female teachers about the realities of teaching students who are likely to hold a different sociopolitical, sociocultural, and socioeconomic perspective.[17,18]

Over the next decade, schools in the United States will be faced with the daunting task of hiring two million teachers. We know that high-quality teachers make all the difference in the classroom. We also know that it is becoming increasingly difficult to find them and keep them. Twenty percent of new teachers leave the classroom after four years, and white women, some of whom will come through the lateral entry programs, will replace nearly eighty percent of the teachers retiring in the next 15 to 20 years.[17]

Some educators believe that a better representation of minority teachers might help reverse the disproportionate numbers of Black and Hispanic students who are suspended and expelled or who drop out of school altogether. Minority students are also over-represented in special education programs and underrepresented in honors and Advanced Placement classes. Regardless of whether you agree with this idea, a diverse teaching and administrative staff in schools give minority children authority figures that look like them. The likelihood that minority students will attend school with a significant numbers of minority teachers is constantly decreasing. As far as Black males are concerned, it is highly possible that a Black male will go all the way through public school without ever having a course taught by a Black male teacher. If having Black male teachers is important to the self concept of Black male students, then the picture Black boys have about themselves will be shaped by white females who have the responsibility, through modeling, to show Black boys how to act and communicate with others. This will undoubtedly be a difficult task for some white female teachers who are struggling with self-esteem issues associated with being effective teachers and their reservations about their ability to reach and teach Black males. [7,16,17,18]

Given the large gap in the academic performance of Black and white students in our country, it is essential that teachers develop competencies necessary to meet the needs of Black males and other students of color. As some scholars have claimed, perhaps it is not Black males who are falling behind or failing. Maybe it is our schools and teachers who are falling behind and failing our students. Teachers and schools, in large measure, appear to be falling behind in terms of their thinking, pedagogy, and curricula decision making, particularly where Black males and other students of color are concerned. Many of the teachers in the classroom across our country simply don't have the repertoire necessary to teach the culturally diverse learners and they don't know how to make curricular and pedagogical decisions that are relevant and responsive to their students.

I am fortunate to have ongoing relationships with several young Black males who keep me informed about the challenges they encounter making sure they receive the quality of education they deserve. Some of these young men have been in my life for a long time and some have recently completed college. For example, if it were not for the insights I gained from my co-authors, Stephon Hall and Stephen Hall, this chapter would have not been possible. Through endless discussions, Stephon and Stephen have helped me and other members of our Mastermind group to question what works best to motivate Black males. While the bulk of the chapter is written from my standpoint, the essence of what is being presented represents a synthesis of ideas that have come alive through my interactions with the Hall brothers.

Successful White Female Teachers Who Have Closed the Gaps

Over the past decade or so, I've met hundreds of great teachers through my work at NCCAT, many of whom are white females who have successfully ignited the flame for knowledge in Black males. Some of their students have beaten the odds and gotten a high school diploma, and others have gone on to college to pursue their dreams. Whereas the backgrounds of these students are varied, one element they have in common is being exposed to good teachers who are qualified and have the right credential to teach what they are teaching. Another element they share is that when white females are successful in educating Black and minority students, they invariably use methods that are radically different and more intensive than those employed by most other teachers. Finally, white teachers who are successful at reaching Black males avoid reducing the Black males they teach to a simple algorithm. They recognize that by giving every Black male you teach X, then you will not necessarily get Y. By contrast, they see each Black boy as an individual, with different needs, styles for learning, and their own compelling reasons for accomplishing and achieving. School, for many of them, is a place to learn and a pathway to a better quality of life where success is the norm. Not only have they consistently discouraged dysfunctional behaviors, they expect all of their students, including Black males, to be fully engaged in their own academic development.

Sue Farlow and the Tenth Grade Problem

Sue is an active NCCAT alumni. She teaches tenth grade literature and language arts as well as English and journalism to juniors and seniors. The demographics for students and teachers at the high school where Sue teaches is typical of many of the schools in North Carolina. Roughly, 35 percent of the students are African Americans, a small percent (2%) of the teachers are African Americans, and the majority of the teachers are white females (over 85%). The school has a number of African American males employed in non-teaching roles (e.g., athletic coaches, ROTC directors, driver's education instructor, school counselor, etc.), and the Black male students at the school seem more interested in athletic accomplishments than pursuing their academic development. While the school might not provide many Black role models that are teachers, it certainly has enough men to establish a mentoring program for Black boys. Moreover, like so many of the other schools where I've conducted workshops, there are many white female and male teachers who are not only interested in mentoring Black boys but capable of being outstanding role models for their mentees. "We care about the boys and are very interested in the well being of all students, particularly the students who need a little bit more guidance. Sometime all it takes is just to have someone smile. They need us and they need to graduate from school and our job is to make sure they become useful citizens. Unfortunately, while in college, we are provided only with information to teach knowledge basic skills, but no one teaches us to reach out to a kid . . . we are just out there alone trying to figure out what works best to reach Black boys. It's so unfortunate that white teachers have to learn this by themselves," said Sue.

When Sue started teaching nearly 25 years ago, she had a nice orderly classroom where everyone was well behaved and nearly all the students were white. There was no need to consider the needs of the few non-white students since their task was to do whatever it took to assimilate into the mainstream culture. The non-white students were humble and felt grateful for having an opportunity to get an education. Today, things are different, and students of color want to the accepted and appreciated for their unique differences and the cultural perspectives they bring into the classroom. "Every boy is so different, and I have to adjust my approach to really reach them. At the same time, I'm teaching them how to see learning and the world they live in from different perspectives. In the end, I am amazed by the quality and creativity of their work. The stories and poetry they produce are always so rich with emotion and I realize that writing about their lives in this way is probably like therapy," explained Sue.

Rather than allow school to deteriorate into a combination of non-engaging academic activities and negative interactions with teachers and administrators, teachers at Sue's school have created a mentoring program for tenth graders, with a special focus on Black males that aims to develop academic and social skills that are relevant to their survival. "We've got to focus on our tenth grade boys because this is when we tend to loose them at our school . . . and without an intervention, many of the boys, some of them real good students and doing well in school, will eventually lose interest and drop out."

Sue and the teachers at her school developed their program based on the idea that Black males want teachers who are hip, cool, and knowledgeable enough about Black culture to modify their lessons plans to include discussions about race and ethnic diversity. And more importantly, they want to feel respected by their teachers, regardless of their home life or performance in the classroom. "It was a lot easier a long time ago to manage the students in our classes because there wasn't too much diversity to deal with, but today a teacher has to go the extra mile to learn about their students and their cultural backgrounds . . . and the three pieces of advice I give to all teachers is that (1) you have to help Black boys learn to respect themselves and their fellows students, (2) encourage them to take pride in themselves and their classroom work, and (3) instill in them the courage to stand up and do in their hearts what they know is right and best," explains Sue. According to Sue, what makes working with back boys easy is the adoption of a "we," rather than "them," mentality. "When the boys know that I'm in the same game with them and that the school, the community, their parents and me aren't going to put up with excuses for poor school performance, then the boys I teach typically rally to the call of duty." So far, things are going well for the tenth grade mentoring program and during my last visit the boys were eagerly discussing Oprah Winfrey's movie, The Great Debaters, staring Denzel Washington and Forrest Whitaker. This film, set in the 1930s, chronicles the journey of Professor Melvin Tolson, a brilliant but volatile debate coach who uses the power of words to shape a group of Black students into an elite debate team. In their pursuit for excellence, Tolson's debaters, who hail from a small African American college in Texas, receive a groundbreaking invitation to debate Harvard University's championship team. The Great Debaters is one of a number of movies depicting Black students who are excelling academically in face of insurmountable odds. "It's important for our boys to see other Black students who are doing well. For many of them, there are no positive Black male role models at home, and our school, just like many throughout the nation, has a shortage of Black male teachers. So we use films as a way to stimulate discussions about some of the issues they face as Black males."

Marie and Her Mom

Sound research and common sense have put to rest the question of whether good teaching matters in the lives of Black boys: It does. But exactly what constitutes high-quality teaching of Black male students? In an ideal world, high-quality teaching of Black male students happens when teachers come to the classroom with a toolkit of knowledge and skills that they employ based on a set of effective practices that lead, over time, to Black males being inspired to learn. Teachers work as part of a professional community within a workplace that supports continuous learning for both Black males and their teachers. In the real world, teachers who effectively provide a quality education to Black males work in isolation with little support from the administration and are often ridiculed by their peers for showing "favoritism" toward Black students. A few decades ago, the services of these teachers would have been quietly terminated, and they would have been forced out of the teaching profession for helping Black boys develop their academic talents. Take Marie, for example. She is a white female who has been teaching for over thirty years, and she told me about her mom, a high school biology teacher who taught during the time when schools were first integrated. "The school my mom worked in was predominately white before integration, and then all of a sudden 40 percent of the students were Black. My mom was fair to all students and pushed everyone to achieve, regardless of their race or color. She was constantly questioned by other teachers, the principal, and parents since Black students in her classes were doing as well as the white students. After being consistently denied funds for laboratory supplies and equipment, her position was terminated. She was told, in no polite terms that she was bringing the standards down for students in her classes."

In today's world, with so much focus on the "achievement gap" between Black and white students, you would think that having a teacher who could work effectively with Black boys would be an asset. That was obviously not the case for Marie's mom, who worked in a predominately white school district where Black students were bused to school. Rather than see the diversity of the school as an opportunity for the teachers to build upon the knowledge that Black children had about their culture, Marie's mom worked in a school that saw Black and minority children as being intellectually inferior with nothing knowledgeable that could be tapped into or shared with white students. "I think my mom was successful in reaching Black boys because she brought important information about Black scientists and their discoveries into her biology classroom . . . she was not a radical person, she just taught the facts."

The current, fragmented continuum for developing teaching expertise for educating Black boys must be transformed into a system capable of supporting and assisting teachers to be the best they can be. It must be flexible, dynamic, and responsive to changing needs of Black boys, a system that "learns" and adapts to change. I have no doubt that there is a lot of great teaching of Black males going on, unsung and unseen. If we can shift our focus from teachers' deficiencies to teachers' strengths, we can start tapping into those talents that motivate Black males to thrive.

In most schools, we do a pretty good job of finding out where our teachers are falling short in reaching Black males. We don't do as good a job seeking out those classrooms where things are going well. What if we made a sustained national effort at asset mapping? What if we found out what every teacher in every school in America is good at in terms of educating Black boys and then encouraged them to develop that gift and to share it with other teachers? We could have classroom teachers leading job-embedded professional development, rather than flying in high-dollar consultants who understand little about a school's context and culture. If we look for the excellence within our schools, we will find that there is nothing wrong with the teaching profession that cannot be cured by what is right with it.

Lack of Support

It's terribly difficult for teaches to continue to believe in the hidden talents and abilities of Black males, when the behavioral routines and grades they see in the classroom are more consistent with slow or low performance than academic excellence. It's just as difficult for these teachers to stay in the profession when they receive little support from their administrators or peers for their efforts to educate Black males. Debra, a sixth grade language arts teacher, for example, had made up her mind to leave the teaching profession because of the lack of support she received for her successful work with Black males at their school. "It was the start of my fifth year when my principal, a white male, pulled me aside following a faculty meeting and told me that I had to tone down some of the activities in my classroom, particularly the spoken-word program that had too many Black boys involved."

What's amazing about Debra's encounter is that the spoken-word and poetry program seemed to motivate Black boys to get more involved in their academic work. In addition, she had data showing that many of the Black students involved with spoken-word were scoring just as well as white students on the reading and writing tests and, in some instances, outscoring the white students. Although Debra presented her principal with solid evidence that boys in the program were doing better academically, he refused to support her efforts and told her in such an unkind way that the school could not have a program solely for Black boys. He suggested that her time would be better spent elsewhere. "He never told me the exact reason for his decision, but I always thought that other teachers had complained or they thought they had to do something, beyond their usual approach, to raise the academic performance of Black students. When I think about it now, I realize that he made me feel ashamed about the success I was having reaching Black boys."

Fortunately, Debra transferred to another school and continued the impressive work she started. Our paths crossed during one of the seminars at NCCAT that focused on the best ways to motivate Black students. I remember Debra talking about how reaffirmed she finally felt having an opportunity to be with other teachers who were committed to doing whatever it took to ensure that Black boys would have the same academic opportunities as white students. What continues to stick in my memory is the tearful story about how alone and unappreciated she felt after being discouraged from continuing the spoken-word and poetry program at her previous school. I have to admit that I shed as many tears, probably a few more, as the other educators while Debra told this story.

Debra is not the only white female teacher who received more criticism than support for her effort to motivate Black males.

Arlene, a fifth grade teacher, received so much ridicule and negative comments from both the white and Black teachers at her school that she decided it would be best to continue her education and become a principal. "I got to the point that I could not take it any more . . . and then I realized that the major obstacle to my work with Black students was the leadership at my school. I was having much success getting Black boys to set higher expectations about what they could learn. It takes time to meet the individual needs of my students, but I was able to build trust with each Black boy I taught and to understand their temperament. For me, the key to motivating Black boys starts with focusing on learning about their personality or style of learning and then being able to relate this to my teaching plans. Many of my boys I taught in fifth grade have gone on to do exceptional work in middle school."

Just like Debra, Arlene was told by her principal, "The school can not afford to have you spend so much time working with Black boys, when there are other students who also need your attention." To me, both of these teachers are heroes because they did not allow the lack of support to thwart their efforts to reach out to Black males and other students of color.

The Phone Call From Jean

Many of the teachers I've met through the seminars at NCCAT have told me that they did not know how to relate to the Black males in their classes. While the impact seems stronger for white teachers during the early phase of their careers, many well-seasoned teachers continue to be naïve about working with Black males. Interestingly enough, the difficulty these teachers have with reaching Black males has little to do with whether the boys are doing well academically or struggling. "I knew that some of the Black boys in my classes were capable of doing better than their grades and test scores showed, but I just didn't know how to get them to express their academic talents. And then a few weeks after attending a seminar at NCCAT, I realized that I was allowing some of my students to fall through the cracks. I realized that it wasn't them, it was me who was accepting all the bull crap about them not being capable," Jean, a seasoned math teacher, of twenty or so years, told me tearfully.

I met Jean a few months earlier while she was participating in our "Young, Black and Male In America" seminar. While I always feel great when teachers, particularly white females, call me about their students, Jean's call took me by surprise because she was in the middle of an Algebra lesson when she made the call. She told me that one of her students, a young brilliant Black boy, probably the brightest student in the class, just wasn't making the connections, and then "out of the blue" he gave up trying and said it was just too hard for him. Jean explained, "This really got to me and I was about to buy into his denial of his abilities . . . and then I broke down and started crying. I told him that there was no way that I could believe that a brilliant young Black man would give up on the idea of using education as a way to excel himself and his people . . . I told him how proud and special I feel having an opportunity to have him as a student. I was crying, smiling, and expressing everything in my heart . . . and I told him that I just didn't know what else to do but to believe in him. He stopped complaining, lowered his head, shed a few tears, and then he demonstrated that he was the brightest student in my class . . . and I want you to say a few words to him."

Jean's story left me speechless, but I found courage in the midst of her tears of joy and sadness to speak to that young man, Jerome. "There is never a reason to give up, no matter how difficult a problem may seem. There is always a solution if you keep looking for it. You have to always expect to do your best." And I told him how fortunate he was to have a teacher who believed that every Black boy and all students sitting in her class are genius." After hearing the applause and comments from the students, it became apparent to me Jean had gathered all of the students around the speakerphone to hear what I had to say to Jerome.

Since responding to that call from Jean, I have received several others from teachers at her school who have asked me to speak with some of their Black male students. While the students might be different, the main issue seems to be consistent: white female teachers wanting a potentially brilliant student to develop a significant relationship with a Black professional male about the value of doing outstanding work. Each time I speak to a young Black male student is special, and over the past five years, I've had dozens of opportunities. While I know that making these connections is important, it does sadden me a bit to realize that I'm being called because there are no Black male role models in many of the schools where the teachers are employed.

Stepping Across the Line Between Church and State

Historically, the church, in addition to being the heart of the Sunday celebration, has been the center of political, social, economic, religious and educational affairs for African Americans. The church was not only spiritually important, but also culturally unifying. It was the heart of the African American community. The church fought against the social injustices that African Americans faced in America. It was also a sanctuary of comfort, where everyone could express themselves freely and unite culturally in their beliefs and life practices. The church was a place to observe, participate in, and experience the reality of owning and directing an institution free from the control of whites. The church was also an arena where group interests could be articulated and defended collectively. The church was a place where Black folk, children and adults, learned to read so that they could acquire an education. For all these reasons and a host of others, the Black church has served as the organizational hub of Black life. The church is influential for not only physically unifying its congregation, but emotionally and spiritually tying everyone together to fight for common causes, like voting rights and the educational well-being of Black children.[19,20,21,22,23,24]

As the center of African American life, the church gives spiritual guidance as well as a sense of equality among peers. Because most African Americans did not feel equal in the presence of whites, the church was a comfort zone where no one had to feel inferior. James Baldwin speaks of his experience as a minister in The Fire Next Time: "Nothing that has happened to me since equals the power and the glory that I sometimes felt when, in the middle of a sermon, I knew that I was somehow, by some miracle, really carrying, as they said, 'the Word'-when the church and I were one. Their pain and their joy were mine, and mine were theirs-they surrendered their pain and joy to me, I surrendered mine to them-and their cries of 'Amen!' and 'Hallelujah!' and 'Yes, Lord!' and 'Praise His Name!' and 'Preach it brother!' sustained and whipped on my solos until we all became equal . . . at the foot of the altar"(33-34). These emotions were not exclusive to Baldwin's church.[25]

Charlene, a white female seventh grade music teacher and member of the choir of a Baptist church with a predominately African American congregation, said, "If it wasn't for the church, I don't think teachers at my school would be enjoying the success we are having with our Black males.

I have witnessed, first hand, the closeness and emotional support the church gives to Black families, and our pastor has gone out of his way to find mentors, tutors, and space in the church for our after school program. Without the church and the protective prayers of the congregation, the Black boys at our school wouldn't have a chance."

The separation of church and state is a legal and political principle derived from the First Amendment to the United States Constitution, which reads, "Congress shall make no law respecting an establishment of religion, or prohibiting the free exercise thereof . . ." The phrase "separation of church and state," which does not appear in the Constitution itself, is generally traced to an 1802 letter by Thomas Jefferson to the Danbury Baptists, where Jefferson spoke of the combined effect of the Establishment Clause and the Free Exercise Clause of the First Amendment. It has since been quoted in several opinions handed down by the United States Supreme Court involving prayer in schools, using taxpayers money to transport students to schools owned by a church, and several other issues where involving the government in church would impinge upon an individual's private religious practices.

To say that the line between church and state is a bit murky, as far as providing services for students in public schools is concerned, is an understatement. As you read through this section, please keep in mind that there are several successful after-school programs that provide space, mentors, and other resources for students attending public schools. I guess the issue is whether state funds are being used and whether these programs associated with public schools are using these opportunity to impinge on the religious freedom of students enrolled in the programs. It is this last issue, more so than any other that brings delight to my consciousness as far as using taxpayer money to fund academic programs in churches. For me, as long as the church does not impinge on any students religious, cultural or social practices, then I personally have no problem with taxpayer money being used to help address some of the problems we have reaching out to Black males. "It takes a committed group of teachers and administrators to open themselves up to criticism from the community by establishing a relationship between a school and after-school activities at a church. We received a lot of criticism, but the parents and community came around to understand that what we were proposing had nothing to do with the religious training that goes on in the church. We just needed a safe place close to where most of the boys lived," explained Charlene.

In addition to providing mentors, tutors, and a safe environment for after school activities, the program that Charlene is involved in offers classes for the parents of the boys. In addition, each boy in the program has to tutor younger children and in exchange are, provided part-time work during the weekends and summer months. By all means, Charlene and the teachers at her school have taken a holistic approach to working with the boys. They let the boys know that they are valuable members of the community. "Part of the reason the boys feel so angry and alienated is that they don't feel that any of us (teachers, parents and people in the community) really want an authentic relationship with them. Personally, I don't think that it's the tutoring or mentoring that has improved their behavior at school or their grades. I think they have improved because they know they are loved, and we have taught them how to discover their talents, what they really want to do with their lives," explained Charlene.

Given a choice, I am apt to agree with Charlene about the reason for the behavior and grade changes among the Black boys enrolled in their programs. I'll take liberty here to go a bit farther and suggest that the love Black boys experience when people take an authentic interest in their lives and helping them grow, and not just school, is probably the single most important factor in successfully working with Black males.

Jackie Burris and the Twins

Jackie Burris, a career teacher with more than twenty-five years of classroom teaching experience, had never taken such an indirect approach to working with Black boys. For the most part, she just did the usual things when confronted with Black males who were underachieving. "I would have a talk with the boy, schedule a meeting with his parents, suggest a few ways to study, and arrange for after-school sessions with a tutor. Most of the time I felt okay because I had tried to help, but with Stephon and Stephen, I felt a need to take responsibility for making sure that they were not going to fall through the cracks like so many of the Black boys that I have taught. I've been with these boys since the ninth grade; I saw that there was something special in them, and they stole my heart."

During their first year in high school, the twins enrolled in an after-school program called Success Through Education and Motivation (Project STEM). The boys soaked up information about the arts, business instruction, self-motivation, self-discipline, academic excellence and, most importantly, the need to believe in themselves. "Project STEM gave us some knowledge about how to get out of the projects, to get out of the box, and allowed us to understand that just because we were poor did not mean that we could not become successful," explained Stephen.

Jackie and several other teachers saw the potential in these eager students. They formed a network of support and encouragement that grew stronger over the years, bolstered by the twins' own growing sense of self motivation and determination and their consistently high grades. "We knew that children like them don't go to college and they don't go on to have successful careers, loving marriages and healthy, happy children. They were supposed to just do enough to get a high school diploma, if they could, and do their best to stay out of jail, but we vowed to do everything we could to not allow them to slip through the cracks," explained Jackie passionately.

I met Stephon and his identical twin brother Stephen before I met Jackie. The twin brothers were juniors in college when our paths crossed. They were supposed to be losers, living, breathing statistics doomed to repeat a cycle of poverty, failure, and hopelessness. The twins' parents divorced when they were 12, and they lived with their father and younger sister. These two African American males, living in the projects in single-parent homes, ambivalent about academia and searching for a future framed only by what fun or mischief the next few hours might bring, were not supposed to graduate from high school with honors nor graduate from college to pursue their interests in communications and law. While their path was difficult and they occasionally had encounters with teachers and peers that caused them despair, they kept on marching because of the support from their father and Ms. Burris. "I knew my dad wanted us to succeed, but he did not have the tools or the ways to expose us to other possibilities. My dad is the best person on the face of the earth, but he had difficulty opening doors of opportunity for us," added Stephon.

After learning more about the twins and the obstacles they overcame to do well in college and graduate with honors, I was convinced that teachers would learn a lot from hearing their story. Besides that, they were attending college at Western Carolina University that is located just across the road from the center.

The first time I had the twins do a session at NCCAT was for a seminar called "Achieving Against The Odds." The aim of the session was to talk with the teachers about what they thought teachers needed to do in order to prepare Black males to achieve against the odds. I remember how intensely the teachers were listening to the twins story about how Ms. Burris came into their lives. I remember Stephon saying something about how Ms. Burris opened up the world for them and how she and the other teachers started placing responsibility on them to learn how to learn. They were talking about how Ms. Burris and her husband, Erich, considered them a part of their family, when one of the participants, asked, "Was she an African American teacher?" I remember the twins looking at each other, quietly contemplating which one of them was going to answer the question, and then Stephon politely said, "Ms. Burris is white." Stephen corrected him, saying, "Ma Burris is white, and she is like a mother to us. She allowed us to become part of her family. We could come in and out of her house, and we were invited to family gatherings. She has pictures of us all over the house, just as if we are part of their family. She kept in constant contact with our father, who was a little reluctant to deal with her, but he came around after seeing how serious she was about helping us get through school."

The silence that fell on the room was so thick as the twins told their story that you could have cut the air with a knife. The group of teachers, mostly white females, were listening so intensely that they seemed mesmerized. "Our father was and still is an inspiration, but there was so much about school and helping us study and stay on top of our academic development that he just didn't know how to handle. We were lucky to have Ma Burris in our lives because we wouldn't be here. She went out of her way to show us how to excel, and that was something no other white teacher had been willing to do for us. Most of the other teachers saw us as at-risk-students, but Ma Burris saw us as Black boys who needed some direction to become great," explained Stephen.

When Stephen and Stephon stopped talking, many of teachers responded as if they did not believe that a white woman, one of their own, went out of her way to get this close to these Black males. I could clearly understand their denial and their discomfort with the idea that they too had to "go out of their way" to establish meaningful relationships with the Black males they were teaching. There were many questions from the teachers, but the most memorable was, "Was there any pressure from other teachers about her relationship with you two?" Both Stephen and Stephon chimed in. "Sure, Ms. Burris got flack from some of the teachers. But she stood up for what she believed in, and she believed that teachers need to know their students if they were going to have some sort of impact. I'm sure she took some heat, but Ma Burris is tough. She did not allow any of her students to push her around, clown in class, or slip through the cracks. She cared about all of us." Stephen talked about a time when Ms. Burris confronted him about not giving proper attention to his homework. "I remember telling her that she needed to call my father and take that up with him. She pulled out a cell phone right there on the spot and got my dad on the phone."

Stephen and Stephon talked about a time when one of Ms. Burris' neighbors questioned them about who they were when they showed up when Ms. Burris was not at home. "I'm sure that old man thought we were going to break into her house, and he acted like we were not welcome in his neighborhood. The next week he just about had a heart attack when we showed up again and let ourselves into the house with the key Ms. Burris had given us," explained Stephon.

The exchange between the teachers and the twins was very emotional at times, but the dialogue was open and honest. The teachers gained much from the exchange, and although they expressed concern about how unlikely it would be for them to develop deep relationships like Ms. Burris, there was agreement about the need for teachers to develop better relationships with Black males. While some of the teachers indicated that their teaching demands would not permit them to attend to the individuals needs of their students, most agreed that dealing with Black boys on an individual basis was the best way to help themselves and Black boys to overcome the stereotypes about their academic capabilities.

Final Thoughts About Using What We Have Written

To improve the academic achievement of African American males in our public schools, teachers, white females in particular, must take a more active role than ever before. With the enrollment of students of color at an all time high—well over 70 percent in some schools and the percentage of male teachers being at an all time low, the role of white female teachers is vital in promoting academic achievement among African American males. My recommendations to teachers, school counselors, mentors and parents are as follows:

- Regardless of how well you have established your relationship with Black males in your life, there will be communication challenges, so be prepared to break down these barriers. Rather than giving into their desire to just do enough to get by or to be accepted by their peers, increase your efforts to push African American males toward greater academic achievement. Much too often, academic achievement is marginalized by teachers and parents for the sake of maintaining the status quo of the relationship with Black males. To help a student see beyond their limiting expectations and beliefs, you've got to push them and, in some cases, you might find yourself being tempted to hold Black males to higher academic standards than other students. If you find yourself in this situation, please don't buy into the hype that "expecting too much from Black males" will damage their academic development. If you have established an authentic relationship with the Black males in your life, you will discover that it is low, rather than high, expectations that have limited their academic achievement. Honest and authentic communication is the one necessary ingredient that will help you motivate Black males to excel. Don't let fear cause you to not make demands on the talents of Black boys you teach. It's so easy to stay in your comfort zone and listen to your own voice of doubt and that of your peers. Sure, you might find yourself wondering whether you are doing the right things or worrying about what others think about your approaches for reaching Black boys. You've got to stop looking for a miracle to help you reach boys and become the miracle! Let go of your fear and become the example of what it means to be a great teacher. By doing so, you might just discover that the Black boys are willing to follow your example, and not allow fear to keep them from making changes in their lives.

- All of us have expectations about the Black males in our lives. Some of these expectations are positive and empowering, while others are negative and disempowering. In today's world, most Black males are part of the Hip hop culture where their acceptance by peers is often associated with them keeping up with the latest fashions. Their appearance, however, usually invites negative stereotypes from teachers and administrators. You've got to keep in mind that your expectations and the stereotypes associated with these expectations can be the greatest source of motivation for Black males. Regardless of style of clothing they choose to wear or the extracurricular activities in which they are involved, you have to stress that academic achievement is their first priority. You have to be willing to see beyond your stereotypes about how a good student should dress and look and the music they listen to. When you do this, you are also helping to set a school wide standard for academic excellence for all Black males.

- I routinely recommend that teachers, particularly white females, create a "wall of fame" in their classroom. The wall of fame is a collection of pictures of the teacher with various young Black male professionals and entertainers that have met at conferences, seminars, and author book signings. If it's true that a picture is worth a thousand words, then a picture of a white female teacher with a young African American Hip hop artist or a professional athlete is priceless. It closes the generational, cultural and racial gaps white teachers encounter with Black male students. While you might not agree with the lifestyle or musical lyrics of Hip hop artists or professional athletes, these are the people who have the attention of Black boys.

- The life of many Black males is far more complicated than teachers are aware. If he's the oldest child being raised by a single mother, then he has family responsibilities that often interfere with his academic success. Just like you, he has challenges balancing his personal life and academic responsibilities. His world is ruled by images, music, and models of manhood that are probably in conflict with those you would consider appropriate for your generation. Chances are that he or his friends have been victimized by gang-related violence. There is a high probability that he has never seen a movie on a Black-and-white television and that the majority of his meals are prepared in a microwave oven. Chances are that you learned to read using Black text printed on white pages while he learned from the bright, colorful, and highly stimulating web pages on the Internet or a computer-based reading program. Hand-held and wireless computing devices and games are a regular part of his daily life, but they may be relatively new to you. To have a meaningful and effective relationship with Black boys, you've got to be willing to, at least, learn about the cultural traditions of Black males. Make an effort to become familiar with their music, their choice of clothing, hairstyles and their favorite television programs. If you don't make the effort, then you will quickly learn how difficult it is to reach back males. You won't have a clue about how they think, perceive the world or make choices about their priorities.

- To achieve sustainable improvements with Black males, attending a workshop now and then about educating Black males cannot be a activity that you simply check off your to do list. Instead, your professional and personal development must be an ongoing, consistent focus. If your aim is to encourage Black males to become lifelong learners, then you've got to remember that they are more likely to emulate your behavior rather than take your advice about how they should behave. Seek out professional learning that promotes continual improvement for yourself and provides you with constant access to a vast array of relevant resources. Today, you have access to great resources that include on-site and online workshops and courses. While on-site workshops which train teachers in a group setting tend to be the prototype, please keep in mind that these workshops typically focus on one topic dictated by the district and occur at one time in one place. Because of their limited scope, workshops often fail to address teachers' daily needs and the finite time period does not promote continual learning and does not include the follow-up necessary for sustainable improvement. In fact, without follow-up, research shows that a traditional workshop only impacts two percent of the attendees. Many educators and parents are turning to online courses as an alternative to one-time on-site workshops. While online courses allow for increased flexibility in terms of scheduling, they do not provide quick answers. After participants have completed a course, they usually move on to something else, whether or not they fully understand the material. Additionally, most participants don't refer back to online course material when they need a reminder. An interesting alternative is on-demand professional learning. On-demand courses have no start or end date, and they are designed to provide instant help. On-demand professional learning is specifically what you need, when you need it, where you need it. High impact professional learning resources are accessed through the Internet for maximum flexibility and convenience. Teachers and parents find the help they need when they need it and can review information as much as necessary. Like online courses, on-demand professional learning utilizes the convenience of the Internet but also provides individualized support for each participant. Regardless of type of professional development you seek out, it's up to you to review what you have learned and seek out additional training related to your particular concerns. My advice is for you to avoid professional development opportunities that are limited to one time or place. Dwell on the fact that learning is not limited to one place or time. Learning occurs throughout the entire year and across a lifetime.

- Unfortunately, racial discrimination is built into the very fabric of our social and political structures and our schools. Many white people, particularly female teachers, perceive Black males as being hostile, untrustworthy, and not capable of sustaining healthy relationships. Most, if not all, Black males have experienced some form of subtle discrimination or blatant racism that makes them feel unworthy, angry, and powerless. Consequently, one of the things that white female teachers or counselors can do is to help the Black males develop healthy and authentic relationships. By extending yourself in this way, you are preparing Black males to cope with real world situations where they have to develop and sustain relationships with people who are different from themselves. Look for opportunities to connect back males to productive activities in the community outside of school. One effective way that you can help Black males make connections to real world issues is through service learning, a form of experiential learning in which students learn through hands-on service projects. The community and economic activities that you help arrange for Black males can provide them with a safe and supportive process for addressing many of the difficult and very political issues around race, class, power, and privilege. Since Black males typically know their community better than teachers, you'll have to ask your students about the assets and the things they wish to change in their community. Ask them about the people they want to learn from and the experiences they want to have to help prepare them for their lives away from school. Just the simple fact that you are trusting Black males to make assessments about the strengths and weaknesses of their community is enough to help them develop their critical thinking skills. Their skills will be enhanced when you invite Black males and community members to answer the difficult questions about why certain needs exist in the community. You will be pleasantly surprised by the solutions that your students suggest and create to help address these needs.

- Study after study shows the single most important factor determining the quality of the education a Black boy receives is the quality of his teacher. Teaching is one of the most complicated jobs today, and having to deal with students from diverse cultural and socioeconomic backgrounds makes it a bit tougher. To be a great teacher demands broad knowledge of subject matter, curriculum and standards; enthusiasm, a caring attitude and a love of learning; knowledge of discipline and classroom management techniques; the ability to establish a safe and motivating inclusive environment with a clear focus on students that establishes learning goals for all students while acknowledging individualized learning needs; and a desire to make a difference in the lives of young people. With all these qualities required, it's no wonder that it's hard to find and keep great teachers involved in the profession, particularly when one of their unwritten responsibilities is to teach Black boys how to be men. Don't shirk from this responsibility because it will cost society less in the long run if you treat Black boys as if they were your own children.[13,26,27,28,29]

- Real school success with African American males begins with the principal. It is the principal who empowers the teacher, encourages the student, and involves the community in ways that have lasting impact. The principal brings it all together by providing the management and instructional leadership needed to trigger the improvement in African American males we all seek. Effective principals have the vision, courage, wisdom, and professional knowledge to lead learning communities that create opportunities for all children to achieve their highest potential. They accomplish these aims by collaborating with teachers on effective practice, professional development, resource allocation, and student learning. Effective principals are the primary gatekeepers of both the process for the best ways to educate and motivate African American males and the outcome. As conveyors of best practice, catalysts of learning, and protectors of the whole child, our nation's principals are suppose to drive schools to lead, learn, and build. If the principal of your school (or that of your child's school) is not taking their responsibility for student learning seriously and they are not continually gaining knowledge to deliver on 21st century learning expectations, then file a formal complaint. Don't just sit by on the sidelines and ignore what they are not doing because they don't have children as their first, last, and primary concern.

- An old adage suggests that if you and going to have a great harvest, then you have to be prepared. You have to plant the seeds, water the crops, and attend to your garden. If you want to have great relationships with Black males and help them unleash their academic gifts, then you have to act as if that is what you really want. If you expect all students, including Black males, to achieve in their classrooms, then you can't give up on them when they underachieve. You've got to be consistent and never let Black boys think that you have given up on them. You've got to realize that it is always worth it to fight for your students to learn. Great teachers are warm, accessible, enthusiastic and caring. They establish a genuine bond and connection with Black males. Teachers with these qualities are known to stay after school and make themselves available to students and parents who need them. They see and treat the student as a person first, then as a student. They realize that if they come out of their comfort zone, their students will do the same. They are involved in school-wide committees and activities, and they demonstrate a commitment to the school, community, parents and, most importantly, the students.

3

Transformational Teaching: Practices for Ensuring That No Black Boys are Left Behind

By Tavares Stephens and William "Bill" Greene

Introduction to Transformational Pedagogy

Educators are part of the three-pronged backbone of inspiration and training that must exist in every community. This three-pronged backbone consists of parents, places of worship, and the school. As frontline servants in schools, educators play a vital role in uplifting and motivating the heart and spirit of African American males. We play a vital role because we stand at the threshold between the preparation for greatness and the propagation of mediocrity. We are individuals who can guide African American males towards wisdom or leave them wallowing in ignorance. Educators, like parents and spiritual teachers, are charged with ensuring that African American males develop the critical skills and character traits essential to their livelihood. We are also responsible for using curriculum and relationship to assist African American males in their evolution as thinkers, doers, and leaders in their communities.[1]

Our task is neither easy nor cut and dry. The era of raised accountability has bred a more intense focus on students of all demographics.[2] The heightened focus on test scores has almost demanded that teachers "teach to the test." Yet the experienced educator knows that education is not merely about passing standardized tests. Education is an experience that should not only sharpen the mind of students but it should expand their souls as well. The decreasing graduation rates of African American males has required that we find ways to keep them engaged in school so that they may be prepared for school's tests (through the sharpening of their minds) and engaged in personal growth so that they pass life's tests (through expanding their souls).[3]

This chapter focuses on philosophy and practices that can sharpen the mind and expand the soul of African American male students. As you read, I ask that you take an inward look and critically analyze your personal commitment to African American males in your school or classroom. Ponder the importance of their success and the role that you might play in it. And finally, consider what would happen if everyone in our society realized the role we play in achieving one another's destinies and then committed to helping each other transform into the best we can be. If we did so, what would our schools look like? Would teachers be less likely to leave the profession after three years? Would schools be better equipped to prepare students for jobs in the 21st century? Would there be greater numbers of African American males graduating from high school and entering college? What would our neighborhoods feel like? Would everyone be happily employed and not worried about the cost of health care? Would there be fewer single mothers raising families? Would our prison populations be as high as they are today? What would our nation and world be like if we aided each other in evolution and transformation as human beings? [4,5,6,7]

I am often called upon to step out of the classroom for a few days to provide training for other educators, most often white females, who need guidance and support in their work with African American males. If it was not for the support of Bill, the co-author of this chapter and my immediate supervisor, neither this chapter nor the professional development work I've done for teachers at NCCAT or anywhere else would have been possible. More importantly, through endless discussions, Bill has helped me and other members of the Champions for Peace Mastermind Institute find answers to the questions above. It is a true blessing for a teacher to have the support of principals and administrators, but it is this very support that empowers a transformed teacher to extend their wisdom to their students. While the bulk of the chapter is written from my standpoint, the essence of what is being presented represents a synthesis of ideas that have come alive through my interactions with Bill.

Beginning With the End In Mind

As each school year began, I would open my class by saying to my students, "The grade you receive in this class doesn't matter to me." The room would become completely quiet and one by one, they would stare at me with incredulous looks. "What does matter to me," I would continue, "is that your mind is sharpened and your soul expanded." I would then say, "If you follow my instructions as I help you sharpen your mind, you'll get the both the grade you deserve and the grade you desire. And if you follow my instructions as I help you expand your soul, time spent with me this year will help make you a better person, more in tune with the wisdom, gifts, and talents living inside of you." This short speech became my opening address as I began my fifth year of teaching. In the summer before that year, I examined myself as an educator, lifelong learner, and servant. I examined myself as an educator because I knew that my role as a teacher tremendously impacted what and how my students learned. I examined myself as a lifelong learner because I knew that I had to been in tune with best practices that made me a better teacher for my students. I examined myself as a servant because I know that teaching is not simply a job; it is a vocation. It is a calling that impacts the life mission and purpose of students and, therefore, has a far reaching impact on a student's individual success and the contribution he will make to an entire community.

I analyzed my strengths and weakness. I contemplated successful moments with my students, as well as moments when the full measure of success eluded our grasp. I realized that the moments of success contained a certain kind of magic that was both intangible and tangible. It was esoteric yet very practical. Yet no matter how this magic was described, it was transformational when put into use. It created an atmosphere of high level learning, respect for learning and for peers, and a spirit of inquiry that made students comfortable with learning and applying success traits. Additionally, the magic always added a sense of family to my classroom. In these moments, students were not only better students but better human beings. And because of the impact the students had on me, I, too, became a better human being and a better teacher. The magic that occurred was truly transformational for the students and for me. Therefore, for the sake of this chapter, this magic will be described as transformational pedagogy with the purpose being to sharpen the mind and expands the soul.

The aim of transformation is to create an environment that fosters emotional, social and spiritual growth or to provide opportunities for personal growth. Clearly, one factor that hampers healthy relationships is the fact that Black males (all males in general) are not encouraged to be self-reflective or to take individual and collective self-inventory. Black males are not alone in this regard because this lack of self-reflection is also one of the shortcomings that hold most educators back from becoming a transformed teacher.[5,8] In this regard, being transformed is like the cultivation of emotional and social intelligence discussed by the psychologist Daniel Goleman.[9,10] Everyone knows that high IQ is no guarantee of success, happiness, or virtue, but until Goleman's work with emotional intelligence, we could only guess why. When teachers and students are transformed, they become aware of their "two minds"—the rational and the emotional—and how they together shape their destiny. The good news is that "Emotional Literacy" is not fixed early in life. Every teacher, parent, mentor, school counselor, and everyone interested in cultivating the emotional and social development of Black boys has a stake in this compelling vision of human possibility.

Pedagogy, defined as the art and science of teaching (Webster's), deals with not only what we teach our children, but how we teach our children. It defines the sense of purpose and power our students gain from the educational process. The pedagogy of our schools and classrooms plays a major role in all students' journey of becoming. When I began to understand my role as a transformational educator utilizing transformational pedagogy (transformational teaching), my effectiveness expanded immeasurably. As I consciously harnessed the magic of transformational pedagogy, I experienced the magic that occurs when teachers empower students. This magic allowed me to be used as an inspirational vessel for the uninspired student and a guide to help the focused student expand his terrain. It enabled me to connect with the shy student and help him evolve into an expressive individual unafraid to display gifts, talents, and prowess that previously lay dormant. It aided me in playing a more intricate role in helping students graduate, earn scholarships, or simply become better at achieving academic and personal goals. Transformational pedagogy helped me make a difference in the lives of my students; and for this, I am forever grateful.

At this point, some readers may be asking themselves, "What does this chapter about transformational pedagogy and being a transformational educator have to do with motivating and uplifting the spirits of African American boys?" My answer to this question is, "Everything." Since 1994, my life has been dedicated to teaching, motivating, and inspiring youth. I've worked as a substitute teacher, after school tutor, and mentor. I've worked as a middle and high school language arts instructor, a trainer of teachers as an Academic Instructional Coach, and a facilitator of mentoring and best practices workshops as an educational consultant. During this time, I've worked with young people of diverse socioeconomic backgrounds. I've worked with rich and poor students, American and foreign students, and students who grasp the power of education, as well as those who don't understand its power at all. Yet amazingly, when I began to understand and accept the role of teacher as transformational vessel, I began to see that the concept of transformational pedagogy cuts across perceived demographic boundaries and enables students of all backgrounds to connect with the concept of mind sharpening and soul expansion. Simply put, I began to understand that I am not in the business of developing children of a specific ethnic background or any other specific demographic, but I am in the business of developing capable, competent, powerful human beings whose specific demographic and destiny bring both challenges and gifts to their life's journey. My goal as a transformational educator is to create an environment where the gifts of these students multiply in such a way that the challenges are met with critical thinking, intelligence, wisdom, and a sense of purpose and destiny.

Transformational pedagogy enables classrooms to become fields of creative exploration where a student's value as a human being remains equally as important as their value as a scholar. It treats the subjects of reading, math, science, history, art, and technology as tools used to inspire and motivate. It treats critical thinking as a skill that all students must master and use to lead purposeful, fulfilling lives. If our nation truly wants to empower African American male students, we must value them as human beings and scholars. On all levels from elementary to high school, teachers must value and love African American males as if they were their own sons. We must challenge them to succeed as if the lifeblood of our nation depended on their success. We must train them to be emotionally and mentally balanced so that they might be leaders of families and communities. Our schools and classrooms must become laboratories of skill acquisition, motivation, and inspiration that place African American males on the track to success. Transformational educators are capable of leading the way on this mission.

Inspiration Quotient and the Social Prophet

Well equipped and inspired students become inspired individuals who seek a higher quality of life and make valuable contributions to society. With that being said, well equipped and inspired African American male students become inspired individuals who seek a higher quality of life and make valuable contributions to society. Yet, in order to make sure that we are equipping and inspiring African American males, we must believe they can be successful and push them towards success at the earliest levels. Beginning at the elementary level, we must assume the role of visionary voice in the lives of African American boys. As visionary voice, we inspire heightened visions of who they are, what they can do, and what they will be. If we see African American males as unable or unwilling to learn, we have instantly lowered our expectation and we will teach them as though they are incapable. If we see them as capable and willing to learn, then our level of expectation has been raised, and we will then teach with an expectation of achievement. It has been well documented that high levels of expectations often lead to success even in many worst case scenarios.

I know that as some of you read, you may say to yourself, "How can my temperament and expectation change the child's temperament? What if he does not want to learn or what if he truly isn't capable?" As transformational educators teaching African American males, we must decide to teach from a level of high expectation and level of high dedication regardless of student's current mindset. We must view ourselves as agents of change in the child's educational process. We are motivator, inspiration, and life coach. We are sage, counselor, mentor, and parent. Just as a sage or counselor or mentor or parent wouldn't stop expecting the best from the person they counsel, we can never stop expecting the best out of our African American male students.

We are, in many ways, social prophets to our African American males. In sacred literature, prophets served as the visionary voice meant to inform, instruct, predict, project, and inspire. As social prophets, we have the power to impart uplifting visions into their lives. We can and must show them that they possess master keys enabling them to script their lives as stories of success. We cannot accept mediocrity in effort. To do so is tantamount to envisioning mediocrity into their lives. We cannot accept mediocrity in their attitude towards learning. To do so, again, envisions mediocrity. Every aspect of our teaching must promote the idea that maximum effort, positive attitudes, and developing habits of success are the only acceptable ideals in our classrooms. As these ideals are imbibed and applied by our African American male students, they'll begin operating with an achievement mind frame. And as they achieve, we should continue to remind them that successive and consistent steps create academic success. While this move towards academic success remains in constant motion, the transformational educator reminds students that success will not only be gauged by academic performance but also by personal growth. They remind them that sound mind and sound character are an unbeatable combination in the game of life. The merger of these two qualities guarantees African American males that if pathways to success are present, they will be able to walk that path. And if pathways to success are nonexistent, they will be equipped to create that pathway and forge ahead until they reach their goal.

Like ancient and modern day prophets, transformational educators also point out harbingers of danger for African American males. We make them keenly aware of the challenges that face any individual who fails to maximize educational opportunities or develop habits of success. We remind them that refusal to develop their natural gifts and talents, acquire career related skills, and hone rudiments such as reading, writing, mathematics, and critical thinking are equal to writing chapters of struggle into the story of their lives. We help them to understand that this story of struggle affects the lives of at least three generations. It affects the lives of parents or guardians who nurture them. It affects their own life and the lives of friends and family who are a part of their generation. Finally, it will affect the lives of their children. When they write stories of struggle rather than stories of success, they miss opportunities where they could become sources of inspiration, leadership, and motivation for the generations their lives directly affect. The transformational educator keeps this ideal in the forefront of the mind of African American males to remind them that their destiny does matter. It will have a powerful impact on a life other than his own.

Using the Classroom and Curriculum to Expand the Soul

As I mentioned earlier, it was my fifth year of teaching when I began fully grasping this concept of transformational pedagogy. Prior to that point, it wasn't that I didn't connect with my students and provide opportunities for the classroom to become a laboratory of academic achievement, inspiration, and personal growth. Actually, I'd done a fairly good job of doing so. I was part of a language arts staff whose middle school students scored in the top three in our district on national standardized tests each of my four years at the middle school. Many parents whose boys, nearly all African Americans, were in my class had given me testimonials concerning the positive impact I had on their sons' lives. Most of the boys who came into my class left stronger academically than when they came. Additionally, my efforts garnered a Teacher of the Year nomination. So, it wasn't that I didn't have a track record of success when working with African American boys. It was that I knew something was missing. I knew that I could give more and, in turn, help my students achieve more. These factors are what made me analyze my work with students prior to my fifth year in the classroom. I desired to produce the moments of transformational learning more consistently and with more potency. It was then that I was reintroduced to a few concepts that, when used in conjunction, make transformational learning absolutely possible.

Howard Gardner's theory of multiple intelligences, Asa Hilliard's theories concerning cultural competency, and my own theory that educators walk in a love-inspired, divine calling changed and enhanced my approach to teaching and lifelong learning. These concepts provided insight that helped me develop a deeper value of the opportunity to serve African American male students, mentor other teachers, and they helped make transformational teaching consistently attainable.[11,12,13,14,15,16,17,18,19,20,21,22]

Howard Gardner suggests that there are at least eight different measures of intelligence that should be taken into account. They are as follows:

- Linguistic Intelligence (Word Smart)
- Logical-Mathematical intelligence (Numbering, Reasoning Smart)
- Spatial Intelligence (Picture Smart)

- Bodily-Kinesthetic intelligence (Body Smart)
- Musical Intelligence (Music Smart)
- Interpersonal Intelligence (People Smart)
- Intrapersonal Intelligence (Self Smart)
- Naturalist Intelligence (Nature Smart)

The concept of multiple intelligences allows an educator to see African American males as multi-faceted beings possessing different gifts and talents. By understanding how those gifts and talents can be used to stimulate learning, I became better able to assist African American male students articulate and achieve their own destiny. Applying the concept of multiple intelligences to my teaching also helped me connect with the soul of my African American males. I was able to use their natural gifts to engage them in learning, ensuring that they worked at the mastery of requisites such as reading, writing, and critical thinking.

Applying the theory of multiple intelligences to my teaching helped me to meet my African American male students where they were, in terms of learning, while allowing me to show them where they had to go. Because multiple intelligences scan the gamut of human creativity and expression, I was able to create an environment where students could find multiple ways of expressing their understanding of lessons and concepts. They were able to be successful on their own terms. Once they experienced success on their own terms, it became easier to guide in them in engaging in the process of trial and error that could produce success on the terms I needed to push forward (i.e., being better writers, better critical thinkers, and better literary analysts). The young man who performed well and received high marks for role plays was then more willing to take steps in improving his writing. The young man who received high marks for an art related presentation was now more willing to risk the trials and errors when honing his critical thinking and literary analysis skills. Competency and proficiency in one area helped them believe that they could be competent and proficient in other areas.

Utilizing the multiple intelligences theory provides a gateway to teaching life lessons that expand beyond the classroom. My students were better able to deal with complex issues when given a variety of ways to express themselves; especially when the expanded mode of academic expression created chances of increased success. Multiple intelligence theory can be incorporated in the classroom without sacrificing skills needed to be successful writers, critical thinkers, and practitioners of math and science. The theory can be incorporated without sacrificing the understanding of history. It can also be incorporated without compromising standardized test preparation. Utilizing multiple intelligences is not an either or proposition. It is simply an infusion of creativity that expands the learning experience for both student and teacher. In essence, it helps content come alive and increases its relevance. Role plays that deal with the themes of love and loss in Shakespeare (Bodily-kinesthetic and Linguistic intelligence in Literature); artwork that deals with the themes of justice and equality in the writings of Martin Luther King, Jr. (Spatial intelligence in History); opinion polls that use statistics to analyze the issues African American boys face in their communities (Logical-Mathematics and Interpersonal intelligence in Algebra); and hands on experiments that deal with issues of health and well being that affect the lives of African Americans (Bodily-kinesthetic and Interpersonal intelligence in science) make learning real and relevant for our boys. Multiple intelligence theory helps them develop gifts, talents, and insight. It helps them hone needed skills. It helps them find their place in the classroom and school, and it helps them find their purpose and destiny.

Asa Hilliard's groundbreaking work in the area of cultural consciousness reminded me of the need to create lessons and a classroom atmosphere that celebrated and affirmed the genius of people of African descent.[19,20] Dr. Hilliard promulgated the idea that proper understanding of their cultural heritage can play a paramount role in African American student success.[21,22] His work suggests that proper knowledge of cultural heritage can help African American males understand that they have a rich and empowering history—that did not begin with slavery in America [emphasis mine]. This rich history is a worldwide history of intellectual achievement, economic and social prowess, military ingenuity, artistic depth and spirituality. Dr. Hilliard's work has always made practical sense to me because, as a child, I was exposed to large doses of African and African American history. Therefore, I've always been aware of the positive, meaningful contributions that people of African descent have made to the world. At an early age, I was challenged not only to be proud of these contributions but also to use my life to make my contributions to the world. I was also challenged to be the best human being I could be. And that meant being loving and kind and a servant to others. In my mind, being an African American was synonymous with achievement, success, love, and service.

I saw myself sharing a cultural link with the mathematicians who built the pyramids and the scholars who made Timbuktu a seat of worldwide wisdom. I saw myself culturally linked to George Washington Carver, Lewis Latimer, and Madam C.J. Walker, and I was supposed to emulate their success. As a young man fascinated by writing, I even wondered that someday, I could move people in the way that St. Augustine or Langston Hughes moved people who read their work. Additionally, my biological family and my communal family (in particular, my church communal family) stressed the importance of developing my intellect, as well as any God-given talents recognizable in me. They helped me believe that success was my birth rite and that if I exercised the desire to work for my success, success would come. Additionally, my hometown was filled with successful African American male civic leaders, business owners, and family men. There images were seared into my mind, so Dr. Hilliard's work made sense to me. I'd lived out his theories my entire life. I grew up thinking that I would be successful not only because of intellectual gifts, work ethic, and a sense of good fortune but also because of a sense of self worth that had been planted in me for as long as I could remember.

Therefore, I decided to use what I learned in theory and what I knew from experience to enhance my classroom. I became more conscious about using the curriculum to change the consciousness of my African American male students. I wanted them to develop a success consciousness. Rather than waiting for success to come upon them haphazardly, I chose to be assertive in terms of showing them pathways to success. As a language arts instructor, I incorporated the African American perspective into the classroom setting by using lessons in district textbooks and outside sources that related to the African American experience. I also consciously made efforts to show patterns of success and positive personal growth in subject matter that also dealt with people of other ethnicities. In this way, the young men in my class were able to see that success and positive personal growth are not ethnic specific. Instead, they are philosophies and habits that can be learned and cultivated.

In addition to using the curriculum to steer them towards success, I also used words and images. We used what I'll term the "language of success." I outlawed the use of words that could create an atmosphere of mediocrity in my classroom. Words such as "can't", "won't", and "unable to" were not allowed in the classroom. Students could only speak of what they could do, would do, and must do. Criticism for derision's sake was not allowed. I taught them what constructive criticism looks like and sounds like (to build up and make better) and that was the only type of criticism allowed. Additionally, students could only use words of encouragement, no matter the situation. I desired to teach my students that words help shape our realities. I would not allow them to bring themselves or others down with the words they directed towards one another. Words could only be used to create successful realities in our classroom.

In addition to raising cultural awareness through the curriculum and using a language of success, I consciously focused on the power of images. The power of images plays a pivotal role in spurring achievement among our African American male students. Images speak to their conscious and subconscious minds in ways that our words sometimes cannot. Our words, whether they are of encouragement or discouragement, can be fought off by our boys with a quick mental argument. But images enter their minds before they have a chance to consciously accept or reject the message the image conveys. I used the power of images in my classroom by creating a wall of fame that highlighted African American male achievers on local, state, and national levels. The wall included all forms of endeavors, from sports to music to art to politics and business. It gave my young men the chance to see the various opportunities that awaited anyone who chose to become addicted to habits of success. It placed imprints in their minds that were able to penetrate beyond negativity and doubt and illustrate what might be possible if skill, faith, and diligent work were combined.

I must share an important point here. During my fifth year of teaching, when I began to utilize transformational teaching, I moved to a new school. With that move, the demographics of my students changed. I went from a school that was 98 percent African American to one that was approximately 75 percent African American, 15 percent Caucasian American, and ten percent other. Most of my classes had students of at least four different nationalities and who spoke four different languages. Therefore, everything I did for my African American males, in terms of making curriculum culturally relevant and using images that reinforce success, I also had to do for my other students. I was stretched to select stories and find images that identified with Asian-American, Native American, and Latino students, as well as my African American and Caucasian-American students. I sought to use both the stories and images and the language of success to help sharpen the mind and expand the soul of every student in my classroom. The curriculum, words, and images served as model for success, its sounds, and its appearance.

My students were exposed to the challenges that different groups of people face on the path to success. They saw challenges people had to confront to become better people. In our laboratory of success and personal growth, we exploded the myth that success is culturally specific because we saw it in so many different people. We exploded the myth that joy and pain of the human experience are what make us all better human. The assertion is ethnic specific because we studied personal growth in the characters and people of different ethnicities. My students learned that success and personal growth are universal philosophies that transcend ethnicity, nationality, religion and social class; and they were able to appreciate success regardless of the background of the person who achieved it. They saw the human experience as a universal experience that touches the hearts and minds of people all over the world in many similar ways and they saw that regardless of an individual's background they joys and pains of life can help us all to be better people.

Being a Vessel of Love

For the transformational educator, teaching is a vocation. It is not merely a source of employment. It is not an exercise in professional advancement from teacher, to administrator, to district or state level official. It is an experience that calls upon the educator to serve their students by engaging heart, mind, and soul in the art of teaching. Some transformational teachers describe what they do as a "divine calling." Others describe it as a "mission of service." Others do not use poetic language to talk about what they do. They teach simply because they care about their students. No matter the description used by a transformational educator, one can tell that they care about students' hearts as much as they care about their heads. Though their students' scholarship is important, so, too is the relationship between teacher and student.

The transformational educator also exudes a fierce urgency that palpitates and percolates inside the classroom. Their students sense this urgency in the transformational teacher's preparation. They see the urgency in the transformational teacher's passion for student learning. And they hear in the transformational teacher's voice that they will not accept failure, excuses, or the belief that their African American male students will not achieve. This combination is nothing less than the manifestation of the love of a transformational teacher.

While some aspects of transformational teaching are philosophical and others are technical, the most important aspect of transformational teaching is love. Love of students, love of teaching and learning, and love of creating an atmosphere where every child's good is sought are hallmarks of the transformational educator. Transformational educators are successful with African American males because of this love. It is this love that leaves indelible and uplifting imprints on the lives of African American males. This love empowers the transformational educator to skillfully and assertively water seeds of success in African American males. It allows them to patiently and vigilantly aid in the germination of habits that make that success tangible. And finally, the love of the transformational educator helps them become sources of empowerment in the lives of African American male students. They guide them and encourage them as they evolve into manhood and success.

The love of a transformational educator is born out of an authentic desire to positively impact the mind and soul of African American male students. This authentic desire produces an authentic concern that African American male students sense and respond to in ways that exemplify the magic of transformation.

This authentic concern yields relationships that enable us to push African American males to their perceived limits and challenge them to go beyond. It yields trust that allows them to show us their weaknesses in order that we might help them become stronger. It yields a common ground on which we can serve as the teacher, mentor, or sage who helps them deal with life's tough questions that center on academic growth and emotional well being, their personal lives, and fears, hopes, and their dreams. This common ground can be cultivated only in an atmosphere of love that demands excellence yet it is non-judgmental. It is full of caring, yet absent of enabling poor habits. It is inspirational and motivational, while, at the same time, practical in fueling the pursuit of dreams. This love saves the lives of African American males. It shows them that there are teaches who treasure them and care about their well-being. It shows them that school can be a place where they are welcomed, affirmed, and embraced. It also provides them a safe place where they can learn from their own mistakes and the mistakes of others.

The love of the transformational educator creates a sacred space where African American male students become free—free to be human beings simply trying to be the best that they can be. With this freedom comes a sense of power, creativity, and determination that is more than sufficient for any Black males to handle the academic demands of any course. The love of the transformation educator saves the lives of teachers and empowers teachers to see themselves as glorious leaders.

Using Transformational Teaching to Close the Achievement Gap

African American males, like all other students in American public schools, are blessed with the privilege of a free public education. They must use their education as a tool of self-empowerment that strengthens their walk as community leaders, fathers and husbands, and individuals dedicated to the greater good of our society. Teachers of African American males are also privileged. They are privileged to touch the lives of young men who are diamonds in the rough, waiting to shine with brilliant luster. They are privileged to help budding stars become better able to use their gifts. They are also privileged to help African American boys grow into African American men who make viable contributions in our world.

In the pursuit of achievement, African American boys are often times on the wrong end of the gap that separates achievers from those who fall short. As they stand on the precipice of underachievement and look across the chasm of challenge that separate them from success, we must guide them in taking leaps of faith that will help them land on the high ground of success. These leaps of faith symbolize the work ethic and belief in themselves and their abilities that African American males must possess in order to achieve. It also symbolizes the work ethic and belief in themselves that teachers must possess in order to successfully teach African American males. The combination of these factors creates transformational teaching experiences that close the achievement gap.

In the following section, I've provided ideas that can serve as blueprints for using transformational teaching to close the achievement gap. These blueprints can be used by any teacher who encounters African American males on a daily basis. The ideas are not static and rigid. They are fluid and flexible and can be used to jumpstart innovations in teaching, relationship building, and touching both the mind and soul of African American male students. Use them. Modify them. Develop ideas that supersede their scope and impact. Most importantly though, take ownership of your relationship with African American male students. Don't shortchange yourself by shortchanging your experience with them. And don't shortchange them by failing to explore how you can help them develop into high achieving students and well rounded human beings. There is a magic that is waiting to happen if we can simply open our hearts and minds to the opportunity to educate, inspire, and motivate young men who play critical roles in ensuring our nation's well being.

Action Steps for Using Transformational Teaching

As classroom teachers make the commitment to being transformational educators, so, too, must building level and district level administrators. Administrators are fulcrums upon which the academic wheel of a district turns. Although teachers are responsible for the translating the articulated vision and mission of a school district, building level and district level administrators provide the blueprints which empower teachers to make learning happen. They are the stewards of funds, generators of programs, and agents of pragmatic creativity that set the academic tone of individual schools buildings and districts as a whole. In this sense, they are the thermostats regulating the mood and temperaments of a district. Building level and district officials who possess a transformational mindset, have the power to empower their teachers to become leaders who cultivate success in their students. If you are serious about closing the achievement gaps for African American males, then you must close the gap between yourself and the administrators in your district before embarking upon a plan to motivate and lift the spirit of African American males. By this, I mean that it is highly unlikely that you will significantly change the behavior of African American males without first changing how you interact with and seek advice from administrators at your school.

William Greene is one those transformational administrators whom I've just described in the preceding paragraph. William Greene has served as a classroom teacher, assistant principal, high school principal, district level coordinator of Social Studies, and a director of teaching and learning for a metropolitan school system with more than 50,000 students. At the time of this penning, he serves as a Principal of the Eula Ponds Perry Learning Center in Jonesboro, Georgia. As colleagues at the Eula Ponds

Perry Center for Learning (William actually serves as my principal) and members of the Champions For Peace Mastermind Institute, William and I have had many conversations concerning ways in which we can address the needs of African American male students. These conversations almost always move from intangible flashes of inspiration into tangible experiences meant to help African American male students and their teachers reach their full potential as a school wide community.

Under William's leadership, our staff has analyzed data and reflected on best practices in order to build upon what works and discard what doesn't. William has overseen the implementation of after school tutorial programs, empowered the staff to build thriving mentoring programs, conducted staff development activities aimed at invoking a deeper reflection on the staff's ability to function as a team with the singular goal of moving students from points A to Z in their learning process. He has empowered the counseling department to build an extremely effective advisor-advisee program that pairs groups of students with a faculty advisor who helps students navigate through issues such as goal setting, conflict resolution, and preparing for a post secondary education. In this way, all of our students (including the African American male students who make up nearly fifty percent of our school's population) are given the opportunity to develop deepened relationships with their teachers. And these deepened relationships are often not only the doorways for helping African American male students develop visions for success but also the doorway to helping them gain the focus, confidence, and skill needed to make their visions real. William's constant mantra is the Masai greeting, "Kassarian Ingera." This phrase translated means, "And how are the children." As transformational educators, we must always have the children and their academic, mental, and social well being in the forefront of our minds. If we do, we will see that the process of transforming our students and ourselves as an inevitable byproduct of an educational process that is as close to our thoughts and actions as breathing is to our hearts and lungs.

Action Step 1: Examine your perception of African American males.

- Love them as if they were your own children and don't operate out of a spirit of fear when dealing with African American males. Expect your best in reaching and teaching them. Expect their best in terms of their academic performance and social/emotional growth.

- Be assertive and kind, demanding and understanding, and tough and gentle. Be a psychologist, teacher, coach, and parent of African American males as you would any other child you have the privilege of teaching.

- Remember that they, like all other children, read body language. They analyze verbal language. Therefore, let your body language be welcoming. Let your words speak empowerment and truth. Let your eyes speak acceptance and love. Let your actions speak respect and expectations of the diligent effort you require from them. Let your teaching speak for a desire to turn weaknesses into strengths and strengths into skills. Let your classroom be the sanctuary where they grow stronger and wiser than they ever imagined.

Action Step 2: Instructional tips that bring out the best in African American males.

- Instruct African American males with high level intensity. Don't let up. Don't accept mediocrity. Show them their strengths and make them use them. Find their weaknesses and direct them how to improve. Demand improvement.

- Utilize differentiated instruction to tap into the skills and talents of African American males. This can be done without sacrificing the fundamentals of reading, writing, arithmetic, and test taking skills. It requires transformational teachers to be more in tune with the individual gifts and talents of their students. It requires that transformational teachers be willing to become facilitators who broaden the learning process.

- Make classroom assignments relevant to the everyday lives of African American males. Curriculum coverage and test taking prep do not have to be altered to infuse themes of real life relevance. But you must adapt lessons to explore African American themes in more depth and detail.

- Make sure that a language of encouragement and achievement is cultivated. Words such as "I can't," "I won't," or "It's not possible," can never be tolerated. An "I am capable, I will achieve," attitude must be the mantra among your African American male students. Praise students who meet high academic demands and encourage others to follow suit.

- Contact their parents to alert them of academic and socially praiseworthy behavior, as well as academically and socially deleterious behavior. Positive parent contact goes a long way in building fruitful relationships.

- Bring in outside speakers who are successful in various fields and highlight African American males who bring forth and reinforce the idea that, "If he can do it, so can I." But don't limit yourself to one ethnic group. Remember that transformational teachers help students learn that success traits are universal and can be applied effectively by any person of ethnic background. Bringing in African American male speakers helps plant images of African American male success in the mind of your African American male students.

- Show films of African Americans who have achieved success in various endeavors. Use these films in conjunction with class discussions, case studies, and special projects that focus on the universal skills needed for high achievement. Some examples of films include *Finding Forrester*, *The Great Debaters*, *Akilah and the Bee*, *Remember the Titans*, *When We Were Kings*, *Ali*, *Eyes on the Prize*, *Pride*, *The Pursuit of Happyness*, *Stomp the Yard*, *Once Upon a Time When We Were Colored*, *Malcolm X*, *Soul Food* (certain excerpts), *Gifted Hands: The Ben Carson Story*, *Men of Honor*, *The Tuskegee Airmen*, *He Got Game* (certain excerpts), *The Preacher's Wife*, *Crooklyn*, *Coach Carter*, and *The Cosby Show* (via DVD).

Action Step 3: Stress intellectual, emotional, and psychological growth through reading.

- On the elementary level, ensure that your African American male students master reading. If we fail them at this critical stage, we have placed them behind the eight ball at the beginning of their educational process. Elementary teachers are on the forefront of the learning process and can give African American males a healthy intellectual start by making sure that they know how to read.

- Encourage African American males of all grade levels to read books of various subject matter. Reading across disciplines exposes their mind and imagination to concepts that challenge their thinking and their world view.

- Encourage African American males to read literature that actually presents African American issues, history, and culture and worldwide issues, history, and culture. This strengthens awareness and appreciation of their culture and the culture of others. Some examples of the literature I'm talking about include: The Autobiography of Malcolm X with Alex Haley, A Knock at Midnight and Strength to Love by Dr. Martin Luther King, Jr., I, Dread Scott and the Legend of Buddy Bush by Shelia P. Moses, Invisible Man by Ralph Ellison, Letters to a Young Brother by Hill Harper, Dreams of My Father and The Audacity of Hope by President Barack Obama, Think Big by Ben Carson, A Treasure Within by Chike Akua, Deep Sightings and Rescue Missions by Toni Cade Bambara, Brothers on The Mend: Understanding and Healing Anger for African-American Men and Women by Ernest H. Johnson, and The Collected Works of Langston Hughes.

- Include literature related to the African American experience in class lessons. This is especially feasible in literature and history classes. Teaching African American themes provides opportunities for exploration and validation that are absent when these themes are omitted.

Action Step 4: Learn from your African American male students.

- Use journal entries, role-plays, and case studies to learn about their ideas concerning academic subject matter and world events.
- Use class discussion as a method to tie academic themes to every day situations African American males encounter. Let these discussions help you to appreciate them and see the world through their eyes. Use what you learn to build positive relationships.
- Provide them with opportunities to develop leadership and communication skills through class projects and presentations.
- Realize that in terms of ideas and beliefs, they are not a monolithic group. You'll find enormous individuality among African American males.

Action Step 5: Be interested in who your African American males are.

- Attend extracurricular activities in which they are involved.
- Learn about their family and social lives (to your level of comfort and always within the realm of professional relationship) and show them that they are more than a student number in your role book.
- Make a habit of asking them about their day and listening attentively when they open up. Let them encounter sincerity and caring when they enter your classroom.
- Attend professional development workshops that deal with issues and themes related to African American males. Find research, studies, or anecdotal stories that illustrate how others have been successful in teaching African American males.
- Talk to teachers who've built positive relationships and experienced high achievement with African American male students. These uplifting experiences create pathways for your personal experience of success with African American males.
- Encourage your African American male students to participate in activities that help them develop their talents into skills. If they draw, encourage them to take art. If they possess dramatic flair, encourage them to explore theater. If they have technological propensity, encourage them to take technology classes. If they possess verbal dexterity, encourage them to join the debate club or mock trial team. Help them learn that talents can become skills that become fulfilling careers.

Action Step 6: Use assignments to employ direct and indirect goal setting exercises (This technique is especially effective in any writing intensive course, such as language arts, history, business/marketing, etc. It can be tailored to fit curriculum specifics of those courses).

- Begin each semester with goal setting and/or dream envisioning. End each semester with an assessment of the student's progress towards fulfillment of his dreams and/or goals.
- Have students write letters to the persons they hope to become in the future. In this letter, students should encourage their future selves to remain committed to their goals and take the necessary

steps to make their goals and dreams a reality. In the letter, the students' current selves should stress the benefits that will come from the pursuit of and accomplishing their dreams and goals.

- Have students write letters from their future selves (who has achieved all of their hopes and dreams) to the person they are currently. In this letter, the future selves should encourage the present selves to remain committed to their goals and dreams and take the necessary steps to make their goals and dreams a reality. The students' future selves should stress the benefits that will come from continuing the pursuit of and accomplishing their dreams and goals.
- Create flow charts illustrating the following:
    1) The steps needed to accomplish their hopes and dreams
    2) The impact of negative and positive decisions
    3) The role education plays in helping them find their life's purpose and achieve their destiny
- Create cause and effect charts that show the results of patterns of behavior (both good and bad) with major emphasis on the effects cause by positive, self affirming, and educationally enriching behaviors (because that is what we must promote as transformational educators).
- Create mock news articles or biographical essays detailing future success in their endeavors.
- Write and/or perform original motivational speeches encouraging others to be successful in the face of challenges or adversity. Students should use their own lives as springboard for their speeches.

Closing Thoughts on The Legacy of the Transformational Educator

Transformational educators possess the unique privilege of motivating and uplifting the spirits of African American males. Our skill, love, and dedication make the indelible imprint that shapes their lives. The moments we share with our African American male students inspire their souls and stretch their minds. Even when our faces fade from their memory, the lessons they learned with us will remain. We are more than teachers merely earning pay. We are life coaches who empower, surrogate parents who ensure growth, and success counselors who push the young men we serve to higher heights. We see their faults yet embrace them, and we remind them that their good can conquer their shortcomings. We see their brilliance and encourage them to convert it into realized success, rather than untapped potential. We serve as their sounding board and their looking glass, their support system and their strongest, constructive critic. And through this process, they grow. They achieve. They become capable boys who become capable men.

For transformational educators, teaching surpasses the scope of grades, test scores, and curriculum standards. It is an act of love and a sharing of dreams. It is the actualized hope of mothers and fathers who pray that skilled and innovative teachers will touch their sons' lives. It is the manifested dream of young men who desire academic success. It is the desired fulfilled of principals who seek competent, energized, and caring teachers who can make their schools sanctuaries of success.

With each moment, transformational teachers breathe life into African American male students. We touch them in ways that help them believe in their mind's power and their heart's inner light. If we are willing to grow with them, learn from them, and allow them to transform us as we transform them, then true education takes place. Our minds and their minds sharpen. Our souls and their souls expand. Both our nation and our world become better and stronger as African American males reach their destinies to bring the greater good to our nation and to our world.

4

Using Character and Culture to Close the Achievement Gap: A Special Message for Beginning Teachers

By Chike Akua, M.Ed.

Introduction

It's been a while since I stepped into the classroom of my first "real" teaching position. I was excited, anxious, and so ready to teach. This feeling of excitement was followed by one of uncertainty and loads of self-doubt, particularly when I considered the diversity of students sitting in front of me. Hines Middle School, the site of my first teaching assignment, was a school in flux. It had recently become 50 percent Black and 50 percent white after being predominantly white since its inception. The principal's commitment to diversity was evident in that I was one of six Black males that was hired that year. She went out of her way to find us. Hines was in the center of Newport News, Virginia, a 21-mile long and 4-mile wide peninsula. Being in the middle of town, Hines attracted middle class students from uptown in Denbigh and economically challenged students from the east end. The east end—once a thriving Black neighborhood near the shipyards before integration—now had all the indicators of urban blight, complete with poverty, drugs, gangs and violence.

My students were an interesting mix whose parents were working class and professionals. In addition, the Tidewater area of Virginia is known for its high population of military families due to the nearby naval and army bases. Demographically, my classes were about 60 percent white and 40 percent Black. While I cared deeply about all of my students, it was also clear that I intended to make sure that my Black students, especially Black males succeeded.

Today, while I continue my work as a teacher of teachers while pursuing a doctoral degree in educational leadership, I can still remember the self-doubt and questions I had about whether I would be an effective teacher. I never doubted my abilities to teach and lead, to inspire and motivate; however, I had a weakness for doing long-range lesson plans. I struggled with day-to-day planning for a good portion of my first year. I was navigating my way through the textbooks, filtering out the unnecessary, and digging for stories and concepts that would capture my student's attention and imagination.

Did I have the knowledge and skills to be in total control of a classroom? What would I do when a student talked back to me? Did I have the knowledge and skills to reach and teach Black males? How would I decide what topics to teach? How should I assess students' progress? What should I do if a student calls me a racist? What was the best way to maintain discipline in my classroom? Would the students like me? They were all valid questions then, and just like me, you will find that as you evolve as a teacher, they are relevant questions now.

As a first-year teacher, you have the exciting challenge of teaching students and learning what it means to be an effective teacher. If you are reading this book, the chances are quite high that you are a white female who has made the decision to be a teacher. Although our paths may be a bit different in terms of how we arrived at the point of becoming teachers, the classroom atmosphere and activities we use to be effective in reaching Black males will need to be quite similar. College courses are filled with theory and a number of instructional and learning strategies that you can use to become a successful teacher. They give you, the future teacher, many ideas that can be incorporate into your classroom, but offer little advice about how to translate these ideas into practice. How do I decide which strategy to use and when? What are some practical tips that will help me in my day-to-day practice teaching Black males? How can I successfully survive my first years of teaching? How can I successfully educate the diverse groups of students that I teach? How can I use culture and character to close the achievement gap?

It may come as a shock to many that there are educators who know how to reach African American students, bring out the best in them, and consistently help them succeed, regardless of the circumstances. Yet, America's schools are replete with committed educators who exemplify this standard of excellence. Over the last decade or so, many have produced some fascinating books, exciting training manuals, and other materials to support the development of their fellow teachers and their students. I found Jawanza Kunjufu's four-volume work, *Countering the Conspiracy to Destroy Black Boys*, to be very helpful in outlining systemic stumbling blocks for Black males in the classroom and providing intervention strategies for Black male achievement in the classroom. Mychal Wynn's work (*Empowering African American Males*; *Follow Your Dreams*, Teaching, *Parenting, and Mentoring Successful Black Males*) has provided me with new insights about how to best prepare African American males for college and how to develop a successful business as an educational consultant. Mychal is recognized as one of the world's premiere authorities on Black male achievement, school improvement planning, closing the achievement gap, and college planning.[1,2,3,4]

Useni Eugene Perkins, *Harvesting New Generations*, is an innovative text full of ideas to foster cultural depth and understanding of my students while increasing skills. Then of course, Dr. Carter G. Woodson's timeless classic, *The Mis-education of the Negro*, written in 1933, thoroughly outlined the crisis of Black children being "mis-educated" to understand, appreciate, and serve the cultural interests of everyone but themselves.[5,6]

The challenges facing African American males today, even since the time of Woodson, has reached epidemic proportions over the years. I take this to mean that educators failed to successfully use the methods shared by these and other scholars. Either way, the purpose of this chapter is to provide you with several tried and true teaching methods for motivating and educating African American males. The element that is central to these methods employs the use of culturally relevant practices to enhance the self-esteem and develop the character of African American males.

It should further be noted that that there was no crisis among Black males in Africa and other places prior to alien interruption and intervention. Therefore, the cultivation of Black males from boyhood to manhood was never left to chance; it was clear, compelling, conscientious, and it's results were tangible. Today we find ourselves in a situation that requires revolutionary, out-of-the-box thinking. It also requires us to keep in mind that the typical Black male sitting in your classroom is the product of over 200 years of psychosocial manipulations.[7] His ancestors, upon being enslaved and brought to America, were conditioned, much like Pavlov's dogs, to respond in particular ways to environmental clues. Much like the fact that drivers of automobiles have been conditioned to stop their vehicles when the traffic light turns red, Black males in America have been conditioned to see themselves as capable athletes instead of capable students who can do outstanding academic work. Our roles as educators, regardless of whether you are a white female teacher fresh out of college or a seasoned African American male teacher, is to help Black males appreciate the true contributions of their people to the rich academic and cultural heritage that makes this nation what it is.

Framework and Philosophical Foundation

Any curriculum, program, or school that intends to properly serve and meet the needs of African American males must contain certain key components. Any teacher, whether African American or non-African American, who intends to make a critical impact on Black boys, must understand and employ these components. These components can be codified into what I call "The Pyramid Paradigm." It is indeed a paradigm for high performance. It is a three-part template and a guide that I developed and utilized with great success in 14 years as a pubic school classroom teacher.

At the left base of the pyramid is the history of our people that must comes first. Dr. John Henrik Clarke taught us that, "history is a clock which people use to tell the time." This suggests that if we do not teach African American males their history, they will not have a realistic reference point or foundation for understanding themselves.

Once we develop an understanding of history, we begin to understand our identity, which is located on the right base of the pyramid. Dr. Edward Robinson has taught us that a thorough understanding of our history gives us a vital nutrient called Vitamin I (for identity). As Dr. Na'im Akbar notes in his seminal work *Know Thyself*, "The first function of education is to provide identity".[8] Identity determines activity. Currently, we are Vitamin I deficient. This suggests that our young men are suffering from an identity crisis. If our young men think they are n___, they will act like n___. If they think they are thugs, they will act like thugs. If they think they are "pimps and playas," this is what they will act like, because identity determines activity.

Conversely, when our young men know that they are the descendents of great masters and builders, they will excel, build strong families, businesses and communities. They will walk with power and majesty, calling forth a new reality, because identity determines activity. Therefore, to know this history and legacy of excellence is not optional. It is essential. Indeed our young men will benefit greatly from this knowledge and insight. The knowledge of this legacy must permeate every discipline. For this to be the case, educators must know the African origins of the discipline they teach.

Just as wise and prudent people supplement their diet with multi-vitamins and other essential nutrients that are not found in many of the foods we eat, it is incumbent upon educators and parents to be sure to supplement the academic diet of our children with the Vitamin I that can be found through a careful study of their own culture across all disciplines. In other words, there are African and African American contributions (both ancient and modern) to all subjects and disciplines. Dr. Asa Hilliard notes, "Today, the formal education of most people of African ancestry is usually accomplished in systems that take us far away from ourselves." This has led many of our young men to assume what Akbar and other scholars call, the "alien identity."[8,9,10,11,12,13]

As the ancient father of medicine and pyramid building engineer and architect, Imhotep has much to say to our young men in the way of excellence and achievement. But they can't hear him because they've never heard of him. Ptahhotep has much to teach our young men about character. But they can't hear him because they've never heard of him, much less studied his writings. Ahmose, the ancient African writer of the oldest mathematics textbook in history, has much to share about the how math is a reflection of life. Sundiata, the Lion King of Mali, has much to teach our young men about courage and leadership. But they can't hear him because they don't know who he is.[14,15]

Dr. Mark Dean, an African American, led a team of computer scientists who built a microchip that does a billion calculations per second.[16] At the ripe age of 35, Dr. Thomas Mensah, a native of Ghana,[17] was one of a few innovative and pioneering engineers who developed the technology that made the cell phone and ATMs possible. Do you think these men, through their accomplishments, might have something to say to our African American boys?

In addition, there needs to be a radical restructuring of the definition of womanhood in the minds of young men, lest they continue to view women as objects of exploitation and pleasure rather than subjects worthy of dignity and respect. Mae Jemison, Maxine Waters, Cathy Hughes, and Queen Hatshepsut (and many more), successful women of African descent, have much to say to our young men about what it means to be a Black woman and the respect Black men should accord them.

We can no longer afford to keep the powerful stories of these monumental men and women from Black boys.

Educators intent on meeting the needs of African American boys must make a calculated effort to constantly and consistently show them images of excellence and achievement. So many of our young men think that crime, violence, incarceration, irresponsible parenting, and sexual promiscuity are the norm. This perception being the case, we must help them transform the norm through the positive, life-affirming images we expose them to. In so doing, we will help Black boys to discern and discriminate between alien self-destructive images and healthy constructive images.

Once our young men understand their history and are rooted in their true identity, their future blooms and unfolds into a powerful destiny: executives, scientists, educators, medical practitioners, engineers, ministers, husbands, fathers, and leaders. Destiny can be defined as, "our place in Eternity." However, Eternity must not be viewed as a far off place that we encounter after death. The Ancestors of ancient Kemet (Egypt) taught us, "If we wish to live for Eternity, we must build for Eternity." And when we sow seeds of history, identity, and destiny into our African American boys, we awaken within them the urge to leave a legacy.

Now we must define the terms inside the Pyramid Paradigm. At the base inside the pyramid is culture. Dr. Marimba Ani defines culture as, "ordered behavior."[18] We are in the process of restoring order for young African American males, their families, and communities. Hilliard further states, ". . . our own cultural traditions provide ample answers to the basic human questions that all must ask. We can start from our own African center in the creation of a future . . . and share it with the world."[10,11]

Rising up from the base of culture is character. An integral part of cultural awareness is character development. We define character as, "the ongoing development of morals, values, critical thinking and decision-making skills." Traditional African systems of education were always infused with character-building activities and lessons. This is why the ancient African writer and philosopher Ankhsheshonqi said, "It is in the development of character that instruction succeeds." This is why the ancient African educator and writer, Ptahhotep said, "Strive for excellence in all that you do, so that no fault can be found in your character."[13]

When young African American males are exposed to proper cultural and character development, a new mental and spiritual phenomenon emerges. We call it consciousness. Consciousness is "the expanded awareness of your place in the universe." Black boys need their character and their culture to speak to their consciousness. When this happens, they will be transformed by the renewing of their minds.

With this new consciousness comes a new commitment—a commitment to actively participate in the resurrection of African people and the redemption of Humanity. Commitment is at the apex of the Pyramid Paradigm because it is the fruit of the culture, character, and consciousness we spoke of earlier.

What we have engaged in here is a brief conversation to illuminate a philosophical foundation. But how do we take these ideas and ideals and turn them into classroom activities and tangible results for Black boys? How do we take the great works of Hilliard, Akbar, Karenga, Ani, Nobles, Wilson, Asante, and others and make the ideas work in the classroom? How do we takes these ideas and make them relevant to the kinds of life experiences that Black boys are having today? How do we accomplish any of this and make sure that the classroom lessons are meeting the educational standards established for the course we are teaching?

From Philosophical Foundation to Practical Application

There are four primary areas that will allow us to actualize the ideas shared in the first part of this chapter. Employing these application strategies will begin to awaken and release the potential within our Black boys. In the first part of this chapter, we discussed curriculum and content. Not only do we find that often the curriculum and content do not adequately serve Black boys, but the methodology employed by teachers does not tap the genius within them.

Sweeping social, cultural and demographic changes in urban schools have caused rapid change in public schools. As a result, most schools of education in the colleges and universities have programs of study that are obsolete by the time the pre-service teacher enters the classroom. There are, however, some basic applications that work across the board when thoughtful, caring and committed teachers employ them.

Ritual: a prescribed set of actions that set the stage for a powerful experience

Student Creed
I am a student seeking to be a scholar.
The standard is excellence, today and tomorrow.
I am disciplined, focused, and on-time.
I am organized, respectful and responsible.
I am on a mission to elevate myself, my community and Humanity.

A significant part of African and African American cultural expression is known as "call and response." This is when a leader or group of leaders speak words of a chant, affirmation, or song and the rest of the group repeats after them. In the modern context, this is most often seen in churches where spirit-filled preachers exhort their congregations to live and love righteously following the teachings of Jesus. The members of the congregation are known to shout "Amen," "Hallelujah", "hey," 'preach," "teach," "go 'head brotha," "well . . . !" It is in the midst of the rhythm of the sermon or song, the cadence of the choir, testifying about how good God is that you will see call and response at its best.

The "call and response" method is effective because it welcomes everyone immediately into the experience. You can use it to welcome all of your students into the experience of being in your class as opposed to any other. This is not elitist or arrogant. But there is a way to let students know, without saying it, that there's something special about being in this class.

The words of the Student Creed above always flowed from my lips and those of my students at the beginning of every class period. These words constituted the deconstruction of negative values and the reconstruction of positive, life-affirming values. I would walk into class and begin, "I am a student seeking to be a scholar . . ." and the students would cease conversation, stand straight, strong and tall, and repeat after me until we had finished the whole Student Creed.

I never asked my students to memorize it, but by reciting it daily, naturally, they did. We took out the key vocabulary words, defined them, and discovered their unique meaning within the context of the affirmation. Soon, usually after the first week of the school year, students would pull me aside and ask if they could lead the Student Creed. It became a teachable moment! Pleased with the request (which I fully expected), I would oblige them. They took ownership of these powerful words, and the Student Creed became theirs, as well as mine.

Oftentimes it was my most challenging boys who wanted to lead the Creed. They craved attention so much. Leading the Creed allowed them to get the attention they craved (which met their emotional needs) and get the leadership experience they needed (which met their academic, social and cultural needs).

When my principal got wind of it, the Student Creed was soon adopted as the school's creed. It was read and recited on the announcements every morning. T-shirts with the Student Creed on the back were printed and sold. Students and teachers wore these shirts on Fridays, and we gradually began to see the climate and the culture of the school change.

In class, the Student Creed became the foundation we used to evaluate the behavior of characters in stories and people in history and current events. They now had a cultural and moral point of reference to draw from and build upon—a point of reference much more palatable than soft-porn videos, violent and misogynistic music, and degenerate talk shows.

Ritual is a prescribed and established set of actions that set the stage for a powerful experience. Using ritual in the classroom, in particular the Student Creed, does several things:

- It establishes order; it lets students know that class has begun.
- It welcomes a spirit of cooperation because the students recite it in unison.

- It makes cooperation natural because everyone knows what to do; students will even correct other students who do not immediately snap to attention.

Transformation Affirmation

Any affirmations that you may choose to use at the beginning of class should serve as a call to order; it must confirm and affirm purpose, values, and goals. Another affirmation that I have used over the years to do this is the rhythmic Transformation Affirmation.

> Love and light, truth and transformation. Healing and harmony, across the nation. Compassion and conviction are the tools for my mission. I open my eyes to see with inner vision. Peace and blessings be unto Humanity. The change begins within; the change begins with me.

The Transformation Affirmation is often done with clapping and a djembe drum, if available. Again, we are deconstructing negative values and reconstructing the positive. This affirmation articulates all of the values I want my students to demonstrate. The spirit and energy that this affirmation conjures up opens the pathway for exceptional learning to take place as we employ kinesthetic techniques of choral reading, body movement, sound and rhythm.

Resurrection Affirmation

We close class everyday with the Resurrection Affirmation, which gives a charge and reminds us of our unique calling and work in the world.

> The resurrection of my people and the redemption of humanity depends on whether I accept the call to higher consciousness.
> Today, tomorrow, and evermore . . . I accept the call.
> The lesson here is that while we enter to learn, we depart to serve our family, community, and humanity.

These affirmations will be particularly helpful, especially for new teachers, to begin to create a climate of achievement in the classroom. Early in my teaching career, I entered class saying, "Okay, everybody sit down, take out your homework/book/a sheet of paper, etc." It would take me five minutes just to get the class settled and ready for the day's lesson. I wondered why I had such a problem with losing my voice several times in the course of the school year. I was working hard but not "smart." You can use the aforementioned affirmations, which are now being used in many schools throughout the country, or you can create your own. If you are going to create your own, consider which character traits and success principles you want to instill in your children. Then incorporate them into your affirmations. Better still, have the students developed their own affirmations or a class affirmation. These affirmations are the call to order and they confirm and reaffirm our purpose for being in school. It immediately creates cooperation because everyone knows what to do once it is established as a ritual.

Rhythm: "the use of syncopated patterns of sound to enhance students' cognitive functioning, memory and understanding."

A-B-C-D-E-F-G
H-I-J-K-L-M-N-O-P
Q-R-S-T-U-V
W-X-Y-Z
Now I know my ABCs
Next time won't you sing with me.

Have you ever witnessed a child tapping his pen or pencil on the desk. I've seen many Black male students create intricate beats and polyrhythms with hands, feet, pens, and pencils. The rhythm of life is flowing through them. Oftentimes their inner rhythms are punished and suppressed rather than appreciated and rewarded. Why not capitalize on these inner rhythms through your classroom activities? All school children in America learn the rhythmic ABC song in preschool or kindergarten. In early childhood education, songs and rhymes are used frequently. For some reason, when children get to middle and high school, this critically effective teaching method is discarded as elementary. Nothing could be further from the truth, as reflected by the rich contributions in this book that shows how the principles of Hip hop are being integrated into language arts, history, social studies, and math courses.

In traditional African societies and centers of learning, rhythm was a foundational element in everyday life. The Master Teacher capitalizes on this and seizes the opportunity to cultivate this into a teaching tool that helps balance the down time when students are expected to sit still and concentrate. In teaching my students the eight parts of speech, I wanted to create a rap that would help them remember the information. What I found was that learning the rap cut my teaching time by more than half and helped them learn to name, define and give examples of the eight parts of speech. Please note that, as a teaching tool, "The Grammar Rap" has each of the eight parts of speech in bold, a definition of each, and examples of each underlined.

Grammar Rap

Good communication skills are essential
The power of the word will make you influential
We need to know the eight parts of speech
Master the language go as high as you can reach.
A noun is a person place or thing
An idea in my mind that makes me dream.
A verb is a word that always shows action.
Like divide, multiply, add, and do subtraction.
An adjective always describes a noun.
Like a big, red truck you can drive around
An adverb usually ends in—ly
Clearly a verb is what it modifies
A pronoun takes the place of a noun,
Like when she, he, and they walk around.
A conjunction connects phrases, clauses and words
And, but, or, nor, and yet—haven't you heard.
Here's a word that's definitely on a mission
Let me give you some examples of a preposition
In, on, from, to, and around, during, after, up and even down
Now we need to learn about interjections
A word with enthusiasm, lots of expression
Like STOP!, GO!, WAIT!, YES!, and NO!

WOW!, GREAT!, AWESOME!, UH-OH!
Now that you know the eight parts of speech, master the language, go as high as you can reach!

I was amazed to see how my sixth, seventh, and eighth grade students took the words to the rap, changed the beat and rhythm, performed it, then wrote and typed a 10-page grammar handbook, with great proficiency. My wife has used "The Grammar Rap" with her second graders and raved about the results. In both cases, the boys emerged ready to take the lead in rapping the lyrics. I even videotaped their outstanding performances, another example of the power of rhythm.

Remembrance

Remembrance is an evolving awareness of the contributions of Africa and her people throughout the world. Black boys are suffering from cultural amnesia. Of course, amnesia is a severe loss of memory. This loss of cultural memory is what has allowed others to supplant African identity with a self-destructive alien identity. The alien identity has become a cancer spreading throughout the community.

When someone loses part of their memory, there are basic steps that are taken to resuscitate the memory. They are shown pictures of great moments from their past. They are told wonderful stories about themselves and their family members. Herein lies the key to remembering a dismembered mind. We must take the responsibility for putting the consciousness back together again.

Knowing the critical nature and need for this type of information to get to our children and young Black males, in particular, I asked long time friend, colleague, and former Teacher of the Year, Tavares Stephens, to co-author *Reading Revolution: Reconnecting the Roots.*[19] It is a collection of 90 reading selections set up in the standardized testing format. The reading selection is on the left column and ten multiple-choice questions are on the right. Our premise was that we can raise comprehension and cultural consciousness at the same time. When this resource was introduced to other teachers, they clamored to get copies to share with their students because they knew of no other resource like it. Dr. Vonzia Phillips, director of Premier Middle Schools for Dekalb County (Georgia) Schools, remarked, "At a time when teachers across the nation are struggling to find that delicate balance between curriculum standards and meaningful content that students will readily identify with, Mr. Akua and Mr. Stephens have definitely hit the mark with Reading Revolution."

Many teachers have remarked that Reading Revolution opened up incredible insight with students on critical issues and inspired their students to strive for excellence. Simultaneously, it increases their understanding and achievement.

We suggest to teachers and parents that their children read one selection per day, something akin to a daily cultural multi-vitamin. Just as a person who takes a vitamin still eats other foods to get nutrients and nourishment, Black boys still need exposure to as much of their history and culture as possible. It is the least that our children should be learning about where they come from.

Co-author, Tavares Stephens remarks, "Reading Revolution is not the first book of its kind. Other biographies covering people of African and African American descent have been written. Yet Reading Revolution possesses unique applications. It is an interdisciplinary text aimed at enhancing test-taking and critical thinking skills, while lifting the mind and spirit through inspirational selections. This text will break cycles of underachievement."

Results with "At Risk" Students

I used this curriculum resource with a group of students who did not pass the state test in reading and language arts. After affirmations, class began with 10 minutes of quiet (with soft music playing: jazz or classical) for them to read the selection and answer the questions. Then we would take 10 minutes to read the selection orally, analyze it, and answer the questions. The rest of the class period was spent on other activities.

We showed these students the structure of the test and how to look for and identify topic, main idea, supporting details, and context clues. We taught them, not to fall for the trick that the test-makers try to play on the test-taker. So they began to notice the patterns of common mistakes that are made. None of these students had passed the state test the previous year, yet 72% of them passed after going through only half of the Reading Revolution exercises. While these results are preliminary, they indicate the kind of outcomes that are possible when Black boys are provided with culturally appropriate reading materials.

Another striking result of using these reading selections is that students began to exhibit increased interest in class. They began to look forward to their daily reading selection. They would see me in the hallway or at my door and ask, "Who are we reading about today, Mr. Akua?" One day during the last period, a young man came to class and asked with a sigh, "Mr. Akua, can't we just chill today?" I had always told my students that class wasn't the place to chill. They could "chill" at home.

With a smile, I replied, "You know you've been waiting all day just to see who we're going to read about today!" His response astounded me. "Yeah," he shrugged his shoulders, "you're right." He sat down, got out his pen, and got ready to read.

Stories of Remembrance and Rediscovery

Another strategy that I use to gain the attention of African American males is to expose them to short stories, fantasies, and fiction pieces where young people encounter ancient ancestors to learn about traditional morals, values, culture, and history. In the first two stories from the book, *A Treasure Within*, the main characters travel back in time to ancient Kemet (Egypt). After completing these stories with a group of seventh graders, our culminating activity was to do a project using ancient Kemetic symbols. I knew the project would have powerful results, but even I was shocked at how tremendous the response was from the students.[20]

Their assignment was to choose from a list of symbols I gave them. They were to type a one-page essay detailing what the symbol meant in ancient times and what it means to them today. This stimulates the affective domain. It is essential for the students to know the meaning of the symbol they chose so that they can begin to imagine the structure of a society in which these symbols had supreme importance and were incorporated into artwork, sacred writings, jewelry, and clothing. Lastly, students had to purchase a fiberglass ceiling tile and carefully, colorfully, and creatively paint the symbol on the ceiling tile. "Those tiles that meet the standard of excellence will be placed in the ceiling of the main entrance to the school. Our ancestors left clear examples of excellence and achievement. We will do the same. Your projects will remain in the ceiling for years to come, long after you leave this school," I explained. James, a seventh grader, decided to do his project on the scarab symbol, which symbolizes the transformations that many adolescent boys are going through at this time in their lives. "I thought it would be interesting to study something that is happening in my life, and I really wanted to know the meaning of it. The scarab lays its eggs in a ball of dung and pushes it in the direct path of the sun until the eggs hatch. Why is this important to me? Even if you're not from a good household and there is crime and your family is poor, it doesn't matter. You can walk in the direct path of the sun. You can transform and be whatever you want to be. You are always in the direct path of the sun and you can transform (change) at any time."

Another student, Ezekiel, chose the symbol of the Third Eye because it represents the ability to see and gain insight with more than just the two physical eyes. He passionately explained, "After reading Mr. Akua's book ("A Treasure Within") about Marcus and Imani, it has shown me how difficult it is to open my Third Eye. It takes a focused mind to reach success in life, and the Third Eye will show you the way. I also chose this symbol because it happens to be the one that interests me the most. The Third Eye is also called the eye of all-seeing enlightenment for mental and spiritual vision. To me, the Third Eye is like the North Star because it leads you in the right direction when you are lost. The Third Eye is important to me because it will keep me from going in the wrong direction. It is like a compass that leads you where you want to go. These things are important in life because I want to be successful."

James and Ezekiel were students in one of my language arts classes that were introduced to the Adinkra symbols of Ghana after reading a story, *Daniel and the Djembe Drum*. This is a story about a 13-year old boy, Daniel who is coming of age and dealing with peer pressure and the untimely death of his father when he was four years old. A Ghanaian elder teaches Daniel the ancient art of drumming and leads him to a transformational encounter. Since Daniel's drumming instructor is from Ghana, I decided to introduce my students to the Adinkra symbols and their meanings (instead of Kemetic symbols) to choose from for their final project. Adinkra symbols were first used by the Akan, Gyaman, and Ashanti people. All the Adinkra symbols are in the language of Twi of the Akan people.

Alfred, a seventh grade boy in my class, chose Nkruma Kesee, which in Twi means greatness. "To me, Nkruma Kesee means more than just the word greatness. It means that everyone, even if you are the poorest person, can do many great things if you put your mind to it. The reason I chose this symbol is because this symbol really makes me feel that I can be great anytime and anywhere. The greatness that I want to achieve is to one day become President of the United States. To me this symbol can show people what greatness really is," explained Alfred.

One of his classmates, Lincoln, a quiet and thoughtful young man, chose the same symbol, but had a slightly different take on greatness. "This symbol (Nkruma Kesee) means a lot to me because I try to achieve greatness in everything I do. I chose this symbol because its circle has no starting or ending point.

The dictionary meaning of greatness is, 'very large, larger in size than others of the same kind, remarkable or outstanding in magnitude, degree or extent; of outstanding significance or importance, chief or principal, superior in quality or character; noble, grand, aristocratic, and enthusiastic. This symbol is important to me because it is so powerful." Given the raw, violent, misogynistic images of Black males in the media, who would imagine young Black boys thinking like this? Amidst the bug-eyed clown-like caricatures that play the tired and timeless buffoon, who would think that Black boys would produce such insights?

The essay by Lincoln reminds me that not all of my students saw themselves as being worthy of doing great academic work. Many of them have misconceptions about the sequence and order of how things works in the world.

Rather than seeing greatness as a trait or consequence that is gained from working to continuously improve a skill, many of my students believed there was a quick way and easy way to become great or that greatness was an exceptional talent for exceptional people like Michael Jordan, Kobe Bryant or the Hip hop artist, Fifty-Cent. It is for these reasons that I persisted in using the ancient symbols as a way to help Black boys understand the values and routines that are required for them to do outstanding academic work. As my student Lincoln stated, "People are too quick to put themselves on the higher level. You cannot be great in a short time. I feel you must continually do good things to have greatness. Greatness is a mark you are left with when you earn it. You can look at some sports stars, authors, and other people to see greatness in many ways. Greatness is something that everyone can accomplish in their lifetime if they try. Greatness is within all of us."

These essays represent just a taste of what the children came up with, not to mention the incredible artwork they did with their ceiling tiles. Their tiles were displayed in the main hall of the school and remain there to this day. When I moved to another school and came back to visit, the security guard said, "Mr. Akua, I meant to tell you something. Whenever parents come to visit the school the first thing they see and mention is how incredible those ceiling tiles look."

Upon reflection, I realize that this simple project was an attempt to turn my classroom and school into a place where African American males felt respected, valued, and a vital part of a community of learners. There is a fine line between art on school walls and ceilings and graffiti on the walls of bathrooms, buildings and bridges in the community. Give a child the opportunity to express and affirm his creativity at school in the proper way and perhaps he won't express it in such a profane way elsewhere.

Repetition

In repeating the successful strategies of Ritual, Rhythm, and Remembrance, teachers will find that students adopt and adapt a higher level of consistency and proficiency in their work. They show more interest, respect, and responsibility. In addition, these strategies transform a classroom into a veritable temple of higher learning. These strategies, for me, changed a school year into a rite of passage. Children entered at the beginning of the year as students. They emerged at the end of the year as scholars. Put simply, it gets results. For example, Philip was tall for his age. At the beginning of seventh grade, he was about 5'9". He had quite a presence in the classroom; he was well-liked and brought energy, enthusiasm, and opinions to every lesson. While he wasn't an outstanding student at the beginning of the year, I saw his achievement improve over time as he saw that the assignments we did and the issues we discussed were easy for him to identify with. He saw himself in the context of our activities, not the textbook, but the unspoken narrative of a group of students who were striving for excellence. Phillip said, "I've learned to display my intelligence, not my ignorance, how to get into the proper mindset to learn, and how to handle responsibility. Those are the important things in life. This has been my best year in school, maybe not grade-wise, but in learning wisdom and not as much book knowledge. Our relationship went past student-teacher, but to father-son and friend to friend. I appreciate that. You know I have no father. It's a joy when I can talk and chill with a teacher and picture him being my father. You gave me the key to my past and future, but now I must open it and explore the things in it. All the things you taught about

Black history were and are not taken for granted by me. I enjoyed learning that the most."

Daryl Brown, another student I had the privilege of teaching, was the son of a hard-working single mother. He missed a great deal of the first quarter due to a neck injury from football. Daryl came to me with fear in his eyes after we completed a unit on Martin Luther King and Malcolm X. He confided that he had a dream the night before. In the dream, he was called to do the same work as Martin Luther King, and he was afraid. I told him that Dr. King was afraid also. I told him that Dr. King didn't even want to show up at his most famous, "Mountain Top" speech just before his assassination in Memphis. I then encouraged him to know that if he was called to do the same type of work—and I believed then and now that he is called to do the same type of work—that he would be guided and protected.

At the writing of this chapter, Daryl is a senior at Holy Cross College. He is a student-football athlete majoring in Political Science with a minor in Spanish. He is determining whether he wants to go to law school, a similar decision Dr. King had to make. Of all the things that grabbed Daryl's attention, it was learning about the contributions African Americans had made to the fabric of life that changed the way he felt about himself. "I learned so many fascinating things about my African heritage and many famous African American brothers and sisters. What makes this information so important is that during all my other years of education, this information was denied me. And I really thank you, Mr. Akua, for really opening my eyes so I could see how great of a people we are," Daryl explained with passion.

Of all my students, Larry went through the most dramatic transformation. He was a struggling eighth grader when he entered my classroom. That year, I was at Huntington Middle School, a school designated "in-crisis" by the superintendent. A call was sent throughout the system for teachers who wanted to teach their to transform the school. Prior to integration, the historic Huntington High School was an all Black bastion of academic, cultural, and athletic excellence. It was known around the country for its prowess in these areas.

Now, it was a middle school "in crisis." I, along with a colleague and friend, volunteered to be a part of an eighth grade team of students who had the most discipline and tardy and truancy problems.

Larry's first quarter grade in language arts was an F. The second quarter, he earned a D. Slowly he began to improve as I gave him individual attention and encouragement. At the beginning of the year, he assumed he would fail language arts as he had done in the past. But I convinced him that he could be an "A" student with just a little more effort. I worked with him on the classroom routines of the daily warm-up, a critical grade in my class. Students had to correct five sentences in the first five minutes of class by adding capitalization, verb tense, and punctuation.

As he improved on the daily warm-ups, his writing began to improve as well. Each of my students had a folder that I kept in my filing cabinet. Inside the folder was a grade record sheet in which the student recorded the date of the assignment/test/quiz, the number grade, and the letter grade they received. Larry began to compare his quiz and test scores with other students. He even began to talk trash about how he could score higher grades than his classmates. I know he was a competitor because I had played him in basketball before. His competitiveness spilled over into the classroom, and he was not to be outdone by his classmates.

Third quarter, Larry earned a C, but was close to a B. I told him that, to get the A, I wasn't going to give it to him, he would have to earn it. And that's exactly what he did. At the end of the year, he not only earned the A, but he received the "Most Improved Student" award.

Over the course of my career, I've seen a countless number of Black males transformed from students who were doing enough in school to just get by into students who settled for nothing less than making the top grade. Not all of my students followed this route, but because enough of them did, I feel confident that I know about the best ways to motivate and educate African American males. While you might be tempted to believe that you can't achieve similar results with the Black males in your classes, you can. And if you are teaching in a multi-cultural/multi-ethnic/multi-racial classroom, then many of the methods described in the chapter will help non-African American students develop a great awareness and appreciation of the contributions of Black people to the fabric of life in America. You will need to put some effort into learning how to use the methods to motivate your students, but the effort will payoff in terms of greater interest in classroom lessons and higher grades. I offer you, in the next section, ten essential lessons about how to use culture and character to close the achievement gaps.

Ten Essential Lessons Teachers Can Use to Close the Achievement Gap

Regardless of whether you are teaching in the inner-city or rural America, and regardless of whether your students are from working-class families or receiving free and reduces lunches, all of them deserve a balanced and quality education to prepare them for their future. Here are my top ten hints for success using culture and character to close the achievement gap that your college professors and texts probably did not mention.

The ten tips will give you a head start on this process by giving you some basic ideas to help you be a successful teacher and to help your students become better learners. Often, experienced teachers, particularly the few African American males (and females), who are doing exceptional work with Black males become entrenched in a day-to-day routine and are so busy with their own concerns that they do not realize that a beginning teacher might need help or support.

Although many school districts have formal new teacher induction programs that include an assigned mentor for new teachers, not all schools have the resources, and few have teacher/mentors who are enthusiastic about teaching in the multi-culture/multi-ethnic/multi/racial classroom. As a consequence, with 2.5 million new teachers expected to enter the field over the next decade and with the growing exodus of seasoned staff into retirement, it is up to you to be proactive about finding the right mentor and how to go about using culture and character to close the achievement gap.

1. Don't isolate yourself from the seasoned teaching staff, particularly the African Americans, who can provide you with a deeper insight about motivating and educating African American males. New teachers are often overwhelmed with the demands of their first teaching job, fear of failure, and uncertainty about the best course of action. What makes this worse is a feeling of isolation and the need to talk about work and the problems you have encountered. Your number one priority should be to have a friend, a colleague on staff at your school who is there to support your growth as a teacher. Without a doubt, it is essential for you to be proactive in developing a support system. Take the initiative to develop personal and professional relationships in your school. If possible, establish a mentor relationship with an experienced teacher, someone who has been effective

in educating Black males. A mentor encourages you to cooperatively seek solutions, increases your awareness of alternatives, provides a sounding board to vent frustrations, and allows you to learn from his/her experiences. By all means, don't buy into the idea that just because you have recently completed your training to be a teacher that you have a better knowledge base about working with Black males than teachers who have considerable experience. Regardless of your ethnicity/race or gender, it's up to you to seek advice from those who know how to best motivate and educate Black males. It is from witnessing your interactions with staff members from different ethnic/cultural backgrounds that your students will come to see you as a person who walks their talk. A mentor, particularly one from another ethnic/racial background than your own who is familiar with district policies and the various testing programs, will be valuable in helping you to understand the rules, regulations, and accepted practices for just about everything that occurs regularly in the day of a classroom teacher. The faster you find the right mentor or coach for yourself, the faster you will start to feel as though you are thriving rather than just surviving.

2. Relax and be yourself and get to know the Black boys in your classroom. Listen, empathize, and, above all be patient. The Black boys, along with all of your other students, are great people and capable of doing superior work. Let them know that you care about them, their lives outside of school, and the quality of their education. Also, let the students know that you are not infallible; be comfortable enough with yourself to admit when you do not know an answer and to be willing to learn with your students. Establish that sense of presence that conveys to students and anyone observing the classroom that you are confident, capable, organized, prepared, responsive to students' needs, able to make the class engaging for all students, and a lifelong learner. And don't act like you know everything about African American culture because even if you are an African American teacher, you don't. Show your students, from your example, how to research and discover new facts about the accomplishment of African Americans and their role in creating the foundation for life in the world today. Most importantly, don't just wait until Black History Month to integrate information about African American history into your curriculum and lesson plans. Your role should be to make the celebration

of the truthful contribution of all people, regardless of their ethnicity, an everyday celebration in your classroom.

3. Without a doubt, Black boys will quickly tune into perceived lack of respect by a teacher. Many Black boys come into the classroom with big chips on their shoulders because of their home life and their previous relationships with teachers. In other words, they are expecting you to treat them as less than intelligent human beings who are valuable members of your classroom. Avoid categorizing them as lazy, bright, unorganized, etc. Rather, look for each student's unique qualities. Do not allow put-downs or sarcasm in your classroom. Show by example that every comment is valued and must be constructive or helpful to others. Make them happy to be in your classroom every day. Think about the difference in the following scenarios: A student has been absent from class for several days. As you greet students coming into the classroom, you might say in a stern and authoritarian voice "Phillip, you have been absent for three days. Your homework is in your folder. You have until Thursday to turn it in." Or as you greet the student, you smile and say, "Phillip, I'm so glad to see you. I was beginning to be concerned. You have been gone for three days. Your homework is in your folder. Please pick it up and complete it by Thursday. You may ask me or your fellow students for help." In both cases, you are the person in charge of the classroom. In one case, however, a positive classroom environment is established where a student feels important and cared for, while in the other, rules and procedure appear to be more important than the child. Which classroom would you rather be in? Remember, you do not know what has happened to your students before they entered your classroom. Maybe they have had a fight with their mom or dad or with a sister or brother before leaving for school; maybe they haven't eaten; maybe they are feeling sick or have been teased in the hallway. Give them a break, and, most importantly, remember that Black boys can be taught responsibility for their own actions by following your example. This means you should always be prepared, return papers promptly, and provide feedback that is quick, helpful, and thoughtful. Chances are that if you respect the Black boys in your classroom, they will respect you.

4. Believe in the Black males in your classroom even if they don't believe in themselves. Treat them as valued members of your classroom, school,

and community. This will enable them to feel hopeful and have the confidence to develop into strong individuals. Don't fall into the habit of accepting lower quality work from Black boys or giving them answers. Don't take over and do assignments; this can cause them to doubt their ability to succeed. It is also important that discipline is not perceived as a personal attack. The act is criticized, not the student who has erred in judgment. We are all learning acceptable modes of behavior. Help them learn. In my classroom, my policy for dealing with discipline was to use a combination of modeling and environmental control. I used classroom rules that described the behaviors I wanted instead of a list of things they could not do. I believe that politeness, promptness, enthusiasm, control, patience and organization are the types of behavior we want students to demonstrate. Students will often model our behavior, so mixed messages confuse students and invite misbehavior. If you want students to behave a particular way, then it is important for them to see you behaving that way. As a rule, my classroom was a warm and friendly place where students felt welcomed and could take a glimpse into my life from the personal pieces of art, posters, and other items in my classroom.

Often times I would tie certain pieces of my art into a lesson and this caused my students to get to know my values and me better, which led to fewer problems with discipline. The room was also arranged to allow a "quiet place" where students could be steered to work on projects and then come back into the main classroom. What's amazing is that even in cases where the student was physically larger and taller than me, the quiet and peaceful nature of my classroom was often enough to turn a potentially threatening situation into a learning opportunity.

5. My room is a learning environment that fosters growth and pride. I often told my students that my room was not a classroom, but a temple of higher learning. I worked diligently to create an inviting environment in even the most uninviting buildings so that students standing in the doorway on the first day would be drawn, like a magnet, to come inside. Over time, I put their work on display to give them ownership of the temple. I took great pride at the beginning of each year, like a shaman performing a ritual, transforming my classrooms into centers of initiation. I would personally make and create displays and posters and banners that could not be found in teacher stores. It sent an unspoken message to the students that this is a place where your creativity and self-expression is welcomed. As a result, I

typically didn't experience any significant disciplinary problems and those that did emerge quickly dissolved. I attribute the rapid dissolution of conflicts and disciplinary concerns to being able to remind students of the behaviors necessary for accomplishing their academic goals. In this regard, most of my disciplinary problems emerged as a result of students feeling uncomfortable and or not having the tools to accomplish a particular assignment. In other words, there was some sort of discrepancy between what they perceived in their skill set and those necessary for accomplishing the task. Typically, there is a tendency for Black males to act out when they experience this type of anxiety and discomfort. But the acting out and resultant disciplinary problems can be avoided by reminding students that they are in school to learn how to learn rather than to just pass a test.

6. Standards are not the curriculum; they are the goals of the curriculum. Standards cannot be ignored and should not be feared. In this age of high stakes testing and stagnant and constricting standards, many teachers find it difficult to maintain their creativity, teach what they feel is essential, and still cover what's on state tests. Remain centered. Understand that you can cover what is essential and still have your students prepared. Be mindful of the tests, but don't be blinded by the tests. You must maintain a sense of what is worth knowing. I found that when I did this, the test scores took care of themselves.

This is not to say that I didn't give time and attention to the standards. On the contrary, I perused the standards to see how/if they fit into what I felt was necessary for my students to learn. Then I utilized them accordingly. There are pressures of test scores and state standards that must be met. Standardized tests are often used to determine school and district performance, allocate funds, and gain public approval. These test scores may even be published. Look at the standards as an aid to good teaching. Standards help you decide what to teach, support your decisions about what and how to teach, convince the public that you are familiar with the subjects your teach, and focus curriculum so that you do not spend too much time on a favorite topic and ignore important concepts that must be taught. By no means does your adherence to the standards mean that you can't include information about African American history and culture into whatever subjects you are teaching.

7. Create objectives for your class that focus on student learning, not on the task you have for the day. For example, discussing how the classic curriculum is connected to Hip hop poetry is a task, which stimulate students to critically analyze the poetry of Hip hop and compare its motifs, themes, and general poetic devices (such as alliteration, rhyme scheme, figurative language, etc.) is the skill you want students to have. Focus on what you really expect students to learn and to be able to do. Thinking about the criteria for student success before giving an assignment will help you determine your expectations. Critics will say this leads to grade inflation, but I disagree. Almost all students want to succeed. Clearly stating your expectations upfront helps students to know what they need to do to be successful and helps to build student confidence in you as a fair teacher. Expectations need to be realistic and challenging for all students. Creating a list of expectations that provides for a range of abilities and skill levels can be difficult; however, students of all abilities must have the opportunity to succeed. Having clear expectations (objectives) will help you focus your lesson plan by allowing you to ask yourself, "How does this lesson or activity bring my students closer to meeting expectations?"

8. You've got to understand your students by giving some attention to their styles of learning. No two people process information in exactly the same way you do. Some people prefer to read about a concept to learn it; others need to see a demonstration of the concept. You have probably noticed that some students prefer to learn by listening to someone talk to them about the information while others prefer to learn by doing something with the information. Learning Style Theory proposes that different people learn in different ways and that it is good to know what your own preferred learning style is. When learning something new or difficult, you naturally tend to use the learning style you prefer. It is good to know what this learning style is so that you can respond most effectively to the material being presented. Even when the material is not presented in the way you prefer, you can use knowledge about your learning styles to adjust and be flexible, no matter who your instructor is or what the topic might be.

Chances are that your students are growing up in a world completely different from the one you grew up in. Technology, lifestyles, economics, and many other factors have created a different world than when you were in school. The classroom environment tends to be very lively and demands the use of technology rather than simple textbooks as a way to connect with students. By all means, students today are different from those of yesterday. They might seem less motivated to learn because of their diverse interests in video games, Internet sites, and listening to music you don't quite understand, but they are eager to learn using the multimedia technology that they are familiar with. The problem is not with the students; the real problem is that teachers are less familiar with the use of technology. Without a doubt, if a Black boy, or any child, is excited about being in the classroom, then there is an increased likelihood that there won't be any major challenges with getting the boy to focus on his school work. Basically, most children learn better in classrooms where they feel happy, safe, and excited. Black boys, even those considered to be at high risk for academic failure, can be lured into being a productive member of an exciting classroom. In most cases, the teachers' use of digital media is what it takes to capture their attention. The capacity of digital media to combine and transform text, speech, and images leads to a more diversified palette for communication; one that accommodates the varied strengths of all students. While printed text has already disappeared in high-impact fields like advertising, entertainment, and communication, in education, its dominance remains. In the years ahead, however, it is clear that text-only instruction will give way to a more deliberate application of multimedia.

Great teachers will use digital tools to tailor media to the task, to different kinds of learning, and to different kinds of students, thereby reducing the barriers and inefficiencies inherent in one-size-fits-all printed textbooks. You can capitalize on your students' energy and enthusiasm by making connections between what you teach in the classroom and their everyday lives. But before you can do this, you need to know what students' lives are like outside the classroom. A good way to learn about your students is to allow them to choose their own topics for projects and the process by which they work on their projects. This gives you the opportunity to see what your students are interested in and helps make the learning relevant. An added benefit is that when students are involved in deciding what to study and how to demonstrate their understanding, they develop a sense of ownership and generally try to exceed your expectations. As with adults, students learn more when the concepts are personally meaningful to them. This translates into a need for authentic learning in classrooms—deep learning, relevant to those outside the classroom—and involving students' use of the key ideas in a production where they have developed a deep understanding that causes them to constantly think about their own thinking.

Using digital multimedia encourages students to think about their thinking (e.g., become meta-cognitive), and, therefore, they approach problems by automatically trying to predict outcomes, explaining ideas to themselves, noting and learning from failures, and activating prior knowledge. Great teachers understand the remarkable features and flexibility that digital media offers Black males. They encourage their students to save text, speech, and images, reliably and precisely over time, and they encourage their students to see for themselves how and where their text, speech, and images can be redisplayed. By encouraging their students to become comfortable with the technology of digital media, great teachers are helping to prepare Black males to participate in today's rapidly changing world.

9. Manage your time. Teachers, particularly beginning teachers, are generally surprised at the amount of time it takes to plan effectively. Determining objectives, deciding on classroom activities, doing research to collect materials, creating exams, grading papers, handling disciplinary issues, and making informed decisions take a tremendous amount of time and effort, more time and effort than you ever thought possible. It is essential that you organize and use your time efficiently. And just when you think you have everything planned and organized, there is an unexpected fire drill, bad weather alert, student assembly, or early dismissal that forces you to adjust your plans. In addition to planning, it is essential that beginning teachers learn to be flexible. Flexibility in time management is also essential to accommodate the diversity of students' background knowledge and the manner in which they learn to process information. Successful teachers are willing to stop and re-teach if necessary or to modify lesson plans if it becomes clear that more or less time is required. It will help if you thoroughly think through your day's activities and objectives, keep careful records and notes, and prepare to explain and give common everyday examples. Don't be afraid to ask for suggestions and opinions. Talk to colleagues. Most teachers are flattered when you ask. Please keep in mind that your students learn from your example. So if they see that you are not organized and delivering lessons that are not well planned or

that critical information is missing, then you should expect them to do as they see you doing rather than behave in accordance with what you say.

10. Get parents on your side up front and quickly. Often, when they see the high standards you set for your students and your willingness to tell them something good about their child, they will back you up in ways you wouldn't imagine. Don't make the mistake of waiting until there is a problem to start communicating with parents. Just imagine that your son, an energetic seventh grader, has been attending school for four months. Based on his reports, you assume that everything is going smoothly. But what he does not tell you about is his bad temper, his fights with peers, and the way he constantly interrupts class. Just image that he's been acting this way for several months and that you receive a letter in the mail, not a phone call or email, but a letter in the mail requesting a meeting to talking about the impending suspension of your son because of his behavioral problems at school. Parents want to know that you care enough to give their child culturally relevant instruction and information, along with the encouragement to be their best. This is not done by stating, "I will give your child culturally relevant instruction and information . . ." Demonstration beats conversation. It is done in the way you carry yourself, the homework assignments, projects, and notes you send home.

In conclusion, effective teachers are constantly learning from their successes and failures with Black males. To be effective, teachers must look back on their practices and assess what works well, what doesn't, and how they might improve as teachers. Keeping a journal is an excellent means of keeping track of your performance, and it can provide valuable information for your own professional development. At the end of each semester, I asked students to write a letter about the most important thing they learned that semester, perhaps an academic or life lesson. Often I saw patterns about what was most impactful for them: knowledge, skills, insights, and experiences. I always incorporated these insights into my plans for the next semester and I suggest that you adopt a similar practice.

5

Honoring the Culture of African American Males Through Storytelling

By Obakunle Akinlana and Madafo Lyold Williams

Introduction

Take watch of your thoughts because your thoughts become words you use to tell your story. Take watch over your words and your story because they become your actions. Take watch of your actions used to tell your story because your actions become your habits. Take watch of over the habits you are acting out because your habits become your character. Take watch over your character because it becomes your destiny and the story your people (your children) know you by. Take watch over your destiny because your journey to the promised land is still long!

The free agency of the spirit equips us as humans with the instrumentality of choice. The choices that we make begin at birth and follow us to our graves. The choices that we make shape the template or pattern that displays our identity through distinguishing attributes. These distinguishing attributes are known as character. In the Yoruba language of Nigeria, it is called iwa. It is our iwa that defines who we are.

African American youth must know their true identity in order to develop the character that reflects who they are. Culture is the essence of a people. Many African American citizens have a feeling of having been left out of the country's dialogue and decision-making process. This community, like any other community, knows itself through its heritage, patterns of everyday behavior, cultural expression, art, and education. A community's identity is defined by what it has excelled in, historically, as well as its recent achievements. Identity also grows from cultural memory and heritage, including the headlines of local history and folklore from griots.

Much of what Black people in America know about their ancient African cultural roots, their identity, was passed along from one generation to the next in the form of stories. Reading and writing was forbidden for Africans enslaved in America and would often result in the ultimate punishment, death. For most African slaves, stories provided a link with their culture. Storytelling, probably, first consisted of simple chants that praised the dawn, expressed the joy of being alive, and were used to ease the drudgery and pain associated with laborious tasks. Later, the storyteller became the community entertainer, combining their stories with poetry, music, and dance. The storyteller also evolved into the group historian. This was the beginning of professional storytelling, but storytelling has always been a part of the African culture. In this regard, storytelling is one of the earliest forms of folkart.[1,2,3]

Madafo's Reflections: The Birth Of Storytelling

Obakunle and I were drawn to the profession of storytelling for many of the same reasons: It was always a part of our lives growing up. As children, our mothers told stories to us every night at bed time, and that was my introduction to storytelling. As a child, I did not understand it that way, but those times with my mother were special. My mothers related stories about growing up in Hemingway, South Carolina, and about family members, some of whom I had not yet met and some I would never meet because they were deceased. It was in those moments that I learned about how powerful storytelling was in soothing my fears and laying the foundation for my identity.

It was through the stories my mother told that gave me a vision of who I am and my role in my family. It was those stories about family that helped me understand the importance of storytelling. For example, my grandmother, the youngest of 18 children, had a tradition where everyone came to her house for dinner on holidays, after church on most Sundays, or when we had something to celebrate or some family business to talk over. Her little house was usually filled with so many family members and guests that there was no place for us children to sit except on the floor in the middle of the room. My aunt, who was the griot of the family, made sure that everyone knew it was time to visit my grandmother. There would always be laughter, fables, songs, and stories. Storytelling was ever-present at these gatherings where it was a tradition to tell stories before, during, and after dinner. The task of the children was to be alert and listen to the stories about our family and to understand why it was important for us to come together.

When I became a father, I began to tell my children the same stories my mother told me. Passing along stories from one generation to the next is a powerful way to pass on family values, traditions, secrets, and any information that needs to be safeguarded by a family. In this way, storytelling is a tradition in my family, and much like Obakunle, storytelling became a natural way for me to help other people understand why it's important for them to keep the memories of their families alive through stories.

Storytelling is the ancient art of conveying events in words, images, and sounds. Stories have probably been shared in every culture and in every land as a means of entertainment, education, preservation of culture, and instilling knowledge and values/morals. Crucial elements of storytelling include plot and characters, as well as the narrative point of view. Stories are frequently used to teach important lessons about life, explain, and/or entertain. Less frequently, but occasionally with major consequences, they have been used to mislead. There can be much truth in a story of fiction and much falsehood in a story that uses facts.

Technology has changed the tools available to storytellers. The earliest forms of storytelling are thought to have been primarily oral, combined with gestures and expressions. African storytellers also used various instruments (e.g., drums, etc.) and dance to convey their stories. Rudimentary drawings, such as can be seen in the artwork scratched onto the walls of caves, may also have been early forms of storytelling. Ephemeral media such as sand, leaves, and the carved trunks of living trees have also been used to record stories in pictures or words. With the advent of writing and the use of stable, portable media, stories were recorded, transcribed, and shared over wide regions of the world. Stories have been carved, scratched, painted, printed, or inked onto wood or bamboo, ivory and other bones, pottery, clay tablets, stone, palm-leaf books, skins (parchment), bark cloth, paper, silk, canvas, and other textiles. They have been recorded on film and stored electronically in digital form. Complex forms of tattooing may also represent stories, with information about genealogy, affiliation, and social status.

Traditionally, oral stories were passed from generation to generation and survived solely by memory. With the advent of written and sophisticated means of capturing stories in various multimedia formats, this has become less important. In recent times, however, there has been a renewed interest in the art of storytelling. Today, professional storytellers tour the world. Likewise, storytelling conferences and festivals abound and attract a wide audience. In formal storytelling, the teller prepares a story to present to their listeners. Some storytellers tell stories from their own imagination. Other stories have been gathered, sometimes adapted from significant cultural events in books or from other storytellers. Regardless of the content of the story, the essence of the stories resides in a rich oral tradition.

Obakunle's Reflections: The Oral Traditions

Storytelling includes the teller and the audience. The storyteller creates the experience using words and gestures, while the audience perceives the message and creates personal mental images. In this experience, the audience becomes co-creator of the art. Storytellers sometimes dialogue with their audience, adjusting their words to respond to the listeners and to the moment.

Oral storytelling is an improvisational art form, one that is sometimes compared to music. Generally, a storyteller does not memorize a set text. Rather he or she learns a series of script-like incidents that form a satisfying narrative arc (a plot) with a distinct beginning, middle, and end. The teller visualizes the characters and settings, and then improvises the actual wording. Thus no two versions of an oral story are exactly alike, but the stories provide a way to preserve important events within a cultural context that revolved around strong family bonds and unity. Unfortunately today, many of the stories about African people or African Americans occur within a context where men are absent from the family. The family unit is quite fragmented because of divorce, death of Black men from preventable health problems, excessive incarceration of Black men, wartime causalities, and other hardships that Black men experience.

When culture is absent from the education of our youth, they are denied the opportunity to develop their complete selves. Culture serves as the compass that directs its people to their character. People without their culture become lost. Our children don't know us, and we don't know our children. And teachers don't have a real sense of the cultural context in which their students are navigating through life.

I (Obakunle) often see my role as an African storyteller as being an educator who has the responsibility of helping teachers develop a cultural awareness of the lives and backgrounds of Africa American males. Without this awareness, I don't believe that a teacher's sensitivity and compassion for Black males would develop. My travels across the United States and around the world have helped me view life through cultural lens.

But what is culture? For me, culture can be viewed as an iceberg with its small visible tip and huge mass below the surface. Most teachers view only the surface aspects of culture—observable behavior—sometimes known as the five Fs: food, fashion, festivals, folklore, and flags. But culture goes deeper than that. It's what is beneath the surface that we need to be aware: factors such as beliefs about raising children, concepts of self, gender roles, connections to peers, beauty and personal space, religious rituals and perspectives, establishing priorities, eating habits, facial expressions, eye contact, work ethic, approaches to problem solving and interpersonal relationships, moral values, cosmology, world views, and personal discipline—to name a few.

Developing cultural competence is a process of inner growth. In order for teachers (or mentors or school counselors) to be as effective as possible with Black male students, they must continuously engage in a process of self-reflection. To be able to know others, especially students as diverse as Black males, a teacher must know him-or herself. They must look within for a deeper understanding of their core beliefs and hidden biases before they can adequately address the needs of their students. Developing cultural competence is a process that comes with experience and engagement and painful lessons that highlight a teacher's limitations and prejudices. To learn about the cultural backgrounds of students takes time and effort; it involves reading about their countries of origin, meeting family members, connecting with parents, visiting their homes, developing relationships with community members and organizations, going to cultural and religious festivals, and being courageous enough to create cultural experiences for all the students in the classroom.

A Story About Obakunle

I did not fully appreciate the idea that schools don't exist in vacuums and that they are situated within communities until I was a freshman at Morris Brown College in Atlanta, Georgia. I was excited about attending college, and it was my first experience away from home. I lived in a campus dormitory, and I met students from around the nation, as well as students from other nations. But the part that I enjoyed best was seeing and meeting so many beautiful women. I walked around the campus viewing the young beauties from everywhere. If you had put a pair of dark sunglasses on me, I could have been mistaken for Stevie Wonder, turning my head from side to side trying to catch a glimpse of the young ladies. I still smile today when I recall those images of African queens, ranging from ebony to ivory.

One day, my father paid me a surprise visit on campus and observed me and my friends sitting on the wall girl watching. He called me to his side and voiced his concerns that I should give the attention that I was giving to the girls to my studies. My father began to tell me a story that I wish to share. Daddy looked me in my eyes and asked me whether I had heard of Oni Eat Them All. I replied no. He then proceeded to narrate to me the story. He said, "You see, son, Oni Eat Them All was the biggest and baddest crocodile in all of Africa. His name came as a result of his reputation that he would eat anything that dared to enter the waters of the Niger River, located in the country of Nigeria."

"There was a family of dogs that lived near the banks of the Niger River. The mother and father of the dogs warned their puppies not to go near the river because of Oni Eat Them All, the fierce crocodile. All of the puppies, except one, obeyed their parents' instructions. One day, the lone puppy went to the river's edge and barked. Oni Eat Them All appeared without any warning and lunged after the unsuspecting puppy. A few more inches and the poor puppy would have been the giant crocodile's dinner. Instead of the puppy being alarmed by the attempt on his life, the young pup laughed, assuming the crocodile was playing a game. Each day, the puppy would go to the river to challenge the crocodile by barking at him and dodging as the great croc lunged after him. This game soon became the puppy's daily routine."

"One day, the puppy went to the river for his daily encounter with Oni Eat Them All. The dog barked and waited for the great croc to appear, but it was to no avail. The puppy barked louder and louder, but still there was no Oni Eat Them All. The sound of another dog's bark came from across the river. The sound was coming from a female dog that was on the other side of the river. The female dog said 'Hi, I'm new around here. Why don't you come across the river to join me and show me around?' The young puppy replied with a series of barks and said to the female dog on the other side, 'You must be new around here, indeed, if you expect me to cross that river and join you. Don't you know that the biggest and baddest crocodile in all of Africa lives there in that river? He is called Oni Eat Them All.' The young dog went on to explain that the crocodile had gained his name from his reputation for eating all that entered the river. If any creature—large or small, man, bird, or beast—entered the river, they would become his meal for the day. The young female dog replied with a series of barks and said to the young puppy, 'I understand. I'll find someone else to show me around'. She lifted up her tail and began to walk away. The young male let out a strong bark and said, 'Stop. I'll find a way to get across and join you.' The female dog stopped, wagged her tail, and smiled."

"The young male dog knew that if anything made a disturbance in the river, Oni Eat Them All would investigate. The dog found a stone and threw it into the river. As it hit the water, it made a loud splash and roused Oni Eat Them All. The crocodile swam past the dog, who waited on the bank of the river. When the crocodile had swam to what appeared to be a safe distance down the river, the young puppy made a daring move. He dove into the river, making a loud splash, and began to swim across the river. Hearing the splash, Oni Eat Them All stopped, turned around and saw the young puppy in the river. The great croc began to pursue the young puppy."

"The young pup knew that he was in trouble. He swam with all of his might in an effort to reach the other side and escape the razor sharp teeth of Oni Eat Them All. The young female dog on the other side recognized the grave situation that the young pup had gotten himself in and began to bark, urging him to swim faster. 'Faster,' she barked. 'He's gaining on you, swim faster.' The young puppy swam faster and faster and finally made it across to the other side."

"The young dog smiled and started to wag its tail. The female dog barked and warned the young puppy that he was not safe yet. His tail still remained in the river. 'Get your tail out of the water,' she barked at him. The young puppy turned around to remove its tail from the river. As he did, the jaws of Oni Eat Them All bit off the young dog's head, killing him instantly."

My father looked into my eyes and asked if I know understood the meaning of the story. I replied, "No."

He then said to me, "Son, you should never lose your head over a piece of tail!" Sadly, too many of our young Black males have lost their heads and their lives running behind women. HIV/AIDS, while having a more devastating effect on African American women, continues to take the lives of far too many Black males before they have had a chance to make a meaningful contribution to life. The HIV/AIDS story for Black women runs parallel to the story of sexual irresponsibility among Black men (See Chapter 14). More than 80 percent of the HIV/AIDS cases among Black women are a result of having sexual intercourse with an HIV/AIDS infected male partner who did not use protection.

Humans often evaluate various situations incorrectly by referencing the effects and ignoring the cause. It is the cause that brings about the effect. With the current focus in education on test scores, medicating low performing students, security, and discipline, it is evident that educators are missing the point. Instead of forming mental stereotypes about the sagging pants these youth wear, I suggest that you look into the eyes of these young Black explorers. Their eyes and faces reveal confusion, hurt, disappointment, hunger, hopelessness, and frustration at their failure to find their place as productive citizens in a system that seems not to have a place for them. Rather than labeling Black males as being at-risk, try referring to them as being at chance for becoming great. There is a sort of self-fulfilling prophesy at play because, as an educator or parents, you are probably well aware that children are more likely to do what you do rather than what you say. In this regard, Black boys will live up to (or down to) whatever level of expectation you constantly communicate. If they consistently receive messages from you that they can't perform well, they will believe the message, and they will live up to your expectations. On the other hand, if you communicate that they are capable, studious, smart, brilliant, and just as good as other students, then Black boys will excel academically, socially, and emotionally.

When students identify with subject matter, they tend to show more interest. For example, if Black boys discover that the banjo and violin originated in West Africa, then their interest in classical music may be stimulated. If they learn that honesty and hard work are recognized as great qualities for males in their culture, then they would value these qualities. If they knew that a Black man invented the major instrument used by rappers, the microphone, then their interest in science, math and engineering might grow. If they knew that most people around the world don't have a clue that a Black man developed the stoplight, then they might be moved to learn about the many other contributions Black men have made to the fabric of life.

African American History Book on a Poster

One member of our mastermind group, Rap Mapp, has focused most of his work on the creation of classroom materials that depict inventions made by African Americans. The Black Miracles poster developed by Ray is the only known quick reference guide to over 200 inventions by African Americans.[4] Organized in an easy-to-read format, the poster provides educators, parents, and others with an effective resource for teaching Black history. "I could have used something like this when I was going through school. I felt embarrassed in front of my white friends about being Black because the curriculum typically emphasized all of the negative aspects of Black life and never taught us anything about the intellectual contributions of Black people. The only mention of Black people was slavery and some limited information about the civil rights movement, while the history of European was glorified," says Ray.

The poster book developed by Ray lists inventions that people around the world use everyday (e.g., electric light, refrigerator, microphone, procedure for open-heart surgery, stoplight, chemotherapy treatments for cancer, laser instrument used for eye surgery, and major components for the personal computers) to make their lives safer and more comfortable. His goal in creating the Black Miracles Book on a Poster was to help young Black people learn about the remarkable intellectual accomplishments of Black people and, in doing so, overcome some of the symptoms of self-hate and self-destruction that are associated with having a distorted and negative view of Black people. "I believe that self-esteem and respect are enhanced when Black males know the truthful history of their people. Also, many of the problems teachers have motivating Black males will disappear when schools and the media accentuate the positive stories about the achievements and deemphasize the difficult past of Black Americans."

Our history is rich with stories about discovery, resilience, courage, economic prosperity, compassion, love, and determination. Every invention listed on Ray's poster represents an important piece of the story of Black people in America. Black boys will never know about these stories unless parents and educators step outside of their comfort zones and teach Black boys the truth about the contributions of their ancestors. "There is somewhat of a myth going on about Black students not being interested in science, technology, engineering, and mathematics (STEM) fields. The truth is that data going back to 1985 show African-American freshmen consistently specifying STEM majors at a higher rate than their white peers. African Americans also enroll in college at rates roughly on par with their representation in the population, so at the very beginning of college, the representation of African Americans in STEM fields is slightly in excess of their representation in the general population." But students often change their plans, and the attrition rates from a STEM major and from college itself are greater for African Americans than they are for the average college student. That leaves African Americans underrepresented among those with bachelor's degrees in STEM fields and even less well represented at every subsequent phase of the career path." Whereas the reasons for the high attritions rates are not well understood, factors such as academic and cultural isolation, low expectations that erode motivation and performance, unsupportive peers, lack of African American faculty and role models that send the subconscious message that you don't belong, and discrimination can all cause undergraduate students to drop out or transfer out of STEM fields. While keeping African-American students interested in STEM and engaged in undergraduate studies is important, no amount of interest can overcome financial problems that tend to be the major reason why Black students leave college. "But who is to say what the impact will be from providing Black boys, from K-12 grades, with information that clearly and strongly depicts the involvement of African Americans in STEM fields."

Madafo: The Role of Community in Our Stories

When I was a young boy living in Wilmington, North Carolina, it was tradition on the weekend for farmers and artisans to come into town to sell their produce. It was the one time during the week where Black men came together to support each other and exchange information about people and events. These Saturday gatherings were like a festival. There was music, arts and crafts, and food to eat. I remember one artist in particular, primarily because of his beautiful daughters and because he made jewelry right there in front of our faces. He made some wonderful jewelry, but his daughter captured my attention. At the time, I had a job as a shoeshine boy, and I remember shining the shoes of Black men who were doctors, lawyers, teachers, and other leaders of the community. I also remember that there was nothing but Black people. Black people doing business with other Black people. For whatever reasons, white people stayed away from these Saturday festivals.

These experience have always stuck out in my mind because they provided a foundation for me to understand that Black men, regardless of the pain and humiliation they have experienced, played a significant role in the wellbeing of their own community. These Saturday festivals showed us younger males how to keep the community intact and why it was important for us to always be on the lookout for ways to improve the community.

It boggles my mind when I think about how tough times must have been for our parents. They sacrificed, knowing that in doing so, a foundation would be in place for the next generation to have a better start in life. That was their motivation. Many times, I heard the phrase, "I'm working this hard so you won't have to."

Our parents, the Elders, believed in the idea that if they made the necessary provisions, their children would be more secure in the pursuit of their goals. Their weapon was education! And so, they bargained with Miss Ann, negotiated with Mr. Man and worked hard to insure Black children would have the opportunities necessary to excel in a society hell bent on keeping Black faces in their kitchens and nurseries. So, the Elders told the untold stories that unfolded the secrets of a people who made a way out of no way. It was in those untold stories, those secrets, coded messages, that we, the children, gained a true sense of self and understood the responsibility being passed on to us. We were constantly being told how capable and bright we were. From every corner of the community, it was put to us that our effort had to be ten times more to succeed. Not one or two times the effort, but ten times more. And in the face of all the odds, we did it! Our communities flourished under the capable leadership, positive role modeling, and direction of Black Men, the Father spirit, the caretakers, teachers, the leaders—the ones who knew, understood and willingly accepted the responsibility of their manhood. Consequently, we seriously embraced school, went to college, graduated with honors, and made our parents and the community proud. We became doctors, lawyers, architects, scientist, and teachers, successful in every endeavor. In spite of the hardships, maybe even because of them, the Black community flourished, and the world took notice.

I remember growing up in Wilmington, North Carolina, where racist ideals akin to the Dred Scot Decision were unspoken laws; Black men where lynched in public, at will; Black people ordered food from restaurants through a window at the back of the establishments; Black children read from books that white school systems considered obsolete; and the infamous "Colored Only" and "White Only" signs were the norm. The images of Black men stepping down off the curb to allow a White man to pass unimpeded are forever burned in my memory. In my life-time, I have observed and experienced this inhumane treatment and wondered how someone, anyone, could profess to be a student of God and commit such cruel, evil and heinous deeds.

What emerged for me over time was a cogent resolve to practice respect for the family and community in which we lived, one that spoke from tradition, history, and culture. The "Golden Rule" was prominently displayed on the walls of my classrooms, at school and church. Teachers read to us from books they purchased for their home library, forbidden books that told the true stories of a glorious history and wondrous culture that dated back to the beginning of time and implanted in our young minds a keener and positive sense of self.

Black men were everywhere then: in the schools as teachers, principles, and presidents of PTAs; they were in the church as Sunday school administrators, ministers, and scout masters and on the playground teaching us sportsmanship. They were in the homes being fathers and positive role models. Black men presented themselves as pillars of the community. The children belonged to the community, and the community accepted the responsibility to properly nurture them.

Growing up witnessing how Black men were in charge of their own communities and families had a profound impact on me. I remember young boys my age being encouraged by their older brothers to respect the norms of the community and to always show respect for their elders. I remember the social and peer pressure being exerted on those boys who ignored their role as a responsible member of the community. Even boys who were raised without a father at home had men who took an active role in their development.

The story has been told thousands of times about how a child committed a wrong somewhere in the community and before that youngster would arrive home, he had been chastised several times by the elders. He received a bop on the head for being so stupid and when he arrived home, his parents had already gotten word and were ready to take care of business. Just the fear of having to walk that gauntlet was enough to scare you straight. Going to jail had nothing on the community gauntlet.

Then, seemingly, in the blink of an eye, everything changed. The Father Spirit disappeared into a puff of smoke with a spike in the main vein. Strong backs that once were imaginary horses for their babies and loved their women with a passion were bent over, in a stupor. Arms, that once lovingly held us, taught us how to catch a ball and change a tire, now reached out, begging for quarters to cop the next fix. Home was a prison cell. The stories of history, once told by mothers and fathers, lost their meaning. Now, they were being read and interpreted by white teachers, people who had little to no knowledge of the secrets and coded messages. To the young, Hip hop mentality, the word "culture" meant old and irrelevant. Striving for excellence was out of the question; that was "a white thang." Stories that reflected the success and pride of Black people were forgotten or distorted. In addition, the one thing that seemed to have made this possible was the disappearance of the father from the homes of Black families.

In addition to my work as a storyteller, I have been mentoring Black males for nearly 20 years. Many of my boys are living up to their potential and have become model students and leaders. The transformations that occurred in the boys had little to do with what was said during out time together, but were brought about because of the relationship they developed with me. It was about trust; me being there for them, on time, listening to their stories and trying to help them make some sense of their pain. From our relationship, they gained a keen understanding of themselves, purpose and direction. They gained an appreciation of their own story and the struggles their parents and grandparents endured so they could have a better life.

As long as the eyes of educators stay focused on the majesty and great potential of Black males, there will be contentment, mutual respect, and motivation to learn. However, if we continue to focus on the problems in the classroom while ignoring the solutions, teachers, parents and students will grumble about every challenge they encounter. Energetic stories about cooperation and unity provide a way for teachers to keep their eyes on the real prize of transforming a Black boy into a lifelong learner.

Educators must review the current curriculum and insist on the inclusion of African culture. Care must be taken not to generalize Africa or the descendants of Africans who were enslaved and brought to America. A consistent curriculum must be designed that will give students a cultural and historic understanding of Africa and her descendants. Educators and parents must help Black boys understand that the history of Black people on this planet did not start with slavery. And learning from an African storyteller is one of the most interesting ways for children to learn and appreciate the history of Africa and her people.

Cultural programs must be presented in schools, libraries, places of worship, and community centers. A Yoruba proverb says: One tree does not make a forest, nor does one thread make a fabric.

Everyone's culture is important. Culture is a valuable educational resource, and storytelling could be a vehicle for helping Black boys to be more open to strategies that allow them to express themselves. Perhaps helping Black boys to find their voice through storytelling about events from their culture is one way for Black boys to feel valued by their peers and their teachers. To feel valued, however, starts when the teacher knows a little something about the story of every student in the classroom. Something as gentle as having children tell the story of where their names come from can create a marvelous amount of love in a classroom.

A Few Easy Ways To Get Children to Tell Stories

The Black boys that step into your classroom each year have a variety of life paths. Looking at their cultural backgrounds with the iceberg concept in mind will help you to be aware of the aspects of their lives that are not in plain view. Like the iceberg, what is in plan view when you deal with

Black boys is rather small in comparison to the vast emotional, social, religious, and economic injustices Black boys have experienced.

This journey of establishing a multicultural learning community in your classroom, with a foundation of respect for all cultures, is ever changing and evolving. Children bring to the classroom rich cultural life experiences, so why not tap into it? This involves a continuous process of research about the lives of the children in your classroom, your own interpretations and perspectives, and, hopefully, the integration of storytelling into your curriculum. The nuances of culture are complex and continually changing, but your classroom is a natural place for all students to learn about different cultures.

- One technique storytellers use to motivate children to tell stories is called spotlighting. This is a getting-to-know-you activity that is great for the beginning of the year. First, ask students to make a list of as many things about themselves as there are students in the classroom. Ask them, as long as they are comfortable, to write things that their friends don't know. Once all students have completed their lists, allow them to move around and talk to one another. The goal is to trade one fact with each student and write the student's first name beside the fact. Next, let the students take turns sitting in a chair at the front of the room, being "spotlighted," while everyone calls out the things they have learned about the student.

- African mask-making exercises. It's always exciting to see students working on their projects and to hear what the mask means to them. In schools that don't have adequate space for the mask-making exercise, we involve students in a storytelling exercise called House Stories. The students are shown pictures of houses from Africa and other places around the world. All of the pictures contain no people, only houses. We ask the students to look into the windows of the house and to tell a story, including at least four characters, that reflects something they have learned from our storytelling workshop about unity, hope, achievement, peaceful living, or family.

- The oldest family member. We often have children tell stories about their oldest living family member. We have them answer questions, such as: When and where was the person born? What kind of job did they have? What was their school like? What kind of car did the person have? We encourage students to discuss what food, clothing, and going to the movies cost today compared to when their relative, usually a grandparent, was a child.

There are endless sources for stories, and you don't have to spend a large amount of money to bring storytelling into your classroom. Students love having an opportunity to tell stories about their heroes, favorite teachers, close friends, funny things that happened to other people, embarrassing moments, best times at school, and their version of stories currently in the newspapers.

Madafo On Using Storytelling To Build Resilience and Hope

Storytelling is undoubtedly a vehicle that can help Black boys be resilient and hopeful while the long-term efforts of school reform proceed around them. Lost in the discussions about school reform is the impact of troubled schools on Black boys who are unlikely to benefit a great deal from the changes being debated and planned. Black boys and their parents are watching and waiting for educators to take the steps necessary to make their schools safe and provide teachers who are well-qualified and committed to teaching Black males. Interesting enough, storytelling, according to the work of the psychologist James W. Pennebaker, is a way for young people facing chronic difficulties to find emotional relief from their stressful experiences. In fact, a number of research studies have validated the fact that writing about difficult circumstances is therapeutic for those unable to change what they must live through. And at this moment in our history, Black parents are feeling discouraged and stressed-out by a system of education that seems disinterested in the alarming rate at which Black males are dropping out of school. Stories on the 6 o'clock news have little to do with the success experiences of Black males or the threats to Black culture and more to do with murders, arrests for drug use, and how some star athlete has fallen onto hard times.[5,6,7,8]

Princeville, North Carolina, is the oldest incorporated Black town (98% of the residents are African Americans) in the United States. It is located in the coastal plain region of eastern North Carolina and lies just south of the Tar River. Settled just after the Civil War in 1865, Princeville was originally called "Freedom Hill" by the freed slaves who had gathered on the Tar River flood plain seeking refuge at a Union Army camp. In 1999, much of Princeville was lost when flooding from back-to-back hurricanes devastated the city. The city's 2,100 residents, many of them descendants of the original settlers, found their homes submerged under water for two weeks. They lost virtually everything.[9,10,11]

The story of the Princeville flood is one of government neglect, even malfeasance. Before the flooding, the waterfront town had been under pressure by developers and land speculators to sell its land and relocate residents further inland. After the disaster, residents were pressured by both the federal and local government to abandon the area. Residents were suspicious—particularly when similarly situated white communities in the region were receiving large sums of money for rebuilding, not relocation.

In Princeville, it was a different story. Some six months after the storm, only 100 of the city's 875 families had moved back into their homes. More than 300 families still lived at the sprawling temporary camper park nicknamed "Camp Depression," or "FEMAville," after the Federal Emergency Management Agency (FEMA) that set up the camper park immediately after the flooding. Here, the displaced families made do with makeshift housing on a landfill next door to a women's prison outside of the City of Rocky Mount. Almost a year later, many still waited for assistance. The nearly 260 families that left the campsite were still living in campers, though this time on their own property, as they began the slow process of rebuilding.

Princeville's business community was virtually leveled. In addition, the town's historic churches—including Mount Zion Primitive Baptist Church, founded in 1876 and built in 1895—were also severely affected. Mt. Zion remains one of the oldest African American houses of worship in the state. It was the only one of the town's six churches not to be torn down.

If the destruction of homes, churches, and businesses wasn't enough, the town was totally devastated by the impact of the flooding on the centuries-old Dancy, Wilson and Community cemeteries: 224 caskets and crypts were dislodged. Critical emergency assistance was provided by the federal government's Disaster Mortuary Operational Response Team, which helped to secure and rebury the caskets and restore the cemeteries.

Although residents accepted that the hand of God, in part, dictated their fate, it was confirmed months later that God received some "assistance" from the nearby government of Rocky Mount. The city opened the flood gates to the upstream Tar River Reservoir Dam just 20 miles away. While state officials were quick in issuing a statement of support of the Rocky Mountain city managers within days of the flooding, city managers have not answered questions about why they had not communicated to any officials downstream, or to the state, that they were opening up a floodgate. This lack of communication from Rocky Mount, the quick support of Rocky Mount by the state, along with the years of speculators pressuring residents to sell their property, raised residents' suspicions. The flood seemed ill-timed, particularly, given the town's pending historic designation, a status that many residents believed would bring desperately needed tourism dollars (an effort opposed by some neighboring and statewide forces). By the time the Federal Emergency Management Agency stepped in, tensions were at a climax.

It has been a stormy road to recovery but Princeville residents have gracefully received the outpouring of support from politicians and others who have spoken out nationally to raise public awareness of the community's plight. In addition to support from private individuals, faith institutions, and other non-governmental organizations, Congress has provided the U.S. Army Corps of Engineers with funds needed to repair a flood prevention levee built in 1967. Former President Clinton established the "President's Council on the Future of Princeville" and set aside additional funds to be used to further study the construction of the dike and evaluate the flow of waters along the Tar River. Although government support is welcome, it is a long way from the estimated $80 million required to complete rebuilding and flood proofing. And it is still significantly less than the public support allocated to predominantly white communities in the region.

A few day after the flood, I (Madafo) received a phone from Doc (Dr. Ernest H. Johnson) who wanted to know whether I knew anything about the flood in Princeville. He was interested in going out to provide some emotional support and hope for the residents. We reached out for help from some of the Black psychologists in the state, but we soon discovered that we only had each other during this journey to Princeville. And it was a journey. Many roads were still flooded, homes were underwater, pets were stranded on rooftops, and one of the few places that had space for people to rest and feel safe was a high school in a nearby town. We told stories, prayed with people, cried with people, offered hope, and did workshops for the students. Many of the residents we spent time with had lost everything, but telling their stories to us provided them a way to reflect on the past, relieve some of their stress, and to focus on the new life they wanted for themselves and their families.

Today, Princeville is still rebuilding from the devastation of the flood of 1999 and is very proud of its unique place within African American heritage and United States history. This unique sense of place and solidarity among the residents of Princeville, along with the destruction of historical documents, made it an ideal community in which to begin the preservation of oral history. In August of 2003, The North Carolina Language and Life Project (NCLLP) began to work with the Princeville community to conduct interviews with long-time residents to tell the story of Princeville's survival through racial prejudice, economic hardship, and near-permanent destruction from Hurricane Floyd.[10,11,12]

Remembering personal and collective stories of which one is a part allows Black males to experience a sense of wholeness, harmony, integration, and a sense of integrity. The story of Princeville is an example of the process of remembering that is a vital dimension of the transformation of consciousness that Black males must explore as an exercise in self-discovery. Memory serves to recollect, reassemble, and reconfigure individual and collective consciousness into a meaningful and sequential whole through the process of narrativization. Remembering is significant because it allows individuals to connect with information lodged in the unconscious soul of a person.[13] Remembering allows Black males to better understand and respond to questions of character: Who am I? How can I contribute to the development of my people? How do I get what I really want in life? What is my place in the world?

Storytelling allows Black males to remember their stories and to examine the beliefs and values that have been handed down to them by traditions and customs. The process of storytelling and retelling stories enable a Black man to identify core beliefs and better understand the people and important circumstances that have contributed to his thinking about who he is. When Black men understand the value derived from storytelling, particular the self-esteem generated from telling their own stories, they can begin to reframe their stories to find common ground with others. Discovering the limit of one's beliefs can be painful, but it provides one with opportunity for growth and respect among family, peers, and teachers. It allows us to heal deep emotional wounds that have distorted our moral vision and our compassion for others. When a Black boy reframes his story, he initiates a process that results in new habits that allow him to accommodate the ethical choices with which one is confronted in the context of his relationships with others.[13]

A story from a white male teacher provides a good example of the power of reframing. On the weekends, he served as a coach for a little league softball team for children ages 9-11. One of his players was a little Black boy who rarely got a chance to play under the previous coach because he could barely catch the ball, and no one had ever seen him hit the ball. Well, the chance came for him to bat for another boy who had gotten sick. The first pitch was a strike. But he hit the next ball out to right field. But after hitting the ball, he just stood there at home plate with the bat in hand. Everyone, including members of the other team, was yelling for him to run to first base. But rather than run to first base, in the direction where he hit the ball, he ran to third base instead and was called out by the referee. What followed was a very angry conversation. The referee was trying to convince the boy that he was out and that he should go back to the dugout. Eventually, the little fellow relinquished his hold on third base, lowered his head, and slowly walked to the dugout. Everyone could see how angry and frustrated he was, and the coach asked him what was going on. The young man said, "That man, the referee, is a bad and mean man. He was mean to me because he's white and I'm Black." The coach then asked, "Well, if he's mean because he white, then what does that make me because I'm white and a man?" The little fella hesitated for a while and thoughtfully replied, "You're different, but you are white and you are good."

As you imagine this story, think for a few moments about the generalized anger and hurt that Black males sitting in your classrooms go through because they might see you as a mean person because you are white. Just like you, they have heard stories about how white teachers mistreat Black boys. Stories they have lodged in their subconscious depict you as being a villain rather than a nurturing provider of knowledge and education they can use to make a better life. Stories about your relationships with Black students and how you have worked to transform them into academically enriched students are important. Those stories will help you connect with Black males in ways that will enable you to gain their trust and respect.

Storytelling is not just a bit of entertainment for students; it can be a powerful way for educators to break through stereotypes they have about race, a platform for meaningful conversations about the meaning of race, and a means to discover precious stories about friendship and commitment between people from different races. Often overlooked are those stories, during the most brutal times of the Civil Rights Movement, of the bond between Black and white people that set the stage for racial healing.

Obakunle's Reflections About The Laws of Life

One program that taps into the universally recognized healing power of storytelling is the Laws of Life essay, which provides Black males and all students with an opportunity to write about the values and guiding moral principles with which they live their lives.[14,15] The Laws of Life essay, established by the John Templeton Foundation, is based on the philosophy of the late philanthropist and financier Sir John Templeton, a man of great spiritual belief and optimism, who felt that most young people were getting positive messages from the caring adults around them. He believed that all they and needed is a vehicle for tuning into their own deepest understandings. As Black boys begin to look deeply at their lives and put their varied experiences into narrative form, they also reflect on the life paths of others and their Laws of Life. This leads them to speculate about their futures. The essay-writing process broadens students' sense of possibilities. Equally important, the parents and educators who hear students' stories often revise their own narratives of the direction of these students' lives.

The program occurs worldwide, with much of the implementation in the United States at the high school level and in communities that are not disadvantaged. But one New Jersey community decided to apply the Laws of Life process to schools in difficult urban circumstances. Maurice J. Elias is a professor of psychology at Rutgers University in New Brunswick, N.J., and the academic director of Rutgers' Civic Engagement and Service Education Partnerships program. He is also the co-editor of *Urban Dreams: Stories of Hope, Resilience, and Character*,[8] that tells the story of the essay-writing project in Plainfield, N.J.

Plainfield, N.J., is an urban district with a student population that is almost entirely African-American or Latino and eligible for free or reduced-price lunch. It has many social and health-related problems and serious, persistent concerns about academics.

Plainfield adapted the laws-of-life concept to fit its community's needs. Fifth and eighth graders were the focus, so that they could begin this reflective process before the stressful transition to secondary schools. To encourage dialogue around the life principles, students were asked to discuss their Laws of Life with classmates and families. High school students and community members were enlisted to help screen and judge the subsequent essays according to rubrics established by the district's Laws of Life committee.

It was no surprise that the Students' Laws of Life essays addressed themes such as peace, responsibility, respect, family ties, perseverance, self-discipline, courage, honesty, and kindness, sometimes in combination. To a certain extent, the programs where students present their Laws of Life essays are like poetry jams (spoken word concerts) where there is a high level of excitement and spontaneity. The program has been credited by educators and school superintendents alike with helping improve students' progress in both literacy and character development. Students had renewed enthusiasm for writing, along with a deeper understanding of the long-term implications of their everyday decisions and actions. Outside the schoolhouse, deeper communication among diverse groups of people has broken down barriers and forged new relationships.

The Plainfield experience illustrates how urban youths, so often the object of remediation and the subject of the pedagogy of poverty, can have their learning energized by reflection and inspiration. When they can address their life circumstances, intense challenges, and share these experiences with classmates and families in an open manner, it reduces the emotional barriers that often hinder their progress.

Every child writing an essay received acknowledgment. Some received extra recognition for excellence through awards donated by local businesses, alumni, community organizations, or residents. Teams of staff members, parents, and students from individual schools also arranged celebratory banquets for participants, honoring the authors of each school's best essays. A similar team then planned a district wide banquet attended by representatives of the school board, clergy, community and parents' groups, sponsors, guests—such as the commissioner of education and the mayor—and, of course, many students and their families. The banquets have turned into extraordinary community-building and fund-raising events.

Those entrusted with the care and nurturance of Black males should ask whether our current approaches to improving academic scores are in the best interest of students or are driven by adults' concerns with accountability. To "leave no child behind" is not an adequate goal; there is limited benefit in being brought to the back of the pack. By relentlessly seeking the advancement of all children, we affirm our commitment to prepare them for the tests of life, not for a life of academic tests. And while the times are changing and we and overjoyed by the election of our first African American president, the statistics about school drop out, unemployment, and life expectancy indicate that it is tough being a Black male in America.

It was not too long ago that the scholarly multimillionaire and Wimbledon tennis champion Arthur Ashe, who died from an AIDS-related illness, revealed that the killer virus was not his heaviest burden. He wrote in his memoir, *Days of Grace*,[16] that AIDS "is a burden alright . . . but being Black is the greatest burden I've ever had to bear. No question about it. Race has always been my biggest burden. Having to live as a minority in America. Even now it continues to feel like an extra weight tied around me. Race is for me a more onerous burden than AIDS."

Storytelling answers the questions of life and gives a young mind a perspective about what has transpired in the past. Stories provide Black males with answers to questions about their self-worth and the role their people have played in the formation of civilization. Through stories, Black males learn about the system of education that their people used to build the great pyramids. They learn about the contributions their people have made to science, medicine, agriculture, and they learn about the hydroponics projects that NASA supports at Tuskegee University so that one day man can grow plants to eat within the confines of a space station.

The key issue for us is that the answers Black boys seek about their identities must come from people who are committed to feeding the wonders of a young Black mind with truth. Unless the person answering the questions is someone who he loves and who loves him, then he will seek answers down another path. All you have to do is look in our jails to see how many of our Black males have found answers that have led them to misunderstand who they are, why they are, and what they are. They don't know the truth about themselves or their people, so they simply take on the answers that reflect all of negativity in our society.

Storytelling helps to remove Black males from these negative images so that they can get the proper guidance on their journey through life. Black men are not the only ones who can give our boys the correct answers to questions about their identity, but there are many advantages for connecting Black Men with Black boys. Educators, including white female teachers, can help provide some answers about the history of Africans in the world, but it's important to help Black males understand that the history of his people started long before slavery in America. If we depend on other communities to raise our boys, then they will be raised in the image of those communities. African storytellers provide Black boys, and all children, with a deeper understanding of the origins of Black people and the important cultural, artistic, intellectual, and scientific contributions Black people made long before slavery in America.

Tips For Teachers and Parents

1. The best way to introduce African storytelling into a curriculum is through in-service workshops where the storyteller spends significant time with both students and teachers. It's not enough to simply have a storyteller come for in-service training with teachers without allowing for opportunities for students (and teachers) to enjoy fully the benefits of listening and actively participating in the stories. If there is a remote possibility that there is some reality behind the statement, "The truth shall set you free," then the intellectual development of Black males will remain imprisoned because their identify is built on false information, much of it passed to them from one generation of teachers to the next. Many dedicated storytellers, like ourselves, have spent decades researching and gathering stories about the contributions of Africans and their descendants to the fabric of life in the world. In-service workshops about storytelling can provide educators with much historical information and insights for tapping into the multiple intelligence of the different kinds of learners in your classrooms.

2. It's important for teachers to recognize that, in addition to providing insights into motivating Black males to perform at higher academic

levels, African storytellers can be used to address problems in schools and communities through stories about how to best deal with conflict, violence, traumatic accidents, and disasters (e.g., hurricanes, loss of homes, etc.). In our case, we have applied our craft to help victims of hurricanes, shootings at school, and the deaths of classmates. We have also addressed the health of children and adults, coping with overweight children, gang violence, homelessness, African American history, the diversity of staff and students, teenage pregnancy, drug abuse, character education, and the healing power of humor.

3. One of the biggest problems that we have witnessed in public schools is that teachers often don't know their students and students don't trust each other because they don't know each other. In many cases, teachers don't even know the names of the Black males sitting in their classrooms. If it's even partially true that one of the predictors of whether a Black boy will be motivated to embrace school and excel academically is the relationship he has with his teachers, then teachers should use storytelling as a means to get to know their students. Students become more comfortable with one another and are more likely to cooperate in class when they know and trust each other. Providing opportunities for students to tell stories about their lives or events in the communities is an invaluable way for both teachers and students to develop a learning community of respect and trust. We highly recommend that teachers have each student gather one fact about each student in the classroom as they exchange one fact about themselves. Then over the course of a month or so, ideally the first month of school, have each student sit at the front of the class while each of their classmates recites the one fact that they know about the student. The process takes only a few minutes of each class, but it will provide you with loads of insights about the students in your classroom.

4. So many students sitting in your classroom come from families where they don't know their fathers and they have a vague understanding of their family history. Encouraging students to gather accurate information, through the oral history tradition, is a great way to help children know their family backgrounds. Teachers can also use the oral history tradition to gather information about other important topics.

In a project organized by one of the few white women presenters in our Young, Black and Male in America seminar, Sandra Worsham had her students, mostly Black males, interview a grandparent from their community who was of an ethnic group different than their own. The purpose of the interview was for the students to gain insights about how older people from different ethnic groups dealt with the challenges of being a teenager. Ultimately, the Black boys learned that there were more similarities than differences. Sandra used an audiotape recorder during the time she conducted the project, but today teachers have access to digital audio/video recorders, IPods, and cell phones. There are several free easy-to-use software programs that allow students and their teachers to create stories from photos—similar to a slide show, but with music, sound and visual effects added. If you are not familiar with the online resources your students are using to accomplish these feats, then ask them. You can read about the online resources or even attend workshops, but you'll have more fun learning from the students in your own classroom.

5. Allowing space for storytelling in your classes can be a valuable way for Black boys (all boys) to vent ill feelings that have been suppressed. No matter how you look at the circumstances, Black boys are exposed; the society in which they reside does not have a consistently positive image of Black boys. They are at the bottom on most indicators of social and psychological wellbeing, and they are consistently discriminated against in the workplace. And somehow, the proportion of Black men in prison far exceeds their proportion in the general population. These and other reasons are the fuel that underlies their anger and hostile feelings. Regardless of the gravity of the situation, however, venting anger outwardly is not adaptive in the society we reside. If you are a parent, it is important for you to create opportunities for your Black male child to create stories about the feelings he is experiencing. If you cultivate this habit in your son, then you can also use storytelling to control negative behaviors, avert disasters, and allow the person telling the story to develop creative solutions. While we are working on the long task of improving troubled schools, we can take immediate steps to give Black males ways to explore and express their aspirations and to overcome the emotional barriers to learning born out of difficult life circumstances. All academic success and social resilience is grounded

in positive, caring relationships, and the Laws of Life essay process for telling stories can help strengthen these in many ways.

6. Black boys today are evaluated from the moment they step into the public schools until they leave. They are constantly tested, questioned, and made to feel that they aren't free to say or do anything without being evaluated. Storytelling provides a means for all students to engage in something at school where they don't have to fear being punished or receiving negative feedback about their performance. As long as a story has a beginning, middle, and an end—and the theme does not use profanity or a put-down of anyone—then the child has successfully told a story. As a teacher, you'll probably have some additional criteria for your stories from students, but keep in mind that you can make storytelling an opportunity for all students to receive great feedback about their performance, which is something most Black boys never experience in school. Regardless of the subject you teach, starting each lesson with a great story is a sure way to get the attention of your students. And keep in mind that something as simple as giving a standing ovation to a Black boy after he has shared a story is a powerful way to build self confidence and to make him feel important. Some teachers have made standing ovations a regular practice in their classrooms with the idea being that all students are deserving simply because of their efforts. In order to strengthen this idea, they randomly select a student and ask them to read aloud to the class one of the slogans on the banners in the room. Afterwards, all of the other students give a standing ovation.

7. The art of storytelling might be changing, but teachers need to seek ways to have children apply what they learn from stories to lessons in math, science, financial planning, health, and the other important subjects. If you look within any story, you are bound to find ways for students to use the story to examine an important academic concept. If you are looking for ways to get the attention of Black boys, then consider using storytelling as a way to hook them (along with the other students) into your lesson plans. The observation that many teachers and parents have made about Black boys not being interested in school might be only partially true. The other side of the story is that Black boys aren't being excited; they aren't focusing on the lessons

being taught. For example, you might not know much about the ten-time Grammy Award winner Kanye West, who began his career producing hits for Jay-Z and Janet Jackson, but Black males sitting in your classrooms know the story about how he achieved triple platinum success. They also know that Kanye, like other Hip hop superstars, has turned his pop artistry into a book, *Glow in the Dark*, [17] that comes with a CD, which includes Star Wars-like symphonics. Crash landed alone on an unknown planet for the entirety of his *Glow in the Dark* set, Kanye West takes you on a musical and visual odyssey that no anti-hero has taken you on before. The book and CD represents another leg of that voyage, giving you a gorgeous photographic ride through West's life, both on-and offstage, as well as into the intimate technologies of his creative process with top visual artists of today. The instrumentals are tracks from his set re-mastered to echo John Williams' famous score ("Jesus Walks" is Vader's theme). In personal sketches and reference imagery, 3-D models of the holodeckian stage, and costume designs (including his Grace Jones—inspired outfits for opening act Rihanna), West once again expands a medium and triumphs in the artist's epic struggle to be creative. While *Glow in the Dark* might not inspire you to pick up a book, it will surely inspire young readers because it's a story written by someone who speaks their language. By the way, if you don't know it, Kanye West is the son of a Black Panther and former English professor, and he is known for his socio-political lyrics and sampling from a wide variety of genres. He also attended the American Academy of Art in Chicago and reflects current trends in art, design, electronics, fashion, and architecture.

6

Addicted to Success: The Secrets for Turning Academic Excellence Into a Habit

By Ernest H. Johnson

Introduction

It's been widely stated that "success leaves clues," but most of the time when we are learning about the secrets for becoming successful, we find ourselves examining the strategies of wealthy white males. For the most part, we have been conditioned, almost brainwashed, to believe that success and excellence are ordained for some people and not others, that successful people are lucky, born blessed with the "right stuff" to be successful, or that success is related to being white. And when it comes to Black boys, rarely do we take a good look at the clues they provide us about the nature of success and excellence. Obviously, we hardly ever see any of them as being academically successful or worthy role models for other boys. We overlook those who are doing exceptional work or performing well beyond our expectations because we are often overwhelmed by the difficulties and problems with the few Black boys that "get on our last nerve."

For the most part, educators and parents assume that the standards for doing outstanding work are set by white students. Our job then becomes an endless struggle to motivate Black boys to act like someone who does not look like himself (a white male) and who is often perceived as the cause of generations of painful memories. In this regard, we are contributing to the stereotype that depicts white students as being smart and Black boys as being intellectually challenged and not capable of doing as well as or better than their white counterparts. Academic achievement and success in general, in the ideal world, should be colorblind. Images of success are guided by principles that transcend race and ethnicity. Although we are a long way from achieving these ideals, Black boys who are struggling academically and socially deserve the opportunity to learn from successful role models that reflect their own cultural values and look like them.[1,2,3]

In this chapter you will learn about the beliefs, attitudes, and mental habits of 40 Black boys who are very successful academically (e.g., making A's and B's in all of their courses) despite the fact that each of the boys was considered a "high risk" child because of their home and family life. Being successful in school was no accident for any of these boys, and they by no means were born into wealthy families. Of the 40 boys, only nine were residing with both their mother and father, while 29 were receiving free-and-reduced lunches at school. Most of the boys had siblings, most often an older brother or sister who had graduated from high school. Nearly a third of the older siblings were currently taking classes at a community or four-year college. While most of their parents (34 out of 40) had graduated from high school, only 11 parents had gone to college and graduated.

Over the course of a year, as I was conducting training sessions for elementary and middle schools across the country, I arranged to have lunch with Black male students who were doing exceptional work. I explained to each of them that I wanted to understand what they did at home and school to make sure they would always make As or Bs in their course work. I also explained that I would eventually use the information to help other Black males become better students. Most of the time, I had lunch with a single student, but on several occasions, I had lunch with a group of two or more boys at the same school. Our lunch discussions were guided by these questions: (1) What are the things you do to make sure you are going to do well in your classes? (2) What advice would you give Black males about what they need to do in order to make As and Bs in their course work? (3) How do you make sure that you are always ready to do outstanding work in your classes? (4) What are your secrets for doing well on exams? (5) What are some of the things you do with your body and posture to make sure that you can stay alert and focused in class? (6) What is the single most important thing you do to be successful at school? (7) Why is it important for you to do well in school and get a good education?

The boys typically talked at length about how doing well in school would help them "make a better life for them than their parents." They revealed very specific pathways to excellence and talked almost endlessly about the reasons for their success. Initially, I thought it would be easy to organize the information I had collected, but the process for organizing the information proved to be a complex task. The task took on some extra burdens when many parents, upon learning how I would eventually use the information, wanted to share their thoughts about their role in ensuring that their son (or grandson) would do well academically. To say I was overwhelmed is an understatement; I really didn't know how I would use the information, but I continued interviewing boys and their parents.

One of the unique features of these boys was that most of them came from single parent homes where there was "more month than money." Many of their parents or guardians were not college graduates or employed in white-collar jobs. They were regular, blue-collar workers who were struggling to keep their families together and were receiving government support to keep their households afloat. Nevertheless, most parents believed that it was up to them to show their children how to become successful. What was so startling about this observation is that, in spite of the failure of the parents to become well educated, they instilled within their children the desire to use education as a means to escape from poverty. Like so many of the parents who had high expectations for their children, Marva constantly reminded her grandson about the value of getting a good education, "Whatever he was going to do with his life . . . he would need an education to do it. I always tell my grandson Jessie that if he wants a better life, then he has to go on to college. I didn't have the opportunity to learn much or to help his mother better herself, but with a college education, he can do anything," Marva passionately explained.

For many of these parents and grandparents, success was the unknown and they felt unworthy and uncomfortable in their pursuits of success. Consequently, they unconsciously started sabotaging their successes to get back to a more familiar level of functioning. For many of them, being "successful" was too uncomfortable, unknown, and something neither of their parents had prepared them to accomplish. "To get out of my neighborhood and do well in college meant that I had to give up too much of who I was and become something I knew nothing about. I had no support, and I always felt out of place," explained Vicky, a thirty-eight year old single mother. After failing to master the important aspects of her personal power—her self-communication—Vicky had no place to go except back home to a familiar situation. Vicky, much like many of the other parents, failed to gain the communication skills and self-confidence that were necessary for her to understand that the quality of her life is determined by the quality of her internal communication.

"I barely got through high school and I had no intentions of going to college, but one of my teachers encouraged me to apply because she thought I was smart. My mother never said a positive word about school. She always talked about school being a waste of time and something for white people to do because they didn't want to work. All she wanted was for me to get a job and work for a living. So, when I went to college, my grades weren't that good and it was a struggle coming up with the money to pay for everything. When I quit, all I could think about was that my momma was right," explained Vicky.

While many parents of highly successful children find themselves walking in their parents' footsteps and committing many of their same mistakes, they continue to have higher expectations for their own children. Vicky, much like her mother, started college and got pregnant, and both eventually gave up on their dreams because of the pressures to support a family. Vicky explained that she didn't like the idea of quitting school but had to drop out of college to support her son.

"Most people thought I would never finish college, and I have to admit that it's difficult to believe in your own worth when everyone, including your mother, is saying they expect you to fail. It took me a while to learn how to think for myself and depend on myself . . . and this is the one lesson about life that I'm making sure that my boys learn."

It seems that parents of highly successful children perceive their own "short-comings" as opportunities to teach their children how to avoid making similar mistakes. One of the biggest mistakes they want their children to avoid is not appreciating the quality of their self-communication. "I am the complete opposite of my mother when it comes to encouraging my two sons about school. I attend every PTA meeting and talk with their teachers on a regular basis. I don't want my boys to have doubts about themselves or their abilities or to go through hell learning how to use the strength of their minds. They don't have to live paycheck-to-paycheck I am making sure they believe that getting a college education is their ticket," Vicky said.

Parents of highly successful Black boys have a strong belief in the idea that the first person a boy has to master communication with is himself. As he learns how to talk himself into making correct choices, he learns that he has the final say about the meaning of events in his life. Rather than dwelling on negative experiences and feelings of anger, Black boys who have mastered self-communication understand that whatever they give attention to is what they are reinforcing in their mind, body, and spirit. By mastering communications, they are learning how to be in charge of themselves and how to harness their own happiness. "I'm teaching my boys to think for themselves and to not allow the opinions of others to rule their lives. I would have made a lot fewer mistakes if my mother or someone had taught me this lesson. I guess my mother just didn't know much about this sort of thing. She was doing all she could to hang on, but children today can't survive unless they learn how to take care of themselves," Vicky offered.

Every Black boy is a winner, but some of them might not look the part. Some might not strive to live up to their full potential, and as a result, they don't produce the kind of results they want for themselves or those that we expect. Other boys constantly produce quality work, regardless of their personal problems or the challenges they face at home, regardless of the pressures from their peers and family, and regardless of the things their parents can't afford. They have learned to be in charge of how they talk to themselves, and they respond emotionally very different to the situations most other children see as problems.

Joanne, a single mother of two sons, said, "I've taught my boys to believe in themselves and to see themselves as the great students, thinkers, and intellectual geniuses that they are. They, like all Blacks boys, have to believe they can do anything if they believe they can." After being married for twelve years to an abusive husband, Joann escaped one night with her two sons in tow. "Leaving my husband was the hardest thing I've done in my life, but my boys deserve an opportunity to grow into the great thinkers that they are. I realized that life would be difficult for us, but I had to leave so that they could learn how to be great men," she reasoned.

What other boys see as problems and opportunities for failure, successful Black boys see as challenges that need solutions and opportunities for them to master new information. Highly successful Black boys thrive in the present moment and the future while others are focused on the problems of the past. Although they have firm ideas about goals they want to achieve, they maintain a cool but obsessive, fixation on their objectives. They are not mentally rigid. In fact, the boys often describe situations where they had to "change their approach" in order to move forward. You might say that successful Black boys have different attitudes, beliefs, and values than Black boys who are not doing well academically, socially, or emotionally. "I have some friends that continue trying the same old things to solve problems even though they should know that what they have been doing over and over again has not worked. But somehow, they just keep doing the same things as if they are not paying close attention to what is going on with themselves," said Brandon, the 13 year-old son of Vicky. Brandon was fortunate that his mother, who allowed the opinions of her peers to shape her decisions, vowed to do whatever it took for her sons to be confident enough in themselves and their abilities to understand whether their actions are moving them closer to or further away from their goals.

Whereas attitudes, beliefs, and values play important roles in the development of success among Black boys, most of the highly successful boys—those making As and Bs in all of their courses—have a number of things in common. First, they know what they desire to accomplish with their lives. They have reasons, a number of strong compelling reasons, almost an obsession, for what they desire.

"I use to be all worried and upset about doing poorly in school, but everything seemed to change after we did the goal setting exercise. Before then, I had some strange ideas about what I wanted to do with my life, but when I set my goals, it was as if everything changed. I recognize that my life has a purpose and everything I do in school is to help me reach my goals," stated Gregory, a 16 year-old straight A student.

Unfortunately, many Black boys are never taught how to set personal goals, nor are they exposed to techniques that enable them to discover their real interests or strengths. Consequently, they never get excited about discovering the various ways they can go about using their strengths to accomplish their innermost goals. They never learn about the power that comes from contemplating or questioning themselves about their ambitions and dreams. Unless a Black boy learns to master his self-communication or his emotional intelligence, then it will be difficult for him to activate his brain so that he can produce excellence from chaos. Emotionally intelligent boys stand out because they have perfected their ability to empathize, preserve, control their emotions, communicate clearly, make thoughtful decisions, solve problems, and work with others. At school, they perform better on standardized tests and help create a safe, comfortable classroom atmosphere that makes it easier to learn.

The second thing that highly successful Black boys have in common is their ability to consistently act responsibly and make decisions that increase their productivity. Regardless of the difficulties they encounter, they never stop searching for solutions. They know that, if their dreams are to be turned into a reality, they have to take actions and have faith that their actions will eventually produce positive results. Some of the boys were taught to believe that having faith in God is all that it takes to become successful but later learned that faith without action is a dream that does not come true. Success for these Black boys is no accident and regardless of how "spiritually aligned" they appeared to be, they experience problems and challenges that sometimes result in failure.

Keep in mind that to live a life of excellence a child (or adult) must learn how to continue in spite of whatever challenges they are facing. This is exactly what highly successful Black boys have learned to do in order to release their full potential. They know that there is no such thing as quitting, and they use failure opportunities to re-program themselves to produce new and more self-empowering results in their lives.

"My mother and grandmother insisted that I go to church to learn about God. I love them, and I am grateful for everything they taught me, but they never taught me that you test your faith by taking actions to accomplish what you want out of life. That was something I learned from my mentor. After he taught me about setting goals, it was if a light went off in my head. I could see the connections between what I was doing and my goals. I believe in God and everything and am very involved in church, but having faith without actions is like having a new sports car with no gasoline," said Gregory.

Gregory's experiences are quite similar to other boys raised by deeply religious parents. For example, Jonathan, another straight A student, was also raised by his mother and grandmother, both Southern Baptists. They taught him to believe that prayer is the answer to everything. "Growing up I was always a little confused about how prayer works. They just told me to pray to God for what I wanted. Later on, I learned that you have to really believe in your prayers so strongly that you act as if everything has already happened. You work your plan, never think about failing, and know that God is walking with you. I still don't completely understand how prayer works, but I know that my belief in the power of God is what keeps me doing well in school."

The third thing that highly successful Black boys have in common is their highly developed sensory acuity and ability to get along with other people in all kinds of situations. What this means is that they pay close attention to their actions to see if their actions are getting them closer to or farther away from their goals. Moreover, if their actions are getting them farther away from their goals, then they make thoughtful decisions to get them back on track. Their sensory acuity, compared to other children, is much stronger and they have perfected their ability to make adjustments and changes to move toward their goals and to enhance their relationships. "My mom expects us to do well in school, and she insists that we learn how to use our minds to stay organized and focused. I've always done well in school, but learning how to pay attention to what's going on has made it a lot easier for me to excel in classes and on the school newspaper, in basketball, and on the piano," explains Jonathan.

When you think about it, most of us adults are off-course emotionally, physically, financially, spiritually, and in our relationships. We struggle to reach our goals primarily because many of us haven't established clear goals, or we allow our emotional reactions or relationship problems to get in the way. Some of us set goals for ourselves but fail to consistently take actions that move us toward our goals. And when our actions are met with obstacles or difficulties we often give up or start working on new goals where we repeat the same cycle. This is in stark contrast to what characterizes successful people who never stop searching for answers until they reach their goals.

Take Jonathan, for example. "I used to be really bad in math. I would try doing the problems a certain way and if that didn't work, then I would just give up and stop searching for the right solution. But after a few intense tutoring sessions with my teacher and mentor, I leaned that there are always several ways to approach a math problem or any problem in life. I guess I had to learn that there is never a wrong answer as long as you keep on trying."

One of the unique features about life is that there will always be conflicts and problems you'll have to overcome to achieve your goals. The big secret is knowing that you can always get back on course and continue teaching your children how to settle for nothing less than being excellent. So, how do we get back on course? How do we change our lives? How do we teach Black boys to duplicate excellence? How do we teach them to be successful in school? How do we get them to adopt habits that will lead to excellence? How do we get them to mimic (model) the behavior of children who consistently make As and Bs in their course work?

As I indicated earlier, success leaves clues, and surprisingly we (educators, parents, mentors, counselors, etc.) have to take a major step to uncover one of the clues required to help Black boys to become successful. We have to admit that we have been programmed and brainwashed, just as Black boys have been, to see Black boys from a less than desirable point of view. If we are to successfully teach Black boys how to re-program their own brains, then we have to learn to do the same for ourselves. When you really think about it, by the time a Black boy enters school for the first time, he has been exposed to hundreds or even thousands of messages that depict him as being intellectually incapable of being an excellent student. His subconscious mind, just like yours and mine, automatically responds to these messages. In time, these messages become the reality that is projected through his attitudes, beliefs, and behavioral routines.[4,5,6,7,8,9]

One of most important tasks we have to undertake in order to reach Black boys is to re-program how they think. This programming has to be so strong that when they are faced with intellectually challenges, these situations will automatically trigger them into feeling resourceful and energized rather than experiencing self-doubt and doom. While there is no best way to accomplish this, it seems that most of us, including Black boys, learn best through imitating (modeling) the behaviors of others. When Black boys learn through modeling, particularly models that are like themselves, it seems that they stand a better chance of turning what they learn into a habit. And as any parent or teacher knows, habits are very powerful factors in our lives. Most habits develop to the extent that they become unconscious patterns that constantly express our character and produce our effectiveness or our ineffectiveness. When habits are strung together, they reflect our knowledge, skills, desires, and our character.[10,11,12,13]

One of the important points to remember is that by teaching Black boys to duplicate academic excellence you are teaching them how to model habits of Black boys who are successful. If you are a teacher or counselor, then you will be working with Black boys who often don't trust their own judgment when it comes to doing excellent work. The reason for this might have something to do with problems they encounter at home, peer pressure, their cultural or racial experiences, or how they have bought into the idea that material things have a meaning. Some of them won't trust you or your methods for enhancing their academic development simply because they don't believe that people, including teachers and parents, can be trusted to follow through with what they say.

Another thing that you have to remember is that Black boys, just like other children, model what they see you doing rather than what you say. So, if you discover that boys in your classroom or those in your own home are being somewhat resistant, then spend a few moments thinking about who they are modeling.

If you are a single mother raising a son, then don't blame the absence of a father figure for the challenges you are experiencing with your boy. Sure, the lack of a stable and positive father figure will lead to some challenges, but you are the primary authority figure the boy will learn from and emulate. Therefore, the best advice is to take responsibility and realize that if your son is not interested in doing well academically, then it's quite likely that his disinterest is a reflection of your lack of interest in dealing with intellectually challenging work. Raising a son alone is difficult, but many single women successfully tackle the challenges and provide their sons the appropriate guidance for them to become successful. Several of the contributors of this book were raised by single mothers and there are many highly successful men in just about every occupation and profession you can imagine that were raised without a father in their lives.

Secrets for Duplicating Academic Excellence

Modeling is what we do to duplicate a person's beliefs, order of their behavioral routines, and how they use their body to complete a task. For example, when people are depressed, they take on a certain posture. Their shoulders are slumped over, they walk slow as if they are carrying the weight of the world on their shoulders, their speech is slow and often slurred, they eat lousy foods, they sleep a lot, they talk about gloomy and sad events, they act like things will never get better, their breathing is shallow, and their eyes are typically focused downward. To duplicate depression, all we would have to do model these behaviors and consistently tell ourselves, "I can't do anything right" and "My situation will never change." On the other hand, people who are vibrant, energized, and happy have an entirely different physiology and posture. They usually talk at a moderate or fast pace and approach life with lots of energy and enthusiasm. They sit up straight and while standing their feet are firmly planted. They look like they are ready to take on the world. They walk with a well-measured gait, suggesting that they are confident about who they are and their purpose in life. Their breathing is full and deep, without all of the sighing of people who are depressed, anxious, and lacking energy. In fact, if you duplicate a person's physiology and do exactly what they are doing with their body, then your brain and body begins to mimic the same physiology.

The point is that Black boys who are making As and Bs all the time are going to be excited about sitting in a classroom. Whatever they are doing to stay focused on their assignments; whatever they are doing to have an "up-beat" energy and enthusiasm about doing their homework; whatever they are doing to be "pumped-up" to make As and Bs, we need to teach other Black boys. Modeling or duplicating any behavioral routine, including making As and Bs, starts with a clear delineation of the specific behaviors, attitudes, and values that make up the behavioral routine. Much like building a house, there are specific building materials needed, and there is a specific order for pulling the pieces together.

Few people would purchase a home from a building contractor who claims to specialize in building homes without foundations or insulation or who claims that outhouses are a necessity for the modern home. Most of us would not do business with this contractor because his values are inconsistent with the established norms we have about how a home should be built. Similarly, few Black students buy into the idea that they can be a success from teachers who aren't interested in showing them the most effective ways for perfecting their academic abilities. Rather than show Black boys the exact behavioral routines for being an academic success, many teachers, and parents simply believe that they can convince Black boys to pursue a good education simply by talking to them. They believe that if they can come up with a convincing argument, then Black boys will somehow magically know exactly what they need to do in order to make better grades. Unfortunately, this is not the case.

Every year, there are hundreds of so-called motivational speakers who are invited into public schools to give students (and staff) a motivation speech to get them "pumped-up" and motivated to live up to their potential. While talking to students and staff is as good a place to start as any, these motivational talks aren't good enough to produce lasting changes. Both students and staff are quite excited and animated during these talks, but little information is transferred to the classroom. After doing a hundred or so of these talks, I got to the point where I had my fill with these assignments and started to turn them down. Although the money was great, I realized that there was no way that I could motivate students to do well on an exam that they were scheduled to take in a few days.

I remember the first time I turned down one of these speaking engagements. I told the principal of a middle school in Orlando Florida, "Save your money and use it all year long to teach students how to discover their own compelling reasons for motivating themselves to do well on the end-of-year exams." In fact, the whole idea of talking to Black boys about why they should do well in school reminds me of a Chinese Proverb that goes something like, "Tell me and I'll forget; show me and I may remember; involve me and I'll understand." If teachers and parents involve Black boys in the entire process of learning, then it is relatively easy for them to do well academically. If someone takes the initiative to show them the specific steps and behavioral routines associated with academic success, then it is easy for them to do well academically. If teachers act as if they really appreciate, respect, and believe in them, then it is easy for Black boys to do well academically.

Black boys who are involved in the entire process of learning easily produce positive academic habits. We have to teach them how to think for themselves, how to establish goals, how to discover the best ways to solve problems, how to determine what works, and how to stay focused and motivated by examining their compelling reasons for their own actions. Trying to convince Black boys that it's important for them to do well in school is a good place to start, but talk is cheap. We're got to remember that Black boys, just like adults, learn most things from imitating family members who are the people who love and care about them the most. Moreover, if family does not demonstrate or know the exact steps to produce excellence and successful academic practices, then we (educators) must be willing to stand in the gap and show Black boys how to become successful. It's great to talk with them about the values, beliefs, and attitudes related to doing well in school and the importance of excellence. These are good staring points, but we (educators) have to make some adjustments in our own attitudes if we really expect Black boys to learn and model habits that will lead to academic excellence. For example, the first thing that some of us have to do is admit that we don't know how to help Black boys develop new behavioral routines or how to help them break bad habits.

You might have some bad habits that you can't seem to break and you have grown weary and tired of trying to find the right way to change. Rather than continue acting the same way and hoping for a miracle, you need to seek help from experts who can teach you to get the results you want and help you understand the foundation for changing behavior. If you really want Black boys to be successful, then you've got to know how to instruct them to duplicate the beliefs, the mental syntax, and the physiology of success to the point that their new behavioral routines become automatic. You've got to make this instructional time so positive and compelling that the instructions themselves cause the boys to transcend any reservations they have about becoming an excellent student. If you really want Black boys in your classes or your own sons to produce outstanding work, then you're got to help them discover the keys for duplicating excellence. These keys can be used to duplicate any behavior, and the principles are effective for children and adults.

Three Keys For Duplicating Academic Excellence

I interviewed a dozen or so Black boys about the behavioral practices they thought were responsible for their academic success. Initially, I thought it would be relatively easy to identify what they did to excel, but I quickly found myself overwhelmed. I was wading through papers, notes, transcripts of audio recording, and wondering how to organize the already massive amount of information I had already gathered. After abandoning the organization scheme I had intended to use, I paid more attention to what the boys had observed about themselves. It was from these descriptions of their self-observations that the keys to duplicating excellence emerged. Interestingly enough, the keys tended to be in sync with the major principles associated with behavioral modeling. Modeling or imitating behavior is also known as observational learning. In this process, learning occurs when individuals observe and imitate others' behavior. There are four processes that influence the observer's behavior following exposure to models. These components include attention; retention; motor reproduction; and motivation.

Attention is the first component of observational learning. Individuals cannot learn much by observation unless they perceive and attend to the significant features of the modeled behavior. For example, Black boys who are not doing well academically must attend to what the excellent student is doing and saying in order to reproduce the model's behavior.

Retention is the next component. In order to reproduce the modeled behavior, the boys must code the information into long-term memory so that it can be retrieved.

Motor reproduction is another process in observational learning. The observer must be able to reproduce the model's behavior. The observer must learn and posses the physical capabilities of the modeled behavior. An example of motor reproduction would be learning how to focus all of one's attention on what the teacher is talking about in class or taking notes. Once a behavior is learned through attention and retention, the observer must posses the physically capabilities to produce the behavioral act.

The final process in observational learning is motivation or reinforcements. In this process, the observer expects to receive positive reinforcements for the modeled behavior. In the case of academic excellence, the boys receive information about the rewards Black boys making As and Bs receive for their academic performance. Therefore, we expect boys who are doing poorly in school to perform the same acts to achieve the rewards; however, there is not a high degree of media exposure about Black boys who are rewarded for excelling academically.

Historically, rap artists and athletes are heroes for many Black boys, and most Black boys have repeatedly witnessed these individuals being rewarded by the media. When Black boys, especially when they are young children, witness this type of media, they attend, code, retrieve, posses the motor capabilities and perform the modeled behavior because of the positive reinforcement determined by the media. As they continue to age, the boys continue to thrive for this attention since for many of them, the positive attention given to rap artists and athletes is representative of the few sources of positively reinforced images of Black males. By contrast, much of the violence displayed by older Black boys was drilled into their personalities during their exposure to violent images as children. The violence Black boys experience in real life is often reinforced by violence expressed in films and television shows which depict violence as an acceptable behavior, especially for heroes who never seem to be reprimanded for their misbehavior. What's so startling is that many of these boys will continue to model the socio-cultural-behavioral aspects of violence well into adulthood and live out their lives in neighborhood surrounded by conflict, high crime rates, illiteracy, decay, and insufficient social organizations. In essence, they will become prisoners of their own intellect and rarely get a glimpse at the world outside of that which they have been conditioned to see.

Whereas it is difficult to determine the full extent that the living conditions of a Black boy influences his academic development, few people disagree with the idea that individuals, especially Black boys, imitate behavior they personally observe in others, the environment, and the mass media. Although there will be many individualized reactions to human behavior and several paths one can take to model behavior, ultimately there are three keys to duplicating any human behavior, including academic excellence.[10,11,13,14]

Beliefs: The First Key to Duplicating Academic Excellence

"Like I tell my friends who ask me about how I keep my grades up . . . you have to believe that you deserve good grades and that your grades will get you that scholarship to college and that great job where you make more than enough money to support your family," Maurice passionately explained. A savvy 16-year-old Black boy who dreams of being a great surgeon "like Ben Carson." Maurice, unlike the typical Black boy that I interviewed, he lived with both parents who encouraged him to make doing well in school a priority. Both enjoyed the rewards of being employed in lucrative fields, and both had college degrees. Growing up in a home with college-educated parents provided Maurice with all the right stuff for him to be well prepared for school. Still, he barely got through grade school, not because he wasn't capable, but mostly because of his beliefs and attitudes about doing well academically. "My parents demanded that I do well in school, but they let me get away with too much. I could act-up in class, not turn in my homework, make bad grades, and get away with my parents grounding me for a few days. But in the end, I knew that they would give me back everything they took from me. I didn't have to work hard to please them, and I thought I didn't have to work hard to get anything I wanted. I felt privileged until the middle of 8th grade and then things changed."

The change Maurice talked about involved the notice that his parents received midway through the year. He would have to repeat the eighth grade unless his grades improved dramatically. "I was surprised that neither of them came to my rescue. They didn't act upset or anything. In fact, they had a meeting with me to inquire about my plans for dealing with the problem. They told me that if I was smart enough to get into this mess, I was smart enough to get out of it. The only thing they would say when I tried to talk with them was, 'Your beliefs about the value of education got you in trouble. You should consider changing your beliefs and getting an attitude adjustment'." Fortunately, Maurice because of his failing grades, had to attend an after school program to learn the skills that would help him handle his schoolwork. Just like Maurice, many of the children in the program were more than capable of doing excellent work, but they lacked the motivation to apply themselves. "Maurice came from a fine family where the last thing you would expect would be for him to be doing so poorly in school. I knew the problem didn't have anything to do with his capabilities or his knowledge about how to study. But to be sure, he, went through the study skills assessment before we started working through the self-motivation exercises," explained Mrs. Whitmore, the teacher in change of the program.

As Mrs. Whitmore expected, Maurice proved to be an exceptionally intelligent student who immediately grasped the idea that you have to believe you can be successful if you want to be successful. Maurice, like the other students, came to the program expecting to be tutored and preached at about why they should do better. Instead, they did a lot of writing and talking about what they wanted to do with their lives.

"Rather than argue with us, the teacher, Mrs. Whitmore, taught us how to argue with ourselves, how to push our own buttons, and how to figure out whether what we were doing in school added to or took away value from what we were planning in our lives. We did a lot of writing about our reasons, our compelling reasons, for our actions. The hardest parts where when we had to take the center seat in front of the class and convince the other students that how we were behaving in school added value to our future plans," said Maurice.

Maurice was indeed fortunate to have crossed paths with a teacher, a white female, who had leaned that the first battle to overcome with Black boys is teaching them to not become a prisoner of their own thinking. "I had the good pleasure to attend a training session with Dr. Johnson where I learned how to engage children in their own goal setting workshop. Rather than focusing solely on their goals and dreams, I leaned how to have students discover the important values and beliefs underlying their goals and their behavior," offered Mrs. Whitmore. It was during these sessions with Mrs. Whitmore that Maurice learned to organize his thoughts and reasons for his academic performance. The first key to academic success that Maurice learned about was his ability to duplicate the beliefs and convictions about doing excellent work. To motivate himself, Maurice had to discover good reasons to accomplish his goals, his passions. He had to find compelling reasons to do excellent work. In addition, he discovered that doing better in school meant that he would learn to mimic the behavioral routines of Black boys who make As and Bs all the time. "Showing me how to study wasn't enough to really help me . . . I had to change my attitude about the value of doing well in school before I made any real progress. Once I did that, my brain got really turned on and I was more aware of how my thinking was holding me back from making good grades," Maurice stated.

Like many of the Black boys struggling to do well academically, Maurice learned that his beliefs are the cornerstones of his behavior. There is an old adage that goes something like, "If at first you want to achieve, the first thing you must do is believe." I have to admit that I was overwhelmed by the simple consistency of the beliefs of successful Black males. Some of the typical and most consistent beliefs are presented below.

Black males who Make As and Bs all the time believe that:

- By having faith in themselves and their abilities, they can achieve their goals or anything in life.
- Getting a good education will help them provide for their family.
- Hard work can be fun, rewarding, and necessary to discover the right answers.
- You can always find something exciting about schoolwork.

- You are supposed to grow up to be better off than your parents and that getting a good education will help me with this.
- You have to get a good education to be successful in life.
- They have a responsibility to show others (e.g., younger siblings and other relatives) the value of being educated and doing well in school.
- They value their own approval of what they are doing, but they get excited by the approval of their teachers and parents.
- Mistakes and failure are an essential part of the learning process.
- It's important to have goals for life, to be ambitious, and to always be a role model for your family, including your siblings and children you will have one day.
- It's important to stay focused and excited about doing well in school and keep the "eventual" rewards in your mind.
- It is important to find new things to learn and work on even if you don't have homework.
- It's important for them to always be prepared for class.
- There is nothing that they can't do if they make up their mind to do it.
- They can always find something "fun and different" about their classes so that they get excited about them.
- No matter how difficult their schoolwork becomes, it's important to do their best.
- By studying hard, they will get better grades.
- Anything worth having is worth working hard to get.
- There is a time for studying and a time for playing and having fun.

As you can clearly see, the beliefs underlying the academic achievement of Black males are quite diverse, but there is some overlap in the central idea that is reflected by many of the beliefs. For example, several items have a focus on the future, while other items relate to being a role model. Other items speak to having fun while doing schoolwork. While having strong beliefs about doing well in school is positive, beliefs alone are not enough to produce As and Bs all the time. The boys themselves indicated they had to take actions and do a number of other things in order to do well in school.

The Behavioral Routines: The Second Key to Duplicating Academic Excellence

The second key for duplicating academic excellence consists of identifying the systematic arrangement of the behavioral routines (i.e., the syntax) that successful Black boys use to excel academically. To a certain extent, determining the order and sequence Black boys use to master intellectual materials is akin to determining the order in which they use their five senses. Most Black boys, just like most adults, are not consciously aware of the order and sequence of events they employ to tackle seemingly simple, let alone complex tasks. However, there is a behavioral routine or syntax for everything we do. There is a syntax for spelling words, driving a car, building a house, doing the laundry, preparing a meal, eating burgers and fries, for being happy or expressing anger, for liking massive amount of pleasure, and responding to failure. In addition, there is a syntax for studying, preparing for an exam, doing a book report, and for making excellent grades. It is, therefore, essential for the child to understand the behavioral routines they are currently using to deal with their academic demands. Once they understand the order and sequences of their behavioral routines and the consequences and rewards (or lack thereof) associated with these routines, and then it is a lot easier to help them change their routines to achieve the results they desire.

Jamal, age 13, was fortunate in that he had an older brother, a sophomore in college, to help him figure out the process for making good grades. According to Jamal, his brother taught him that the first thing you have to have is a special notebook, journal, or something you can use to keep up with homework and class assignments. "I have a special notebook, like a planner, where I describe all of my homework assignments, when assignments are due, and when we have tests. I have notes about things I don't understand and need help with . . . and the phone numbers of others students in my classes that I might need to call to get help. Sometime I might have notes about how the assignment is like other stuff I'm studying and learning about. I have many notes about what will be on the tests. My brother taught me that you've got to make sure you understand your assignments and what will be on the tests or the report you have to write. If you understand what you've got to do and what's required to make the high grades, then it's a lot easier to get everything right. And I always talk to the teacher after class to make sure I understand the assignment."

In addition to making sure that he understands his assignments, Jamal takes a lunch to school most days, has a snacks when he arrives homes, and does not waste much time before starting his homework assignments. "We have a special room we call the learning center at home where I do my homework shortly after I get home. I spend at least three hours doing homework or studying in the learning center everyday. It's a real cool room where we have all of our school supplies and everything you need to work on projects. The room is quiet and clean, and we don't have music playing or a television in the room to distract us. I can work on projects, leave stuff laying around, and not worry about loosing anything." The process Jamal described for handling his homework has worked well. He maintains a solid B+ average while working at a grocery store part-time after school and on weekends.

After much discussion with Jamal and several other boys, it became clear that the process for making good grades started in their mind. They have a vivid understanding of exactly what they have to study and the requirements for making the best grade. In addition, they study shortly after they arrive home from school in a quiet place where distractions are minimal. "In a very strange way, I feel almost like I am cheating when I take exams. By the time I sit down with the test, I have already figured out exactly what will be asked. I've done all my homework, questioned my teachers about the material, and studied everything. Sometimes I've studied other stuff related to what I will be tested on. When I study like this, I know my grade before I even start the test. I know exactly how well I am going to do," Jamal said.

The process Jamal goes through to organize his assignments and prepare for tests is similar to what Andrew, the older of two boys being raised in a near poverty situation by a single father, utilizes to maintain his high grades. "I make sure that I take my notebook, the one where I describe my homework assignments, home with me every day, and it is the first thing I look at when I get home from school. In middle school, I was always forgetting to do my homework, so my dad bought me this daily planner, like the one he uses to keep up with his delivery schedule, and I have been using it ever since to keep up with my assignments." Andrew, age 15, is the prototype of the Black boy who has survived tough circumstances. A drug-addicted burglar murdered his mother and younger brother the day before he celebrated his thirteenth birthday. Andrew discovered their dead bodies when he arrived home from school.

Of all the boys interviewed, Andrew had justifiable reasons for being angry and upset about his life circumstances, yet he did not allow his academic work or his plans to be affected by losses he had suffered. He consistently makes high grades in all his courses while handling the responsibilities of being the class president and a active member of the literary club. "I can't change what I've been through in my life, but I can take pride in how I am preparing myself for college. My mom taught me a lot about being discipline, organized, and how there is a time for studying and a time for having fun. I guess I am lucky and blessed that I have friends who I can study with and teachers I can call at home if I have questions about my assignments."

During my interview, it was obvious that Andrews's maturity was far greater than what you would expect from a 15-year-old Black boy. In addition to be an excellent student, he maintains a busy schedule filled with extracurricular activities and an exciting social life. "I lost focus when my mom and little brother were murdered. My grades went down, and I had a hard time concentrating in class and doing my work when I got home. Usually, when I got home from school, I would eat a sandwich and have a glass of milk before studying, but for a while, I did not feel like eating or doing anything. I guess what kept me going was thinking about what my mom used to tell me about how I have an obligation and responsibility to show my brothers and other boys that, even if you live in the projects, you can get a good education." Like so many other Black boys being raised in poverty, Andrew's motivation for excelling in school seems tied to the idea and belief that he has a responsibility to do well because he is a role model for other Black boys, including his younger brother. "There is so much that I wouldn't even think of doing because I have a little brother who is looking up to me to teach him about right and wrong. He wants to be a good student because I do well in school. If I don't teach him how to study and stay out of trouble, then he will be out here in this world all by himself. I get sick thinking about how much we miss our mother and brother, but I know that they would want me to keep my focus on doing well and showing my little brother how to be the best than he can be."

It is never easy for Black boys to dismiss the frustration and humiliation they experience as a result of being treated unfairly by teachers, particularly when they have experienced traumatic events like those Andrew have experienced. The natural reaction for many Black boys is to strike back at someone to vent some of the frustration, but that is exactly the kind of reaction that lends itself to the harsh disciplinary actions that Black boys encounter at school. "I was so angry after my mom's death, and all I wanted to do is give people a hard time or pick a fight. But I didn't do any of this because I knew that, in time, I would get over how bad I was feeling. It was hard curbing my anger and helping my little brother get over losing our mother and brother, but getting mad at the world was not going to bring back my momma and brother. When I get home from school, I sit down and have a sandwich with my little brother. We take a walk outside for a while and talk about schoolwork, but when we go back inside, we go straight to the books."

It is easy to say in retrospect what a Black boy should have performed in school or how he could have handled his feelings about family problems. The truth is, though, that many of them are simply behaving like other boys they have observed. Many Black boys often feel as though they are in a double bind. The predominate view is that their teachers don't expect them to do well even though they (teachers) are quick to point out what they should have done to do well. What's so ironic is that even though most teachers are quick to ridicule Black boys about their failures, those same teachers provide very little specific guidance or support. The guidance and support Black boys need are cognitive strategies, appropriate relationships, coping strategies, goal-setting opportunities, and appropriate instruction both in content, discipline, and how to identify and install the behavioral routines that are aligned with producing excellent academic grades and test scores. Unfortunately, most Black boys don't get anything except criticism for not living up to their potential and stronger reasons for disliking school.

The following list includes those behavioral routines that were consistently revealed during my interviews with Black males who make As and Bs all the time. As you examine the list, keep in mind that a particular boy might start his routine at either of the points, but most eventually engage in all of these behaviors. The key for these boys is that they have learned to create patterns of movements that create confidence, a sense of strength, flexibility, fun, and a sense of personal power.

The behavioral routines of Black males making As and Bs consist of:

- Having a healthy snack before starting their homework.

- Carefully reading over notes about homework assignments before leaving school.
- Spending a little time outside (e.g., taking a walk, sitting out on the porch, etc.) when they get home from school.
- Talking to someone about their day at school when they get home, either a parent, grandparent, or older sibling.
- Taking a short nap or just daydreaming (e.g., just sit in their room for a while and do nothing) before starting homework.
- Spending time thinking about their assignments for the day before starting their homework.
- Studying immediately after having a snack or after a short nap.
- Checking their planner or notebook to determine the homework assignments that are due before leaving school.
- Devoting a certain amount of time to studying every night, even when they don't have homework.
- Having a specific dinner and bedtime, even on the weekends.
- Always sitting at their desk or a special place at home that is organized and neat to do their work.
- Not listening to music, watching TV, eating snacks, or do anything to distract themselves while they are studying.
- Not doing "fun stuff" before studying; they wait until they have done their work. They know there is a time for studying and a time for having fun.
- Asking their teachers for other information about what they are studying.
- Asking for assistance when they don't understand the information.
- Having a network of friends they talk to about their school assignments and the instructors.
- Asking themselves questions (Who, What, When, Where, Why) when they are reading, studying or doing homework to get a better idea about what they need to do.
- Spending time imagining how they can use the information they are learning.
- Making learning fun by playing with the information they are learning, thinking about it and trying to figure it out while they are doing their homework.
- Taking pride in getting their work completed on time.

- Taking pride in the appearance of their work.
- Making statements to themselves such as "This is easy, all I've got to do is figure it out," or "I know that this is important and I want to have some fun, so how can I have fun while learning this."

Physiology and Movement: The Third Key to Duplicating Academic Excellence

The third key for duplicating academic excellence consists of identifying what successful Black boys do with their bodies and physiology (posture, breathing patterns, facial expressions, muscle tension, etc.) to stay alert and excited at school and while completing assignments at home. The way Black boys use their body and physiology when they are in a "learning mode" determines which parts of their brains is being activated. Everything they feel about what they are doing and learning results from how they use their bodies. Even small changes in their facial expressions, gestures, or how they are moving their bodies causes shifts in the way they feel, the way they evaluate, and the way they are behaving.

Every emotion a child experiences has a specific physiology linked to it: posture, breathing, patterns of movement, and facial expressions. The challenge for most Black boys and most adults is that we are not aware of what we do with our bodies and physiology to shape our behavior or emotions. Once we learn how to use our bodies in certain emotional states, we can return to those states or avoid them simply by changing what we do with our bodies and physiology. If Black boys repeatedly use their bodies in weak ways (slumping over their desks, slouching in their chairs, and not listening to and giving their full attention to their teacher) the likelihood of them make passing grades is low. How could they do otherwise? Their body is producing an emotional state of boredom and disinterest in school, which then affects their and emotions. Low and behold, they have created an endless loop of boredom and disinterest in school that leads to poor grades that generates boredom and disinterest in school that results in poor grades!

You have probably heard the old adage, "Someday you'll look back at this and laugh." If that is true, why not laugh today? Why wait? More than anything else, Black boys who excel academically have learned to create pleasurable emotional states for themselves no matter what is happening. They smile and laugh a lot in class and while they are probably not aware of it, they are automatically triggering part of their brain and creating neurological pathways to pleasure that eventually become habitual. In essence, they have learned that just by changing their physiology (posture, breathing pattern, facial expression), they can change their level of performance and the ease by which they can handle mentally demanding work. What is so amazing is that they have made feeling good, being cheerful, acting playful, and having fun while learning at school a habit. They don't have reasons for feeling good; they just feel good for no reason and enjoy the new level of confidence and energy they have created for focusing on their schoolwork.

Wilson, age 12, is quite fond of the world-renowned golfer, Tiger Woods, and even tough Wilson has never held a golf club, he has a vivid mental image of what Tiger does with his body and physiology when he sinks an incredible putt. Tiger's smile is infectious, and the way he moves his body, clenches his fist, and pumps his arms triggers an emotional celebration for just about everyone who witnessed the event. "I love watching Tiger Woods on TV because he makes everyone feel his happiness when he makes one of his tough shots. I figure that if people feel so happy watching him, then I would also feel happy too doing the same thing he does with his movements . . . you know, he has that big smile and he makes that hammer movement with his fist and arm. It makes me feel good to act the same way when I've done something good in class." In addition to emulating how Tiger moves his body when he has accomplished an important task, Wilson always pays close attention to what his teachers are saying, and he is typically the first person to raise his hand to answer questions in class. "My mother always tells me that smart people look smart and so I always sit-up tall, take notes, and look like I am excited about being in class. I never talk out in class, but I am always ready to ask questions or give answers. But sometimes my teachers say that I am acting out in class."

Most of the Black boys who talked about what they do in class to stay alert and focused say they were made to feel like they were "doing something wrong" when they showed enthusiasm about their classroom accomplishments. "My teacher would get upset with me when I showed how excited I was about doing well, and she treated me a lot different than the white boys who acted the exact same way in class that I did when they got the correct answer to a question or when they got their text scores," angrily explained Wilson. The frustration, humiliation, and shame that results from such situations is intense and generally provides much fuel for the anger than burns deep within Black boys. But, rather than express their frustrations inappropriately, Black boys like Wilson have a way of looking pleasant, content, and happy even though they feel angry and upset about the unfair treatment they received.

The situation that Wilson describes is similar to the situation with Daniel, age 14, one of the few Black males enrolled in the honors program at his school. "I've always had teachers tell me that I get too excited about doing well in class. Some have even suggested that I might need to talk to a psychologist to learn how to sit still and be less excited in class. I get tired of being told how to act, especially when the teachers don't ever single out white children who do the same things. They keep saying that they don't have problems with my grades or test scores, but they don't like how I behave when I'm proud and happy about some exceptional thing I've done in class. So rather than blow up and get in trouble, I remind myself to relax, stay cool, and to sit up like I am the son of a king."

In talking with Wilson and Daniel, it was clear to me that, in addition to mastering the behavioral routines related to making good grades, they have learned to curb their emotional reactions to being treated unfairly by their teachers. In essence, they often find themselves in situations where they feel like they have to put up with more emotional distractions than white students do in order to be successful at school. "Sometimes I'm squirming around in my chair just to find a way to be comfortable . . . and it does not help if the teacher is boring. So I get singled out for disturbing the class when the only thing I'm doing is trying to figure out what to do with my body to stay alert. But when a white boy does the same thing, the teacher lets it slide. He gets away with it and suffers no consequences for what he did," explained Daniel. Given these and other circumstances that Black boys face in the classroom, one has to wonder how they go about cooling off emotionally so that they can do what is necessary to stay focused on their schoolwork. How do they cope with the anger they feel when they are treated unfairly? "To cope with what happens in class, you have to be cool and not allow yourself to get worked up about how the teacher or other students are going to respond to you. Sure, you are going to feel upset, but being cool is the rule. And if you know that you are smart, then prove it by making the highest grades in class. I make good grades to prove to them that I can do my work even if I am treated with no respect, and when I make the top grades, I act like I am proud of the work that I have accomplished."

Although many of the Black boys interviewed feel the constant pressure to do well in classrooms where they are oftentimes mistreated, rarely do they allow these pressures to ruffle their feathers. Instead, they keep their cool and continue to be excited about what they are learning. They seek strength from within their families, which enables them to stay focused on their higher purpose: doing quality work so they can go to college. "It's difficult at times to not look sad or upset, but I just give all of my attention to my studies and that helps me to block out some of the ill feelings I might be having about how one of my friends or myself is being mishandled by our teacher. I just keep studying and being ready for any information they throw at me. I know that I am capable of learning everything and doing well on any test they give me; I just wish my teachers treated me with more respect," reasoned James, a perceptive high school senior who plans on going to medical school.

James' behavior is typical of a number of Black boys who have leaned how to stay mentally alert and excited about school even though they are experiencing tremendous emotional discomforts. Perhaps the greatest challenge facing Black boys in school today is figuring out when the expression of emotions is right. Although African American students constitute 16 percent of public school enrollment, as a group they are expelled, suspended, and retained (repeat a grade) at rates of 13%, 43%, and 21% respectively. Further, Black boys are at higher risk for these exclusionary disciplinary practices. Given these disproportionate rates, one has to wonder about the extent to which the cultural clash between Black male students and white teachers, most often a white female, contributes to the seemingly unfair treatment that Black males endure. Could it be that some of the verbal behavior (facial expression, eye gazes), paralanguage (voice tone, pitch, speech rate), and proxemics (personal distance, hand slapping other students, or giving 'high fives') that characterize clashes between Black males and their teachers can be explained as a cultural misunderstanding or the simple attempt by Black males to engage their physiology and body movements to remain alert in class. Obviously, these cultural misunderstanding contribute to negative teacher-student interactions that often result in inappropriate behavioral referrals. What is amazing is that there are Black males who consistently make As and Bs, in spite of the being exposed to teachers who abuse their position, power, and prestige as a way to control and exploit Black males. Although the boys revealed many things they do to stay excited about school or to celebrate their accomplishments in class, the following list includes only those behaviors where there was consistent agreement between the boys who make As and Bs all the time.[15,16]

The physiology and movement of Black males who make As and Bs consist of:

- Looking pleasant, smiling, and sounding excited about learning, even when you have been treated unfairly.
- Celebrating (e.g., giving high-fives, etc.)when they do something well in class.
- Being relaxed and mentally alert.
- Giving their full attention to the teacher and "always" looking at the teacher when the teacher is talking.
- Always sitting in the front row so they want be distracted by other students.
- Sitting up tall and straight and never slumping over their desks.
- Always trying to be the first person to raise their hands when the teacher asks questions. This is done with enthusiasm so that the teachers know they want to be called on.
- Answering questions with enthusiasm and self-confidence.
- Keeping their hands busy and making sure they are always holding a pencil or pen to write down everything the teacher says is important, even if the teacher has prepared handouts.
- Standing up confidently to ask questions or before speaking in class, even when standing up is not required.
- Being active outside of the classroom (i.e., activities and clubs at school or church).
- Being relaxed and not anxious in class—so that their breathing is fuller and deeper.
- Having hygiene that is above par and taking pride in feeling fresh and knowing that they are clean.
- Eating "real food" for lunch and dinner to maintain their energy and stamina.
- Having a "real" breakfast at home or as soon as they arrive at school—cereal and a piece of fruit or scrambled eggs and toast.

- Staying away from junk foods and sweets.
- Getting enough sleep.

How to Duplicate the Beliefs, Mental Syntax, and Physiology of Successful African Male Students

When you consider the characteristics of champions, the one that is relevant for duplicating excellence and academic success in Black boys is strategy. You're got to have a strategy for using all of the great information you've learned and a definite course and path for helping Black boys cultivate their passion and beliefs about their academic goals. I hope that by now the question you are asking yourself is not "Why should I do these things for Black boys in my classes or my child at home or those boys at my church?" Instead, I hope the question you're asking is "What strategy can I use to get my child (or Black boys in my classes) back on course?" If you are still struggling with this first question, then I encourage you to spend a few quite moments thinking about the fact that nearly 50 percent of Black boys currently in ninth grade will not graduate from high school. If this does not stir you into action, then consider the fact that as a taxpayer, you help pay approximately $38,000 a year for each young Black man incarcerated for a crime he committed out of ignorance or his inability to find a job because he did not graduate from high school. I don't know about you, but I'd rather spend my tax dollars paying for after school programs or increases to teacher salaries than for jail.

Discovering the successful beliefs, behavioral routines, and body movements/physiology of Black boys who are successful was a dream compared to devising a strategy for instructing other Black boys how to duplicate what I had learned. As you are probably well aware, many of the goals that adults make, regardless of their self-assessed importance, are never achieved. While many factors determine whether a person will follow through and accomplish their goals, it is typically the compelling reasons for the goals that distinguish people who accomplish their goals from those who don't. If the reasons are strong and ignited by an intrinsic need, then the individual tends to have a relentless focus on their goals, regardless of the obstacles they face. In essence, if you really want to help Black boys excel academically, then you have to teach them how to uncover their compelling reasons for accomplishing their goals. No matter how interested you say you are in helping Black makes achieve these aims, it all boils down to your willingness to show them how to associate a massive, almost unbelievable, amount of discomfort and pain to not working on their goals. The issue is not whether the child is capable of achieving their goals, but whether they are sufficiently motivated to take actions that moves them toward their goals. Whether they are motivated comes down to their ability to create so much emotional discomfort about not working on their goals that they absolutely must work on their goals to avoid these harsh and uncomfortable feelings.

To develop this type of leverage, all you have to do is teach the boys to ask themselves some pain-inducing questions. The key to this exercise is giving them irrefutable reasons why working on their goals must be a regular part of their lives immediately. Below are some "Negative Power Questions" that can be used or modified to help discover the compelling reasons for accomplishing goals:[10,11]

- How will I feel about myself knowing that I failed to adopt the attitudes, values, and beliefs reflected by my goals?
- What is it already costing me emotionally to not work on my goals?
- Ultimately, what will I miss out in my life today and in the future if I don't work on and accomplish my goals?
- How has not working on my goals affected my relationships with people I care about and people who care about me?

You've got to help the student picture in graphic detail how much their failure to work on their goals will negatively impact his life. If they have an aversion to writing, then I suggest that you have them use an audio tape recorder to capture their responses. Just remember that your main objective is to show them how to make the pain of not working on their goals feel so real, so intense, so immediate that they can't put off changing how they are dealing with their goals. You will know when it's real enough, when the student has reached their pain threshold, because their attitude will become more somber; they might even shed a few fears.

If the child does not feel motivated to work on his goals, then encourage him to continue with the exercise. Have him read aloud his responses to the pain-inducing questions and imagine how not working on his goals will negatively affect him and the people who are most important to him. Have him picture in detail how his life will be five, ten and twenty years from now if he doesn't learn to work on his goals. Have him think about all of the messy personal and family problems that he will cause by his failure to change.

Now that you have taught the student how to link a massive amount of emotional pain to not working on their goals, the next step is for you to show him how to use pleasure-association questions to link positive sensations to working on his goals. Again, we will use questions to open the pathway to his subconscious feelings and thoughts about the benefits he will gain by working on his goals. Use the "Positive Power Questions" below to help the student discover all of the real joys that he wants for his life:[10,11]

- How will I feel after accomplishing my goals?
- How will I feel about myself by adopting the attitudes, values, and beliefs reflected by my goals?
- How will my relationship with important people in my life (my parents, other family members, my teachers) grow or change because I accomplished my goals?
- How much happier will I be by making time to work on my goals a regular part of my life?
- What will I gain mentally, emotionally, physically, financially, and spiritually by accomplishing my goals?
- Ultimately, what will I gain in my life today, tomorrow and in the future, by dedicating myself to accomplish my goals?

Change can take a few minutes, a few hours, a few days, or longer. It all depends on a person's willingness to change and their level of motivation (or compelling reasons) to change. If the child you are working with is not driven to make working on their goals a regular part of his life, then you haven't helped them discover enough leverage. All this means is that you need to spend some additional time working with the child before moving forward. Please don't misunderstand me. There's nothing wrong with you or the child; neither of you needs to be "fixed." All of the resources that you'll need to help them change how they are working on their goals are within you right now; you've just got to help them dig a little deeper and focus on the reasons for accomplishing their goals!

When Black boys use these power questions, they are actively learning how to generate reasons that are strong enough to ignite their own intrinsic need to be relentless in making the beliefs, behavioral routines, and physical actions a part of their lives. Their mastery of this technique resides with their willingness to associate an almost unbelievable amount of discomfort to not adopting the success routines. The pain has to be sufficient so that not making the success routines a part of their lives is incredibly painful while adopting the beliefs, attitudes, values, and actions associated with the success routines is perceived as being attractive, fun, positive, and pleasurable. Although we might like to deny it, the fact remains that what drives the behavior of Black boys is instinctive reactions to pain and pleasure, not intellectual calculations.

Intellectually, a Black boy may believe that not doing his homework is bad, but he'll continue to avoid doing his homework. Why? Because he is not so much driven by what he intellectually knows, but by the fact that he has learned to link pain and pleasure to his actions. It is the associations he has established in his nervous system that determines his actions. Whereas we would like to believe that it's his intellect that really drives him. But in most cases, it is his emotions and the sensations that he has linked to his thought about school that are truly driving him to avoid doing homework.

The process that Black boys embrace to avoid engaging in behavioral routines that result in academic success is no different from what adults go through when they want to lose weight. Intellectually, we know that eating sweet deserts and those "super sized" lunches is bad for us, but we still reach for that doughnut (or favorite piece of sweet junk food) and a cup of coffee that is loaded with sugar. Why? Because we are driven by the pleasure that has been linked to the sweet, calorie rich food, rather than what we know intellectually. The truth is that you have to link pain to your old eating habits and pleasure to your healthy eating habits if you really want to eliminate your poor diet and eating habits. Basically, all of us will do more to avoid pain than we will to gain pleasure. The Black boys who make As and Bs all the time believe that nothing feels as good to them as when they ace an exam or turn in a super project. Similarly, nothing tastes as good to healthy people as food that nourishes their bodies and minds.

Black boys can be taught to condition their minds, bodies, and emotions to link pain or pleasure to whatever they choose. Teaching them to change what they link pain or pleasure to will instantly change their behavior. This simple secret is what underlies the science underlying the most effective strategies I've discovered for transforming at-risk Black boys to A and B students who perceive no other possibilities for themselves other than going on to college to have a professional career. You've probably heard of the conditioned-response experiments conducted by the Russian scientist Ivan Pavlov. His most famous experiment was one in which he offered food to a dog, thereby stimulating the dog to salivate, and pairing the presentation of the food with the sound of the bell. After repeating the conditioning experiment enough times, Pavlov found that merely ringing the bell, even when food was no longer available, would cause the dog to salivate.

What does Pavlov have to do with teaching Black boys how to make As and Bs all the time? By teaching Black boys to consistently link pleasure to the beliefs, syntax, and bodily movements/physiology that leads to academic success and pain to their absence, they will develop a conditioned response, a habit, that will be difficult to change. It's the idea that if Black boys engage in specific behavioral routines related to academic success, they'll enjoy rich rewards today, tomorrow, and in their future. Advertisers clearly understand that what drives us is not our intellect as much as it is the sensations we link to their products. As a result, they have become experts in using exciting or soothing music, rapid or elegant imagery, and a variety of other elements that evoke emotional states; then, when our emotions are at their peak, when the sensations are most intense, they flash an image of their product continuously until we link it to these desired feelings. The net result is that people feel that they absolutely must have the product. The big question is whether you are willing to use similar procedures for encouraging Black boys to become addicted to success.

Advice to Educators, Parents, Counselors and Mentors

Turning a Black boy who is doing poorly in school into an A or B student does not happen overnight. Even Black boys who are doing average work and making passing grades go through progressive stages to make As and Bs all the time. The process takes time and you've got to be patient with yourself and the boy. You have to be committed to using the time to improve the relationship between you and the boy. If this is where you are, then here is my advice.

First, have the boys write down a number of actions they need to take, but have been putting off in order to do better in school. In most cases, these actions will either be a belief, a behavioral routine or some bodily movement similar to, if not identical to, those that have been identified by boys who consistently make As and Bs in their course work. Most boys have created barriers that interfere with them having an authentic relationship with their teachers, mentors, and parents so don't be surprised if there are communication challenges. If you back away from dealing with these challenges, then you are doing a disservice to every Black boy in your life. Although they are part of the "now generation" which is fast-paced and fueled by glitter and instant messages, they want to believe that they are somebody, that they are special, and that they are worthy of being accepted, loved, and educated by someone—a teacher or mentor or parent—who cares about them enough to go out of their way to make a difference in their lives. Communicating from the heart will break down all barriers and enhance your relationships regardless of how challenging you believe them to be. You've got to set aside all of your stereotypes about what society says they "can't do" and raise his expectations. They might act as if you are the enemy and that you can't possibly understand their world, but they want to know the secrets to your success. They want to be like you. The real hero for Black boys is the teacher who balances his or her personal life with his or her professional life while, helping a classroom full of potential geniuses develops their abilities. Black boys might not ever admit it to you, but they are in awe of your ability to see their greatness in spite of all of the problems and difficulties they bring into your classroom.

Second, under each of these actions, have the boys write down and discuss the answer to the following two questions: (1) Why haven't I taken the action? (2) In the past, what pain or frustration have I linked to taking this action? Answering these questions will help them to understand that what has held them back is that they've associated greater pain to taking the action than to not taking it. Encourage them to be honest with themselves. If you want to have an impact, then you've got to show the boys you're working with that you are a lifelong learner who has also struggled with bad habits. You've got to help them learn from your mistakes and see how you've overcome obstacles that were holding you back from moving toward your goals.

Third, under each action, have them write down all of the pleasures they've had in the past by indulging in behaviors associated with not doing their academic work. Have them write down and discuss the answers to the following two questions: (1) What have I gained from not taking the action? (2) In the past, what good things have been linked to not taking the action? Helping them to identify the pleasures they've been getting will help them know what their target is. Just like you, Black boys have a difficult time balancing the pleasures they receive in their personal and family life from what is happening in their academic and professional life. Trying to figure out what is right for the moment is like being tempted by chocolate cake when you are trying to diet. Just like you, Black boys know the right thing to do in most situations, but there are times when good intentions are not enough to overcome temptations. If you are going to help Black boys handle this issue, then you've got to let them know that you too have experienced situations where you gave up or delayed doing something that was good in order for you to accomplish an important goal.

Fourth, have the boys write down what it will cost them if they don't change now. What will happen if they don't stop daydreaming when it's time to study? If they don't stop ignoring what their teaches are discussing in class? If they don't stop staying up late to watch television rather completing their homework assignments? What is it going to cost them if they don't study everyday? What is it going to cost them over the next two, three, four or five years? What is it going to cost them in terms of their self-image or self-respect if they don't focus their attention on doing well in school? What is it going to cost them in terms of how society thinks about them? What is it going to cost them in terms of what their mother, father, and other family members think about them? What is it going to cost them financially in the future, if they don't change how they are dealing with school? What is it going to cost them if their lack of a good education results in them having a low paying job or no job at all?

Just looking back over these questions should be enough to help you understand the power you are helping Black boys to unleash. In most of my work with Black boys, it has been their personal discoveries at this step that has caused them to question their internal beliefs about the effort they put into doing better at school. You've got to remember that change does not occur overnight. But it can happen the instant you help Black boys raise their expectations about their ability to achieve. This chapter, along with the others in this book, provides you with a number of reliable ways to help Black males see beyond the prison of their intellect. Your role as an educator, parent, or mentor is to be a guide who is knowledgeable enough to have the courage to help a young man develop his potential to live his dreams. Also, keep in mind that the strategies you are teaching Black boys apply to making changes in every aspect of their lives today and in future. There is no way to help them avoid the uncomfortable circumstances that will arise in their lives, but you can give them the tools to effectively deal with whatever comes up.

Fifth, have the boy's rate each of the beliefs, behavioral routines, and physiology/body movements of Black boys who make As and Bs all the time: (1) Top priority and must be done immediately, (2) Extremely important and should be started soon, (3) Important, but it can wait, (4) Not so important. Have the boys take each of their "Top Priority" items from each of the three categories (Beliefs, Behavioral Routines, Physiology/Body Movements) and have them think about, write out, and discuss with you their compelling reasons why they have to make each of these items a part of their lives. Keep in mind that your goal is to help them discover about all of the great reasons why they have to adopt these beliefs, behavioral routines, and physiology/body movements associated with academic success. Equally or more important is your work with the boys to help them discover all of the negative things that can happen if they choose to not adopt the top priority items associated with academic success. To accomplish all of this, you might consider having the students work on one of their top priority items from each of the categories each day. Repetition is the mother of all skills. In fact, as you continue to work with the procedures for duplicating academic success, it will become obvious that some boys reap huge rewards shortly after they start using the procedures with a few of their Top Priority beliefs. Other boys require a longer conditioning period. What seems to speed up the process is whether you have interjected enough discussion to help the boys see the connections between their behavior today and the real world opportunities that await them at school and in their communities.

Most teachers who are committed to working with Black boys will soon discover that it is easier to work with one boy at a time. There is far greater control over the implementation and continuation of the work with the boy. The academic benefits are likely to emerge earlier and the relationship between the teacher and student grows rapidly. The major disadvantage is that the teacher or counselor has limited him or herself to working with one Black boy while there are countless others who desperately need the same attention. Some teachers have modified the procedures for duplicating academic success, making them part of their in-class and homework assignments for all of their students. Others have relied solely on the time immediately after school to work with a small group of Black boys or to introduce the procedures to staff working with Black boys in after school enrichment programs. Although working with a small group can be challenging, it allows Black boys an opportunity to learn from each other and to have the experience of being part of a group dedicated to increasing academic achievement.

Sixth, repeat steps one through five until you achieve the breakthrough that you and the boys are seeking. For some boys, the changes will occur rapidly. You'll experience resistance from some boys and you, too, might not be totally convinced that these procedures will work. When you have these experiences, and I am certain you will, then don't hesitate to contact me through the phone numbers and email address found in the back of the book.

While working with Black boys, I have found it useful to have incentives that are linked to their self-development work. In most cases, spending an hour or two at the movie theater or simply enjoying popcorn while we watched a video was an invaluable time to talk about life, school, and the pursuit of happiness. Although many of the boys that I've mentored were initially doing poorly in school, what I soon discovered is that they were starving for opportunities to interact with Black men more than they were starving for study skills. Consequently, the use of social reinforcements as a reward for following through with their self-development work was by far the most valuable tool. Another useful tool that I have used routinely to help strengthen my relationship with Black boys is "bonding beads." Each boy and I make a necklace or bracelet using a leather chain and glass beads that we exchange with each other as a sort of seal or commitment to honor our relationship.

Many parents and teachers experience tremendous anxieties and fears when they attempt to make changes in their own behavior or when they attempt to change the behavior of children in their lives. They feel awful because they have internal conflicts about whether they believe the child is capable of changing. Others are in conflict about the right way to encourage the child to change, but they don't have passion, a consuming reason, or an energizing purpose that causes them to do everything they can to help their children or Black boys in their classrooms become great. Regardless of where you are with important goals in your life, don't let fear rule your relationship with Black males. Even if you don't know exactly how to handle a situation, it is best to let the boys you are working with see you attempt to deal with the challenge rather than see you avoid it because of your fear. You've got to remember that they learn from you and that they are just as fearful as you are about making changes in their lives.

Some parents and teachers really don't have any faith in their children's abilities, and they have set narrow limits about what they expect. In the end, the academic performance they get out of the child is just as limited as their beliefs. This happens because their beliefs and interactions feed on and interact with one another to provide the fuel to push dreams into a reality. While having fuel for your work with Black boys is great, fuel without a vehicle or strategy is like having electricity with no outlets to plug in your appliances. You've got to use a strategy that will move them in the direction of excellence if you want your work with Black boys or your own children to be effective. While there is no one best place to start, I strongly recommend that you follow the six steps. Be patient, but expect big results because inside each Black boy is a great man waiting to blossom. By the way, I have used these steps to empower fifteen boys to discover their academic gifts. Initially, neither boy had what you would consider "good grades" and a few were close to being kicked out of school while some were waiting to reach the age where they could dropout. Since becoming their mentor and taking an active role in their lives, all boys have graduated from high school and all but two have obtained a bachelors degree from a four-year college.

7

Early Exposure to Reading and Positive Male Role Models

By Pryce Baldwin, Jr.

Introduction

When it comes to African Americans, we have not always had the pleasure of reading. "Roots," by Alex Haley[1] revealed that slaves were often beaten when they were caught reading or even trying to learn to read. Even more drastic measures were sometimes taken. During Jim Crow and segregation, African Americans were denied access to libraries and were denied voting rights if they could not pass required reading test. African Americans went to segregated schools that received second-hand books from white schools.[2] That was problematic enough, but often the stories depicted in these books projected an inferior and negative image of Black people. Historically, our nation has devalued all African Americans but the male more especially. Frederick Douglass, Booker T. Washington, and Marcus Garvey became prolific writers, leaders, and proponents of African Americans in spite of their situations. A lot of the history of the African American in America exists because men like these risked their lives learning to read and write and encouraging others to do the same.

I was born during segregation. My public school education and college was segregated. My mother finished high school but my dad completed 8th grade. My mother earned a bachelor of science degree at 52 years of age and a Master of Divinity degree at 56. My early experiences in reading included the Bible, my Sunday School Book, the Bobsey Twins, Davy Crockett and second-hand books at school. My love for reading started at an early age and my parents bolstered it with books and magazines. My mother did domestic work and she brought home books and magazines that were being discarded from the homes that she worked in. All of us, including my father, were glad to get those books and would spend hours pouring through them, looking at pictures and reading. Unfortunately, the circumstances that I encountered while growing up is not typical for Black boys today. Many of them are born into poverty, and they don't have two parents at home who are concerned about their academic development. Books are not part of the household inventory and mindless hours are spent watching television rather than reading. Consequently, many Black boys loose out on the opportunity to make reading a fundamental part of their day-to-day experience.

This chapter will discuss the power of reading and its relationship to writing and self-confidence. It will also offer advice to both parents and educators about the best ways to motivate Black boys to fall in love with reading. Finally, the chapter describes the process for establishing a mentoring relationship with Black boys and how mentoring programs can be used to encourage reading.

Reading Builds Vocabulary

Whether one is traveling, working, or just being, reading is a lifeline to the world. The word is the act that allows one to connect to humanity. Aside from seeing another human being, words are the connector to others. The arrangement of our words, the pronunciation, and the manner of delivery denotes to another our capabilities. Everything that depicts who we are as African American males starts as words. We teach African American youngsters that they really live in two worlds, the African American culture and the American culture. There is a standard in both that he must master. In his real world, he must be able to withstand the peer pressures and environmental pressures that surround him. His language here is casual, colorful, full of symbols, secretive, and almost tribal. In the other world, he is obliged to know, read, speak and write the King's English. Yet if he cannot traverse that world he is doomed to being bullied, crushed to the point of recoiling into his own world of darkness, video games, even gangs.

An advanced society, with technological discoveries, demands that he be able to read, think, and interpret at a rapid pace in order to compete. We must assure that every child can read, and does read, well. Supplanting the notion that one must develop socially and not educationally is a disservice to the child, as well as to the system. Schools and society at large must compel the powers to ensure that we fully educate every child. Of all the basic skills a child must master, reading is the cornerstone and motivating children to master reading at the earliest grades is the key to success.

One of the major features of No Child Left Behind, Reading First, is a $6 billion federal program to help struggling readers in the earliest grades, particularly those where a high percentage of the students live in poverty. Based heavily on the 2000 National Reading Panel report, the Reading First program require schools being funded by them to focus their reading instruction on phonemic awareness, phonics, developing fluency, vocabulary, and text comprehension. The panel report's underlying research deemed these elements essential to ensuring that children were reading well by the end of 3rd grade.[3,4]

Although there is controversy about whether the program is effective, many states have reported increased reading achievement among poor and minority students.[4] For example, in North Carolina, the state's K-3 students from all subgroups in the 90 Reading First schools made double-digit gains in reading comprehension in the 2007-08 school year, with proficiency rates for 1st grade Black students rising from 26 percent to 75 percent. The proficiency rates for 3rd grade students on free and reduced-price lunch rose from 58 to 72 percent. Similar results were reported for Florida, where most of the 583 schools in the state have implemented the Reading First program. The state's top schools showing the greatest improvement in K-3 reading had seven characteristics in common.

1. Strong leadership.
2. Dedicated teachers convinced that all students could read regardless of language barriers, limited home support, or low socioeconomic status.
3. Regular discussion of reading data from a variety of sources.

4. Effective scheduling that included a 90-minute reading Black, plus time beyond that for intervention.
5. Professional development for teachers.
6. Scientifically based reading programs that included a variety of material and computer-based intervention.
7. Parental involvement.

The literacy gains through Reading First[3,4] are encouraging, but there are still low-performing schools that struggle in their efforts to motivate students, particularly Black males, to increase their reading comprehension. In addition, little attention is being given to older students who did not have the opportunity to master reading at the earliest grades.

National reading achievement data continue to indicate that as a group, African American males, particularly adolescents in middle and high school classroom, are not performing well. Several solutions proposed over the past decade specifically address the literacy needs of African American adolescent males. They include providing culturally responsive literacy instruction that links classroom content to student experiences; developing character development programs, rites-of-passage programs, comprehensive literacy programs, and academically oriented remedial programs; and establishing all-male academies or alternative schools and programs designed specifically for African American males. All the proposed solutions emphasize a meaningful curriculum reflective of student experiences. Yet the most vulnerable African American adolescent males remain in public schools in which literacy instruction is not responsive to their needs.

A review of research on the education of African American adolescent males revealed a glaring omission: the role of text in literacy development. Although curriculum is often a significant consideration for improving education outcomes for African American males, specific texts and text characteristics that should inform curriculum selection are strikingly absent.

This is problematic because educators who are seeking to identify ways to engage African American males in reading-related tasks have little guidance in doing so. By selecting appropriate reading materials, teachers can engage African American adolescent males with text, particularly those students who have not mastered the skills, strategies, and knowledge that will lead to positive life outcomes. This productive shift in literacy takes into account students' four literacy needs—academic, cultural, emotional, and social—and relies on instructional practices that have proven effective with African American males. The big problem is that African American adolescent males currently have limited exposure to this kind of quality literacy instruction in school. Many complete school unable to identify texts they find meaningful and significant to their lives. This is one of the great tragedies of American public education. A meaningful program should include texts that shape a positive life trajectory and provide a roadmap that can help students resist nonproductive behaviors. This is part of a larger goal of literacy development that aims to shape positive life outcome trajectories and reawaken their minds in order to move them toward self-determination.[5,6,7,8]

Building Relationships Through Reading

When children come to school, they bring with them their own notion of what schooling is going to be. The school also has expectations of the child. Too many times these expectations don't complement each other and one expectation is often overlooked; the more power oriented one, the school. Consequently, the child becomes lost in a setting that does not look like his idea of school and he loses interest. By the third grade, the dye is cast. The two worlds collide for the African American boy and he finds security in neither.

For African American boys, this scene is too real. Because the teacher is often white and female, the Black boy has no one to latch on to, to look up to, or to become a buddy. He turns to acting out or just doing nothing at all. He has no role model that he can see, touch, or relate to. Although his acting out is not much different than his white peer, his consequences are more serious.

If we expect African American boys to excel, there must be a support system that provides insulation from the cries that "he's acting white," "he's a nerd," or "he thinks he's better than us." Therefore, his teachers would do well to remember that and seek ways to provide that security blanket and support system, not only for Black boys but for all students. In addition, white teachers should be aware of their own perceptions and prejudices as they try to understand the African American boy.

Because few role models that look like the African American boy are found in schools, teachers can supplement this by inviting African

American men to school to read to boys, mentor them. Churches, social organizations, professional organizations, fraternities, even motorcycle clubs are places to begin recruiting. Role models in the classroom are essential to the success of African American males in elementary and middle school.

We want the boys to see, talk with, and literally touch successful African American men, so they might know and see their possibilities. I can't tell you the numbers of times that I've walked into a school, passed a class walking down the hall and watched as the little boys follow you with their eyes and wonder, "Whose Daddy is that?" They know that they are being denied something as basic as a role model that looks like him.

There are other ways that men can contribute and many are doing that, but not nearly enough. Role models/mentors can share lunch, coach a team, job share, share a hobby, etc. The boy needs to see the adult male doing positive things in order to know his destiny. For many boys, there are no real images of Black males doing positive things to achieve their destiny. To combat that, have them read biographies of successful Black males as a way for them vicariously learn how they too can overcome odds and achieve success.

Building a solid relationship with a boy is essential to being a role model or mentor. Relationships are what boys treasure most. It often happens around something that the boy and the man have in common. Just as essential is trust. One must do what one says he will do. Most boys have had men in their lives only to see them come and go. When we don't keep our promise with boys we are saying, "You are not worth my time." Being a role model/mentor is not for everyone. There are other ways to help. Don't start unless you are committed.

Mentoring can be a unique way of passing on what you know about working to success. It's your legacy. Dr. James Comer, Professor of Child Psychiatry at Yale University, says, "No significant learning takes place without a significant relationship." It's the little things in relationships that really count. Reading with young boys and reading to them is a sure fire way of creating and maintaining a relationship. The possibilities are endless. Boys like to read about sports, adventures, making things and stories that reflect their lives. Find places and things in your area that are an extension of the reading. Work together to make something that you read about. Play a game together related to what you have read. Let the boy teach you something that you don't know. Share time.

For those who want to assist children in learning to read, read Marva Collins' "Marva Collins' Way." It's not the reading that she teaches but rather the relationship that she builds with each child. It is obvious that building a relationship with another is paramount to teaching anything. It is the "you can do anything" attitude that permeates to the very core of our being that prompts one to strive to do their best, if they have been told that they can.[9]

It is through storytelling, reading, and writing that children are given another world to exist in. As sad as it sounds, many men learn to read in prison. For example, Malcolm X explains that reading. enabled him to escape the confines of prison. He wrote, "I supposed it was inevitable that as my word base broadened, I could for the first time pick up a book and read and now begin to understand what the book was saying. Anyone who has read a great deal can imagine the new world that opened. Let me tell you something; from then until I left prison, in every free moment I had, if I was not reading in the library, I was reading on my bunk."[10]

Brother Malcolm, like many other Black men, learned to read and acquired a good part of their education while in prison. Malcolm was a great student while attending public school, but he turned away from the power of reading and education when one of his teachers, a white man, told him he was crazy for thinking that, one day, he would become a lawyer.

We need to take an honest position with regard to the literacy development of African American adolescent males. Neither effective reading strategies nor comprehensive literacy reform efforts will close the achievement gap in a race-and class-based society unless meaningful texts are at the core of the curriculum. In addition, educators need to ground literacy instruction of African American males in larger ideals and take students' present condition into account.[8] In his novel Convicted in the Womb, Carl Upchurch wrote,[11] "The text taught me how to look at myself . . . they told me regardless of my condition, regardless of the circumstances I came from, I was a legitimate human being and a child of God. But I also learned that society considered me inferior because of my color—and considered any rights and privileges I have as a Black man to be the gift of white men. I decided that I had the responsibility to stand up for people who hadn't yet learned to think of themselves as human beings." (p. 92). Beyond any doubt, the texts Upchurch read gave him capital, but he did not appreciate reading until he was imprisoned and lost in the penal system.

Reading helps one to escape for the moment and provides entry into another world, a world read and dreamed about, a world we they can see themselves through the extraordinary lives of men like Malcolm, Martin Luther King, Jr., Ben Carson, George Washing Carver, L.L. Cool J, Sean Puffy Combs, Barack Obama, John H. Johnson, Will Smith, and Denzel Washington, to name a few. We need to shore up the resilience of African American adolescent males by providing them with reading materials about Black men they can identify with. This is strongly needed for struggling readers attending public schools in low-income areas. Identifying texts that can shape positive life outcome trajectories for African American males—who constitute 7 percent of the school-age population (4 million of 53 million)—is a significant challenge.[12]

Introducing Black males to books and other text that encourage empowerment, resilience, and success through literacy is obviously not the only panacea for addressing the literacy needs of African American males. What's also needed are teachers, parents, mentors, and school counselors who are familiar with these texts so they can engage Black males in caring, supportive, and cognitively challenging discussions. In this context, these texts can provide Black adolescent males with the capital they need to be resilient in environments in which they were previously vulnerable. Not only can this practice improve the reading outcomes of African American adolescent males, but it can improve their life outcomes as well.

Reading, Writing, and Speaking Go Hand in Hand

A good reader develops a command of writing because the vocabulary grows as the mastery of reading evolves. The more one reads, the more one knows, and knowledge increases both the ability to write and speak. Carl Boyd says,[13] "No one rises to low expectations!" Teachers must challenge students' ability to retain this knowledge and gather even more. Master teachers create high expectations and then encourage children to meet them. They understand that everyone loves a pat on the back, particularly when they have achieved a goal that at first seemed beyond their reach.

African American boys have a special talent, verve, which allows them to be very creative. Rappers and hip-hop artists are just some examples of this talent. What that talent needs is the space, safety, and security in the classroom that high achieving boys must have to be successful. Allowing flexibility in context and content allows success for the boy. Teachers must recognize the cultural and societal learning styles of each child, both general and specific. Allowing for that difference in the writing and rewriting process allows for a win-win situation. Encouragement and support of the original creation and providing assurances of success opens the youngster to another world. For boys, tailoring the subject to areas they like helps the process. It is important to be gentle because boys have feelings too!

Reading Is Not Just For Boys

This is pure myth. Ask any boy who enters school why he's there, and you will know that his craving for learning is as great as any. We have to start assuming and act on the assumption that every child wants to learn and do well in school. Black boys are no different. Because their behavior in the classroom and the playing field are different from girls, their desire should not be misread as representing a disinterest in learning. Sure, it is true that language and the mastery of verbal behaviors occur developmentally a bit earlier for girls than for boys. But regardless of the developmental delay in reading, boys love to read. Their preferences might be very particular and strangely different from what girls prefer to read, but they want to read. What boys read is significant. Elementary age boys' preference is broader in terms of content. These guys will read anything that involves movement and action—if they can read. The trick is to determine their interest and supplement their reading with books and articles that meet that need.

This is a special time to immerse the boys into reading for life. Their thirst for knowing and learning is unmatched. If you watch young boys, their energy is endless. This boundless energy must be guided through words and books that adults must provide for boys. In this way, reading becomes a vicarious way for Black boys to vent some of their endless energy through the adventures, characters, and circumstances they are reading. In addiction to seeing themselves in some of the adventures and stories, reading helps Black boys develop social and problem solving skills. Moreover, reading is the basic building block for success in the new technological world. Although the lives of boys today are filled with electronic gadgets, computers, and all sorts of multimedia applications, reading continues to be the basic skills they will need to be successful. The earlier that one begins this process, the better Black boys will perform in the classroom and in life. Catching up later takes twice the energy, time, and money. So it's a no brainer that getting Black boys hooked on reading during their early years is best.[8,14]

In a conversation I had with an eight year old, he revealed his likes and dislikes of school. He loved math and gym. So I asked, "Do you like reading?" He hesitated and said, "No." "Why don't you like reading?" I asked. "You read stories, don't you?" "I read this story about a fish," he said. "Did you like it?" I inquired. "I didn't like the questions at the end," he muttered. Are we taking away the desire and the love to read all for the sake of testing or some other national legislation? This young man loved to read because he told me the story, ending with, "It was a short story," he volunteered. Every opportunity that I get with him, I encourage reading, library visits, reading aloud by him and me, giving him books.

Advice For Parents

Parenting skills develop on the job, unless you trust others' experiences and adhere to them. Most parents, if they pay attention, become experts after the fact. Being a parent and an educator, I will offer some tips for parents of Black males. My experiences span the era of segregation and integration. I have taught elementary and middle school and have been an administrator for a mentoring program for African American boys. But there is much about reading that I did not know simply because I did not learn these lessons from my parents. For example, until just a few years ago I was unaware of the tremendous research showing that babies can read. A baby's brain thrives on stimulation and develops at a phenomenal pace; nearly 90% during the first five years of life! Therefore, it appears that the easiest time for children to learn a language is during the infant and toddler years, when the brain is creating thousands of synapses every second. Perhaps, the current practice of waiting to teach reading skills until Black boys start school is too late. The earlier a child is taught to read the better they will read and the more likely they will enjoy it. If Black boys are taught to read during the natural window for learning language, from about birth to about age five, it will be easier for them to learn any type of language including spoken, receptive, foreign and written language. Early readers have more self-esteem and they perform better in school and later in life. I was not able to seize this small window of opportunity with my children, but you can.[15,16]

Provide children with books to read and put the books where they work and play.

I loved to read so much that when my mom or dad would say, "Lights out!" I would cover the lamp with something to hide the light. Once I covered the lamp with a sweater. My mom asked, "What's that I smell?" The sweater was on the bulb and it was burning. Needless to say, that was probably my last time reading after "lights out!"

My parents read to us and with us. In their own way, they encouraged reading. I have a son and a daughter, and while we taught them early and often, the system that they entered into created roadblocks and challenges. For my son, he was an avid reader at first. A change in location for our family, from Brooklyn, New York, to Raleigh, North Carolina, was the culprit. Although I was born and raised in North Carolina, my return was at the onset of integration. My son began struggling at the middle years (6th-9th grades). He always had female teachers, mostly white. That became an increasing problem and developed into serious challenges by high school. As much as he loved to read sports section of the newspaper, sports magazines, and novels that provided suspense he was failing an average English class. We requested something more challenging and his teacher agreed, and he had more success in Advanced English classes.

Parents must be strong advocates for their children.

Know your child's potential, from having worked with him, and in a kind, gentle way, express that to his teachers. Remember, you may have some differences with the school, administration, and teachers, but chances are your son will remain in that school. Get to know your child's teacher before problems arise. Volunteer if you can and if you can't volunteer, offer whatever you can to the teacher and his class.

Read to your children, and let them see you reading.

Children model what they see, not what you tell them. Pediatricians claim that babies in the womb can and do detect sounds around them, most of all, their mother's voice. Aside from being called crazy, it's worth the chance to read, recite even talk to the baby in the womb. There are few activities as joyous for parents and babies as reading 'play' sessions.

Reading is the basis of all learning and the acquisition of knowledge and success go hand-in-hand. By teaching your baby how to read, parents can open the door to learning to the world.

A baby's brain thrives on stimulation and develops at a phenomenal pace . . . nearly 90% during the first five years of life. The best and easiest time to learn a language is during the infant and toddler years, when the brain is creating thousands of synapses every second—allowing a child to learn both the written word and spoken-word simultaneously, and with much more ease. The current practice of starting to teach reading skills in school is too late and children benefit greatly from getting a much earlier start since a child has only one natural window for learning language—from about birth to about age four. During this period, it is easier for a child to learn any type of language including spoken, receptive, foreign and written language. The earlier the child is taught to read the better they will read and the better they perform in school and later in life. Early readers have more self-esteem and are more likely to stay in school.[15,16]

Parents must insist that academics precede athletics.

In 1988, the Washington Redskins were the Super Bowl Champions. On that team was a very talented tackle, Dexter Manley. Dexter grew up in Texas, went to public school in Houston, and later played football for Oklahoma State University. In 1989, Dexter Manley admitted on national television that he could not read above the second grade level. How could this happen? Public school, 12 years, college 3-4 years and he could not read. If it wasn't for his ability to play football, Dexter Manley would just be another Black male with little prospects for a professional career.[17] He is one of the lucky ones. Today, the odds are low that a Black boy, regardless of how great an athletic he is, will play college sports and end up on a professional team, if he can't read.

AAU teams are great places for students, but insist that your son(s) and his coaches know: Academic Before Athletics. Rather than have sports use your son, insist that he use sports to gain knowledge and intellect. If your son is good enough athletically, and you persist, someone will step up and help him. Without the ability to read, there is no success in life. Many boys don't like to read school assigned books for many reasons. It is not a macho thing (they haven't seen it modeled at school or at home) to do. Because boys often emulate the males they see on television, video games, and the Internet, they have no visual record of African American men reading. While this whole notion of seeing someone model reading is significant, it is not to be taken lightly. A newspaper's sports section, an auto manual, magazine is a good substitute as long as they are reading.

Advice For Teachers

Having been an educator for many years, as well as a director of a mentoring project for African American males, I have identified a number of significant points to aid teachers as they aspire to teach African American males. The external factors that influence and motivate African American males lie in your domain. It is important that you have a complete view of the Black boys you are teaching, their views of you as a teacher, and their expectations about doing well in school.

Visit the student at his home.

Home visits are a thing of the past, but it works for the teacher and the student. Too risky? Try his church on Sunday morning. Two things happen: (1) You will learn a lot about the African American culture, and (2) You will find a different child. I remember one boy that I mentored in elementary school. Once a week I would visit him at school and he was always in one of three places: the principal's office, another teacher's class, or isolated in his class. I happened to visit his church one Sunday and guess who ushered me to my seat? He was surprised that I was there, and I used the opportunity to speak with his parent and his pastor. I later suggested to his teacher that she visit also. She did. I never found the youngster out of or isolated in his class again.

Read research by African Americans on what works for African American boys

I was the coordinator for the Wake County Public School/Community Helping Hands Project, a mentoring project for African American boys in elementary and middle school. Reading was a vital part of our project. Not only did we provide books, but we also offered books of relevance for the boys. Several come to mind: Ben Carson's, *Gifted Hands*[18] and *Think Big*;[19] *The Pact*[20] by Sampson Davis, George Jenkins, and Rameck Hunt; Mychal Wynn's, *Follow Your Dreams*.[21] In most instances, boys in grades 4 through 8 can read the books with ease. Where students found difficulties, we had volunteers to work with them. *The Pact* shows that if we want boys to read, the content must be relevant and the environment must be safe and supportive. Peer groups make it safe and supportive. Out of that kind of reading, the boys created collages, poems, raps and short essays that summarized not only the readings but what the readings meant to them. Teachers should be alert to how they respond to boys. Remember that they have feelings, too.

Connect the text to the real World

Text should be connected to larger ideals such as cultural uplift, economic advancement, resistance to oppression, and intellectual development. The African American abolitionist Frederick Douglass' work, the poetry of Paul Laurence Dunbar, and the literature of other African American authors provide this kind of uplift and empowerment for African American boys. I used these authors and their works in our public speaking contests. Surprises abound when students read what is relevant to them. Even discussions that followed these readings provided opportunities to analyze their realities and develop strategies for overcoming. In middle and high school classrooms, their voices are often absent in conversations about their literacy-related successes and failures. Today, as I write these words, I realize that there are many "must-read" texts for Black males. When considering text, however, you should keep four things in mind: (1) The books and other materials need to be intellectually exciting for both students and teachers, (2) they should serve as a roadmap and provide apprenticeship, (3) they must challenge students cognitively, and (4) they ought to help students apply literacy skills and strategies independently. More specifically, must-read texts should:

- Encourage students to have real and authentic discussions in which they can discuss strategies for overcoming academic and societal barriers.
- Honor the students' cultural characteristics while addressing their emotional, psychological and social experiences.
- Make sure the text addresses the interconnections between the social, emotional, economic, and the political nature of the world of the students.
- Acknowledge that developing skills, increasing test scores, and nurturing students' identities are fundamentally compatible.

- Serve as soft role models in the absence of physically present male role models by providing motivation, direction, and hope for the future and suggesting what is worthwhile in life.

Identifying reading material for Black males, however, is not sufficient. Teachers need professional support to help them mediate texts with students, and the students should provide input about the value of these texts.

Note the language and reading skills that children bring to school.

Helping Black boys recognize the differences in those language skills that are acceptable at home and those applicable in the school and the work place is a sensitive matter. While teachers may want to remedy it, one does not want to discourage the student entirely. Worse yet is to give the impression that what the student brings to school is worthless. One does not want children to feel that their world and its language is devalued, rather every effort must be made to make school inclusive. One way to obtain this is by teaching children how to "switch," often referred to as "code switching." As long as they are aware of the language rules for casual and formal situations, then when they are at home, in a casual setting, or just "chilling" with friends, they can use their own language and break all the verbs they desire.

In the school and work place, there is a formal language that is the standard. This formal language is necessary in order for business to take place as well as learning in the classroom. So that African American boys can feel their worth in the school setting, teachers would do well to be creative in making their language inclusive. Teachers might have a fun activity where students teach teachers their language. Another activity would be to develop a dictionary of terms that students use in casual language and list the formal way of saying the same thing. Students must be made to feel that they are an integral part of the process or they will turn to negative ways of being included and ultimately become excluded. The same can be said for discipline.

The one thing that gets African American boys in trouble in school is breaking school rules. School rules say, prohibit fighting, and cursing, and mandate that students stay in their seats, keep their hands to themselves, etc. In the boys' world, these rules don't exist. Parents tell their children, if someone hits you, hit them back. What parents and teachers should teach them is that there are two sets of rules—school rules to be observed at school and another set to be observed at home. Teachers must also make sure that all students are safe from harm and protected at all cost.

Many teachers see in African American boys what they refer to as an "aggressiveness." In many cases, these boys are the sole male in the family or worse, they are the male protector of the family and are left to make adult decisions for other siblings. Teachers fear this student because they do not recognize nor understand the cultural aspects of what the boy is saying or doing. He is simply defending his turf the only way that he knows and responding to a perceived threat. Rather than ignoring how the boys is acting or pretending that it means something else, teachers need to build trusting relationship with Black boys. By building a relationship with the student, one will find out that he is still a child struggling with identify issues and only wants to be treated fairly. Teachers must establish and maintain that it is their role in the classroom and the school to keep everyone safe. Boys will generally buy into that notion. At the first sign of unequal treatment, however, the boys will revert to his standard of self protection.

Encourage summer reading

The single summertime activity that is most strongly and consistently related to summer learning is reading. Most children, regardless of their gender or ethnicity, who make great strides during the academic year, lose what they gained over the summer break. Although education policymakers have done little to address this issue, there is a long history of research showing that summer reading setback is a primary source of the reading achievement gap and might explain the nearly 80 percent reading achievement gap between poor and non-poor students at age fourteen.[22] Teachers who work hard and long hours throughout the year are often blamed for academic difficulties Black boys experience, but it really does take a whole village of people (e.g., parents, grandparents, teachers, siblings and peers who value education, administrators, athletic coaches, Sunday school teachers, community libraries, community organizations, etc.) to create a supportive environment for Black boys to be successful at school and in life.

Reading is clearly the key, but for many Black boys, there are some severe restrictions to their access to books and other reading material. Black boys from low-income families are likely to have fewer books in the home, and city libraries not easily accessible to children. Research supports the commonsense notion that easier access to interesting reading materials increases the likelihood that children will read and several studies have shown that increasing low-income students' access to books during the summer months seems likely to stimulate reading activity and thereby minimize summer reading loss.

To motivate Black boys to read during the summer months, schools should rethink how they limit access to books. Typically, the collection of books in the school libraries are the largest and nearest collection of age-appropriate books for students in grades K-8, but in many schools there is no access to the library or classrooms during the summer months. Teachers and parents should acknowledge the role of popular culture in the lives of Black boys. Rather than denigrating series books or books derived from movies or video games, it is important to build on this prior knowledge to create communities of Black male readers who share, discuss, and swap favorite books. There are probably loads of creative ways to put books into the hands of Black boys during the summer months, but whatever you choose to do, don't overlook the need for Black boys to mimic your behavior. Chances are that if they see you (teacher, parent, counselor, and mentor) constantly reading and discussing books, then they will mimic this behavior and follow your lead. But access to books is the key.[23,24,25,26,27]

Whether a child reads fiction, comic books, a biography, instructions on a package, text messages or the cereal box, it is essential for all children to be able to read and to read for pleasure and knowledge. I want every African American male to real all throughout the year, including the summer. Summer is a great time for African American males to explore their interests by reading about different topics and chances are that your Public Library offers many free opportunities for fun reading adventures during the summer. I strongly encourage parents and students to make the Public Library a destination for your family during the summer. Some cities have summer reading kickoff where children can register for the summer reading program, enjoy free food and entertainment, and take home a few free books. Making a phone call to your city or county library is a good place to discover events in your city. In addition, regardless of how you approach summer reading, here are some useful tips for reading with children:[28]

1. Model Reading: Show your child that reading is both fun and useful by reading books, magazines, and other materials. Assist your child in discerning important/main ideas in a text. Discuss the main or "big ideas" in a story. Talk about the many ways that reading is important. Model how to preview a text. Do "picture walks" through a storybook. Model thinking and wondering aloud as you read a story to your child. Mention what you think the character looks like, or wonder why a character did what he did. Guide your child is making predictions and inferences. Guide your child in logically ordering and sequencing events, identifying problems, relationships and details. Guide your child in drawing conclusions. Help them use stated or implied evidence to draw and support their conclusions.

2. Time: Set aside time each day for reading. Some schools have time set where all students drop everything and read (DEAR Time) and families can do the same thing during the summer so that the entire family will have a special set time to read.

3. Read Aloud: Parents often stop reading aloud to children, as the children become better readers. However, by reading books aloud you can help your child learn new vocabulary words, concepts and ways of telling stores or presenting information. Having time to read aloud will provide you with opportunities to introduce and pronounce difficult and unfamiliar words before and after reading aloud. You can utilize a word wall or whiteboard to post words from a story and encourage your child to use these words in other contexts. Encourage your child to use words that name and describe characters and settings (who and where) and words that tell action and events (what and how). Provide opportunities for discussion about and reflection upon a text. Pose higher order questions to your child before, during and after reading to synthesize and/or use relevant information within a text or extent or evaluate the text. What was the most interesting part of the story? What was the most important part? What details support your answers? Were the characters believable? Why or why not? What examples and details support your answer?

4. Choice: Allow your child to choose the books he wants to read for the summer. Help them select books that provide literacy experiences that are relevant to their interest, everyday life or

important current events, while also exposing them to new ideas and situations through literature. Introduce a variety of genres including narrative, adventure fiction, mystery, historical fiction, folklore, modern fantasy, poetry, biographies, autobiographies, journals and memoirs. Help your child make connections from the text to themselves, their outside experiences and knowledge and connections between texts ("Think about a character that did something courageous. How was that experience like . . ." Or "How is this story or character similar to/different from . . . ?). Show your child how to use Venn diagrams and graphic organizers to determine likes and differences.

5. Comfort: If your child reads smoothly, use expression and can accurately tell you what has been read, then the book is probably at a comfortable reading level for your child. If your child makes five or more errors in reading a page of about 50 words, the book is too challenging.

6. Video: Read a book and watch the video together. Make books available in movie version. Talk about the similarities and differences and which version you prefer.

7. Writers: Writing postcards to friends, keeping a journal, noting books that have been read, encourage your child to write about his summer experiences.

Black boys need your support

Every student in school needs to have at least one adult in that school that he can relate to, go to as an advocate, find it easy to talk to. Therefore, relationship building should be at the forefront of the minds of every school administrator, teacher and other school employees. I've visited many schools where the custodian, who was often African American, advocated and related to African American boys in ways that teachers never could. Schools must find role models, mentors for African American boys. It is as essential as reading itself. Most of us copy what we see others do. Because African American boys don't see anyone in the school setting who resembles himself reading and excelling in achievement, they reason that it is unimportant, not relevant, and unnecessary for the American dream. Ask any African American male in any public school in America what he will eventually do in life and often you will get this response: "I am going to play professional basketball," or "I'm going to become a professional football player," or "I am going to become a rapper." None of the above is equated with doing well in school.

We must help students see the importance of work and service through role models. Dr. Jawanza Kunjufu, in a recent book, "An African Centered Response to Ruby Payne's Poverty Theory," cites evidence that the professional sports and entertainment field is not as available for participation as many of our young people think.[29,30,31]

- 1 million boys have a desire to make it into the NBA.
- 400,000 make high school teams.
- 4,000 make college teams.
- 35 are drafted into the NBA.
- 7 start.
- 4 years is the average career length in the NBA, 3 years in the NFL.

We must be able to show students that the majority of us work, including Black men. Further he states:

- A rapper sells one million CD's at $18 for $18 million.
- Distributors receive 50 percent ($9 million}.
- Producers receive 40 percent ($7.2 million).
- Rapper pays studio and video costs ($800,000).
- $1 million remains. IRS receives 50 percent.
- $500,000 remains. Rapper buys Lamborghini or Bentley.
- $0 remain.

Encouraging Reading Through Mentoring

I was a mentor long before I was given the title. It began when I lived with my sister and her family, including her son Jay, in New York. Jay was a real joy, full of energy and always eager to go. I would take him to Prospect Park and the corner store, to friends' homes, to Met's games, and even on trips to our parents' home in North Carolina. I really didn't know then what I was doing other than being family. Even though he was not my biological child, he was my child. I taught Jay, and he taught me. When I married my wife, Yvonne, I continued to share with her nieces and nephews. We always had a child even before we had our own children. Out of this bunch, I chose Dwight, the oldest of Yvonne's sister's children. Sometimes

I took Dwight and Jay on excursions, and they became friends. Once I decided to take my nieces and nephews to the Macy's Thanksgiving Day parade. Looking back now, I think maybe I was a little insane-eight nieces and nephews at a Macy's Day Parade amid an enormous crowd and frigid weather, but the children had a blast. All of these children had mothers and fathers, but it was a deep-rooted notion of "villages raising children" that drove me to share time and things I enjoy with a child. All that was vague in my memory, until a year ago when Jay, now married, living in Ohio and the father of one daughter, Ramah, flew to Raleigh to visit his parents. He brought Ramah with him, and everyone marveled that a father would travel alone with his child. The family concluded that he had learned such behavior from his Uncle Pryce. At that moment, I could understand how I had come to mentoring so easily. Every adult Black male is a mentor—either through his formal involvement in a mentoring relationship or because of the simple fact that children, including those not in our families, observe and mimic what we do.

Being a mentor is not a sophisticated task. It means being spiritually and physically in tune with others around you. Mentoring is giving. Mentoring is providing a living legacy. Children learn what they live. What is truer still is that in giving, we receive. One of the joys of teaching, mentoring and parenting is seeing the results of our giving. I marvel at the adults whom I have taught as children. Yes, children do grow up. Yes, that child whom you mentor may well be the one who reaches out to you when you need a helping hand.

During the middle part of my career, I was the program manager for the School/Community Helping Hands Project created by former Superintendent Dr. Robert Bridges, who was the first African American to serve in that capacity in North Carolina. Its purpose is to counter many negative images that African American males encounter in their communities, the school, and the larger world. It is these negative images that lead to getting in trouble at school, dropping out, and even going to prison. In studying data from the school district, Dr. Bridges found that African American males were not only dropping out of school but becoming a penal statistic as well. The project was to become a standard-bearer in the district to overcome some of that deficit. It began in the 1987-1988 school year and exists today. Over the years, it has evolved to provide not only mentoring but also assists boys with reading, test take skills, public speaking, and becoming leaders in their schools and communities. Under

Bill McNeal's leadership as superintendent, the project was recognized in the school community as a must for the county.

Helping Hands arranges school system mentors for small groups of boys in elementary schools. It should be noted that the number of adult African American males in schools, especially elementary schools, is steadily dwindling. These groups meet after school and on Saturdays to tackle the problems of educational achievement, peer relations, and self-esteem. The community volunteers serve these groups in one-on-one situations by spending an hour per week with them on the job, at the park, at home or in any activity where the boys can see how a successful adult behaves. The project provides for large group activities such as workshops for student partners, parents, and annual academic and athletic competitions for the students. In June, we have a graduation with presentations and receptions for students and parents.

Our search for mentors is never-ending, especially in the outlying areas of the county. Principals, counselors, teachers, and even parents constantly call seeking mentors for youngsters as early as kindergarten. The need is great. For adults, the choice is whether we want our tax dollars to continue to go toward building prisons—the "cure" that provides no real positive influence in the community—or the "prevention" where volunteers spend one hour a week with a youngster who, without some positive influence, will grow up to be a man who thinks manhood is making babies, acting tough, and carrying a gun.

What Is A Mentor?

Mentoring is as old as the world. In Biblical times, we find Moses being a mentor for Joshua. A great civil rights leader, Dr. Martin Luther King, Jr., had Dr. Benjamin Mays, President of Morehouse College, as his mentor. Each of the contributors to this book had mentors who encouraged their academic and professional development. As you read this and think back on your life, you can probably identify someone who mentored you. It is through this process that you have become what you are today

A mentor is an advisor, advocate, provider by example, gate opener, and most of all, a friend. Mentors are role models who are kind, concerned adults who offer their protégés support and guidance while providing them with some type of assistance. Even if you don't see yourself as a role model, you are. Whether you are a good role model or a bad one, you are a role model. Children only do and say what they see and hear other adults do. For those in the public eye, professional athletes, entertainers, teachers, politicians, we are all role models for Black boys.

In order for a mentor to be able to help a boy, he must be able to connect with the child. What the mentor is saying is you are worth my time because you are a special creation. Marian Wright Edelman, Executive Director of Children's Trust Fund, says, "Our children are the measure of our success."[32]

More and more children are in need of role models, especially African American boys. Many boys have as their role models men who are athletes, artists, men that they only see on television and never have an opportunity to touch or interact with. But they need role models that they can see, talk to, and share with on a regular basis. Having been a mentor and the coordinator of a mentoring project, I have learned that a mentor of the same sex and ethnicity is most desirable. In the real world, however, that is not always possible. I believe that any positive mentor is better than no mentor. I have approached many organizations about providing support in the form of mentoring. Often their talk was impressive but their actions were less than desirable.

What Makes a Good Mentor?

African American men are often found coaching youngsters in basketball, football, and soccer. Coaches make some of the best mentors, but they must insist on "academics before athletics." They must be concerned about the total boy, not just his athletic abilities. For those who would be mentors, consistency and commitment are crucial. Too many of our boys have become victims of men coming in and going out of their lives. Whether it is their on-again-off-again fathers or their mother's boyfriends, boys get messages about how men behave and eventually they will behave like the men they have observed. Remember, if you are not committed to the long term, don't start.

Boys need men to show them how to become men. They need to know a proper way to relate to females. They need to know what man's work is and how to become a positive force at home and in the community. When men fail to carry out this mentor relationship, it says to boys that they are not worthy of the mentor's time. This absence of a positive male role model/mentor leaves the boy to develop his own concept of manhood or worse to seek advice from his peers who know no more than he does.

For those contemplating establishing a program, whether it is group mentoring or one-on-one, deciding the age group that you will mentor is important. For a mentoring project, consider first the support for such a project. Where will you get the financial and personal support? What will be the age group? Will it be group mentoring or one on one? Depending on the experience of the group, one might want to begin with a group mentoring effort with members of the group assigned special tasks (i.e. mentor activities that should be varied to include some academic tasks, projects for the boys, outings, etc.). Remember boys prefer activities that involve doing things of interest to them. Sitting and listening to lectures are not things that boys love to do. Basketball and football are not the only options. Mentors should introduce what they enjoy also.

Our summer program consisted of half days of academics and half days of activities. The activities included non-traditional sports such as swimming, tennis, golf and photography. I believe it is important to introduce the boys to things that they have not tried. We discovered that many of the boys had a natural affinity to these non—traditional sports.

If one-on-one is what you decide to do, make sure that the men commit to at least one year of mentoring. If the match is good, the relationship will last much longer. In order to get the best match, the mentor must make his selection, of things to do as well as the mentee. This helps to make a better match.

Boys in elementary school are generally just happy to be with a man. They are open to just about anything that is exciting, from reading to playing games and learning new things. I recall the many times that I have visited elementary schools and noticed how African American boys watched my every move. Men, know that you are a role model to boys. Whether a mentor or just a visitor, African American males represent just one percent of teachers across this country. Some boys go to school for 12 years and they never have an African American male teacher. This is all the more why African American men need to become mentors.

For middle school boys, the choices are fewer than at the elementary level. Middle school boys are beginning to develop their own preferences for what they like to do. For a mentor, that is a good place to begin. Sharing one's own interests with the mentee, tempered with new ventures, is suggested. Reading books and articles that are relevant to the boy and engaging in discussions about life issues can provide a base of guidance that all boys need.

Choosing to mentor young men in high school should be centered on career choices. The match is all important. As coordinator, I tried to match mentors with boys who were interested in the profession of the mentor. The mentee can learn what courses in school relate to that profession and get a first hand view of a professional does. The mentor can also become an advocate, as well as a resource of references, for the young man. Ultimately, every adult who cares about children has a role to play. Beginning with parents, the first line of care for children, to the mentor/ role model, teachers, adults, we all have a part to play. While it may be difficult in today's world to engage young people that we encounter, we must make the effort. Raising children must not be left to the public institutions and public support; rather it has to be a community effort. Each one of us must reach out and touch the lives of young people in order for them to be prepared to become adults. I've often heard it said, "teachers live on through their students." We all do. Every effort spent with a child may be the one that directs one into a life of service and support for someone else. In addition, when a mentor empower a Black male to read and read well, it's like the gates of heaven opens his mind to an ocean of possibilities for a life that often times is beyond his wildest dreams.

Summary and Conclusions

The success of African American males in school and the larger society is dependent upon two factors. There are internal and external forces at work. Internally, African American males have the same foundation as all children. What's added by family is both cultural and ethnic. As educators, we need to know the cultural and ethnic makeup of these boys and incorporate this into instruction. Boys have taste when it comes to reading and it often is the opposite of what girls like to read. Girls have feelings and so do boys. African American boys put on a mask that says I'm tough and I'm not afraid of you or anything. The classroom must remain consistent when students are dealt with. Most of all teachers must have the desire to want to see all students being successful. In order for that to happen teachers must love children, all children. Teachers must love to teach and realize that they have the power to transform a child's life. The teacher's greatest payday is when the teacher encounters a former student who they had forgotten about and that student lets them know how much of a difference they made in their lives. If you don't fit that mold, leave teaching now before you destroy another life.

For parents, stay in the race. It is never too early to begin the process of educating your son. The sooner, the better, especially with reading. It has to be academics before athletics. Find a mentor, tutor for your son if there is a void in his life. If a positive adult male is not a part of your son's life, make it so. Women can raise a Black boy, but a boy needs a man to provide him with the skills to negotiate his way through the social, cultural, political, spiritual, and economic forces that can either empower or destroy him. For the past three decades or so, Black boys have been exposed to texts at schools that have been characteristically disabling. They largely ignore the cultural context of Black males and their desire for self-definition, focusing instead on reading skill and strategy development. This shift is largely influenced by policy decisions to administer tests to measure reading output. Unfortunately, our policy makers didn't see the need to include reading materials that were interesting to Black males, and as a result, the reading development and test scores of Black males have suffered.

Some of the dire effects of not meeting the reading needs of Black boys include academic tracking, disproportionate referrals for disciplinary action, retention in grade, remedial curricula, assigned to special education placements, and a resistance to school-related tasks. Moreover, many Black males experience school as an assault on their identities and on their masculinity. They have been made to feel as if their existence at school simply doesn't matter and they see little reason to navigate this path of humiliation. Many end up dropping out of school, unable to read, and incapable of cultivating a life that is filled with hope.

Of all of the academic skills, I believe that reading is the key, but Black boys need books and other text that reflects the often overlooked and rich contributions of Black men to the fabric of life. Just as exercise is essential to healthy minds and bodies, reading materials written by and for African American males is essential for African American males.

Recommended Books

Elementary School Level
- During the early year, the focus needs to be on the fundamental of reading, and the books should be ones that fully capture the attention of African American males.
- One exceptional collection of books for children of color can be found at Brown Sugar and Spice Books.[33] Elementary school age children of color will enjoy seeing themselves in each of the 56 African-American children's books. Many are true stories about African American history and people of color. Brown Sugar and Spice has a series of 12 books just for boys. This delightful set of paperback children's books, each one depicting an African-American boy, is sure to please! Easy reading levels and everyday experiences will entertain and educate children. Titles include:

"A Day With Daddy"

"Hurry Up!"

"I Can't Take A Bath"

"Sunday Best"

"Don't Hit Me"

"No Boys Allowed"

"The Low-Down, Bad-Day Blues"

"The Mystery of the Missing Dog"

"The Two Tyrone's"

"Stop Drop and Chill"

"Shop Talk"

"Mommy's Bed"

Activities at the end of each book extend the meaning. African American boys typically have fun doing the follow-up activities that make the reading experience even more beneficial. Each book is written and illustrated by an African-American and a short bio and photo is included.

Middle School Level
- *With Every Drop of Blood: A Novel of the Civil War.* James Collier and Christopher Collier. (1992). New York: Laurel Leaf. A 14-year-old white boy from Virginia, attempting to bring food to besieged

Richmond, is captured by Black Union soldiers, one of whom is a former slave his own age. The boys ultimately become friends.

- *47.* Walter Mosley. (2005). New York: Little, Brown. The narrator remembers himself as a young slave named "47," living in Georgia in 1832. A mystical runaway slave called Tall John inspires him to fulfill his destiny and lead his people to freedom.
- *Handbook for Boys: A Novel. Walter Dean Myers.* (2002). New York: Harper Trophy. A 16-year-old is given the option of participating in barber Duke Wilson's "community mentoring program" instead of serving time in a youth rehabilitation center. The teen's gradual change in perspective shows the value of adult mentoring.
- *The Beast.* Walter Dean Myers. (2003). New York: Scholastic.
- A young man leaves his neighborhood in Harlem to attend a college prep school and confronts his anxieties about his future when he returns for winter break to discover that his girlfriend has become addicted to drugs.
- *Nightjohn.* Gary Paulsen. (1993). New York: Laurel Leaf. Nightjohn, a new slave on the Waller plantation, sacrifices his chance for freedom and risks punishment to empower other slaves by helping them learn to read and write.

High School Level
- *Yo, Little Brother: Basic Rules of Survival for Young African American Males.* Anthony C. Davis and Jeffrey W. Jackson. (1998). Chicago: African American Images. In direct, down-to-earth language, this book offers advice for African American youth from their older counterparts.
- *Reallionaire: Nine Steps to Becoming Rich from the Inside Out.* Farrah Gray. (2005). Deerfield Beach, FL: HCI. A self-made millionaire and philanthropist at age 20, the author tells his personal story of growing up on the South Side of Chicago and rising to success.
- *There Are No Children Here: The Story of Two Boys Growing Up in the Other America.* Alex Kotlowitz. (1991). New York: Anchor Books. A Wall Street Journal reporter tells the true story of two brothers, ages 11 and 9, who live in a violence-ridden Chicago housing project.
- *Workin' on the Chain Gang: Shaking Off the Dead Hand of History.* Walter Mosley. (2000). New York: Ballantine Books. This essay

about Americans' enslavement to the economy describes a nation ruled by a small power elite and shows what liberation from consumer capitalism might look like.

- *The Pact: Three Young Men Make a Promise and Fulfill a Dream.* George Jenkins, Sampson Davis, and Rameck Hunt. (2002). New York: Riverhead Books. This true story tells how the three authors grew up in poverty in Newark, New Jersey, became friends at a magnet high school, and made a pact to attend college and become dentists.

- *A Hope in the Unseen: An American Odyssey from the Inner City to the Ivy League.* Ron Suskind. (1999). New York: Random House. A Wall Street Journal reporter follows an African American through his last two years of high school and his freshman year at Brown University.

- *Rite of Passage.* Richard Wright. (1994). New York: Harper Trophy. Set in Harlem in the late 1940s, this book tells the story of a bright 15-year-old boy who suddenly learns that he is a foster child and is being transferred to a new foster home. He runs away and struggles to survive in a harsh world.

- *The Measure of a Man.* Martin Luther King, Jr. (Originally published in 1959 released in 2001). Minneapolis, MN: Augsburg Fortress. This book by Dr. King answers the question about what it means to be a man.

- A Knock At *Midnight.* Edited by Clayborne Caron and Peter Holloran. (2000). New York: Warner Books. This is a collection of eleven of Dr. Kings most powerful sermons, from his earliest to his last, delivered days before his assassination.

- *The Black Male Handbook.* Edited by Kevin Powell. (2008). New York: Atria Books. This is a collection of essays about the ways that Black males can empower themselves politically, spiritually, economically, culturally, and in areas of physical health and mental wellness.

- *Brothers On The Mend: Understanding and Healing Anger for African-American Men and Women.* Ernest H. Johnson, Ph.D. (1998). New York: Pocket Books. This book discussed the problems caused by anger and ways to manage anger and conflicts that arises at work and in relationships with people in your life.

8

Using Poetry and Spoken-word to Motivate Black Males

By Jerold Marcellus Bryant and Phillip "Professor Pitt" Colas

Introduction

Spoken-word—a contemporary literacy tool, representing a new take on the traditional, age-old poetry reading phenomenon—has found a home in pockets of major cities, with some artists preferring to perform, rather than merely recite, their poetry. The term, Spoken-word, was adopted by college circles in the early 80's to recognize a wave of new word-based performance art that emerged from the Postmodern Art Movement.[1,2]Spoken-word was a catch-all category to lump together anything that did not fit into the already well established categories of performance: music, theatre and dance. Spoken-word often included collaborations with other non-word-based art genres or works created in collaboration with artists from non-word-based disciplines. Some word performance art had been around for eons—storytelling, sound-emphasis poetry, African American toasting, reggae, but these forms just had not received much attention and suddenly the well-educated acknowledged the exclusion. Most word artists have historically been and currently are rebel artists; often they are marginalized people or social change activists. These artists resent academically minded experts defining their work and suspect a link to those who would streamline art as a commodity. Therefore, there is no simple singular definition for Spoken-word, and maybe there shouldn't be.[2,3,4,5,6,7]

The goal of Spoken-word artists is to execute their thoughts with sharp, unapologetic color, realism, and emotion. Local cafes, restaurants, coffee shops, theaters, centralized areas of shopping malls, bookstores and university campuses have become spoken-word hot spots. The gatherings are provocative and by the end of an event, those in the audience have become active players in a spiritually charged play. Spoken-word poetry delivery has become more prominent since HBO's hit "Russell Simmons Presents Def Poetry." A spinoff of Simmons' uproariously crass "Def Comedy" program, "Def Poetry" has catapulted many unknown poets into the literary spotlight and brought poetry, particularly the poetry slam, into the consciousness of young African American males. While there are some poetry-slams that have been around for nearly twenty years, the philosophy of the movement (an art and entertainment form open to all people from all walks of life) remains the same.[7,8,9,10]

In a poetry slam, poets have a limited time to present their work, which is rated on a scale of zero to 10 by a panel of judges chosen from the audience. Poets are not allowed props, only their poems, written or memorized. The competition, or slam, aspect of the event is not intended as a game of one-upmanship. It's not about the points; it's about using poetry to deliver a relevant message about every topic imaginable. Slams are where you can hear a wide variety of poetry. Some poets work in meters, but others work in forms that are more open. It's one of the places where you will see traditional writers and free verse writers in the same place. While the audience is part of the process, they are urged to have respect for the poets, reserving their feelings for the judging table.

Slams are also the only forum where audiences can see teams of poets performing the same work together. Ultimately, spoken-word poetry is about showing people that vocabulary and alphabets have evolved. The poets are a mostly young, highly energetic breed of new-age entertainers. They are as diverse in appearance as in ideology; an African American male in a dashiki with dreadlocks, denouncing the war in Iraq, might be followed by a white woman with blond hair wearing a basketball jersey and sneakers professing her unconditional love for her man. While each poet or team has its own agenda, they do have something in common: capturing the listener's attention with catchy rhymes, infectious vocals, and expressive gesticulation. In addition, for many of the poets, spoken-word is therapy because it allows young people to articulate some of those things that a lot of people aren't able to say for themselves. Poetry allows young people an opportunity to offer up their rhymes in an effort to make some spiritual, mental, or even physical connection with the crowd. In this chapter, we will discuss the key elements that are essential for integrating spoken-word poetry into the classroom.

The many hidden aspects of poetry and spoken-word help teach us how to read, and write, as well as introduce science, history, economic, and mathematic lessons to children. Anecdotes as simple as nursery rhymes, as modern as hip-hop rap songs, and strangely enough, as useful as medical and scientific mnemonic devices are being used by teachers to connect students to classroom lessons. These devices don't have to rhyme; they just need to have rhythm and stand apart in style and delivery. Many fans of spoken-word know when they have heard something enlightening. They can always revert back to the delivery of the points of interest. That enlightening moment can be as subtle as a whisper in a performance or ring as loud as a siren in your memory. These techniques used in nursery rhymes, rap songs, and mnemonic devices are excellent tools for developing comprehension, oral language, phonics, fluency, and vocabulary, as well as improving the ability to analyze and synthesize information. The power of the word in poetic expression can motivate all children. But with respect to young African American males, we must give colossal attention to motivating them to learn through relevant means. The hip-hop culture is where we must learn and where these young males refuse to be ignorant. As educators, we must be proficient in the ever-moving and uncontainable parameters of the hip-hop culture. It is where young African American males get information. It is where Black males find their foundations in communications and social aspects of life. The greatest common denominator is that the hip-hop culture is built upon poetry, spoken-word, rhythm, and experiences.

Jerold on the Intersections of Rhythm, Rhymes and Poetry

My (Jerold) career path is directly related to the earliest forms of rap music. I had a favorite song. I loved the rhythm and I had to memorize the lyrics. I would listen, rewind, press play on my cassette player, and write the lyrics until I had the entire song. Once finished, I would recite sections of the song, and then recite the entire song without looking at my notes. Now, after 25 years of using this technique, I can still recite the words to this song, and I still use this technique to memorize excerpts and to learn poetry and spoken-word.

As a poet and spoken-word artist, my ability to write, recite and learn is analogous to young African American males' desire to grasp the message inherent in a piece performed by a rap artist. My desire to understand the intersections of rhythm, words and style is similar to what young African American males favor as a culture. We find it easier to learn when these intersecting concepts are used. I am not saying to teach everything with Hip hop rap concepts. What I am saying is that in order to break through barriers of learning, we must infuse interest and avenues designed specifically for and by African American males. Some teaching styles we use can be referenced back 150 years to educators who may have never had to deal with a young African American male, especially those associated to the Hip hop culture. We need to implement new supplemental techniques that build the desire to learn. The motivation is the fuel that runs the intellectual minds. The motivation we are trying to pull out of our young males is the same motivation that we pull from within as educators. The motivation and the guts to use derivatives of the Hip hop culture as a supplemental piece even being driven enough to develop a core curriculum based on the Hip hop culture is where I see our future as educators. In my research, I have found school systems and teachers who have integrated Hip hop experiences into their classrooms. My co-author and I will expound on some of these success stories throughout this chapter.

When teachers attempted to bring my interest in poetry and rhyme in the classroom, I was motivated to see if he/she knew exactly what she was talking about; I even challenged him/her. Simply decoding a rap song, memorizing the flow and the meaning was my motivation, and I used this self-taught technique to comprehend text. It is important for all educators to motivate young African American males. We must use our most influential aspect of our culture to teach. It amazes me that there were thousands, possibly millions, of people who were memorizing the same song that I had decoded, learning a new culture by an old concept. In the final determination, it was simply a new interest to read, listen, comprehend and recite.

In an inspiring article, *Weaving Multiple Dialects in the Classroom Discourse: Poetry and Spoken-word as a Critical Teaching Tool*,[11] Shiv-Raj broadly expresses much of the enthusiasm I have for using written text from people of color in a school setting. Much like myself, Shiv-Raj points out that he should have been exposed to this sooner—long before he started college. As I reflect back on my experiences, I often wonder why wasn't this part of my schooling. Even, in college, I had one class where we read and discussed spoken-word poetry and listened to spoken-word artists. For the first time in my school experience, I was discussing topics that I could relate to, such as family life and issues about Black males. What I soon discovered is that spoken-word articulated a style that demonstrated how intellectually stimulating people of color could express what is going on in their world.

Much like Shiv-Raj, spoken-word poetry touched my soul like no other type of literary form. When I listen to spoken-word it was like looking in a mirror and seeing myself—and wondering about what life has is store for me. The revelation is startling when you have gone through elementary, middle and high school and you discover on a college campus what you really missed in school. In my case, I often wonder about whether I would have been a better student in middle and high school if I had teachers who were comfortable integrating spoken-word into the curriculum. Whenever it starts for your students, your attitude should be to help them use the experience to reach their highest potential.

Enter Professor Pitt

Like Jerold, I can relate to times using the cassette player to listen to and learn lyrics of songs. Jerold was learning the lyrics while I was listening to and memorizing the beats, rhythms and rhymes. Since I was 14, which was somewhere in the middle of the golden age of Hip hop, I've been an MC and rapper, and I'm still active today. As a teenager, I had nothing too much to worry about except completing my homework and being cool with my peers. MTV came along at a time when I was experimenting with ways to promote my work using multimedia sources other than the radio, which was expensive. Until then, radio was the only way to reach out to young people unless you were lucky to be on one of those televised variety shows like American Band Stand or Soul Train.

As a teenager, I was encouraged to find my passion. For me, what I saw on MTV turned me on like nothing I had ever experienced. There was excitement, rhythms, and creativity. For me, Hip hop became the means for expressing some of the passion about my insights regarding how society was imprisoning the minds of Black males.

What opened me up to the power of the rhythm of Hip hop was the way that people responded, as if they had no choice, to the music. It was clear to me that the beat mattered more than the words of songs for capturing the attention of young people. This worried me because, as my mama would say, "Son, you ain't nobody's fool, so do what you choose to do because it's what you choose to do rather than what somebody else wants you to do." Although I was in love with Hip hop, there was a growing awareness inside of me that Hip hop could be potentially dangerous, particularly, if the artist producing the rhythm and rhymes was not conscious of the way they were embedding messages into a person's mind, body and soul. If the message is about violence and disrespect, then the person goes out into the world with these embedded thoughts and acts out situations without being aware. What a powerful medium and what an opportunity it offered to the few of us who were interested in embedding messages of compassion, wisdom, love, understanding, forgiveness, and grace into the hearts of young Black males. And as far as poetry is concerned, there is nothing as powerful or creative as when young people analyze the poetry of Hip hop and compare motifs, themes, and general poetic devices (such as alliteration, rhyme scheme, figurative language, etc.) to the "classic" poems traditionally studied (by writers such as Frost, Dickinson, Keats, Langston Hughes, etc.).

While I was managing a Hip hop club in Oakland, my life path crossed with Matthew Fox, a 35-year educator and author of several books on spirituality and culture.[12,13] He talked almost non-stop about his inner need to take the lessons learned from teaching and designing pedagogy for adults and invent ways to use these processes among younger people. For most of his career, he has been designing, teaching, and administering programs for undergraduate, masters, and doctoral students. Early in his teaching career, he set out to reinvent the way we approach education, convinced, as he was that the heart, along with creativity and intuition, were sidelined by mainstream educational pedagogy.[14,15]Upon our first meeting, he saw my meditation music video and said he had never seen anyone make meditation interesting, fun and entertaining at the same time. He viewed this as a bridge for using ancient information and the language of multimedia to reach our young generation. From there, we co-created an after school program called Y.E.L.L.A.W.E (Youth and Elders Learning Laboratory of Ancestral Wisdom Education). Matthew Fox provided the bulk of Ancestral wisdom, and I provided a new way of teaching through multimedia. We are convinced that post-modern children require and deserve post-modern forms of education and that pedagogy that has worked wonders with adults will work even greater wonders with children.[16]

Much like Fox, I believe that education will most likely be reinvented by inner-city children, who are most likely to be victimized by the tired and modern forms of education that are still in vogue today. The alternative model that we have created does not compete with the school system (since it meets after school hours), and in time, I believe the essence of how we are getting children to absorb character and education lessons through music, song, and martial arts (kung fu) will become one way that education is reinvented.

Professor Pitt on Comparing and Defining Spoken-word and Poetry

The simple difference between spoken-word and poetry is that one is heard and one is read. The complex difference between spoken-word and poetry is that words are interpreted differently when heard aloud, as opposed to being read quietly. Spoken-word artists bring voice inflections, movement, rhythm, and style. While poets write by way of their inner voices, the reader will read either exactly as the poets' inner voice suggests or in their own voice, which may or may not rhythmically flow or even make sense to the reader. Here are two analogies to describe the differences between spoken-word and poetry: Consider poetry the lyrics of a song and spoken-word the concert or video for that song. The other analogy is to consider poetry the script and spoken-word the actual speaker delivering the speech.

For me (Professor Pitt), spoken-word represents a culture of poetry where the responsibility is to speak from heart about issues that are affecting humanity. Hip hop, on the other hand, which started with a similar mission, has become a bit removed from speaking about issues and has evolved into an international business where the bottom line is all about making money. Don't get me wrong; all artists have to eat, but when what's being eaten up is the dignity of the artist and their capacity to help humanity deal with some of the problems we face, Hip hop has the potential to be explosive and exploitive. In my mind, I see no line between poetry and spoken-word. In the gold era of Hip hop, Boogie Down Production put out a song that said that real rap is poetry. The crosswords where these forms of expressions meet are the actual performances.

According to articles and books referenced in text and footnotes, there are several other definitions of spoken-word, several of which are my favorite. Spoken-word is a form of poetry that utilizes the strengths of our communities: oral tradition, call-and-response, home languages, storytelling, and resistance. Spoken-word poetry is usually performed for an audience and must be heard. Spoken-word expresses a shared language with the audience and demands that we see our community and ourselves in a new light. In addition, spoken-word is a type of poetry that bonds the poet with the audience to an end, whatever that may be. Spoken-word affirms passionate, even shocking, expression and offers ethical insights for solving the most severe problems plaguing society.[17,18]

The actual definition of poetry is a form of art in which language is used for its aesthetic and evocative qualities in addition to, or in lieu of, its ostensible meaning. Poetry may be written independently, as discrete poems, or may occur in conjunction with other arts, as in poetic drama, hymns, or lyrics. Spoken-word is a form of literary art or artistic performance in which lyrics, poetry, or stories are spoken rather than sung. Spoken-word is often done with a musical background, but emphasis is kept on the speaker. The basic definitions may never change for these terms, but new artistic formats will appear, such as performance poetry, slams, and Hip hop rap. Become aware of the new genre of poetry and spoken-word, because just like technology, it is always changing.

Relevant Artists, Styles, and History for Jerold

Soon after my introduction to poetry and spoken word, the famous poets came to my mind because they were Black men, such as Langston Hughes, James Weldon Johnson, Paul Lawrence Dunbar, Countee Cullen, Etheridge Knight, Jupiter Hammond, Claude McKay, W.E.B. Dubois, and James Baldwin. The contemporary poets who are still creating beautiful work today, James A. Emanuel, Forest Hamer, Imamu Amiri Baraka, Yosef Komunyakaa, Quincy Troupe, and Cornelius Eady are just a few of many writers. When it comes to spoken-word artists, however, there is one man who stood above many. His name is Gil Scott-Heron. "The Revolution Will Not Be Televised"[19] is a perfect example of the strength of spoken-word. Gil Scott-Heron's voice and style encapsulated his experiences and the meaning of his time. He was more than a legendary entertainer. He was a social and political visionary that helped to inspire generations of young gifted and talent poets, spoken-word artists, rappers, and a global cadre of musical and cultural satirists that have contributed to the transformations of the mindsets of hundreds of millions of young people around the world. While his death leaves a void in my heart, his work will be forever remembered.

Very few people have listened to Langston Hughes' spoken-word editions. He did record his poetry, and compared to today's spoken-word artists, he embarked on the beginning of a revolution in the art form. To motivate young males, we must bring forth the greats and the contemporaries. The great singer and civil rights activist Paul Robeson even embarked on spoken-word. He presented a concert over the telephone from Wales, when his passport was denied for eight years because of his stand on civil rights. Paul Robeson recited the Langston Hughes poem, Freedom Train. The Freedom Train and The Welsh Transatlantic Concert are true examples of poetry and spoken-word bringing history to life. Just to listen to this exchange of Robeson, the choir, and the audience in Wales shows a young Black male the roads that civil rights activists had to cross.[20,21,22]

In my search for spoken-word artists, I found the work of contemporaries, such as Nikki Giovanni, Maya Angelou, Gill Scott Heron, Tracie Morris, Melvin B. Tolson, Sekou Sundiata, Jill Scott, and Saul Williams. There are, of course, some greats like Countee Cullen, Hughes, and Rita Dove who have recorded their poetry. There is no denying the many women writers who can influence young men (Maya Angelou, Nikki Giovanni, Gwendolyn Brooks and Phyllis Wheatley), and I encourage you to use them in teaching.

In the future, expect more and more rappers to slow down their careers and step into the spoken-word genre. Rappers, such as Mos Def, Nas, KRS One, LL Cool J, will undoubtedly influence the spoken-word world by venturing into the art form. Some will say that Kanye West is a spoken-word artist and rapper. His poetry, voice and style have reminded people of a time when Gil Scott Heron's voice influenced a movement.

True spoken-word artists that don't float the lines of rapper and poet are Carl Hancock Rux, named by The New York Times as one of thirty young artists "most likely to change the culture in the next thirty years;" Jessica Care Moore, a record-breaking five-time winner of the Apollo competition; and Saul Williams, co-scriptwriter and star of the feature film "*Slam*,"[23] winner of the Grand Jury Prize at the Sundance Film Festival and the prestigious Camera D'Or at Cannes. The performance artists that have graced the stages of Def Comedy Jam and Slams nationally, such as John Goode, are finally being recognized for their talent. Superstars such as Jill Scott, Dave Chappelle, Common, Savion Glover, Lauryn Hill, Wyclef Jean, Alicia Keyes, Eve Ensler, John Legend, Phylicia Rashad, Smokey Robinson, and Kanye West have reunited with spoken-word performances and have expressed their talents for the command of poetry.

Former rappers are now contributing to education. An upcoming educational artist is Shawn Brown, formerly known as "The Rapping Duke." He has decided to educate children, pre K through 6th grade, by movement, spoken-word, and rapping. He created the Super Fun Show and tours the country entertaining students using poetry, puppetry, rap, and spoken-word. There is even a group, appropriately named H.E.L.P. (Hip hop Educational Literacy Program) that was designed by rapper Gabriel "Asheru" Benn that uses Hip hop lyrics to supplement the regular coursework. We will discuss more of Benn's work later in the chapters.[24,25]

There are many new poets and spoken-word artists yet to evolve into the mainstream, but these that I have mentioned will ignite interest within our African American males. Sometimes even the mention of a performer gets the attention of the entire classroom. Let's use these people's work to motivate and direct attention to what needs to be learned.

Relevant Artists, Styles, and History for Phillip

I really appreciate the historical flavor that Jerold has provided about the relevant artists in his life. To a great extent, many of the same artists have influenced me. LL Cool J, Mos Def, Nas, and KRS One are rappers that have influenced how I think about spoken-word. The stage performances of James Brown and LL Cool J have given me much inspiration because of the energetic nature of their one-man shows. Both are animated and put everything into their shows. Both are like a ball of fire to me and have provided models for me to emulate when I perform. Before LL's first album, he opened for several groups and convinced me he had a stage presence I wanted, and brother James had a way of moving the crowd that appealed to me. De La Soul was the first group to come out and be serious about rap. They broke the mold about rapping and everything about them was original. They produced great music, and they were not concerned about what others thought. In time, they received much criticism, but the groups survived. For the stylish ways that lyrics are organized and delivered, I lend towards Organize Confusion, Rakim, Slick Rick, Black Thought (from the Roots), Gang Star and KRS One. There a dozen or so other artists or groups that have influenced me, but down in my heart, I am Hip hop. Hip hop, though has changed into something damn near the opposite of what I represent and constantly propagates human behaviors that lead to mental, physical and spiritual misery. Although this musical culture has become devoid of some of its empowering features, I feel it still posses the power to lead to happiness and inner wisdom.

People are often surprised when they discover that I, all 6'4"of me with my long dreadlocks, use the mellow sounds that flow from the Harp I play, to accentuate my spoken-word performances. They are equally stunned that I am a martial artist who has devoted his life to the peaceful practice of meditation as a way to get beyond the conditioned, "thinking" mind and access the deeper states of awareness brought about through relaxation. Meditation often involves turning attention to a single point of reference. It is recognized as a component of almost all religions and has been practiced for over 5,000 years. It is also practiced outside of religious traditions. Different meditative disciplines encompass a wide range of practices which may emphasize different goals—from achievement of a higher state of consciousness to greater focus, creativity or self-awareness, or simply a more relaxed and peaceful frame of mind.[26,27]

For me, Hip hop is the new language for ancient teachings that will usher our society into the age of Aquarius from the age of Pisces. The age of Aquarius stands for free flowing knowledge of mind, body and spirit. The question is how to get the next generation, or any generation, to integrate meditation or any other empowering mental tools into everyday life.

I don't have all the answers, but I do believe that part of the answer depends on our ability to weave the use of technology and media into spoken-word and rap performances. In my case, I have produced works that range from full length CDs, televisions shows, films, comics, and after-school programs to innovative experiential views on an array of internal and external martial arts and ancient healing practices. And for those of you who think Hip hop is dying, just remember that just as the blues spawned rock 'n' roll and gospel gave birth to soul and R and B, we stand at the dawn of a new age where Hip hop and spoken-word are giving birth to new art forms that don't yet have names.

Integrating Spoken-word Into The Classroom

I (Jerold) have presented literacy solution workshop for educators from one end of the country to the other. In most cases, educators have positioned a few elements of spoken-word in their language arts curriculum as a hook to get students interested in reading and writing. I have observed that the level of their success has heavily depended on the extend that spoken work is integrated in the classroom. If it's integrated in a superficial manner, then few students demonstrate any sustained interest in reading and writing. On the other hand, when spoken-word is fully worked into the curriculum during the pressure-filled and testing-driven educational climate, then the results are outstanding. One such example is the Voices on High program that Gerald T. Reyes brought into the classroom of elementary students to change young minds and to improve the teaching experience.[28]

When Reyes entered the classroom full time, he brought the poetry of his life into the learning community that extends beyond the walls of highstakes numbers and testing to determine readiness for graduation. He allowed the poetry of the youth to guide him into his decisions about how to take advantage of opportunities to infuse poetry into the lives of his students. What's so amazing about his work is that everything was not planned from the start. But like language and life itself, the poetic culture he initiated evolved through time. Poetry was integrated into his classroom by having his students read and study pieces about various ethnic groups (African American, Native Americans, Chinese, Mexicans, etc.) or even the ancient Chinese philosopher Confucius. He even found a home for poetry in remembering the mathematical order of operations. And when that was not enough, he created an opportunity for students to perform for a real audience as part of the school's Spoken-word poetry festival.

Voices on High was open to the entire upper elementary school including fourth through sixth graders. Mr. Reyes knew that his class with its culture of poets was unique, so he had to devise a plan that got student poets not in his class interested in participating in Voices on High. He solved this dilemma by the creating an after-school program, Enter Poetic High, which became a hip cultural identity and location where poets could perfect and perform their work.[28]

The Enter Poetic High after-school program was fashioned to uses elements of the regular class in an after-school setting and the fundamental mission is to cultivate a culture of poets. Rather than have a program where students were depending on the teacher for feedback about their work, student poets and writers learned how to rely on each other to answer questions that can improve their work.[28]Similar to the spoken-word workshops I conduct, student poets and writers are encouraged to use the power of questions to understand their work from different perspectives. For example, "Is this piece good enough?" is the typical question student writers ask about work they have completed. Basically, there is nothing "wrong" with this questions, but the answers will provide a limited view of the work and offer little guidance to make the work better. What Gerald Reyes did with his students, and I agree wholeheartedly with his approach, was to transform them from passive students with narrow views and narrow questions about life, into poets who would eagerly seek different perspectives about learning and life. He got them to ask questions that empowered them to feel like an authority—questions that opened their minds to see the fullness of what they are writing about. He got them to understand that it is the nature of questions ("Have I been honest about what I wanted to say?" "What do I want people to think about when they read my work?" "Did I say everything I had on my mind?" "How do I want people to feel about what I've said?" "What do I want people to do with what I said?") that opens their minds and hearts to a much richer writing experience. When student writers answers these questions, they are no longer being passive, but creating an authentic experience for themselves and their audience. To help students find their voice and the confidence, they have to write. Once they are writing about what they want to write about, they can ask themselves some powerful questions to keep their writing authentic and interesting. However, regardless of how interesting the pieces are that students (spoken-word artists) produce; they need to create, refocus, practice, and refine their work before performing it for an audience.

Over the course of my career as a spoken-word artist, I have observed various formats for offering students writing workshops. For the most part, these workshops offer students a linear opportunity to create pieces, but they often don't include elements for building a culture of poets and spoken-word artists. Just like the teacher, Gerald T. Reyes,[28] we believe that a culture of Poets has to be built around a well-organized and writing experience (spoken-word workshop) where young writers can freely express their ideas and receive feedback to help them become better writers and performers.

The Spoken-word workshop (sometimes referred to as a wordshop) is a writing and exploratory process with a definite beginning where artists (or students) are encouraged to find their authentic voice through writing. The process ends after a performance. While there are many elements that can make up a spoken-word workshop, these tend to be the essential elements:

- Discovering One's Authentic and Expert Voice: The authors real voice about his experiences, his perceptions, and his thoughts
- Mini Lessons on Specific Poetic Techniques: Showing young writers how to use a technique to capture their own voice.
- Writer's Rights: The process of making revisions to work that is based on feedback from others and yourself
- Move the Crowd: The excitement that a poet experiences while performing for an audience.

While these elements have unique names, essentially they utilize basic pedagogical principles: assess prior writing experiences; conducting a mini lessons; guided practice sessions; independent practice; analyze and critique, feedback and revising; creating authentic products; and performances with real audiences. While these basic pedagogical principles support the sequence of events and skills needed to teach, it is, however, the philosophical paradigm behind these elements that is at the heart of the Spoken-word Workshop. The elements focus on empowering, creating experts, and ultimately helping young writers to bring forth the language of their lives that describes their perception and how they experience events in their lives and those of others.

Discovering One's Authentic and Expert Voice

A curious mind is needed to help student writers to discover their authentic and expert voice—a mind that is willing to make personal connections between ideas, personal experiences, and what is happening in the world around them. Big general questions are a key component in this process because it allows young writers to be able to respond in the way that resonates best with their personal experiences. "What are you worried about?" "How do you feel knowing that we have a Black man as president?" "How would you motivate other Black males to fall in love with reading?" "What are you so angry about?" "Why do you act differently around some teachers?" "If you had your way, what would a model school look like?" "What would your teachers need to do to get you and other Black males excited about school?" Whatever the general questions are that allows Black males to talk about their lives, what takes place is a group discussion where there is mutual respect for each young poet because they are already experts about the topic. Black male students already know their lives and they produce some rich results when they are allowed to use spoken-word and poetry to help other to see their view of the world.

Quite often, the teacher is viewed as the only authority in the classroom. But in the Spoken-wordshop the teacher is not the only one with something to say. After all, if we are going to reach Black boys today, then we have to be willing to help them discover something they already have ownership of and a story they feel compelled to tell others. It's a noisy and loud world they live in and yet, their voice is maybe the only way they have to get people to stop whatever they are doing and take notice of their poetic work.

If you really took time to set everything aside to listen, like many of the contributors of this book have done, you would be amazed by what young Black male poets and writers have to say about politics, education, health care, wars in foreign lands, retirement funds, and just about everything else we are concerned about.

It is difficult to sit still and give total attention to poetic verses that are weaved between complex rhythms and musical beats that seem to be going nowhere but ends with you feeling emotionally, physically and spiritually charged. These young Black boys sitting in your classrooms have something to say, but it is so powerful and at times confusing, that it has to be said in a nonlinear way accompanied by these complex rhythms, rhymes and beats. Often times, what is hidden beneath their poetic work is the pain and anguish they have experiences during their short time on this planet. In most instances, their pain is so great that they have to use musical beats to capture its meaning because there are no words to describe the meaning of what they have to say.

Getting into the discourse allows your young poets, particularly Black males, to contribute to the discourse that published poets have already been having. It is through discourse that knowledge evolves, so why not allow youth to participate in that? Let them connect with Nikki Giovanni. Let them connect with Langston Hughes. Let them connect with Tupac Shakur, with Saul Williams, with Naomi Shihab Nye. Encourage them to make these connections and they will be energized to create poetry and projects that provide new insights about certain problems that continue to plague humanity. This is a lesson we always give to teachers, particularly those, attending the seminars at NCCAT where the aim is to empower them so that they can empower African American males.

These connections allow young poets to feel like they have ownership of their voice. It validates their ideas because they can see similarities to someone whose poetry has been published. It allows them to find a role model. These connections invite young poets to know that they are not alone and that their ideas, no matter how radical and different they are from others, are important.

When a Black boy understands the work of a famous Black poet and see connections between the challenges the poet faced and their own, then you can clearly say that you have brought life to words on paper. It's not as powerful as Jesus walking on water or resurrecting Lazarus, but if you can get a Black boys to see connections between his life and successful Black poets, then you have a hook you can use to help him free his mind. There is no doubt that "Poetry brings clarity to thought, language to life, and each of us to each other," as embraced by James Kass, the founder and director of San Francisco's Youth Speaks.[29]Since 1996, Kass has been connected with the pulse of young writers and poets by steering Youth Speaks to set a national standard for creative writing, poetry, and spoken-word programs for youth. James has facilitated workshops in over 350 high schools, numerous universities, public library systems, juvenile detention centers, and youth service agencies throughout the extensive international Youth Speaks/Brave New Voices network. For many Black boys, poetry can produce deep insights about life and an understanding of self like that gained from a person undergoing psychotherapy.[30]

Mini-Lessons on Specific Poetic Techniques

Mini-Lessons are often created to give instruction on a specific poetic technique and provides a writing opportunity to apply it. The instruction usually has a model poem from another poet where the student poets can observe a technique, form, idea, or frame in context. The model poem also serves a potential guide for students who need extra support in writing a piece or to help them learn about the social and political forces in place when a poem or short story was written. For instance, I (Jerold) have used one of my poems, *I Write Black*, to help teachers develop a better appreciation of the pain and anguish that Black males have had to endure to survive in America. However, it was the 1998 interview that Charlie Rose conducted with the Pulitzer Prize winning novelist, Toni Morrison that helped me to understand why I write about the experiences of black people.[31]

In the 1998 interview, the host, Charlie Rose revisited a discussion of questions raised by critics. One critic asked her why does she only write about Black characters and can she imagine writing a novel that is not centered on race. The quintessential Morrison reply was with a snap and tone that appeared to rip into Rose's intellect, "Yes, I can, but it is insulting for someone to believe that I can't write about anything without reference to race. Even before becoming the first African American to win the Nobel Prize for literature, I never played it safe in the books I wrote. I learned early on that if change is to occur, one must be willing to think and do the unthinkable." Her answer made me proud and inspired this poem, and healed any doubt about my creative ability. Her response was grand, unforgettable, and far more in depth than the statement above.

Since then, I have recited the poem I wrote to many people who smile when I mention the inspirational moment and then relate to the fury and pride inspired by her response.

> I Write Black!
> I write Black to show the spectrum, Because without Black, No stars shine, No shade cools, No word reads, No man lives, No color exists, No truth told of how evil and beauty comes two-fold. I write Black thoughts, dreams, tragedies, and miracles.
>
> I write Black love, hate, sin, and spirituals, I write Black fertile organic words that eyes only hear. White minds search for understanding. Black visions see clear. Remember the first and last color before the Sun? I write Black so you can see every color as One.
>
> I Write Black! And I Write Black! And I will always Write Black!
>
> I Write about the Black skin. The Black Men. And The Beautiful Black Women. I Write about the Black Drama. The Black farmer. And the Grandchild raised by a Grandmama! I Write about the Invisible Fathers. The Lonely Mothers. And the Slaves. Chased into Horror!
>
> I write Black. And I write Black. And I will Always, Always, Always, Write Black!

I've recited this poem hundreds of times and each time it seems to remind me of the spectrum of things of which we, Black males, can have some type of ownership. In some ways, it reminds me of what Malcolm X said after being imprisoned, "You can lock up my body, but you can't lock up my mind."[32] It reminds me that when Black men had nothing, they still had words.

As educators, I realize it might be difficult to believe that there was a time when Black men were murdered for learning to read, but that is part of our history. Regardless of how painful our experience was, we wanted to communicate and to capture our thoughts. We wanted a way to express ourselves. Black males today are no different, in this regard, than Black males from the past. In my case, writing has always been a way for me to vent and get rid of some of the ill feelings I experienced simply because I am a Black male. Just like everyone, I have had problems figuring out the reasons for racism. Every time racism found its way into my life, I immediately thought about children fussing-and-fighting on a playground. I always wondered whether the adult in charge would come and stop this madness or was the adult in charge responsible, in some way, for the conflict.

When conducting workshops for teachers I use my poem, *I Write Black*, as a model, to help teachers see the need to encourage their students to write about something they are passionate about. I removed the word Black and certain key adjectives and nouns, and replaced them with blanks for students to fill in their own ideas. After allotting a specific amount of time to write, I give the young poets an opportunity to share a few of their favorite lines they have written. If you are planning to do something similar with your students, please allow enough time for each of the young people to present their work. Encourage them to develop questions to ask the person performing their piece, and have ample time for the young poets to talk about the impact of the work.

Writer's Rights

There is no easy way to say this—if you are thinking about a piece of poetry, then you have to write it, and then you have to rewrite it to make it better. Young writers are encouraged to follow the rites of the writing process as it relates to their classroom assignment. They might freewrite. They might prewrite. They revise what they write. They read what they have written. They write. They think on the page. They manifest ideas onto paper. They write. They write by themselves. They write with each other. They talk about what they have written. They write. There is no other way to put it. The point is to create an emotionally comfortable setting where students feel OK about sharing their work and getting feedback from other young poets. One prerequisite to sharing is that it is the piece of poetry that is being reworked, and that the poet is not to be attacked. The focus is on having rules for making the piece better. These rules could be in the form of a student contract or a poet's bill of rights. Either way, make sure there is a ritual in place before students share their work. Sharing allows others to provide feedback about the work and young poets, in my experience, need encouragement more so than criticism to revise their work—and revision is what writer's rights is all about.

Revision is about viewing the original vision of a piece. It's about using feedback about the piece to make sure the piece expresses what you want. It is about trying to see what has been written and whether it is on track for what was originally envisioned or whether it needs to be refocused. To a great extent, revision happens all the time. Sometimes, depending on the writer, it never ends. Why? Because a written piece can always be improved or changed around to express some new ideas or to evoke some different emotions.

Revision is about making something better. It is not a correction process. Everything done to build the culture of poets cultivates re-visioning. Because a student poet wants to make his writing as good as possible, he revises. Because a student poet knows that his work will be published in an anthology, he revises. Because a student poet discovers he has ownership of the language of his life, he revises. And sometimes the revision means improvising by adding sounds and music. For example, while participating in the Best Practices seminar at NCCAT, I (Professor Pitt) got to work with Tavares Stevens who is a gifted poet and lead author of two chapters in this book. Tavares did not know that, in addition to my work with at-risk adolescents, I play the harp. I joined him while he was doing a spoken-word performance, and much like what happens when Jazz musicians get together, we improvised and created something that went well beyond the original vision of his poetry. Something as simple as having students create a rhythmic beat using their hand on the top of the desk is all it takes to cause a poet to revise their work.

With a community of poets, everyone must understand that the ability to receive and give feedback grows into responsibility—the commitment to help every poet succeed. There are countless ways for student poets to get feedback about their work, but nothing is more powerful than a writer's circle, which allows the community of poets to give specific and meaningful feedback to the writer that is sharing. Again, it is key to create a protocol for poets' responses so that each poet knows what is expected. When we get to the performance phase of wordshop I conduct I say, "Give the poet all of your attention," which means to put pencils down, turn off cell phones, face the speaker, make eye contact, but be quite and keep still.

And sometimes, to hear what you are listening to, you've got to close your eyes and focus, like a laser beam, on every word and sound that comes from the poet. Do not take for granted what it means to be attentive. Be explicit in teaching it, practice it, and expect it every time. With that relentless pursuit, focusing on the poet becomes part of the culture that everyone not only expects, but respects.

Move the Crowd

Poets, comedians, storytellers, and great public speakers know about the power of the audience. While knowing about the power of the audience might be a new concept for language arts and writing teachers, students are well aware of what it means to take center stage. In order for them to be comfortable presenting their work, they want to know who the audience will be so they can adjust their message and style. Most importantly, they want to know who the audience will be so they will know how to convey their piece for maximum impact.

One group of teachers, chorus and band directors, know the power of audience. Why do students work so hard practicing the same passage repeatedly, week after week? Because the audience is coming for the performance. But who is the audience for 99 percent of the work students do in school? The teacher! If you happen to work with students who are eager to win their teachers' approval, you won't need to do much to motivate them. But more and more students, particularly Black males, come to class with no desire to please their teachers and no vision of the role school might play on their journey through life. Black males often come from families where no one has used education as a vehicle on the road to success. In addition, the crowd (audience) for many Black males tends to be a gang of some sort that has a strong loyalty to the rhythms, rhymes, and lyrics from songs that speak about a life of pain, shame, and hostility.

Spoken-word poetry is about the crowd, which is the audience. Moving the crowd is an effective way to engage Black males in learning about every subject imaginable. The acceptance and feedback from the crowd—an authentic audience—gives them a sense that someone else (besides teachers and parents) cares about their work. To complete their work, they need to have a vision of a final product. They need to develop skills to complete the product. They have to abide by rules for revising, cooperating and getting feedback from other students, and for presenting their work. In other words, they must demonstrate the emotional and social intelligence that is necessary to move a project from the start to the end while receiving feedback from others to make the final product better. I don't know about you, but for me, this sounds like the type of skills that young people need to be successful in any endeavor in the 21st century.

Moving the crowd is about having student poet's work towards an authentic spoken-word poetry show where their word will be published in written form or recorded on a CD. Moving the crowd is the magic that a poet feels when he hears the applause. Moving the crowd is the energy and excitement a spoken-word poet experiences after he realized that the master of ceremonies has introduced him to an energized crowd. Moving the crowd is the non-stop round of applause a poet received after a performance. Moving the crowd is that expanded sense of self-worth and pride a poet experiences when members of the audience wants to meet him after a performance. Moving the crowd is being asked by someone to sign the CD cover of your work. Moving the crowd is that sense of belonging that all Black males seek from people they want to love them—teachers, parents, and peers. Moving the crowd is a powerful process for Black males to feel like they are valuable members of the classroom and school community.

Building the Language of Discourse and Identity

Black males, like other students, want to feel like they are an important member of the classroom and school experience. They want teachers to know their names and something about their lives. They want to feel like they are somebody important, just as important to the teacher and classroom as other students.

If educators truly want to create an authentically identity for Black male students, then they must relinquish the idea that they are the only experts in the classroom. All too often, teachers will ask students to help them when they are at a loss about how to handle some complex technical issue with a computer application. Some are wise enough to appoint these computer savvy students to the position of tech experts for the classroom. Teachers have to draw from this example and understand that students want to be known as experts in other areas. And the one area that they know the best is the story of their own lives. They might not have mastered the poetic and writing techniques to compose a flawless piece about their lives, but the desire to share who they are with the world is strong. And some of the best therapy you can offer these students is to refer to them as poets or spoken-word artists—titles reserved for adults—while they are preparing pieces for a classroom or a school-wide performance. With this change in the language, we give our young poets the opportunity to "live the questions now" as Rilke[33] described several decades ago in his letter to young poets.

As teachers and parents, we have to give Black males and other students of color the opportunity to construct their own meaning. We have to encourage them to use the power of the answers to their own questions to guide their own lives. We have to teach them that asking purposeful questions has the power to liberate themselves from depending on other people to determine the direction of their lives. When we show them how poetry can be used to execute a peaceful resolution of the pain they are experiencing, then we have shown them a powerful means to express themselves.

Ask any Black male in your classrooms today about what it means to be president of the United States and they are likely to say something about Barrack H. Obama. They are likely to say something about how having him as the first Black president means that other Black men can become presidents and leaders in America. The answer to this same question a decade ago would have been very different because, as a whole, Black people thought the chances of a Black man becoming king of England was greater than a Black man becoming president of the United States. I recently witnessed a black male students perform a spoken-word piece about Obama and I was amazed by the complexity of the rhyme schemes and the amount of Black history that the young man delivered. In his poetry, he answered questions about the presence of kings in Africa before slavery and the value of education. He answered questions about the proportion of Black people who voted in the election and the historic signing of the voting rights legislation. He addressed questions about tolerance and bi-racial children. He used his poetry to talk about the legacy of pain that our president inherited because he is an American citizen.

Asking questions allows students to be thinkers, to be discoverers, to be life-long learners. With purposeful questioning and calling our youth poets, we start helping them realize their identities, so that someday they "will gradually, without noticing it, live into the answer."[33] Giving Black males this opportunity to find themselves within the culture of poetry helps them to become the person they want to become. Building this culture takes us one-step further in helping Black males become authorities, to feel active in their own education, and to take control of the language of their lives. Each teacher and adult a Black male student encounters is a parental authority—this is true by commission or omission. When we fail to be explicit in our instructions to Black males or fail to see them as authorities about their own experiences and perceptions, we are failing to show them that we value them as part of our human family.

Still Searching for Poetic Highs

Imagine a place called "The Poetic High" which is more about the journey within and the progress made outwardly by inspiring writers. The experience is so infectious that it stimulates the young poets to search for new and empowering ways to use poetry and spoken-word to express themselves and to reach other people. The Poetic High is about loving the process of life through language and communities that intersect with minds, hearts, and, of course, voices that rise up to warm us all.[28] Poetry reveals the process of life, and since that first year, "Finding the Poetic High" has revealed some amazing insights about students and their world view. Gerald T. Reyes, the creator of the program has worked with youth ranging from fourth grade to eighth grade. He has conducted teacher training for Poetic High through the Bay Area Writing Project, AmeriCorps, KIPP Schools, and Bay Area Scores with pre-service teachers, new teachers, and veterans who have served over 30 years.[28]

The Poetic High experience shows that there is a method of implementation that must be used to maintain interest and develop a following in the schools. Some high schools in Miami-Dade and Broward County, Florida, have collaborated with a local library and two local community-based organizations to offer students literary and life lessons. Hundreds of public school students have participated in Wordspeak, a program sponsored through Tigertail Productions.[28,34,35]

Teachers recruit student, many of whom are from inner cities, to engage in workshops with poets, refine language skills, perform their pieces, and most importantly, feel empowered to express themselves. The main goal of the literacy program is to help students learn how to get their thoughts on paper. To do so, they also learn discipline, respect for others, tolerance, and how they can plan for a life in the 21st century. The students also learn how spoken-word is utilized as a critical teaching tool to foster critical thinking skills, dialogue, and action—in other words, how students can reflect and articulate their experiences while envisioning new possibilities for themselves and the world.

In a project conducted that at the University of California in Los Angeles, a class call PEACE (Political Education, Art, and Critical Expression)[36] was created for at-risk students enrolled in GEAR UP (Gaining Early Awareness and Readiness for Undergraduate Programs).[37] This class was designed to draw from the cultural capital of students while reinforcing their cultural values. Through key readings and music that speaks to the realities of racism, classism, sexism, heterosexism, and other forms of oppression, the aim of the PEACE class was to engage GEAR UP students in developing a critical consciousness and commitment to social justice. In addition to serving as an praxis for social transformation, it was believed that the PEACE class would help to build literacy for economically disadvantaged students of color.

When utilizing spoken-word poetry, teachers and students are able to engage in a discussion that draws from the lives of all participants, while facilitating collective dialogue about local and global events. In the classroom, spoken-word poetry can serve to illuminate generative themes, or points of connection and movement between oppressive realities for the oppressed and the oppressor alike. Within an educational context, teachers must be willing to sacrifice their power in order to make possible the surfacing of student knowledge and voice. Because teachers possess the power to engage in socially reproductive and reductive forms of teaching (and learning), they must become aware of and be willing to sacrifice their position of power to the possibilities of those on the margins. In essence, teachers must be willing to step outside of their traditional and historical roles and acknowledge that they can learn from their students, thus allowing their students to have an authentic voice of authority about their lives.[38,39]

As Dr. Michael Dyson[40,41] points out, rap allows the rest of America to "consume and eavesdrop" as rappers verbalize their perspective on a range of issues—social, cultural, political, and economical—to tell their stories. The same is true about spoken-word artists. Educators must learn to become literate in interactive-auditory discourse in order to facilitate critical engagement with their students. Unless teachers are able to employ interactive-auditory discourse, they will fail to connect with and acknowledge their students' realities. A failure to acknowledge the realities and experiences of Black male students is a failure to acknowledge the possibility of connection and movement within and outside the multiple discourses that come into the classroom. Furthermore, this failure renders the students' experience and perception of the world as illegitimate. It is imperative that Black male students begin to enhance their interactive-auditory discourse so that they, too, can learn from the perceptions of their peers, as well as the tools that their peers may employ in making sense of the world.

Through the use of spoken-word, we are better able to understand what issues Black male students are facing, what subjectivities students identify with and how students persevere. If we are willing to create a space where students are able express and discover their deepest and most intense feelings, then, perhaps, we as critical educators may find a more effective means of interacting with our students. If we don't listen to our students and fail to create a space where they can articulate their realities, how can we expect that they will do the same, both in and outside of the classroom?

A great result of listening and observing our students gives us the opportunity to change our philosophies and add additional tools to our teaching bags. The Hip hop Educational Literacy Program (HELP) provides a supplemental tool that should be used by all schools that have problems engaging students in literacy. In 2005, Gabriel Benn, a teacher and rapper, partnered with Rick Henning, a founder of the Rock Creek Academy of Washington, D.C., to create a curriculum that uses rap lyrics to improve vocabulary, fluency, and reading. This tool is designed for the 21st century student, and it promotes non-traditional strategies. As we observe the influence of the Hip hop nation, we notice that teachers must evolve to understand how to use rap in the classroom. H.E.L.P. is a series of supplemental reading workbooks designed to guide students of all reading levels through the innovative usage of Hip hop lyrics for critical analysis, multicultural relevance, and effective literacy instruction.[42,43]

Since hip-hop includes such concepts as metaphor, rhyme, hyperbole and allusion, the program originally used music as a way to teach literacy. Certain words were picked from songs as vocabulary and questions were asked about the poetic phrasing of the artists. From its initial success as a reading tool, Benn expanded the program into other subjects.

H.E.L.P. addresses the needs of deficient readers and increases the literacy skills of students, particularly between the ages of 13 and 18. All research-based lessons align with standards set forth by the National Council of Teachers of English and the International Reading Association. The program includes innovative activities that blend the five core literacy program elements identified by the National Reading Panel in 2000: phonics, phonemic awareness, fluency, vocabulary, and comprehension.[44]Developed by a team of educators and literacy specialists, the workbooks address the range of reading proficiencies that can exist in a single classroom. Each book is divided into four studios, with each targeting a different reading level. The result: An entire class can use the same text. Each teacher guide contains a biography of the Hip hop artist, the lyrics of a song, a glossary of vocabulary words, and a scope and sequence for the 60 activities located in the student guide. The teacher guides also include supplemental activities based on the Multiple Intelligences, writing rubrics, and answer keys for each studio. H.E.L.P. has been adopted by schools in Washington, D.C., New York City, San Francisco and Los Angeles.[42,43] Individual teachers have purchased these materials directly to keep up with the shift in teaching that occurs everyday. Professional development, research, and the unrelenting search for a better way pushes the edge of change in our classrooms. H.E.L.P and similar programs will become staples in our classrooms.[45,46] They will employ the basics of rap to build interest and motivate students using the combination of poetry and spoken-word.[47,48,48,50,51,52,53]

Benn's use of a more culturally relevant lesson plan eventually helped to overcome the many of the challenges students had learning new material. Students were more respectful of the teachers, they participated more in the classroom, and they felt more comfortable with the material. In addition to the increased reading scores of the 10th grade English classes at a Southeast DC high school, teachers began to sense an overall change in attitude after implementing H.E.L.P. The program has since taken off, and in just five years H.E.L.P. has spread across the nation to places like Oakland, Atlanta, Ohio and Florida. His goal for the future is to initiate virtual classrooms.[42,43]

The appeal of Hip hop and spoken-word as a tool for educators was first established at the college level focusing mostly on the history of the movement. In 2006, Youth Speaks-Wisconsin was regarded as the first university-based spoken-word and urban arts center in the country.[54]

University of Wisconsin at Madison emerged as a leader in putting Hip hop to work in school curricula. William Ney, executive director of the Office of Multicultural Arts Initiatives, predicted that the effectiveness of spoken-word in the classroom would spread the appeal of Hip hop to teachers across the nation and around the world. "By better understanding the positive potential of Hip hop to engage students through art forms they value and trust, teachers and community organizers will be better equipped to counter high dropout rates and academic underachievement of all students, especially students of color struggling to keep up with their peers," he says.[54] Since 2006, the growth of Hip hop and spoken work in the classrooms from kindergarten through college has been explosive.[45,46] You name the subject—science, math, English, history, chemistry, social sciences—and you will find several brilliant ways that educators have weaved Hip hop and spoken-word directly into their curriculum. The next step for the movement is to push districts and school boards to make the invest in this new art form that has the potential for motivating and lifting the spirits of students who are at-risk for dropout.

In August of 2007, we lost a great spoken-word poet, Sekou Sundiata, a professor and performer.[55,56,57] Sekou Sundiata was born Robert Franklin Feaster in Harlem but changed his name in the late 1960s to honor his African heritage. Sundiata's works combined poetry, music and drama. His poetry and performances explored slavery, subjugation and the tension between personal and national identity, especially as they inform the black experience in America. His musical influences included jazz, blues, funk and Afro-Caribbean rhythms. His plays include *The Circle Unbroken is a Hard Bop*, *The Mystery of Love*, *Udu*, and *The 51st Dream State*. He also released several albums, including *Longstoryshort* and *The Blue Oneness of Dreams*. The *Blue Oneness of Dreams* was nominated for a Grammy Award.[55,56,57]

After reading his works and listening to interviews, I believe that the colleagues, friends, family, and students of this man witnessed the epitome of examples of how spoken-word can be used and created to give voice and rhythm to sooth the soul.

Every teacher who uses poetry to teach should hear the words that Sundiata spoke. They should hear his forms of delivery and the consciousness of his message. The opportunity for gaining diversity is administered with the sharpness of a needle and the soothing of an ocean wave's journey into morning. Sundiata is the perfect introduction to this genre. If you are a parent, a teacher, spoken-word event planner, or even a student reading this work, take time to hear Sundiata speak through his interviews and his writings. Follow up on this man's journey into the creative writing world. The flexibility of his work fits into the mindset of young African American males. Where the claustrophobic atmosphere of English and traditional approaches literally kill our students, Sundiata figured out how to relate education to rap, music, poetry and spoken-word, creating an art form that transcends barriers of learning, racism, and, most importantly the interest of students.

Conclusions

This idea of using poetry and spoken-word to motivate Black males is intriguing because motivation is truly determined by interest. With the dropout rates, imprisonment, and test scores of Black males looking dismal and disturbing, one solution for connecting Black males to academic relies on a central activity of the Hip hop nation: spoken-word poetry. It is up to leading minds in education—the upper elementary and middle school teachers or the inner city Title I school curriculum specialists—to develop the tools to bring poetry and spoken-word into the classroom and create the interest points that will connect Black males to their own academic development. We have to believe that the solution is available and the remedy is worth the investment of time and resources. The emergence of programs throughout the country will benefit everyone involved in the social and emotional development of Black males and other students of color.

Maya Angelou once said, "Everyone has a story to tell." It makes perfect sense that the most troubled group in the education field is drawn to the likes of poetry paired with music. This is because everyone of these males has a story to tell and looks forward to hearing a story told. They listen to poetry for hours on top of hours everyday. Sometimes its in the form of Hip hop and rap, but it's poetry nonetheless. It is obvious that we must find the bridge that connects the students into the mainstream without souring their interest in Hip hop, rap, and spoken-word These young men are smarter than we are willing to admit. They are using lyrics, rhythms, and rhymes is some complex manners to make connections to their life experiences. While we might not see the world as they do, we have to believe in them and know that within them is a brilliant student.

How do we connect? We connect by joining the crowd and working the angles to gain more experience in this ever moving nation of Hip hop. We revert to the simplistic form by undressing the glamour of Hip hop and promoting poetry. We integrate the interest and flow into our traditional paths of learning. The interest in learning is always there among Black males, but we must figure out how to capture these students' attention. We have failed them because we do not know what they are experiencing. We have to be unconventional and recognize the consciousness of relevant messages. They know their struggle, and they want to tell their story and listen and learn from other stories. Black males want to be on top of their experience, but sadly the administrators have not met their needs.

The conventional attitudes are changing as more students from the early MTV era become teachers with intimate knowledge of Hip hop and the power to use multimedia tools to teach their courses. Slowly, the unconventional will become a mainstay, and the bridge will be built as the teaching profession evolves. In the meantime, we must save those young Black males who will encounter teachers and districts that do not have a clue about what motivates African American males. Force feeding the uninteresting strategies to these students will damage the learning opportunity. Set in motion will be a vicious cycle where the more effort put into these ineffective ways of motivating students, the more damage will be done to the learning opportunities of African American males. We must understand that "open minds create the wonders of the world, and closed minds trample the life in wondering." We must push for the unconventional usage of poetry and spoken-word. Teachers, administrators, districts, professors, and universities must have open minds because Black males and other students of color will lose their opportunity to succeed without relevant intervention. Rather than look for some new gimmick, we have to take a close look at what is capturing the attention of Black males and other students of color—poetry and spoken-word.

Advice to Teachers and Parents

1. We strongly recommend using the most popular forms of spoken-word or poetry to build interest and motivation. The performance artists who have been featured in the critically acclaimed Def Jam Poets and National Slams should be able to bring age appropriate poetry to your students or children. Analyze the various performances that can be found on the

Internet via youtube.com and through video rental houses. Discuss the content, style, rhythm and delivery of the poetry. Ask questions, such as: What is his problem? To whom is she directing this message? Are there any awkward parts of this poem? What does this mean to people of different cultures? This is an indirect way to introduce children to the art form. Since Television rules, why not bring the medium that these students are familiar with to the classroom or to your living room?

2. Research the various artists who were at the top-of-the-charts at various times in history. Recognize the highs and lows of poetry in the mainstream media. Do not limit yourself to just spoken-word artist, use Rap and Hip-Hop artists, jingle writers, storytellers, and classical writers.

3. Learn the basic forms of poetry. This may call for a refresher course in literature, but you can make this easy.

4. Establish an environment for young poets to polish and present their work. The space can be in a classroom, library, living room, a corner of a used bookstore, central location in a shopping mall, or a coffeehouse. The students, parents and teachers will have a great time creating the environment and performing their work.

5. Encourage students to accentuate their poetry and spoken-word performances with rhythmic beats from musical instruments. If musical instruments aren't available, as it was for several projects I worked on, allow the students to drum on table tops or large tin cans. Also, Flocabulary[46] has some recorded beats and rhythms, without lyrics, that students can pair with their poetry.

6. Praise is good in all things that are completed with dignity. Make this a non-threatening exercise where everyone is applauded for performing within your rules. Students will often challenge the guideline established for a spoken-word event, but you must make sure the language, content, and performances respect everyone.

7. Allow the students to be fully involved in every aspect of the program so that they have a sense of ownership.

8. Encourage young poets to read the work of the established poets. If reading is a gateway skill to doing well in other subjects, then encourage young poets to read about the lives of other poets and writers.

9. Encourage young poets to keep a journal to capture their thoughts and feelings about events in their lives. Help them to understand the therapeutic nature of journaling to help capture the essence of their thoughts from different viewpoints. Help them to understand that journaling is a

great way for them to capture their life story, know themselves better, solve personal problems, reduce stress, and to let go of anger, rage and depression. Interestingly enough, each of the contributors to this book use journaling as a way to stay focused and to gain deeper meaning from their life experiences.

10. Work with your students to organize a spoken-word and poetry performance—and have fun learning how smart and articulate Black males can be when they are given an opportunity to be the center of attention.

9

Why Is It Important to Cultivate an Interest in Creativity In Black Males?

By Anthony (Tony) Goldston and Vandorn Hinnant

Introduction

When you really think about the arrival of Black men in this new land called America, you realize that they had nothing. They were slaves, bought and sold just like livestock, listed as property of their owners, with less value than livestock. Stripped of every thread of human dignity and trained to obey their masters, the only freedom Black men had was their thoughts and a desire to start a new life. As you can imagine, the life for those first Black men in American was tough, and the main task of their owners was to condition their minds so that all thoughts focused on pleasing their masters and obeying all rules. Fortunately, thoughts of freedom and starting a new life were resistant to change, and it's amazing how resistant the need to create and adjust to a new life has been for Black men who were armed only with their thoughts.

Black men have come a long way since the days of slavery and it's difficulty for many young people to imagine a world where they would be hanged if they were caught learning to read. They can't imagine being denied entry into restaurants and other public buildings because of the color of their skin. Given the election of our first African American president, it is almost inconceivable for Black boys to believe that there was a time when literacy laws were enacted to keep Black men from voting. The process that a Black man goes through today to register to vote is a far cry from the humiliation he experienced just a few years ago as he failed the voting-rights-questions about the number of feathers on a chicken or the number of pennies it takes to fill a half-gallon candy jar. What's amazing is that if those were legitimate questions then the majority of, if not all, white people would have also been denied the right to vote.

Vandorns' Reflections

As artists, our thoughts are in alignment with this idea advanced by the poet Kahlil Gibran, "A pearl is a body built by pain around a grain of sand. What pain built our bodies, and around what grain?"[1] We believe the need that Black males have to create grew out of their need to record the painful experience of life in America. A perfect example is the blues. Black men sang the blues when they had nothing but their own pain and suffering. They sang this beautiful music as a way to sooth their tired and weary bodies. The blues was a cry for hope for a better day. Clearly, this beautiful and powerful art form grew from the pain and suffering Black people experienced.

Nearly two decade ago, Tony and I crossed paths, while we were students in college. At the time, we were drawn to teaching art to children and helping young people use art as a way to resolve personal conflicts. My journey as artist began at a rather early age. I was drawing as early as I could hold a drawing instrument, and my years in elementary school were colored with drawings that teachers had me create for bulletin boards. My earliest art pieces were attempts to make some visual record of experiences I had in dreams or while day dreaming.

Tony continued his work in the public schools while I pursued a career teaching at the college level, and then it happened. I encountered a retired physicist named Robert Powell, Sr. and began to study a rather obscure body of ancient knowledge conveniently labeled by Westerners as Sacred Geometry, and known to some as The Geometry of Life. Upon the occasion of our meeting in 1989, I pulled from my pocket a fresh sketch for a new composition that I intended to soon formalize. It was a rather poetic and organic geometric abstraction of two polyhedron (a pentagon and a hexagon) having in common one of their sides. With great enthusiasm Robert Powell invited me to a workshop/presentation he was conducting the next day. What has grown out of that fate-filled meeting is the subject of a forthcoming book to be titled," The Rest of Euclid."

As a result of my art studies at NCA&T State University in art design and my study of Sacred Geometry, I have developed an eye for patterns and relationships within patterns in our everyday world. What fascinates me is how two-dimensional and three-dimensional geometry appears to be a kind of shorthand writing for the energetic matrices in matter we have come to observe via modern technologies such as the electron microscope, and earlier magnifiers such as microscopes, and telescopes. Many of the free-hand sketches I have done bear a striking resemblance to images I have seen of magnified atoms and molecules. I believe that spending time in silence through meditation has helped to sustain my childhood ability to sense and to see energy patterns in and around objects and people.

In 1994, the revered and celebrated African-American artist John Biggers came to visit my home. He stepped into the living room and was greeted by a room full of my work on the walls. The first words out of his mouth were: "Man, you are dealing with pure Spirit!"

My encounter with Dr. Powell kicked me into a deeper appreciation and understanding for how geometry is at the foundation of all patterns, including the organic world. I started to understand more of how the mind forms thoughts and how the creative potential is hindered by how the mind is conditioned to see reality.

Artists are often accused of seeing patterns that other don't see, but after my encounters with Dr. Powell, I started to understand that we exist in a universe where everything is connected to everything, where any action or thought has an effect on everything. I began to see that there are no boundaries that separate us from each other since we are in a constant and divinely intimate relationship with everyone and every world that lies beyond the boundaries of our perception. Through my work with Dr. Powell, I understood that there is a constant give and take relationship between everything and everyone in the universe and as I took in a breath, the universe had to exhale.

When artists focus on the truth that they and everyone are divine spirits, which are not separated by skin, bones and this human form, we can see more clearly that everything is consciousness. Only then can we really understand that everything about us started first as a thought and that thought, consciousness, is what creates the unity between us.

The old adage, "everything starts as a thought," should make it easy to see that everything that Black men have created in America started as a thought. Having clear and powerful thought about what you want to create for yourself, your family, and your culture is what makes us strong as Black men. Out of nothing, we used our creative intelligence to contribute to life in this new world.

Today, our task might seem a little easier, but we've got to continue to cultivate creativity in Black boys. To help you see this differently Tony has to tell you his story about how getting involved in the creative arts changed his life. In fact, much of the chapter is about Tony's life and I thank him for allowing me to contribute some of my thoughts to the chapter.

Tony's Story

The ability to create art opened up many areas of my life that were not available to me as a child growing up in a small town. I was a small, bright-eyed child that did not seem to fit in the world around me. I always felt out of place with my emotions and my feelings. School did not feel like a place where I could be successful or a place I wanted to be. I am the oldest of five children. There was a lot of love and support in our family; however, there was a lot of alcoholic dysfunction and chaos in our family. There was enough love to go around, but little else.

As an adult, I understand that people are always doing the best they can, at the place they are in their lives with the information they have. There is no blame or shame or pointing fingers at anyone. My parents did the best they could to put a roof over our heads and food on the table. But I was a dreamer. I had thoughts of creating a life for myself that was expanded beyond the mill villages and the cotton factories located in our town.

The thoughts of escaping my small town and creating a life on my own were important to me. I did not want to work in one of the local cotton mills and become a lint head, and didn't want to become the semi-functioning alcoholic, walking in the shadows of life, that I had seen many Black men of neighborhood become. As a child and even as a young man, I watched how these men, once powerful and proud, full of dreams, hope and ambition were reduced to ideas that were not their own. This seemed hopeless and painful. It was a pain I would later feel deeply and profoundly in my own life.

As a first grader, I attended a school in my community. During my second year of schooling, however, our school was closed, and we were bused to the local white school. It was my first time riding a school bus and it was also the first time I was told to sit in the back of the bus for no apparent reason other than the color of my skin. Oddly, the bus stopped at the homes of every white child, to and from school, but the children on my road were picked up and dropped off at a common place, whether it was raining, snowing or a hurricane was coming our way. It did not seem fair, but the unspoken rules of conduct for Black people during that time kept us from protesting. To make this situation even less understandable, we were ushered to the back three rows of the bus and packed into seats like sardines, though there were empty seats throughout the bus.

In my second grade classroom, an amazing thing happened; regardless of intelligence, we were separated by color. The white children were placed in regular reading and math groups and the Black children were placed in the "slow" reading and math groups. This type of grouping, systematically placing children of color in remedial groups seemed to follow many of my classmates during our high school career. This practice seemed odd to me, as we were not pre-tested to see how well we could perform the three Rs. It was apparent that we were placed in the "slow groups" because we were Black. During this time, the one thing that helped keep me focused on doing well in school was art. As a child—and even as an adult today—I could not understand an educational system that labeled and tracked children on the assumption that their color, social or economic status influenced their ability to learn. Today, I believe the system is no better, if not worse, than it was 30 years ago. We are still judging children by the way they speak, dress, their physical size, and the economics or occupations of their parents. This practice is especially true when we are talking about Black boys. As a 20-year veteran pubic school art teacher, I know this is a serious problem that we are facing today.

How do we give our young Black boys the wings to soar to become academic achievers when they are told that they belong in the underachieving sub groups? How do build self-worth and self esteem so they can succeed in the 3 R's? How do we turn rejection into acceptance so they will cease with buffoonish behavior that is borne from watching too much television? This scenario is repeated over and over again in every school in this country. This was my story. I became a buffoon and a class clown to fit in with the other children in the class. It was very easy and crafty to misbehave to get the attention of the teacher in the class. I thought I was being mischievous and playful by being a class clown; however, this behavior was being interpreted by my teachers as lack of intelligence, desire, familial concern, or motivation. In hindsight, the message I think the message my teachers were sending the Black children in those classes was, "You are not very important and the thought, dreams and God-given talents you have aren't equal to similar qualities of any white student in this class. You will belong in the slow group in life because white is right and all things Black are wrong."

This was an attitude, a false belief system, which I adopted as a child because it was the system that I had known all my life. As a child, I believed that these white teachers were right. Maybe I belonged in the slow reading circle where we read, "See Spot Run" and "Dick Likes Jane" as third and fourth graders. What a waste of time and creative energy!

As I entered junior high school, this negative believe system was firmly implanted in my psyche. I expected to do less, I expected be in the slow reading and math groups. I subconsciously remained the class clown and the low achiever to feel the acceptance of the other students and to hide the pain of growing up in a dysfunctional alcoholic family. Black boys, just like all other children, want to feel good about themselves. In my case, I became good at making other children laugh, but the problem was that they were laughing at me instead of laughing with me.

In junior high school, I was an extremely shy and manipulative child. It is funny now, but to illustrate how manipulative I was as a small boy, I would pretend to have to go the bathroom, only to go to the gymnasium to steal the needle out of the record player to escape the square dancing lessons that were held every Friday. What a strange dichotomy! Wanting the love and attention of my teachers and classmates, however, I was afraid to let people know me or get close to me.

Looking back, I realize many of the things I did were cries for someone to help me unload the hellish secret of alcoholism that, like an honor code, bonded me to believing that I was a nobody. To cope with the chaos that I felt inside, I drew, created, and learned to appreciate art. This was the greatest thing I could do the escape. When I was not drawing, I would lie in the grass and look at the clouds or take long walks in the cow pasture with my dog, Tree, and dream of being a great artist. I dreamed of leaving all the pain, humiliation, and shame behind. Art helped me at that time to find a sense of self and a sense of hope. It provided me a comfortable place where I could share my thoughts.

Many things seemed hopeless and impossible, but a wonderful miracle happened in the seventh grade. I met the first of many mentors that would guide and shape me into the person that I am today. Mr. Manning was a true Renaissances Man. He was a man of letters; a lover of classical music, which he played in class; a mathematical genius; a scientist; and a wonderful artist. He was always impeccably dressed, with his hat, necktie and socks always matching. Up until this time in my formal education, all of teachers had been white and female, but Mr. Manning was a strong Black man who expected excellence from all of his students regardless of their race, social background, or life circumstance. He expected and gave respect to every one; he expected students to tuck their shirts in their pants and to brush their teeth and comb their hair. If a child did not have a toothbrush or a comb, he would give you a quarter to buy one. There were no excuses! All excuses and poorly done papers were promptly placed in "file thirteen," otherwise known as the trashcan. "Knowledge is power" was his favorite quote. Mr. Manning taught me the power of art and how it can transform and empower one's life. He taught me how art was to be shared to help lighten the load of people that are hurting. He taught me that if I used art coupled with a few common courtesies, such as saying, "please, thank you, and you are welcome," that my life would be a gift to God, myself, and to others, regardless of my color. I used these lessons and others that I have learned from other mentors to live in this world today.

I left junior high school with a new set of expectations and a new set of values. Art was at the center of that belief system. Mr. Manning had taught me an important lesson about the power of information. He also instilled in me the belief that I was somebody important because God did not make any junk.

Academic tracking seemed to follow me from primary and junior high school. In high school, I was enrolled in a brick laying class and textile training class to prepare me for my future. During English class, most of the Black boys were placed in non-reading classes to watch filmstrips entitled, "Man in Cars" and "Man in Sports" while the teacher, usually one of the athletic coaches, read the Sports Illustrated magazine. Another approach to curbing the academic development of boys was for the guidance counselor to suggest to every Black boy that a life in the Army was the way for them to learn to "be the best you can be." Again, without my knowing it, I was placed in the "slow group." This was a tough time for me, as it is for all adolescent Black boys who are confused about who they are, their place in society, and their teachers' negative expectations about them. Many of my friends had nothing to hold onto, nothing to keep them afloat, as they navigated through these difficult times. Fortunately, I had art and without the peace and freedom of choice that art offered me, I am certain that I would have never survived these turbulent times.

Entering my senior year of high school, I realized that I was not going to be a gun-carrying soldier or a lint-head in the local textile mill. Somehow, through the creative experiences I was having with art, I starting to see how there were different ways to complete my art projects and different ways to look at my life. I remember the day I realized that I had choices about what I wanted for my life. I asked the guidance counselor to help me apply for colleges. I thought I had been a good student—at least I was subservient and did not ask difficult questions—but the counselor told me that I was wasting my money and her time by applying to college. Man, what a shock! I had taken all of the classes they had assigned to me, I had good grades in, "Man in Cars" and bricklaying, but I was still 240th out of 300 students in my graduation class!

Since I did not become a gun toting solider or a local lint-head in the textile mill, my only option after graduation was to attend the local community college. I met some wonderful teachers, some who have become life-long friends. After completing two years there, I was equipped a new sense of confidence and was ready to attend art school at a major university so that I could become a teacher. I had arrived and all of the lessons from Mr. Manning and from other mentors were firmly in place. I was a man on a mission and for the first time in my life, I was able to meet other young Black men who were doing some positive things in their lives. Many reflected the social, spiritual and academic interests that were only dreams for me. I was a part of challenging environment, and I felt completely alive. After successfully completing and maintaining a high grade point in my coursework in the school of art education, and after completing the first of my student teaching projects, I was discouraged from pursuing my interest in becoming an art teacher. I was told, in not so kind words, to pick another major. "Black men don't teach art." In retrospect, I recall that I was the only Black male in the art education program and regardless of my grades and abilities to create art, the instructors and students treated me like a stranger, as if I had no business thinking that I could ever teach art in the public schools of North Carolina. This was a very confusing time in my life. I had done what was required to teach, I had done everything I knew to be an outstanding citizen. I did not have a police record, and I wasn't an unwed welfare father. What went wrong? I was being placed in the "slow group" again, but this time I was equipped with a college degree from one of the best universities in North Carolina.

After completing my college degree in art, I returned home morally and spiritually beaten. I had played the game, but there were no rewards for doing well in college and no job waiting for me after I had earned my degree. I was frustrated and angry, and I had no idea about how to turn my situation around. The one thing I had was the same thing that had worked for the men in my community. It made them happy and allowed them to forget about the things that seemed unfair in life. The solution I used to erase all of my problems was alcohol and drugs.

For many years after completing college, I was unemployable, underemployed, and drinking almost everyday to erase the pain and humiliation, I experienced. Being treated as if I was slow and stupid by my teachers and classmates, all of whom were white people, had left an emotional marks on me. Rather than rewards for doing well in school and not becoming a thug or criminal, my entitlement was an emotional problem that pushed me to the point of a breakdown. Without a way to cope with this pain, I knew I would lose my mind. Drinking swept away the wasteful years of bricking laying classes during high school. It swept away the discrimination I felt as a college senior when I was told that I was not smart enough to teach. It was a way to kill the pain. But becoming an addict destroyed everything that was important in my life (relationships, joy, hope, peace, and love) except for art.

In the end, ART was the answer. Today, I have been sober for 18 years and art led me back to myself. It has opened more doors for me than I ever could have dreamed. I have been able to use art to travel around the world and learn about different people and different cultures. Art has allowed me the privilege to work at different zoological parks and major movie studios around the country where I have created and sculpted props and helped to design natural habitat enclosures for animals. Art has allowed me opportunities to conduct creativity workshops across the country. Today, I have been a public middle school art teacher for twenty years. Without me, many of the Black boys in our public schools in North Carolina would have experienced the same shame, humiliation, and confusion I experienced from not having a Black man to talk to about life.

Art has given me the confidence of self-expression and the ability to believe in myself in all circumstances. It has enhanced my life and has influenced the way I relate to the people and the world around me.

Mr. Manning was right: "Knowledge is power," and art is the keystone for me to access that power in my life.

Tony's ideas about why is it important for Black boys to create

Creativity is important for many reasons as it relates to the development of African American boys. When a person learns to create, they are looking inside themselves for the answers that may help them survive. So what happens when creativity and art is suppressed? What happens when our African American boys don't learn this new and innovative language of self-expression? Often, when children, especially boys, are not allowed to create or express themselves, they implode and form a negative belief system that does not serve them well in school or in life. Often this belief system is false; however, it appears real and worth trusting since the foundation for what's there came from people who care about and love the child. I believe we all live by the rules and regulations we have learned in our families and the communities in which we reside. Even if the systems around us are flawed, they become the foundation from which we learn to see the world. As a teacher in a middle school, I have witnessed the difficulties African American boys have expressing themselves socially, academically and verbally. Once this happens, a negative belief system is welded in place by the reinforcements received from his first contacts with teacher. If the boys are not helped to learn more empowering ways to communicate their concerns, the boys will be destined to behave and act out to seek attention in ways that are not accepted in school or in society. But creating art and learning other modes of self-expression, our African American boys learn a new language. With this new language, the child is able to express his hopes, his frustrations and his dreams to himself and the world around him. That is purpose of art.

I have taught many young men during my teaching career, and many seem to get lost in the system because no one taught them how to discover their talents or how to set goals for themselves. These students seem to go from class to class without a purpose, disrupting classes and hindering the learning process of other students. The end result for many of these boys is that one of their teachers will just get tired of their rambling or unbridled energy and have them confined to in school or out of school suspension. What's so troubling about this sequence of events is that many of the teachers, most often white females, have admitted to me that they often send Black boys to in-school suspension because they don't know how to channel the creative gifts of these young men. Often these young men are street-wise and have acquired coping and learning skills that are important to survive in an environment outside the arena of school, but these skills are translated or perceived as being rude, disrespectful, and adding no value to what is needed in the classroom.

This year, I have a young Black male student in my seventh grade art class named Terrell. Even though this young man is only thirteen years old, he considers himself a man, and by many standards of society, he is a man. It almost seems that Terrell has become a man by default. He goes home alone everyday to an empty house that is in the middle of a drug-infested neighborhood. His father has never been a part of his life and when mother is around, she expects Terrell to be an adult, rather than a thirteen-year-old boy, who needs protection and guidance to handle his untraditional and difficult relationships. Terrell has to get up each day and dress and feed his younger brothers and sisters, when and if there is any food in the house. Attempting to be cool and to feel cool and to stand out from his peers, Terrell came to school one day wearing his pajamas and a pair of bedroom slippers. It seemed appropriate to him, and he was sending the message to his fellow students that he was unique and special. He was also sending a message to his teachers that he was above the rules and procedures of the classroom.

Because Terrell lacked the socialization skills and the ability to find acceptance in the normal classroom setting, he became an emotional and physical bully to his peers and to his teachers. In fact, he was a bully to anyone who tried to help him become successful in school. He was an angry and frustrated boy who was looking for a way to express his concerns about the conditions of his life. After many attempts to change Terrell's behavior (e.g., out of school suspension, in-school suspension, boot camps, many trips to the principal's office, etc.), Terrell was finally given an opportunity to enroll in my art class. He was placed in my class because he had become an uncontrollable force, and I was someone the principal felt he could form a trusting relationship with. He felt powerless and was unable to express himself in his classes. In art, however, he thrived and became a more self-confident young man. Not only did his behavior change in his other classes, he also became a better student overall, making mostly Bs on his final report card.

These few lines from the poem, "A Dream Deferred," by Langston Hughes illustrates what happens when we feel our lives are meaningless.[2] "What happens to a dream deferred? Does it dry up like a raisin in the sun? Or does it explode?" When creativity and art are not used to help boys like Terrell, does the will and desire to be successful in other areas of life suffer? I believe so. There was no rational reason for this young man to improve in his other classes. The only thing that changed was to have him placed in my art class and I allowed him to explore new avenues of self-expression. In time, he felt better about himself and he had a purpose to come to school. Art enabled him to experience being successful and to connect this experience to his own behaviors, which was something unavailable to him in his other classes. I believe art provided Terrell the rare opportunity to work at his own pace without the fear of failure and ridicule of others. As he became more efficient and polished in his ability to create art and in his ability to see himself as a successful person, he became a better student. For the first time in his life, Terrell was not a bystander in the educational system that he perceived as useless; he was an active participant in his own education.

Art itself was not the miracle that transformed this young man's life, but through art he found a vehicle that allowed him to become a more powerful and thoughtful person. Once he started to feel and achieve some success in art class, I believe that he started to believe that he belonged in our school. He did not have a need to wear his pajamas and bedroom shoes to school. Just like our other successful students, Terrell started to believe that he belonged in school and that his contributions (e.g., attendance, behaving well in class, and respecting teachers and other students) to school were important. Just like any successful person, Terrell discovered that belonging is the cornerstone to become a successful person. We all have the emotional need to belong and a desire to fit in, to feel valued and respected. By coming to art class, Terrell was able to find himself and he became a better student and a better person.

Without art and forms of self-expression, the soul will indeed dry up. We are seeing a lack of success in English, Math, Science, and History in every school across this country. Often the picture of what is considered successful academically and socially in most classrooms are too narrowly defined. I have seen many African American male students fail in the school environment because they have not found a place of where they can express themselves or to experience what it feel like to be successful. Does this shortage of artistic and creative outlet cause the minds of young boys to disengage from learning? I believe so.

Every human being has a need and a desire for self-expression. So what happens when students like Terrell aren't given the opportunity to create and share their gifts to world? What happens when creativity and other forms self-expression are not fulfilled? Often these young men turn to other outlets, organizations and places for creativity and a sense of belonging. In my school, like many others across the country, African American males, desperate for a sense of belonging and respect, are seeking membership in gangs. We all desire to belong to something or someone, and these young men are ruining their lives and the potential to become respected leaders among their peers in their misguided efforts. Ill equipped to be adult Black men, these disruptive adolescents are thrown away by the schools and society that refuse to save them.

A couple of years ago, a young man named Carlos was in my art class. Carlos was a gifted artist; however, he always enjoyed being the center of attention, and being the best athlete at our school provided him much attention. In art class and on the playing field, Carlos was extremely successful; he was able to show his creativity, style, and ebullience for life. He was able to be the person he wanted to be. He was successful and he felt a sense of belonging. I wish I could tell you that this confidence translated to success in his other classes, but it did not. Carlos came to school to create art and to play ball. The sad thing about playing ball in a middle school is that once a student is fifteen years old, he is no longer eligible play. Carlos stayed in school because he enjoyed being a part of our art class, but he felt "worthless and stupid" in his other classes. To escape the pain, real or imagined, Carlos started to sell and use marijuana at school. By doing so, he once again belonged to a group or gang that was important in his eyes.

Today, after spending some time in prison and being under-employed, if at all unemployable, he occasionally comes by the school to see me. He is a sad and broken young man who has had a difficult life. Proudly, he tells me that he still draws and that it kept him from wasting completely away in prison. That is power of art and creativity. Even when the situation is difficult to understand and accept, the self-expression and peace from creating art can have a transforming effect on a boy living a troubled life.

If our young men are not allowed outlets for creativity and self-expression, they will find ways to vent their feelings. This is what happened to Carlos. Selling drugs gave him a purpose and a sense of belonging; however, it was self-degrading and destructive.

As a middle school teacher, I have observed African American boys use many forms of creativity to gain acceptance, a sense of personal power, and self-respect. Many of my students are excellent spoken-word artists who can put complicated words and phrases to music. Others have found (or experienced) self-expression by performing with the step and drill teams at our school. By doing so, they are learning how to use their bodies in a productive, fun, and creative way. By using the arts, we are helping our students unlock the creative vistas that were previously unknown to them. And the confidence gained with every new step or every verse they learn or create will translate into the mastery of better grades and a higher level of acceptance by others as they become mature adults. There are also the performing arts that help some of our young men successfully connect with the world around them. One of my former students, a young man named Reggie, is currently an off-Broadway actor. I believe that every type of art is important for the success of our African-African boys. It keeps their dreams alive and we all need dreams to love and live by.

Vandorn's ideas about the creative ways to help Black boys express themselves

As Tony has indicated, without art, many Black males would not have a way to connect to the world around them. Clearly, our children are our greatest gifts from God. Creativity is the greatest gift we can give our children. To help our children develop into mature and productive citizens in a growing and changing world, it is important to teach them to be creative problem solvers. Without creative solutions to help guide them toward self-awareness, we allow them to struggle and stumble under the assumption of rules they do not understand.

God has given each of us the strength, courage, and creativity to be of ultimate service to Him and to our fellow man. And to help our children become maximum service to God and to others in their world, it is important to help them understand how to be creative problem solvers. One of the major obstacles Black boys have to overcome to tap into their creativity is a sense of belonging. We belong to one another just as the atoms of the air and the molecules of water belong to one another. There is no separation except through what we have been told and what we have chosen to believe.

If we really perceived ourselves as we really are, we would never see ourselves as different from anything in the universe. We would understand that as we breath the universe exhales. What is so fascinating about all of this is that there is an intelligence that is always at work recreating the divine order that makes us up. This intelligence is spirit, it is consciousness. It is alive, it never sleeps, it never runs out of energy, it never gets a cold or grows old; it is eternal and immortal. The universe that we exist in is alive and everything in the universe is influence by every action, no matter how small or large; including what you and I do and say. Everything that you and I do has an effect on the whole universe. If each of us accepted and lived by this fact then most of the problems we have motivating and teaching Black males would be solved.

Living in harmony, being supportive of each other, and having a healthy and prosperous life are choices that many people don't realize. What seems to cast the dark cloud over this idea is the notion that each of us is born separate but equal. But there is no separation between either of us. How can there be boundaries between us if we are dependent on one another for every breath of life? The answer is very simple; there is no separation between either one of us. We belong to each other.

Belonging

We all have a need to belong to a family, a team, or a group. We all have a need to share. Think of this as a need of connectedness or a need for love. Many Black boys have difficulties with the expression of this natural need to love others and to feel loved by others. This is partly due to the frustration caused by the impoverished circumstances they experienced being raised in fatherless homes. For some, their frustration has turned to anger, often too intense to control, because of how they feel about being abandoned by their fathers. And while this is not the case for all Black boys, most have been made to feel unwelcome by the one institution, school, where they spend the bulk of their times. Others have built a wall of rage around themselves that seems impenetrable or assessable only through membership in a gang. How do we teach Black boys to love and connect to their creative selves? Why is this process of connectedness important for potential growth of young boys into young men?

How often have you listened to Black children talking about how they want to become a professional athlete or a professional rapper in order to make a living and to "become" somebody? For many Black boys, these are the only positive examples they see of Black men in the larger society. They connect their ability to run a football on Friday night or being a Hip hop superstar with success. We see this dilemma often as Black males talk about how to become successful without sports or music that often carries negative messages about sex, achievement, women, and manhood. How can we teach our children to believe that they belong to their schools that they are gifts to us, and they are stewards to dreams of a creative God who gives them each wonderful gifts of creativity to serve him and others in a unique and inspired manner? How can we use creativity to give our children a sense of purpose? I believe we can best serve our children by allowing them to grow and to use the natural gifts that they have. With guidance and practice, we as adults, parents, and teachers can help our children to use and express their natural creative tendencies to achieve a sense of belonging in the world in which that they live.

Some examples of creativity and self-expression that contribute to a sense of belonging are writing stories to explore feelings and self-awareness; interpreting symbols as a listener; and writing and publishing poetry or short stories. Drama can also be used as a tool to gain to be awareness of the power of speech and vast differences between verbal and non-verbal behaviors. Debate clubs; speaking and interacting with others as in a moot court; participating in plays they have written to explore positive and negative themes in their personal lives, school and social worlds; and dance are other forms of creative expression that allow Black boys to feel a sense of belonging. Largely, it does not matter which creative outlet a Black boy explores as long as he feels compelled to excel.

The life and work of one of my favorite people, Dr. Martin Luther King Jr., offers us a glimpse of how to take pride in everything we do and offers us a sense of belonging that is essential to personal growth and a sense of well being that is important to everyone.[3,4,5] It is especially important for us to assist children in feeling a sense of belonging in today's world. He believed that we should encourage children to aim for quality no matter what the task. Shouldn't this be the purpose of any creative endeavor we pursuit? Shouldn't this be the purpose of our role as educators? If one is called to be a street sweeper, he should do it with such pride that everyone would notice how well the streets are being swept. I believe that is our role as parents and teachers is to help our children, especially boys, believe that they can use their inherent creative abilities to manifest a life of connectedness to their school, their family, and most importantly, to themselves. If we don't allow Black boys to use their creative intelligence in ways to develop positive connections with school and society, then many will end up being ill equipped to face the obstacles they will face on their journey toward manhood.

Tony's Ideas About Self-Expression, Art, and Academic Achievement

As an art teacher for 20 years, I have seen many Black boys who have transformed from being uninspired and nearly failing in their schoolwork to highly motivated students who take pride in their academic accomplishments. Patrick entered my classroom as a sixth-grader who had struggled academically. His teachers felt he was not capable of achieving success in the classroom and had even referred him for exceptional children's services. He did not qualify for those services, but he had internalized their opinions of him and allowed himself to simply coast through school, not trying to rise above their expectations. I saw a spark in Patrick the moment he picked up a paintbrush. Much of Patrick's inner creativity was unleashed through art. He found a means for channeling his talent and energy. Patrick was initially resistant to the praise I offered him, having grown accustomed to being overlooked in class. He had been convinced, programmed even, to believe that he was inferior to his peers and lacking potential.

I had the honor of teaching Patrick for three years and watched as he experienced a myriad of tragedies and struggles in his personal life. His father was in and out of the home and abusive when he was present. He watched his mother go from one low-paying job to another and often went to bed hungry so that the younger children at home could have a meal. Art was the one constant that Patrick had during those crucial middle school years. Not only did Patrick grow personally through his positive experiences in art class, but he also found that he could be successful in other academic areas as well. As an eighth grader, this once seemingly under-achieving young man found himself being inducted into Beta Club. Many would have predicted Patrick to be a high school dropout, ending up contributing to all that is wrong with society; instead, Patrick went on to complete high school and continue his academic pursuits at our local community college.

Josh is another example of a student whose life was changed because of his involvement in art. He came to me as the known terror of the sixth grade. Teachers dreaded seeing his name on their roll based solely on the stories that preceded him from elementary school. Josh suffered a traumatic brain injury as a small child when a tree landed on his head. He was physically disabled following the accident and was also identified as behaviorally/emotionally disabled. But Josh had the uncanny ability to visualize space in a way that many mature artists cannot. He was a talented builder; constructing objects through multiple media was engaging for Josh. The tediousness of model car construction was a passion for Josh, an opportunity for him to escape to his own world. While Josh was finding success in my classroom, I was also coaching him in ways to find success in other areas of his life. While he was piecing together an art project, we were talking about making wise choices. Those conversations made a difference to Josh as he started to find positive ways to express himself and he started realizing the importance of academics to his future. Currently, Josh is a productive high school senior, deeply involved in the automotive and repair program. He has found a potential career he enjoys and through which he can make positive contributions to society.

Tony's Review of How Art Changes Lives

A growing body of studies presents compelling evidence connecting students learning in the arts to a wide spectrum of academic and social benefits. In addition, these studies show that what students learn in the arts may help them to master other subjects, such as reading, math or social studies.[6,7,8,9,10] Students who participate in arts learning experiences often improve their achievement in other realms of learning and life. In a well-documented national study using a federal database of over 25,000 middle and high school students, researchers from the University of California at Los Angeles found students with high arts involvement performed better on standardized achievement tests than students with low arts involvement.[7] Furthermore, the high art-involved students also watched fewer hours of TV, participated in more community service and reported less boredom in school. Similarly, several studies have shown a positive relationship between college entrance exams scores (SAT) and involvements in the arts. High school students who take arts classes have higher math and verbal SAT scores than students who take no arts classes. Moreover, the relationship between SAT scores and arts involvement tend to co-vary and suggest that the more arts classes, the higher the scores. On a more personal level, as I reflect on my experiences, I have to admit that without the involvement of arts in my life, I would not be where I am today[10,11,12,13]

I grew up in a family with lots of problems. Being a bit shy and withdrawn provided some emotional relief from the problems at home, but being a loner didn't give me many opportunities to enhance my self-esteem and self-confidence. Despite these difficulties, I discovered an interest in art, which provided an emotional insulation from some of the pressures and conflicts I was experiencing. Basically, I was a decent student growing up, but the arts provided me an opportunity to have success experiences and to generalize those experiences to other areas of my life. I've made it a habit to extend these same experiences to my students, most often through my one-on-one encounters with them in my classes. As you will soon discover, thee are many great research students that examined whether the arts have an impact on academic performance on large groups of children.

Vandorn's Review of the Interrelationships Between Reading, Language, and Art

More than 65 distinct relationships between the arts and academic and social outcomes have been documented. They include such associations as: visual arts instructions and reading readiness; dramatic enactment and conflict resolutions skills; traditional dance and nonverbal reasoning; and learning piano and mathematics proficiency. One of the methods for assigning these outcomes are standardized exams, sometimes referred to as "paper and pencil tests." While not always deemed the best or the most valid measure, standardized test results provide arts educators with important information about the interrelationships between the arts and academic achievement. [6,12,14]

Constellations of process are involved in the development of literacy skills. Children learning to read and write must be able to associate letters, words, and phrases with sounds, sentences, and meanings. Certain forms of art instruction enhance and complement basic reading skills, language development and writing. For example, dance has been employed to develop reading readiness in very young children, and the study of music has provided a context for teaching language skills. The use of drama enactment through plays has been used to affect story understanding, reading comprehension, and topical writing skills. Studies have shown that when students, particularly young children who are reading below grade level, have an opportunity to engage in a dramatic enactment of a story, their overall understanding and comprehension of the story is improved.[15,16,17] The use of drama in the classroom can also be an effective method to develop and improve the quality of children's narrative writing. For example, in one study, second and third grade students showed improvements in their writing when given an opportunity to use poetry, games, movement, and improvisation to act out their story idea as part of a warm-up writing exercise.[16] Clearly, these studies indicate that the use of drama in the classroom helps motivate students to learn.

Interrelationships Between Mathematics, Critical Thinking Skills, and the Arts

There is no doubt about it; math is right up there with history as being one of the courses students don't like. Interestingly enough, there tends to be a strong link between math aptitude and music. There are over 4,000 published references on this topic.[6,7,8,14] Certain types of music instruction help develop the capacity for spatial-temporal reasoning, which is integral to the acquisition of important mathematics skills. Spatial temporal reasoning refers to the ability to understand the relationship of ideas and objects in time and space. Among the strong body of evidence linking student involvement in music to high school math proficiency are two large-scale studies.[13,18] The first, based on an analysis of multiple studies, confirms the finding that students who take music classes in high school are more likely to score higher on standardized mathematics tests such as the SAT. One explanation is that musical training in rhythm emphasizes proportion, patterns, and ratios expressed as mathematical relations. Another explanation is that arts learning experiences increase a child's critical thinking or cognitive problem solving skills. In the second study, students who were consistently involved in orchestra or band during their middle and high school years performed between in math at grade 12. The results were even more pronounced when comparing students from low-income families. Those who were involved in orchestra or band were more than twice as likely to perform at the highest levels in math as their peers who were not involved in music.[13]

Participation in other arts forms, such as dance or visual arts, also lends itself to the development of critical thinking skills, as evidenced in these examples, which also ask the question of whether such skills transfer to other subjects. In an experimental research study of high school age students, those who studied dance scored higher than non-dancers on measures of creative thinking, especially in categories of fluency, originality, and abstract thought. Whether dancers can use their original abstract thinking skills in other disciplines is an important area of exploration.[16] In another project, a group of 162 children, ages 9 and 10, were trained to look closely at works of art and reason about what they saw. The results showed that children's ability to draw inferences about artwork transferred to their reasoning about images in science. In both cases, the critical skill is that of looking closely and reasoning about what is seen.[22]

Certain art activities promote growth in positive social skills, including self-confidence, self-control, conflict resolution, and social tolerance. Research evidence clearly show that the arts can play a key role in developing social competencies among economically disadvantaged youth, who are at greatest risk of not successfully completing their education. For example, in one study a group of boys, ages 8 to 19, living in residential homes and juvenile detention centers for at-risk youth experienced an increase in their confidence and self-esteem after learning how to play guitar and performing for their peers.[23]

The research suggests that the opportunity to perform may be a powerful tool to help youth overcome fears and see that they can succeed. In a similar project, significant gains in self-confidence, tolerance, and persistence occurred among a group of 60 adolescents, ages 13 to 17, who participated in a jazz and Hip hop dance class twice weekly for 10 weeks.[22] Clearly, dance and other art forms can affect the way juvenile offenders and other disenfranchised youth feel about themselves and impact whether they dropout of school.[24] In a project I (Vandorn) conducted, a mathematical application of art was used to build team spirit in a group of children from a low income and crime riddled community. The students were part of an enrichment program where they had to create collaborative art projects, but there were conflicts and too much anger to make any progress. They needed to develop a positive team spirit. To do so, they were given a 7-foot long string with a pencil tied to one end and their task was to draw an intersecting set of circles, one for each student in the group, where each student had to draw a circle and there could never be an occasion where two students were not involved in drawing the circle. It might sound complex, but it's a simple exercise where the pencil is passed along from one student to the next until each student is standing in the middle of a circle that intersects with other circles. They had to communicate with each other and depend on each other to complete the project. From this exercise, they learned about the mathematic principles involved with drawing circles and how each circle was interrelated with the others. Standing in the middle of those circles the students talked about the reality of the words "my space" and how each circle represented an individual. More importantly, their involvement in the project led to a reduction of antagonizing and bickering behaviors as reflected by the efficiency and team spirit they demonstrated while working on their art projects.

It is evident to me that The Geometry of Life used as a teaching tool is a platform for attending to the dormant or latent spirituality in our youth. The best teaching is by example. I dare suggest here that the clearest examples of relationship are to be found in geometry.

When we show students, with physical examples and through living experience, that the concept of relationship rises out of geometry, they are able to see with their eyes and sense with their minds, bodies, and hearts the living/tangible evidence of what the word relationship means. With geometry as the reference for learning about relationship, we can best illustrate principles of mathematics and arithmetic. Given this understanding, Black males are equipped with the foundation for critical and clear thinking, and prepared to navigate the complexities of relationships with respect for themselves and others.

Interrelationships Between The Motivation To Learn and The Arts

Art learning experiences contribute to the development of certain thinking, social, and motivational skills that are considered basic for success in school, work, and life. The arts nurture a motivation to learn, as it did in my case, by emphasizing active engagement, discipline, sustained attention, persistence, risk taking, and other competencies. Let's face it, all children enjoy the process of creating something.

Creativity and Life in the 21st Century

To prepare Black males for work and life in the 21st century, educators must cultivate must cultivate student's creativity.[21] Many of the fastest growing jobs and emerging industries will rely on the workers capacity to think unconventionally, imagine new scenarios, and produce results that are both adaptive and flexible. Many of the emerging industries will generate jobs that do not even exist and workers will need to imagine the unimaginable and hone their creative skills.

Creativity expert, Robert Epstein, a psychologist and author of several books, and both scholarly and popular articles, has identified four competencies essential for creative expression:[25,26,27,28]

1. Capturing—preserving new ideas.
2. Challenging—giving ourselves tough problems to solve.
3. Broadening—boosting creativity by learning interesting and diverse things and people.
4. Surrounding—associating with interesting and diverse things and people.

Of the four competencies, Epstein says that capturing is the most important. In the classroom, educators need to provide a ways, on a daily basis, to capture the ideas of Black males in an idea folder or idea box. Encourage Black boys to keep a journal for jotting down new ideas when they pop into their heads. In this way, you are giving them permission to have these ideas and letting them know that their ideas are important. And keep in mind that Black boys develop creativity not when you tell them to, but when you model creativity and imagination through your teaching. When students are engaged in challenging projects, they produce impressive work and, more often than not, the best projects came from students who were not necessarily the best and brightest.

As discussed earlier, art is related to a number of academic skills. But, creative exercises should not be confined to the arts. Creativity is at the heart of problem solving and Black boys will always have personal and work-related problems to solve. By helping them develop creative competencies, you are preparing them to be better equipped for the world.

Conclusions and Advice to Teachers and Parents

The evidence is clear and strongly indicates that students' involvement in the arts contributes to academic achievement and success. What is less clear is how to ensure that Black boys have the opportunity to learn about and experience the arts in schools. Despite convincing evidence and strong public support, the arts remain on the margins of education, often the last to be added and the first to be dropped in times of strained budgets and shifting priorities. Our Black boys pick up a football or basketball and we encourage them. They pick up an art set and we cringe. Why? Social constructs encourage and re-establish stereotypes of what a Black man can do to be successful in life. Art is typically not part of that stereotype. Parents, however, should be contributing to the long-term success of their Black sons by encouraging, even fostering their interest in the arts. And as many of the contributors of this book will attest, art was part of the foundation of their early education and while neither of them considers themselves an artist, having an art background contributed to their academic development.

Parents should understand that art offers an outlet for creativity, a place for self-discipline to develop, and an opportunity for young men to grow in their understanding of life, culture, and humanity. Through artistic endeavors, young men can experience success in a classroom that will spill over into other academic areas. All young people seek to find a way to contribute and belong. Without a positive way to do this, often Black boys fall into the trap of becoming involved in negative, detrimental, and dangerous behaviors and activities. By participating in artistic endeavors, energy and enthusiasm that might otherwise turn negative have a way to be funneled into positive, productive, and creative pursuits. Engagement in the process of creation through an artistic outlet keeps our young Black men off the streets and involved in productive interests that will contribute to them becoming well-rounded citizens. Those same interests may even lead to fulfilling career opportunities or life-enhancing hobbies that will follow them throughout their journey through life.

Teachers often belittle the arts, referring to them as 'electives' or 'specials' rather than academic courses. By embracing the arts programs at their schools, teachers are supporting courses that give students a way to release energies in a positive way and fuel their creative juices, which will enhance their performance in all their courses and support the development of the whole child. Arts should be viewed as essential building blocks to successful academic programs in all schools spanning all grade levels. If all teachers would work together to integrate curricula and support all areas of learning, test scores would increase, discipline incidents would decrease, student work samples would improve, and schools could achieve what should be their ultimate goal: creating students who appreciate the world around them and who have a strong desire to contribute to that world in a positive, meaningful way.

Parents, teachers, mentors, role models, and other adults who are given the awesome responsibility of influencing young Black men during their formative years should support the arts as a viable means of providing life lessons, educational lessons, and social integration for a productive life. Art, as a creative endeavor, offers our Black boys a much needed and long overlooked opportunity to grow and develop in ways that other academic classes miss. We challenge you to embrace your artistic side while encouraging those you influence to do the same. Art can change the lives of Black boys.

10

The Impact of Mentoring and Critical Thinking Skills on Achievement

By Tavares Stephens

Introduction

We live in a world where cynicism concerning our youth has gained full momentum. We see images of students of all ethnicities and backgrounds who exhibit poor behavior, lower test scores across the board, and are filled with a sense of apathy that will not produce capable leaders but misguided citizens.[1,2,3] And this description occurs far too commonly among African American males. Their parents are at a loss, their teachers are grappling for new ideas that can inspire and encourage, and school systems, at best, are unsure about how to motivate and uplift the twenty-first century African American male. In our society, many individuals see only the impossibility of change for the better. They see a crisis, rather than opportunities to dare to make a change for the better. They forget that, if we choose to view the world as capable and enlightened individuals, we possess power to change what we see. We possess the power to influence what we experience. We possess the power to create new realities in the lives of young African American males through the faith, work, and persistence.

250

For every African American male student I have taught that seemed to be a fallen angel, I have taught two who were to be enlightened souls. For every one who seemed unconcerned about his own education, I've taught two who sought to improve and strengthen their minds and their abilities. More times than not, working with the enlightened soul also helped the fallen angel embark on a journey to his improved self. If I didn't purposely seek to see the light in my students however, I think I would become trapped in the bubble of cynicism and I would only have been of use to the students who were already on the right path. My own experience has taught me that the bubble of cynicism can explode, and its power can be rendered impotent by intentionally seeking to create experiences of inspiration, motivation, and achievement that lift the spirits of African American male students.

One particular path I've chosen to help provide inspiration, motivation, and access to doorways of achievement for my African American male students is mentoring. Like others involved in mentoring.[2,4,5,6,7] I had my challenges dealing with difficult boys. Throughout my entire educational profession, I've mentored in a multitude of ways, shapes, and forms. I co-founded a non-profit organization whose mission was mentoring through rites of passage programs. I mentored young men I encountered in schools and at my place of worship. I've been blessed with the opportunity to train teachers and adults interested in starting formalized mentoring programs. I've mentored young men and women through a writers and performance group. And in addition, I learned how to turn the experiences of classroom teaching and coaching into opportunities to mentor. I've even had the opportunity to write freelance articles on the virtues of mentoring. Now through this amazing project, I have the opportunity to pen a chapter, and share with you readers ways mentoring can uplift and motivate the hearts and minds of twenty-first century African American males.

In this chapter, you will find insights, personal reflections, and vignettes that will illustrate the power of mentoring. You will also find a list of twenty "How To" mentoring tips at the end of the chapter. This information is meant to serve as a theoretical framework and a personal testimony as to how mentoring can and will work if one faithfully commits to the task. As you read, I pray that you are inspired to act. As you act, I pray that you will act in faith. And as you act in faith, know that you will help make a young man's life become better now and in the years to come.

- When our jobs become vocations, we are able to share our gifts in ways that leave a positive and permanent impact on both modernity and posterity.

When people find out that I am an educator, somehow the topic of African American male student achievement always arises.[5,6,7] I am continually asked the question, "Why are such large numbers of African American males underachieving academically; and why do they not seek to further their education beyond high school?" Many recent studies show this phenomena is increasing. As an educator and African American man, the fact that this question continually surfaces is bothersome. In a society barely one generation removed from Jim Crow laws and still grappling with its remnants, one would think that nearly 100 percent of school age African American males would approach their education in ways that help them become leaders, community builders. Yet too often, this is not the case.

In order to gauge the depth of the problems pertaining to the lack of African American male student achievement, it would be wise to list examples of African American male students who do achieve. Perhaps, in that way, light can be shed on why others underachieve.

In ten years of working with middle and high school students, I've taught African American males who at age fourteen were burgeoning academicians and musicians (mastering multiple musical instruments while maintaining A averages). I've encountered students who have become All-American athletes while remaining in the top ten percent of their class. I've seen young men leave lives of crime to become law-abiding citizens and matriculate through college. I've witnessed students become scholars, writers, entrepreneurs, solo flight pilots, martial arts champions, award winning visual artists, and honor graduates from high school at age sixteen. The list of achievements is endless.

In each of the aforementioned scenarios, there are three consistent factors present in the achieving students' lives. These factors include mentorship, the students' understanding of the relevance of education, and the students' decision to seize opportunities to improve their own lives.

Mentorship—whether in the form of biological parents, guardians, or caring adult figures—helps any child excel. With my African American male students who have sought and found academic success, the consistency of mentorship created an aura of confidence and self worth that when blended with their innate abilities, inspired achievement. And when this process occurred, an understanding of education's relevance took place. Whether this understanding was the repetition of an adult figure's view of education or the students own view, the fact remained that education became relevant. Ideals of achievement were birthed, and these young men sought and found ways to achieve during and after high school. Of course, there are exceptions. There are students with the support and mentoring who still underachieve and students without it who overachieve. Yet more times than not, in the presence of mentorship, the student understood education's relevance. They then conceived and attained meaningful academic and extracurricular goals.

Many of the answers to questions concerning the underachievement of African American male students lie right in front of us. And if surveys were done, I would take an educated guess that mentoring and understanding education's relevance significantly affects the achievement levels of not only young African American males but young males of other races, as well.

Our communities must accept the challenge of seeing all students as our own. We must realize that whatever any of our students achieve reflects our commitment to perpetuating vital, thriving communities. Of course, students must accept the responsibility of making their own achievement possible. And parents, teachers and the community-at—large must do the same. We can never afford to leave any child untended. To do so would not only be callous but also irresponsible. We must care about every child whether or not their reflection looks like our own. We must train and mold even in hours when a child's will and effort seem to waver. If we do so, the gain will be immense. If we do not, loss is imminent. And then who will truly be to blame, the children who should be molded by the leaders of their society or the society who should have taken time to mold its children into leaders?

- I came into this world knowing how to move and breathe. I needed no guidance in these feats. Yet when it came to using my mind to construct a life filled with beauty, I needed molding and shaping. Thank God, there was someone there who showed me how to shape my mind and use its power.

Mentors serve as a teacher or guide. They uplift, encourage, and show the way towards making potentiality and reality one in the same. There are no special qualifications needed to be a mentor except a desire to be in a child's life in ways that are consistent and promote positive growth.

If we spend time around any child, we engage in the process of mentoring. We either mentor consciously by commission or unconsciously by omission. Children watch us and learn from what we think, say, and do. The conscious mentor realizes this and mentors intentionally. They mentor through consistent dialogue, trips to places of interest, or even structured activities under the auspice of a specific program aimed at mentoring. We also mentor unconsciously, or by omission, by just being around a child. Children watch to learn how they should or could be as they evolve into adulthood. Even though we may not purposely influence a child's growth in specified ways, the mere fact that they watch how we think, what we say, and what we do creates an unspoken mentoring relationship that influences a child's life.

Both mentoring by commission and omission can help a child manifest the beauty of their potential to. When we mentor by commission, we know with certainty that we are exposing children certain ideas and concepts that can propel their lives towards success. Yet, when we mentor by omission, we are leaving children's opportunities for maximizing their life, gifts, and purpose to chance. As one who has practiced both forms of mentoring, I recommend mentoring of the conscious variety. I've seen the difference it can make. It can turn a lost child into a living pearl of wisdom who adds immeasurable wealth to our society. If this were done for all children, imagine the beauty and joy that would be ushered into our world.

Following is the story of Coach James Livingston (known by many as Coach J) and the Morrow High School Mustang Men's Basketball team. From 2002-05, I had the opportunity to serve as study hall tutor, ninth grade head basketball coach, and varsity head assistant coach of the Mustangs. The account of Coach J and his ability to inspire coaches and student-athletes to achieve at an optimum level is an account of a master mentor at work. Accounts, such as the one that follows, take place every day in our country. They can and will become more commonplace when more of us decide to dedicate our lives to uplifting young men we encounter on a daily basis.

Coach J and His Band of Gentleman

"The I must die, so that We can win." This was the mantra of Coach J—head coach of the Morrow High School Mustangs Men's Basketball Team. Coach J was not your average basketball coach. In many ways, he was not your average person. For him, teaching the skills of the game of basketball came secondary to molding young boys into men. He understood the game of basketball extremely well and possessed the gift of teaching it equally as well. Yet, Coach J firmly believed and always shared, "Coaching the skills is the easy part of coaching. Coaching the mindsets and attitudes of players . . . now that's the real challenge." He always stressed to his coaching staff and players that every thing the team did—from practice, to games, to summer camps and summer practices—was meant to build and mold the character of men. He felt that without the development of character and the growth of boys into manhood, none of the athletic success mattered. Without strong players, the number of games won and lost counted for nothing.

During his own personal journey, he'd been an artist, a professional athlete, a budding theologian, and a head coach. And through his life experience, he'd developed into a philosopher and he readily—sometimes to his players' chagrin—shared his philosophies openly with his players. Actually, they received a steady dose of philosophy along with his extensive knowledge of the game of basketball. Coach J often told his players, "Your participation in the basketball program represents people who've built a legacy of excellence. But the legacy of excellence you build has to be not only on the court, but in the classroom, at home, and in your community, as well." With the help of his dedicated staff, Coach J's players bought into his philosophy. They listened. They learned, and they built a legacy of excellence that would revolutionize the life of every player to wear a Morrow Mustang uniform.

During coach's tenure at Morrow High, nearly every student who came into the program and remained in the basketball program until his senior year graduated on time. Rarely have students been declared ineligible because of grades or behavioral missteps. (During my four-year association with the team, only one varsity player out the nearly 40 players we coached was declared ineligible for a portion of any season. That particular young man was able to return to the team the next year and remained in good academic standing the entire year). The team's overall GPA was always at least a B, and during his tenure as head coach, twelve players earned collegiate athletic scholarships.

Many of the former Morrow High School players often visit the school and check on Coach J, the staff, and the current players. Some of the former players still live and work in the city. Others live out of town and in other countries. Yet whenever they have the opportunity, they stop by and thank Coach J for his work and encourage the younger players to listen to the guidance and admonition of their coaches. They also encouraged current players to uphold the traditions of academic and athletic excellence of the Mustangs. Coach J's tenure has been marked by extreme success. The Mustangs have made the state playoffs during eight of his ten years as head coach. These trips to the state playoffs include a Final Four appearance, two Sweet Sixteen appearances, two regional tournament championships, and a regular season regional championship. Ironically, Coach J, his staff, and his former players never talk about things like championships when they address current players. The only things they spoke of were having strong character as human beings and strong characters as basketball players. The rest, they always said, would take care of itself. By looking at the excellence displayed by the students who encountered Coach J and his staff of assistants, the rest does take care of itself, and a foundation of achievement that inspires and motivates young men to seek to better men has become the normal order of the day.

Coach J is not merely a coach. He is a master mentor who imparts in his student-athletes a spirit of excellence, an understanding of purpose, and a desire to think, dream, and be the absolute best. Coach J chooses his assistants carefully and makes sure that part of their mission in life is helping young people reach their full potential as human beings. Both he and his assistants become heroes and fathers to some. What they do is life enhancing and life affirming. They tap into the wealth of the human spirit living in every child they encounter and bring this wealth to the forefront in meaningful and tangible ways. And by doing so, they help create a perpetual cycle of self-worth and achievement that will last a lifetime. Coach J and his staff realize that young men they encounter come into this world knowing how to move and breathe, yet they need guidance in molding and shaping their minds in order that they might get the most out of life. We can do the same in our communities through volunteering to mentor at our places of worship, schools, community centers, and civic organizations. The tangible results will help set or keep a young man on a course yielding a lifetime of success.

- There are times when you are to serve as seed sower and others when you are to serve as harvest reaper. Remain attuned to the movement of life that you may work effectively both in times of sewing and reaping.

Before a farmer sows seed, he or she first tills the soil. In this process of tilling the soil, the farmer makes sure that the soil has been cleared of debris that might prevents seeds from firmly rooting in the soil. They clear the land of weeds and rocks and all things of the like that might hinder proper growth of the seed. They then make sure that the soil has been rowed properly so that seeds will have a place to grow. Then afterward, they sow seeds. Eventually, the seed takes root and grows. Both the farmer and nature water the soil. Sunlight also touches the soil, causing further growth. As the year passes, the harvest steadily manifests. Throughout this process, the farmer monitors growth but has no true idea how fruitful the harvest will actually be. Though the farmer can use past years as indicators of harvest, they must take a literal walk of faith each year new seeds are sown. They must work diligently with nature, to provide opportunities for the crop to grow and fulfill its destiny.

A child's mind is analogous to the soil the farmer tills. His mind is ripe for cultivation. A mentor serves as a tiller of a young man's mental soil by clearing the mind of the weeds and debris. Through the relationship with a mentor, the mentee learns to discard erroneous information and ill-conceived self-concepts. A mentor helps that same young man arrange his mind into rows of disciplined, clear thought where seeds of positive self-concept and ideas germane to success can be planted. He helps this young man plant the seeds of success fro which he's dreamed. The mentor guides and encourages during drought or plenty, and he keeps the young man he mentors focused on the fact that expanded self-worth, a realization of gifts and talents, and the discovery of one's mission and purpose are key to a life that is filled with both satisfying and enriching harvests.[1,2,3,5,6,7]

In the summer of 2003, I had the opportunity to experience the power of seed sewing and harvest in the life of a young child. In May of that year, I received an email from Sonia Solomon, a former colleague. The email was in reference to her son Dorian's graduation. She wanted to invite me to share in this special occasion with Dorian and their family. Sonia and I had worked together as teachers at Stephenson Middle School in Stone Mountain, Georgia. The year before she joined the Stephenson staff, I had the privilege of serving as language arts instructor for her son Dorian. At the time, Dorian was like many African American eighth grade males I'd encountered. He was trying to find his way through adolescence, trying to listen to more wisdom of his parents than the words of his peers, and trying to walk that fine line between being the cool kid who did just enough to get by and the un-cool kid who showed off his high level of intelligence. His language arts grade and overall grades at this point were average. Yet his potential bespoke of a young man who was far above average intelligence and academic proficiency.

Sonia requested that Dorian be placed with our team of teachers because we had a reputation for working well with all of our students, and I had a reputation of success with young African American males. Sonia was a master teacher in her own right. So I must admit that I felt a little pressure having her son in my class. But I ignored the feelings of pressure and gave him my all as a teacher and mentor.

Each day Dorian entered my classroom, I reminded him of his inherent greatness. I did so by applauding him when he performed well, pushing him (and showing him how) to do better when he missed the mark, and by making sure that I reminded him (as I did with all other students I encountered) that education must be used as a pathway to holistic success in life. Holistic success means using education to develop the intellect, heart, and soul. Holistic success means that education will lead to discovering not just one's occupation but one's mission in life. Holistic success means that, eight hours a day for 180 days in a year, school would be used as a vehicle to develop tools utilized in achieving lifelong success.

After Dorian had been in my class for a couple of months, I noticed that the proverbial light seemed to turn on in his mind. I witnessed his evolution as a student and as a human being. His shyness, in terms of displaying intellectual prowess, began to wane. He began to feel comfortable in his individual skin. His grades continued to rise in my class and in other classes, as well. He also blossomed socially and became the cool kid who got good grades. Dorian graduated high school with honors and he attended Florida A&M University.

In using my classroom as a mentoring vehicle, I was able to see young people like Dorian make monumental strides towards actualizing their potential. In Dorian's case, I was only one of many people who poured goodness into his life. He was reared by a loving mother and father and had a support system that is lacked by many African American boys. And I was one of four dedicated teachers he saw on a daily basis. The reason I share his story, as one of my personal testimonies as it relates to mentoring, is because when Dorian left my class at the end of the year, his mother made a point to tell me the difference I'd made in his life. She wanted me to know that there was a spark living in him that was not ignited until our encounter in the classroom. And I had to take this mother's thoughts and words for what they were—confirmation that I'd made a difference that would help lead a child to success.

Some may read this story about Dorian and say, "Well, he had a support group. What about children who don't? He also had a nuclear family in tact. What about those who don't?" The fact that Dorian had a strong nuclear family and a group of caring adults who dedicate time to helping him be successful does not dilute the effects of mentoring. It actually illustrates exactly why it's important to form support groups that nurture success around all young African American men regardless of whether they come from the traditional nuclear family, single parent family, or are without family at all. The support group spurs achievement. It gives focus. It under girds the foundation of young men searching for identity and meaning in their lives. And it helps young men find that identity and meaning in ways that yield positive, reoccurring benefits. And for every Dorian who had a nuclear family in tact, I've encountered a John or Carlos or Malik who had a disjointed nuclear family but also had a mentor or mentors who invested time in their lives. In most cases, time invested yielded results that made the lives of these young men more fulfilling. It turned would-be sad stories into stories of triumph and achievement. Whether they were young men in juvenile detention centers who decide to leave lives of crime and become high school and college graduates, young men who decide that academic success is the only option, or young men who had bright ideas about how to live their lives in a creative and prosperous way but simply needed proper guidance to do so, I've witnessed mentors help them move toward the actualization of their dreams. I've seen firsthand that the sewing and harvesting of dreams when dream sewers and dream harvesters play their respective roles in helping a young man's mind become a fertile field of right thinking, right living, and bountiful achievement.

- I am because we are. Because we are I am. I can do nothing without you. You can do nothing without me. We are one.

We live in a world where individual beliefs, actions, and concerns affect not only our individual existence but also that of the collective world. What happens to the doctor affects the lawyer; what happens to the custodial worker affects the high-level executive; what happens to rich affects the poor; and what happens to my neighbor affects me. For the mind that struggles to grasp this concept, think of the parents who lost a child because of someone else's reckless behavior or the family spared tragedy because of the heroic actions of a kind bystander. In every aspect of life, truths and realities of our individual world are affected by the world at large and vice versa. Though the effect is sometimes indirect, this reality plays a tremendous role in shaping our children's lives. Mentors, by intuition or by experience, grow to understand this interconnected nature of the world. They understand how this interconnectedness or lack thereof affects the growth and develop of the children they mentor. They use their time, gifts, and talents to infuse life into their community by making positive, life affirming connections with the young people they encounter and others who are committed to mentoring African American males.

I had the opportunity to work with Mr. Lamont Littlejohn during my first training session for teachers at NCCAT. At the time, Lamont was a high school history teacher and he had been running a mentoring project, The Distinguished Gentlemen's Program, for African American males for the past three years. What was exciting about Lamont's program is that he had data based on the end of year test scores to prove how successful the program was in raising academic performance and closing the Black-white test score gap. Another amazing feature of the program was the process by which it was introduced to Black males at the high school. "I was determined that the school year was going to be different for Black boys at my school and that creating a mentoring program was the means to reach some of them that needed help. The big challenge for me was that I didn't want the program introduced with the usual negative baggage and failure expectation that is associated with programs to help Black boys with their academic development," passionately explains Lamont. That was back in the summer of 1997 before Lamont embarked on the adventure to create the "Distinguished Gentlemen's Mentoring" program for Kings Mountain High School.

Like many schools across the country, Black males at Kings Mountain were scoring substantially lower on every measure of academic achievement and the graduation rates lagged behind all other ethnic and racial groups. Five years later, however, the situation had changed, and Black males not only outscore all other students at school on the states standardized end of grade assessments, but their scores exceeded the states average scores for all students. What made this possible wasn't some new way to teach or more vigilant attention to academic skills or tutoring, but the establishment of a compassionate and trusting relationship between the boys and their mentor, Lamont Littlejohn, Jr.

Littlejohn created the mentoring program exclusively for Black boys and the program paired them up with the few available Black teachers to give the students extra help. Sounds like a good plan to me. In fact, it sounded like such a good plan that Littlejohn was baffled about why it didn't have the support of all of the teachers. In fact, when you consider the fact that a high percentage of Black males drop out of school in comparison to other groups, then it is difficult to believe that any educators would argue against creating a program that could possibly help Black boys in the future. "At times I could not believe that some teachers thought that having a mentoring program solely for Black boys would have a negative impact on the self-esteem of the boys. But after thinking about everything, I started to understand that their concerns were similar to my own. No one wanted a program where Black boys felt isolated or stigmatized," explains Lamont.

With these concerns in mind, Lamont convinced the principal and teachers at his school that he needed to have a pre-launching or advertisement period to get all the students interested in the program. He also insisted that there would be no mention that the program would only include Black males. The program started, at the beginning of the school year, with weekly and sometimes daily, announcements about a new, exciting, and distinguished mentoring program for boys who had to be nominated by a teacher to enter the program. The students leaned about the after school activities, ways to earn extra money after school, weekend trips, and summer fun that were scheduled for the participants. After several weeks of these positive announcements, there was a run in period of three days where the announcements were intensified to let the students know that the program, Distinguished Gentlemen, was about to select its first nominations. "There was so much excitement about the program. It seems like every boy at school was wondering whether they would be offered a membership in the program. What they didn't know is that we had targeted boys who had not performed well on the previous year's end of grade tests. None of the boys had a clue about this, but many of their classmates were envious about their invitation. I remember the amazement on the faces of that first group of boys as they looked around at each other as if to say they could not believe they had been nominated for the program," explains Lamont.

During our time together at NCCAT Lamont presented data based on his work. I remember how impressed I was the first time I saw data from this young man who had created a mentoring program that was so powerful that Black boys were now outperforming all other students at their school. Lamont didn't have a chance to complete his presentation before the questions started—How is this possible? Were the boys from the gifted program? Did the program include only those boys who wanted to excel and do better in their schoolwork? How did you force the boys to do the work? How much tutoring and extra work did they do in order to do so well?

Lamont, being the gentle soul that he is, put the teachers at ease as he explained to them that the boys were students who were not doing well in school. He explained the "run-in" and marketing process for creating a positive image for the program. Lamont also told the teachers that he thought the relationship he established with the boys was probably the most important factors in their academic success. "Rather than assume that the boys only needed tutoring, we placed our faith on the strength of the reasons the boys had for wanting to be a part of the program. Most of the boys were capable of doing better, but most teachers didn't believe in them and they ended up making the poor grades that everyone expected. My main goal was to show them that I cared and to help them set higher standards for their own school work." Although the mentoring program provided several academic enhancement activities after school, each participant signed a contract agreeing to maintain a certain grade point average and to adhere to the rule of the program. They also understood that Lamont would be receiving weekly reports from their teachers about their classroom behavior.

As you can imagine, the program didn't start without there being a few problems. There was the issue of "release time" where the principal had to give permission for Lamont to be released from teaching one of his courses in order to visit the classes of the students in the program. "My principal understood that the program couldn't be successful without this support and so he gave me his blessings. For most of the boys, all I did was acknowledge them when I collected progress reports from the teachers. The boys never knew exactly when I would come by and I think this contributed to them being more focused because they wanted to please me by being attentive in class."

A more pressing issue that Lamont had to deal with was the concerns that some teachers, including Black teachers, didn't like the idea of signaling out Black boys for the program. For example, upon hearing about the plans for the program, several teachers reasoned, "it is a form of racial profiling in the public school system. What they're doing here, under the guise of helping more Black boys, is they're singling them out and making them feel inferior or different simply because of their race and gender." This was precisely the attitude that Lamont wanted to avoid. All you would need to determine how well Lamont anticipated and dealt with this issue is look at the number of boys, both Blacks and whites, who wanted to get into the program. "I was utterly amazed that a program that started out to have only twenty boys had over sixty who wanted to be part of things. So rather than limit the program to twenty boys, we decided to increase the number to forty, but during the first year we only included Black males," explains Lamont.

Rather than give-in to the pressures against starting the program, Lamont created a mentoring program for Black boys that eventually became so successful and popular that it typically had more boys, including white males, wanting memberships than there were available spots. By the third year, the program started accepting white males and then something happened that nobody anticipated; jealousy from the girls and female teachers started some heated debates about whether there was a need for a similar mentoring program for girls. Eventually a mentoring program for girls was started, but from the beginning memberships was available to all girls regardless of their ethnicity/race.

There is so much talk about the Black-white difference in test scores these days that most educators believe that Black children, particularly boys, don't stand a chance of performing as well as their white peers. I remember being as mesmerized as the teachers were by Lamont's presentation, and from the look on some of their faces, I could tell that they did not believe what they were looking at either. As is the typical case at NCCAT, most of the teachers were white females, but of all the seminars they could choose from, they had selected to attend a seminar to learn about ways to motivate and teach Black boys. Furthermore, the teachers who participated in this particular seminar also agreed to attend with the principal or assistant principal from their school or another member of their schools' academic improvement team. Consequently, one would assume that most of the teachers were at least open to the possibility of learning about programs purporting to show how Black boys could improve upon their academic performance, but this was not the case. From the looks on their faces and their questions, it was easy to see they did not believe it was possible for a group of Black boys to outperform all other students at their school and score higher than the state averages in most subjects.

As recently as three generations ago, many people lived in communities where the idea that love and respect for our selves and the world around us mattered more than anything else that pervaded social consciousness. There were neighborhoods and schools, although racially segregated and socially independent from one another, were comprised of extended families that enforced this ideal. Neighborhoods existed where the father of each family on the block was the father for all children on the block. Neighborhoods existed where the mother of each family in the cul-de-sac was considered the mother of all children in the cul-de-sac. Black children attending schools often had outdated textbooks that rarely mentioned anything about Black culture, but their teachers were leaders of the community who made sure that children understood the value of education and the contributions of their people to the fabric of life. There were elders in these segregated Black communities who were watchpersons. They could give mothers, fathers, and school teachers sound guidance about important decisions concerning family and community. They could correct children when they were out of line or out of place. From this environment grew self and community respect that said to every Black child: My behavior affects the entire community. It said, When I commit actions detrimental to my well being, I am harming not only myself and reputation, but also that of my entire community. An atmosphere of personal and communal self-worth permeated the actions of those living in the community. This self-worth provided interconnectedness and motivated Black boys to excel in school because education was the doorway to freedom and for becoming a leader.

The mindset of communal responsibility at one time propelled the success of our nation. Though suffering because of its shameful past treatment of Black people, our nation had to foster the ideal that self-sufficiency and community empowerment of all people had to be linked together as closely as breathing and oxygen. This is another one of the key points experientially or intuitively understood by mentors, regardless of their own ethnicity, race or gender. They understand that Black children must be given the blueprints of self-sufficiency, community interconnectedness, and personal and social responsibility in order to build successful lives. When this is done, Black children are empowered by legacies of communal sufficiency, growth, and achievement that serve as stimuli for the dreams, goals, and legacies they will build. Every Black child we encounter may one day be our leaders in education, government, business, and social activism or the young adult who will marry our sons and daughters. They might provide the missing knowledge for sustaining life on another planet or that piece of technology for running an automobile engine for 1,000 miles on a gallon of gasoline or vegetable oil. And their destinies can be influenced profoundly by the roles we decide to play in their lives and our ability to transcend the race and social status of all children we teach.

The following story illustrates why mentoring is not only important in cultivating the destinies of our children but also important to the future success of society as a whole. The story illustrates why it's important for teachers—regardless of their race, ethnicity or gender—to transcend all divisions between themselves and the students they have been entrusted to teach. It illustrates why self-sufficiency and community empowerment are inextricably linked. One cannot exist without the other, as both are essential in each other's proper functioning.

The Sacred Breath

In a time and space where life evolved in patterns similar to the ones that dictate the lives we live, there was a pristine planet. The planet thrived with lush, verdant fields, life giving waters, and air so pure that to breathe was to experience ecstasy. Yet as time passed and the mores of its inhabitants changed, the once vibrant world began to die. Its land began losing the ability to sustain life. Its waters, rather than being ponds and streams of healing and nourishment, became cesspools. The air that once invigorated life forms of all kinds now usher impurities into the very heart and soul of beings it formerly sustained.

The people of this formerly vibrant world were also near extinction. Although technologically advanced, nothing within this people's power could be used to save their planet or themselves. The power and ingenuity that fueled their most advanced machines had been rendered impotent in the fight to help their world sustain itself. Eons of under appreciating and living in ignorance and disdain of the life force that sustain their planet had come back to haunt this people. And now their only option was to wait for extinction and bide the time until no one and no place filled with life existed on the planet. Many of their leaders had seen this time approaching, and, for years, they had searched for solutions but failed. Now, on the brink of extinction, they were beginning to consider the possibility that their search for solutions failed because of their inability to trust and respect others who were different from themselves.

One day, the Elders assembled the people of this dying world together in a final effort to salvage both hope and life. They reverted to the ways of the Elders whom they called the Ancient of Ancients. These Elders were Priest-Kings who held the belief that their world had been created by a benevolent Spirit who they called the Maker of the Universe. They believed that the Maker caused every living being to animate with life. They believe that the Maker created destiny and could change destiny if the Maker so chose. With all hope lost, the Elders had assembled the people together in order to ask that each soul earnestly pray to the Maker of the Universe for help. Nothing in their own power could save them. Though there was some doubt in the people's heart, they still greatly revered the Elders and trusted their judgment. If the Elders were advising that the people enact the ritual of prayer as their last resort, the people of this planet did as they were asked. They prayed with purpose, clarity of vision, and the sincere hope that their prayer would be answered. And miraculously, almost instantly, their prayers were answered. Just as people began to open their eyes at the close of their prayer, a portal opened in the sky. Through this portal emerged the most beautiful, radiant beings anyone on the planet had ever seen. These beings were aglow with a golden, bluish light as brilliant as their twin suns. Yet the light was not blinding to the eye. In fact, it seemed to strengthen all who gazed upon it and allowed them to see more clearly how vastly different each being appeared. Its rays penetrated into their being bringing a mixture of peace, awe, and anticipation.

As the radiant beings descended, initially, there was silence. Then there were loud shouts of praise and thanks to the Maker of the Universe for sending these beings who many hoped would be the answer to the prayers to save this dying world. The people of this planet believed that the Maker of the Universe answered prayers. The legends passed down by the Ancient of Ancients said that when the Maker answered prayers, emissaries of light were used to accomplish the task to be performed. The beings now in their presence were filled with luminous light that caused the differences in their appearances to vanish.

As the people of the dying world celebrated, the minutes seemed like hours. Anticipation pulsed through the crowd. The radiant visitors simply stood silently as the people jumped about. They were observing and appeared as if they were smiling. Finally, one of the visitors approached the assembly of Elders and the crowd began to hush. As silenced finally prevailed, to everyone's amazement, he spoke in the dying planet's language.

The visitor introduced him self as Kana. He and his companions were former residents of the planet Inspirar. He explained to the Elders and the people of the dying world that he and his companions were interstellar nomads. Their home planet was located in a galaxy several light years away. He explained how the inhabitants of his planet had heard the cries of the people of this planet and felt compelled to assist them in avoiding the catastrophe they now faced. Shouts of joy and jubilation went out from the crowd. The visitor continued, explaining that the culture of his planet differed from many of the planets in the universe. He said that it even differed from the culture of this people he and his companions now proposed to help. While other planets live by a cultural mindset of stark divisions by race and ethnicity and survival of the fittest—with weak succumbing to the strong, Black people feeling inferior to whites, and individuals of various ethnic origins and nations engaging in constant conflict because no one feels that he or she has enough—he explained that the culture of Inspirar was based solely on the principles of love and sharing. Every action of every Inspirarian was based on these principles. It was for this reason that they answered the prayers of this dying world.

Kana further explained that Inspirarians were not bound by space or time. They could be everywhere or anywhere in an instant. That is how they came to the aid of this world so quickly. Because of the nomadic heritage of the Inspirarians, no one from the planet stayed on their home planet forever. From their day of birth, their children are cultured in rituals meant to bring Inspirarians into full maturity. Once they reach maturity, they leave their world never to return. This was not a sad thing, for they left their world to pursue their mission. The mission of every Inspirarian was to spread the gift of life. They truly believed that no being in the universe could live without the help of another. Their only law was simply to adhere to the dictum "I am because we are.

Because we are, I am. I can do nothing without you. You can do nothing without me. We are One."

Sometimes the Inspirarians landed on dying planets like this one. Other times they landed on developing planets that were at the crossroads of becoming true civilization or becoming a tale of destruction. Still, there were other times, and these times, Kana said, were a favorite of his people. When they met, entire planets of people ready to truly live as elevated beings. The Inspirarians gave them the gift of life to make this possible.

The head Elder asked Kana to explain this gift of life and how it works. Kana proceeded. The gift of life was a thing the Inspirarians called the "sacred breath." It was a special gift that could not be forced upon anyone. It had to be willingly accepted. To share the sacred breath, the Inspirarians first had to concentrate on being completely filled with love and light-which for them took a matter of only seconds. After being filled, they would simply embrace the being nearest to them without any hesitancy about their race, ethnicity or social class and blow the sacred breath into that being. Once this was done, the sacred breath was passed and the life of that being sustained and enhanced another. It was beautiful and life affirming ritual, yet it had to occur every eight hours of each day or every Inspirarian would die. Once this gift was given to other beings, they had to follow the sacred breath ritual or, they, too, would perish. It was for this reason that the entire Inspararian culture was based on love and sharing.

After this explanation, Kana expressed to the Elders that he knew that the Elders and their people might need time to discuss whether or not they would embark upon this new journey, this new way of life. But before he could finish his sentence, cries of "We accept" arose from the assembly and from the Elders themselves. This cry continued until it reached a fevered pitch. Kana and his fellow Inspirarians moved toward the inhabitants of this world and began to extend themselves in light and love. And with that, a dying planet was reborn and a dying people received the gift of life

> as they embraced not only the Inspirarians but their belief:
> I am because we are. Because we are, I am. I can do nothing
> without you. You can do nothing without me. We are One.

Children's lives are inextricably tied to the roles adults play as nurturers, caretakers, and leaders. Our purpose as nurturers, caretakers, and leaders are inextricably tied to how we treat our children. Just as Kana and his companions, in the preceding anecdote, devoted their lives to sharing the gift of life and pouring the sacred breath into all they encountered, every adult in every community on the planet must show this same devotion in sharing the gift of life and pouring sacred breath into each and every child on this planet. This sacred breath is the time spent nurturing children's emotions, intellects, and spirits. It is in the cultivation of their ideas, dreams, and goals. It is actively creating communities that will serve as vehicles through which children build legacies where love of self, love of family, and love of community are encapsulated and released in thought, word, and deed.

The concept, actions, and results of effective mentoring can change the world if we let it. When this oneness of purpose—the purpose of elevating children to attain possessions of riches and glory living inside their being—comes into realization, a power arises that makes children's hopes, dreams, and realities synonymous. The actualizations of their success becomes unlimited, and the mission of mentoring moves one step closer to bringing what Kana calls true civilization into our midst—that is, a civilization where every human being lives to their full potential.

Each time I'm asked to speak on mentoring or conduct a mentoring training, people ask the question, "How do I become a mentor?" Listed below, you will find 21 "How To" Mentoring Tips. The tips are not static rules meant to be followed in a regimented fashion. Rather, they are flexible guidelines that can be used to point you in the right direction. They are practical guides to help you become involved in mentoring. As you read this list of ideas, allow them to seep into your mind and heart and let them compel you to find the time to pour knowledge, wisdom, and guidance, into the life a young man who needs it. You'll be making an investment that ensures a young man's success and his prosperous and dynamic future. Go out and make a difference. Let your journey as a mentor begin.

Tips for Becoming a Mentor

1) Become an active member of a group such as Big Brothers-Big Sisters of America.

2) Volunteer as a mentor at your local schools.

3) Contact the Boys and Girls Club or YMCA and become a volunteer.

4) Mentor a young man in your family or in your neighborhood.

5) Establish meaningful relationships with young men you encounter in places of worship, at the barber shop, in the grocery store, etc.

6) Always have a positive or encouraging word for young men you encounter (even if the encounter is a random one).

7) If you are spiritually inclined, volunteer to mentor young men at your place of worship through study classes, community service activities, or activities designated for youth.

8) Start a formalized mentoring or rites of passage program at community centers or places of worship.

9) Volunteer at community centers or even juvenile detention centers.

10) Partner with a school, faith based, or community based organization to give seminars introducing young men to professional occupations; ways to succeed in school; blueprints for obtaining post secondary education; practicing sexual responsibility in the face of high pregnancy and the age of life threatening STDs; how to become effective managers of their money; cultivating wealth building and entrepreneurial skills, etc.

11) Establish a mentoring initiative through social clubs, professional organizations, or fraternal orders of which you may be a member.

12) Serve as a volunteer coach at local recreation centers.

13) If you are the father of boys, be actively involved in their school life, social life, and moral/spiritual development.

14) If you are the father of boys, develop, cultivate, and maintain positive lines of communication with your son(s).

15) If you are the uncle, older brother, or cousin of younger men, become actively involved in their school life, social life, and moral/spiritual development.

16) If you are the uncle, older brother, or cousin of younger men, maintain positive lines of communication with these young men.

17) Start a "Boys to Men" book club or discussion group. (Use the club or group as a platform to cover issues related to the journey from boyhood to

manhood. You can invite speakers or experts to conduct workshops and talks on issues relevant to manhood).

18) Encourage other responsible men to become mentors.

19) Be a source of support for single mothers and fathers raising young sons.

20) Don't complain about the problems plaguing young, African American males unless you are willing to lend a hand in being part of the solution.

21) Believe that mentors make a difference and decide to help make a difference through mentoring.

Final Points to Remember:

- Mentoring is not static and regimented. Find out what your mentee(s) need and simply seek to provide it.
- As a mentor, sometimes you are a seed sewer. The harvest may be reaped by someone else at a later time.
- Children inherently seek guidance and acceptance. They will either find it at home, in the school, in places of worship, and places where positive mentors or role models are present or they will find it through gangs or through affiliation with friends who delve into drugs, apathy, and alcohol. They need positive mentors and role models. We must decide which path we're going to allow our children to follow!

11

Why We Must Encourage African American Males to Become Financially Literate Entrepreneurs

By Winston Sharpe and The Champions for Peace Mastermind
Institute

Introduction

There is an old proverb that tells the story of a young Black man who
had lost his way in life, ruined relationships with his family and friends,
and lived on the streets begging for coins to feed himself. Rumor has it
that the company he worked for abruptly downsized and he was one of
the first people fired. He was the sole breadwinner for his wife and two
children who had moved in with relatives to be safe from his angry and
drunken outbursts after losing their eight bedroom home to foreclosure.
Some say he was brilliant and creative but lacked financial intelligence. He
agreed to refinance the home loan on his mortgage, nearly doubling his
monthly payments. He paid for everything with credit cards that charged
outrageous interest rates, and he only paid the minimum due at the end

of the month. He once took elaborate trips to exotic places and bought expensive gifts for his friends, but those days were long gone. With no savings to depend on, he felt like a man standing at the edge of a cliff with raging bulls headed his way. He was alone with nowhere to go and no means to support himself. On most days, he thought death would be an improvement in comparison to how he was currently living.

Day after day, he sat alone holding a tin can with his grimy hands hoping that people passing by would have some compassion and give him a few coins for his next meal. On most days, he sat for hours before his collection of coins was enough for a meal. But one day, early in the morning, a man of great financial means saw the beggar on the street and stopped to talk with him. The wealthy man asked a simple, but powerful, question "Would you prefer that I give you a few fish to eat or teach you how to fish?" The young man, shocked by the attention of this well-dressed man, didn't know what to say. Slowly, the young man replied in a soft, timid voice, "Sir, if you have some fish, I would love some, and if you can show me how to catch my own fish, I will be forever grateful to you for such kindness. But, sir, I need some food now."

Chances are that you have not experienced the frustration, shame, and humiliation that come with this type of situation. It is possible, however, that you know of someone who has been in a similar situation, someone with everything going wrong for him and none of the right connections with people of influence who could open doors to a better life. With the sudden changes in the housing market, lack of available credit, and the fragile world banking situation, chances are pretty good that you know someone who has experienced a sudden change in their economic status because the job they depended on for their income no longer exists or the person had to take a pay cut to continue with the company. Today, as you read these pages, this is the situation for many people, many of them smart and well educated, who believe that their job should be the sole source of their income. Today, it is becoming increasingly clear that having multiple sources of income, as is the case for entrepreneurs, might be more favorable.

This chapter is the product of Winston Sharpe, formerly an assistant vice president of FHA Collections and Loss Mitigation at Wells Fargo Home Mortgage, and some of the men, many of whom are successful entrepreneurs, who have contributed other chapters to the book. While we all believe it is best to teach a man how to fish for his own food, we offer you the perspective that it's best to teach Black boys how to have their own pond so that they can fish anytime they choose. We believe it is crucial for the next generation to use principles of cooperative economics to build and maintain businesses that benefit the Black family, our communities, and our nation. If we do not show African American males the secrets to wealth and business ownership, then some of them are likely to cost us $20,000 to $40,000 a year (our tax dollars at work) while they are incarcerated. The choice is simple: I would rather have a productive global citizen walking the streets than a person with limited education and financial means who could potentially bring harm to me or my family and friends. Entrepreneurs are global citizens who bridge the gap between their communities and the world. They are catalysts for producing jobs, creating wealth, and stimulating economies around the world. United by the power of ideas, they are creating new industries and growing strong economies for a brighter future.

The Meaning Of Entrepreneurship

Entrepreneurship is the practice of starting new organizations or revitalizing mature organizations, particularly new businesses, generally in response to identified opportunities.[1,2,3,4] Entrepreneurship is often a difficult undertaking, as a vast majority of new businesses fail. Entrepreneurial activities are substantially different depending on the type of organization that is being started. Entrepreneurship ranges in scale from solo projects (e.g., selling cookie or posters at a flee market) to major undertakings that create many job opportunities, such as what is happening in Hip hop, multimedia, and internet based businesses.

Entrepreneurship is often associated with true uncertainty, particularly when it involves bringing something into a previously unknown market. Before the Internet, nobody knew the market for Internet-related businesses such as Amazon, Google, YouTube, Yahoo, etc. Only after the Internet emerged did people begin to see opportunities and market in that technology. And as you read these pages, something similar is happening as far as economic viability of "green" jobs are concerned. There was a small interest in recycling and the impact of pollution on the planet, but then former Vice President Al Gore introduced us the *An Inconvenient Truth*, a film that makes the compelling case that global warming is real, man-made, and its effects will be cataclysmic if we don't act now. The evidence is undeniable, and the vast majority of scientists agree that global warming is the result of our activities and not a natural occurrence. What's also undeniable is the number of new business opportunities that are being created to address global warming. In addition, what the future holds for this emerging industry resides solely with the creativity and desire of young entrepreneurs to carve out a niche for themselves.

Global warming, rising fuel prices, and the rise in job loss seems to be on everyone's mind and on the front page of the news. But instead of letting it consume your life or that of Black males, do something unique in your classroom. Encourage your students to consider having a green career that focuses on the well-being of the environment and poses practical solutions to those problems for businesses and local residents alike.

The Green Jobs Act was signed into law in December 2007. Since then, various green job organizations have been fighting to secure federal funding for green job training. The great news today is that Congress passed the final version of the Economic Recovery Bill. And guess what? $500 million for green job training is included in the package.[5]

What Types of Jobs Are Available for Green Entrepreneurs?

Many green entrepreneurs might already know a great deal about the industry, and some become consultants to share their own knowledge and skills. If you don't have the experience to dive into a successful business, you can get ahead by offering your services for free to friends and colleagues in exchange for a reference or referral. It will also help work out any kinks in your business before taking it mainstream.

Encourage your students (or children) to consider applying for jobs at green businesses to gain an insider's perspective and make a name for themselves in their community. Teach them how to entice future clients by donating their own time to green projects and national organizations.

President Barack Obama has discussed plans for a national service plan for young people to earn money for college by volunteering at community organizations.[6] Encourage your students to seek out green businesses that are participating in this program. And remember to help your students understand that being an entrepreneur, even a green one, is a business that requires hard work and the day-to-day managing of marketing, books, finances, and ongoing education to stay on top of new development. While there are many emerging industries where green jobs will be developed, we believe that the following represent the top ten green jobs for entrepreneurs.

Solar Energy—Know something about solar energy or someone who does? Invite these individuals to give presentations at your school. If you don't have access to someone who knows about the complexity of the topic, put together your own presentation and information on the benefits of solar power. If you are looking to earn extra money (like most teachers and parents), consider approaching solar businesses and inquire about work as an independent consultant or sales representative.

Rooftop Landscape Designer—Many cities showcase ingenious rooftop gardens to cut down on cooling and heating costs within the building. The gardens can serve as a natural cooling mechanism and shade on even the most blistering days. If you've got students who are interested in gardening, encourage them to research rooftop gardens, study models, and contact local designers to be a mentor. There might even be a space at your school for students to try their own hand at creating a rooftop garden.

Green Infopreneur—Even in today's society where global warming and environmental issues are a major focus in the media, many don't know where to start to do their part. There is a growing need to have young people design brochures, booklets, e-books, guide books, and describe speaking engagements to help communities take a step toward green living. I bet there are some talented Black males at your school who could create an effective booklet that offers lists of easy things people can do around their home to go green. The booklet could also list shops and restaurants in the area that adhere to environmental standards, keep tabs on recycling plants, and offer breaking news on the latest products and trends, and more. Having students sell those booklets could be a great way for a school to raise funds to make up for losses due to budget cuts.

Green Travel—Consumers are confused by how their carbon footprint will be affected by how far they travel. Several business have been started that cater to green travelers by offering carbon calculators, links to reputable carbon offset websites, and customized green itineraries. Green travel companies would also offer their clients suggestions on green hotels, activities, and transportation. These new green travel companies are likely to work with chambers of commerce and tourism boards to devise plans to attract green travelers.

Farmer's Markets—Some people residing in urban areas have started their own Farmers Markets as a result of their frustration at trying to find fresh produce. In most cases, these businesses have proven to be wildly successful and respected, especially for residents who wanted to buy locally and organically grown produce that are pesticide-free. If this is something you are interested in doing, start by contacting your local courthouse or city hall to find out how to get started. Choose a location, make an announcement for vendors, and start organizing. And make sure that you use vendors that are willing to provide opportunities for young people to earn extra money working on weekends.

Organic Chef—It is apparent to all of us that chefs are very different from ordinary cooks, and the typical chef makes a good living. Organic chefs are in a class all by themselves and in high demand—not just for their flavorful food but for their ability to identify environmentally friendly and healthy options. When some of you were going to school, there was a course called Home Economics. Now, it is called various names, including Culinary Arts. Invite organic chefs into your school and encourage your students to research the training requirement and job prospects for chefs. If you are a great cook looking to reclassify yourself as a chef, then consider holding presentations in your local recreation center, in your home, or at client's homes. Market your services as not only a chef but also as an educator who teaches others about healthy eating and environmentally friendly methods. Position yourself as an expert and make more money by selling a self-published organic cookbook or seasoning.

Organic Textiles or Clothing—If you love fashion, making clothes, or even knitting, you can start an organic textiles or clothing business. Use only the best in organic materials and peddle your wares from flea markets to boutiques, working your way up the commercial ladder. I bet there are thousands of sewing machines and knitting needles sitting idle across the country. Some of them are located in homes where some extra income could make a tremendous difference. Look into the possibility of using your skills to grow a business and teaching others about the organic textile industry.

Waste Consultant—New business, or old ones trying to revamp their environmental policies, need someone to put a waste system, including recycling, hauling services, and waste reduction, in place. Encourage your students to develop a recycling plan for your school that minimally includes paper products, cardboard boxes, used books, printer ink cartridges, and metal cans. Invite speakers to talk to your classes about how to draft a plan of attack customized for each client's needs.

The Vision of the Entrepreneur

Entrepreneurs share some of the same character traits as good leaders, managers, and administrators who are said to be less methodical and more prone to risk-taking. The entrepreneur must employ a disciplined self leadership approach that also focuses on empowering those that believe in the vision. Influencing clients and employees alike is a key character trait that often makes the difference in whether the entrepreneur succeeds.[1,2,3,4,7,8,9,10,11]

- The entrepreneur has an enthusiastic vision that is a driving force for a enterprise.
- The entrepreneur's vision is usually supported by an interlocked collection of specific ideas not available to the marketplace.
- The overall blueprint to realize the vision is clear; however, details may be incomplete, flexible, and evolving.
- The entrepreneur promotes the vision with passion.
- With persistence and determination, the entrepreneur develops strategies to change the vision into reality.
- The entrepreneur assumes the initial responsibility for making the vision a success.
- Entrepreneurs take prudent risks. They assess costs and market/customer needs, and persuade others to join and help.
- An entrepreneur is usually a positive thinker and a decision maker
- An entrepreneur thinks "out of the box" and seeks creative ways to generate wealth by providing a needed service or product.

The Role of Entrepreneurs

Entrepreneurs dream and their dreams drive the economic engine of the world. Are you a dreamer? Do you dream of freedom, wealth, or of changing the world? Entrepreneurs are people who have made a payroll; people who have known victory and defeat and dreamed their own dreams; people who know how to make dreams become real; and people who can teach you how to make your dreams become real. As we take a look at history, we can see clearly how the roles of entrepreneurs have shaped America and provided civilization with many of the things that we categorize as necessities today. Where would we be without the automobile, the telephone, the personal computer, the traffic light, the guided missile, or peanut butter? All of these inventions were the results of entrepreneurs filling a void and capitalizing on opportunities. In fact, we owe our very existence to the profound and often unnoticed inventions of entrepreneurs. Early entrepreneurs, not unlike Madam C.J. Walker,[11] the first African American female millionaire, created their own markets. As you discuss entrepreneurship with your children, consider the following roles that entrepreneurs play in our modern society and the future growth of our world.[8,9,10]

- Develop new markets. Under the modern concept of marketing, markets are people who are willing and able to satisfy their needs. In economics, this is called effective demand. Entrepreneurs are resourceful and creative. They generate customers or buyers. This makes entrepreneurs different from ordinary businesspersons who only perform traditional functions of management, such as planning, organization, and coordination.

- Discover new sources of materials. Entrepreneurs are never satisfied with traditional or existing sources of materials. Due to their innovative nature, they persist in discovering new sources of materials to improve their enterprises. In business, those who can develop new sources of materials enjoy a comparative advantage in terms of supply, cost, and quality.

- Mobilize capital resources. Entrepreneurs are the organizers and coordinators of the major factors of production, such as land labor and capital. They properly mix these factors of production to create goods and service. Capital resources, from a nonprofessional's view, refer to money. In economics, however, capital resources represent machines, buildings, and other physical productive resources. Entrepreneurs have initiative and self-confidence in accumulating and mobilizing capital resources for new business or business expansion.

- Introduce new technologies, new industries, and new products. Aside from being innovators and reasonable risk-takers, entrepreneurs take advantage of business opportunities and transform these into profits. Therefore, they introduce something new, or different, or exciting that meets the needs of individuals, groups, or communities. Such entrepreneurial spirit has greatly contributed to the modernization of economies. Every year, there are new technologies and new products. All of these are intended to satisfy human needs in more convenient and pleasant ways.

- Create employment. The biggest employer is the private business sector. Millions of jobs are provided by factories, service industries, agricultural enterprises, and small-scale businesses. For instance, super department stores employ thousands of workers. Likewise, giant corporations like IBM, Apple, and SMC are great job creators. Such massive employment has multiplier and accelerator effects in the whole economy. More jobs mean more incomes. This increases demand for goods and services. This stimulates production. Again, more production requires more employment, and more employment means more spending.

Advantages of Entrepreneurship

Every successful entrepreneur benefits not only himself/herself but also the municipality, region, or country as a whole. The benefits that can be derived from entrepreneurial activities are as follows:[12,13,14,15,16]

- Personal financial gain
- Self-employment, offering more job satisfaction and flexibility of the work force
- Employment for others, often in better jobs
- Development of more industries, especially in rural areas or regions disadvantaged by economic changes

- Encouragement of the processing of local materials into finished goods for domestic consumption, as well as for export
- Income generation and increased economic growth
- Healthy competition, which encourages higher quality products
- Increased goods and services around the world
- Development of new markets around the world
- Promotes the use of modern technology in small-scale manufacturing to enhance higher productivity
- Encouragement of more research/studies and development of modern machines and equipment for domestic consumption
- Development of entrepreneurial qualities and attitudes in others to bring about significant changes in the rural areas around the world
- Freedom from the dependency on the jobs offered by others
- The ability to have great accomplishments
- Reduction of the informal economy
- Emigration of talent may be stopped by a better domestic entrepreneurship climate
- Providing future entrepreneurs with disciplined examples of self leadership
- Career satisfaction
- Nepotism

Why It's Important for African American Boys to Own Businesses

In today's economic times, African American boys have to understand the responsibility and commitments that owning their own businesses brings. Many of them need to develop the business acumen, as well as the leadership characteristics needed to manage a successful business.

- Owning your own business helps you control your own economic destiny
- Owning your own business enables you to leave a financial legacy for your children.
- Owning your own business helps you teach your children the virtues of hard work, leadership, long term planning, and personal achievement that is intricately tied to benefiting others.

- Owning your own business helps you create and maintain positive business relationships.
- Owning your own business provides you with a sense of accomplishment and empowerment that translates into community pride and involvement.
- Owning your own business causes you to focus on both short and long-term visions. Everything you do now is done in order to impact your family, your business, and community five to 100 years from now.
- Owning your own business helps you to empower your community because you are able to provide jobs for other people.
- Owning your own business opens doorways to civic leadership. Business owners are important to their communities because of the service, goods, and innovations they provide.
- Owning your own business is an expression of creativity, insight, and leadership that can increase belief in one's self. It is both an inspirational and practical experience of personal growth.

How Do We Encourage Entrepreneurship Among African American Males?

The one thing that is unchanged about children today is that they want access to their own money, but few people are willing to create exciting ways for children to learn about money or to uncover ways for them to become entrepreneurs so that they can earn their own money. To ensure that future entrepreneurs and all students make sound financial decisions as adults, financial education has to become a standard part of the curriculum for all students.

As the economic downturn has spread throughout the United States and many nations around the world, some schools have been looking for strategies to help students deal with the real economic world so that it doesn't overwhelm them after they graduate. A 2008 survey of personal financial literacy of high school seniors showed that students scored an average of 47.5 percent (according to the Jump$tart Coalition for Personal Financial Literacy), indicating that the 2008 score for seniors is the lowest on record. In some sates, schools districts are now requiring students to take a semester-long, stand—alone course, before graduating from high school while others have incorporated information about financial literacy into existing programs.[17]

The efforts of one inner-city school in Cleveland have put many of its students ahead of the financial literacy curve. Located in a neighborhood dubbed by national media as the epicenter of the foreclosure disaster, Cleveland Central Catholic High School offers a variety of personal financial classes to its 560 students and their families, half of whom are considered poor, for the past six years.[18]

The school's program recently won recognition from Ohio's treasurer and it's Department of Education as an exemplar for schools seeking to fulfill the state's financial literacy mandate by 2010. Students are exposed to the tools (e.g., checkbook simulation exercises, recording ATM and debit car transactions, researching interest rates of credit cards, creating a savings account, etc.) they will need in order to be financially successful. In addition to learning to understand the difference between financial needs and wants, they are learning to use a budget as a tool that adjusts to meet a person's or a family's changing circumstances.

In ninth grade, students and their families attend a workshop in which they learn the basics of banking and finance. In tenth grade, the same students take two semesters of personal finance. In 11th grade, they enroll in accounting through the school's business department, and as seniors the students take a course called, "Banking Systems and Investing in the Future." Even if students only take away one aspect of their course-work in financial literacy, they will benefit greatly once they get out in the real world.[18]

Many kinds of organizations now exist to help young people become financial literate and support would-be entrepreneurs, including specialized government agencies, business incubators, science parks, and some non-governmental organizations. Many universities offer specialized training and degrees in entrepreneurship, and some middle and high schools have created successful entrepreneurship clubs for young people.

Many of the contributors of this book have involved African American males in business ventures. Some of the projects have been launched in after-school programs, while others have been run during the summer months. In one project, African American boys, ages 12-14, were offered an opportunity to form a business that designed tee shirts and to develop creative ways to market and sell the shirts. Two groups of ten boys were involved in this summer project that lasted for ten weeks. Both groups were provided a small budget, barely enough money to purchase 100 shirts and to cover part of the expenses for printing designs on the shirts. To turn the project into a successful business, the boys had to develop an organized business plan, decide on a name for the company, elect officers for the company, open a bank account, make decisions about the designs to print on the shirts, contact and negotiate with companies that sold tee shirts and those that printed designs on shirts, develop a marketing plan, set prices for their product, determine where and how to sell the shirts, and organize how profits would be split between the company and the ten boys in the company. At the end of ten weeks, each boy had earned nearly two hundred dollars. Our role was simply to provide the boys with a place for weekly meetings and discussions about how to establish an effective business.

Some of us have worked one-on-one with African American males to teach them entrepreneurship skills. The boys created companies that sold cookies, posters, and school supplies, while others provided services such lawn care, garage cleaning and organization, dog washing, installing computer software, reading to blind people, tutoring, babysitting, bicycle repair, and organizing weekend parties.

Some of us involved our mentees in investment clubs where they purchased and traded penny stocks. Our more art-minded educators have taught Black boys how to make jewelry or how to use technology to create personal greeting cards, the quality of some items being great enough to be purchased by outlet stores in a shopping mall. Collectively, the goal of our work has been to show them the connections between what they create and making money and to help them understand the value of saving and investing.

For the most part, the boys were able to create and run their businesses while maintaining good grades. What's amazing for a few of the boys is that, in addition to running a business and keeping their grades up, they were active in team sports at school or some other after-school program. But the one thing that was central for all boys is that they experienced what it means to create a produce and exchange it for money. Some of the boys also learned how to negotiate with business owners to acquire raw materials they need to create products for their own business. While working with Black boys one-on-one is a lot easier than working with a group, the group work is far much more exciting, and it allows Black boys to polish their communication skills, work on a team, and learn how to deal with conflict in a peaceful manner.

Building the Foundation for Entrepreneurship Through Kwanzaa

One approach for bringing entrepreneurship into the homes of African American boys is the incorporation of the principles of Kwanzaa, the only original African American holiday and festivity that has its roots in the Black Nationalist movement of the 1960s. Kwanzaa was established as a means to help African Americans reconnect with their African cultural and historical heritage by uniting in meditation and the study of African traditions and common humanist principles.[19] Dr. Maulana Karenga, an African American scholar and social activist who created Kwanzaa in 1966, said his goal was to "give a Black alternative to the existing holiday and give Blacks an opportunity to celebrate themselves and history, rather than simply imitate the practice of the dominant society." The name Kwanzaa is derived from the Swahili phrase "matunda ya kwanza", meaning "first fruits." The choice of Swahili, an East African language, reflects its status as a symbol of Pan-Africanism, especially in the 1960s. Since its humble beginnings when only a few African American celebrated Kwanzaa, the holiday has become part of the fabric of life for many African Americans—and the American people as a whole. In 1977, for example, the first Kwanzaa stamp was issued by the United States Postal Service. A second stamp, created by the artist Daniel Minter, was issued in 2004. It bears seven figures in colorful robes symbolizing the seven principles. In addition, the first feature film about Kwanzaa, *The Black Candle*, was narrated by Maya Angelou in 2008.[20,21]

Principles of Kwanzaa

Kwanzaa celebrates what its founder called "The Seven Principles of Kwanzaa," or Nguzo Saba (originally "Nguzu Saba: The Seven Principles of Blackness"), which Karenga said "is a communitarian African philosophy" consisting of what he called "the best of African thought and practice in constant exchange with the world." These seven principles comprise Kawaida, a Swahili term for tradition and reason. Each of the seven days of Kwanzaa is dedicated to one of the following principles:

- Umoja (Unity): To strive for and to maintain unity in the family, community, nation, and race.
- Kujichagulia (Self-Determination): To define ourselves, name ourselves, create for ourselves, and speak for ourselves.
- Ujima (Collective Work and Responsibility): To build and maintain our community together and make our brothers' and sisters' problems our problems and to solve them together.
- Ujamaa (Cooperative Economics): To build and maintain our own stores, shops, and other businesses and to profit from them together.
- Nia (Purpose): To make our collective vocation the building and developing of our community in order to restore our people to their traditional greatness.
- Kuumba (Creativity): To do always as much as we can, in the way we can, in order to leave our community more beautiful and better than we inherited it.
- Imani (Faith): To believe with all our heart in our people, our parents, our teachers, our leaders, and the righteousness and victory of our struggle.

If you are a parent reading this information, consider Kwanzaa as not just an African American holiday; look at it as a way to guide yours sons and daughters toward the ownership of their own businesses. If seeing them as owners of their own businesses is too much of a stretch of your imagination, then consider using the seven principles to encourage the development of values and attitudes that will enhance their character and contribute to their becoming successful students and productive citizens. Whatever approach you take will require that you engage your son (or students in your class) in some systematic discussions and writing exercises that explore compelling reasons for incorporating the seven principles into their lives. Spend a week or so with each principle. Have your sons read the principle and write out their compelling reasons for making the values and attitudes reflected by the principle a part of their lives. If you consistently encourage these actions, then the words will seep into their subconscious mind and your sons will soon began to align their behavior with the attitudes and values reflected by the seven principles.

Developing Entrepreneurship Through, Unity and Cooperative Economics

For most people, financial literacy was not taught at home or school. If you are like us, most of your financial education was learned from hanging out with friends and trying to scrape up enough coins to buy a bag of penny candies (which are now a dime), watching your parents pay bills, and hiding money under the mattress or seeing your grandmother stuff wads of money in her brassiere.

Children that grew up during the Great Depression era learned from their parents and their own personal experience about the need to be fiscally conservative. Those children later became parents and then grandparents who instilled core financial values from the hard lessons they learned. Although the average white parent did not play the stock market and the average Black parent was never allowed to enter due to racism and Jim Crow laws, they felt the full destructive force of the Great Depression era. When jobs were scarce and unemployment on the rise, Blacks and Latinos were the last to receive wage paying jobs. The results of this type of financial discrimination necessitated minorities turning inward and reinvesting in their own communities. No matter how bad the situation got, Black men found a way to generate income. Many became self-sufficient during these times and realized that their dollars had power.[22]

After an awakening of the understanding of economic power many Blacks understood that their dollars were a vital part of the economic landscape. Children came to realize that saving and financial conservation equated to educational, political and social advancement opportunities. These same children later became the vanguards of the civil rights movement and measured equality through economic development, as well. Since the 1990s, the buying power of African Americans has increased 116 percent nationwide. With this newfound power comes a responsibility to educate our youth.[23]

In these turbulent financial times with the mortgage meltdown, financial companies being bailed out by the government, the American automobile industry facing extinction, home values dropping, and increased credit card debt pervading our society, each of us has a personal responsibility to educate our children and actively manage our financial lives and destinies and to be conscious about the consequences of financial decisions we make. Combine global economic forces, political shifts, and societal pressures placed on children through mass media advertising, and you have a convergence of forces requiring that our children be taught and given the tools to make sound financial decisions rooted in knowledge, ethics, and a deep understanding of financial history. Fortunately, the tools needed to teach parents and children of all walks of life are now readily accessible. This chapter is designed to be one of those tools. Improving basic financial education at the elementary and secondary school level can provide a foundation for financial literacy, helping younger people avoid poor decisions that can take years to overcome.

While it has become clear that teaching financial literacy is vital, it has become increasingly challenging for educators, policy makers and parents to develop this skill and make it teachable. Schools that are already struggling with the lack of resources cannot add another life skill to their core curriculum. At the foundation of the need for financial literacy are the parents of the children and adults that lacked the knowledge of financial literacy themselves. In many instances, a parent's financial planning amounted to telling their children to "save your money for a rainy day" or "don't spend so much," followed by a stiff pop to the back of the head.

Growing up in an immigrant household, I had a chance to visit Jamaica and learn to appreciate the amenities and financial opportunities that resulted from my parents' immigration to America. In Jamaica the limited availability of educational and financial resources created an environment of scarcity coupled with an awareness that education, specifically financial literacy, equates to an improved quality of life.

My father worked three jobs: cook, office cleaner and taxicab driver. He actively participated in what most people from the Caribbean call the partner or capital accumulation system, where members of the community create a joint banking account. All members contribute a fixed amount of money to the account weekly and at the end of the week or some fixed period of time, the total amount in the account is paid to one member.[24]

This is an honorable arrangement in the Caribbean, and all members of the partnership continue their membership until each has received a weekly payment. At that time the partnership can be dissolved, but what usually happens is that another partner is started the following week or month, additional members are added and, some prior members may drop out. Many of the participants, like my father, worked low skilled jobs and contributed a significant portion of their income.

In many cases, the weekly payment, which can range from hundreds to thousands of dollars, are used for significant life changing investments and purchases, such as a home, start-up capital for a business, or a college education, which leads to increased earning opportunities or other investment opportunities. In my father and uncle's case, they used them to purchase homes to generate rental income. Today, those homes are paid off and produce incomes that pay for their lifestyles and additional investments.

At the foundation of the partner system is the understanding that trust, cooperative economics, financial literacy, and education will create opportunities without having to rely on credit. Parents can reinforce financial responsibility in their children by demonstrating some basic financial principles:

Live below your means. My dad always told us that we did not have to "keep up with everyone else" and the only way to make money was not to spend money on anything that could not pay you or enhance your life. My father's car paid him every time he drove it and taught me a valuable lesson that I incorporate in all my affairs. My first home was less than fifty thousand dollars. Although I was approved for three times that amount, I quickly looked for programs that would assist me with the purchase of my first home. Parents and teachers can educate their children about government and privately backed programs that require them to attend classes that teach financial literacy. One example is the Habitat for Humanity "Homeowner in Process" series that incorporates motivational, self improvement, parenting, financial literacy, and community resource information into a six-month curriculum. This curriculum emphasizes living within a budget.[25]

- Make paying off credit cards and eliminating debt a priority. Financial advisors agree that anyone with credit card debt should take steps to pay them off. The long-term cost of credit cards can be illustrated to your children in many ways. For example, a $2,000 flat screen T.V. purchased on credit will cost $6,198.26 paid over 20 years if a person pays just the minimum payment amount. If you have several cards, choose one and pay it off by making larger payments on it and smaller payments on the other cards. Repeat this process until you have paid off all of your cards.

- Trade unmanageable debt for manageable debt. Old debt with higher interest rates and higher payments can take away your ability to make monthly payments on time. There are a couple of ways to reduce monthly debt payments: reduce the principal amount, lower the interest rate, and extend the repayment terms.
- Don't make guesses about your finances. Create a budget and keep up with your income and monthly expenses. By creating and living within a budget, parents are teaching their children to prepare for future and unpredictable expenses. Budgeting will also allow parents to identify items that are costing too much. Having and sticking to a solid budget allows parents to control their finances, rather than having their finances control them.
- If you don't have enough money saved to handle your monthly expenses for 6 months, then don't use credit for any of your purchases. It might mean that you have to cutback and forgo purchases that are not essential, but in the long run you will have enough case stashed away to get you through tougher times.
- Have some rule for making purchases based on things you need and those that you want. Many of us have far more than we need, but we make impulsive purchases based on what we want. A good rule of thumb about purchasing what you want is that you have to pay for it with cash and if you use a credit card, the total cost of the item has to be paid off within 30 days.

Tips For Bringing Entrepreneurship Into The Classroom

Over 50 years ago, the National Council on Economic Education (NCEE) saw a serious gap between what young people needed to know about economics and what they were being taught. NCEE surveys show that nearly half of our young people don't understand how to save and invest for retirement, don't know how to handle credit cards, and don't know the difference between inflation and recession or how government spending affects them. The NCEE adopted the position that if we (as a nation) fail to act now to improve economic literacy, our children will be at risk for crippling personal debt, for making costly decisions at work and at home, and lack competitive skills in a fast-paced global economy. As a consequence, they took action and established comprehensive programs that equip teachers with tools to get economics, personal finance, and entrepreneurship into the classroom. NCEE has built a unique network of state councils and university-based centers to provide resources for teachers who are seeking ways to make practical economics a core component of the curriculum.[26]

Growing interest in the economy and in financial markets, elementary and secondary education, international education, and educational standards has contributed to the NCEE's commitment to provide teachers with resources for the classroom. If you are looking for supplemental economic, personal finance, or entrepreneurship lesson plans for your K-12 classroom, then every NCEE lesson uses activities, simulations, multimedia content, and background readings to give your students an applied experience with economics principles for all ages: elementary school, middle and junior high school, and high school. In addition to these resources, the Ewing Marion Kauffman Foundation and the U.S. Department of Commerce's International Trade Administration (ITA) are pleased to welcome you to the new online resource intended to help build economies that foster entrepreneurship worldwide.[27]

Web sites www.Entrepreneurship.gov and www.Entrepreneurship. org are part of a new public-private partnership focused on leveraging entrepreneurial leadership to advance economic growth around the world. These sites serve to connect and inform the global community of entrepreneurs while linking them to policy makers, sources of funding, and business development resources needed to grow entrepreneurial economies.

These are exciting times for entrepreneurs, and we should increase our efforts to provide teachers with effective methods and materials to help young people learn about economics, personal finance, and entrepreneurship. Investing in teachers has proven to be the most effective way to get into the heads and hands of the nation's young people the right materials. Teachers are in the best position to provide Black males the most well-rounded entrepreneurial experiences for being competitive in the global economy.

In addition to the curriculum resources provided by NCEE, the list below includes other suggestions teachers can use to increase Black males interest in entrepreneurship.

- Connect entrepreneurship with the history of African Americans. Emphasize African Americans' inspiring ingenuity and innovation and open discussion about how their thoughts and dreams became a reality. Reorganize history classes to examine the most successful businesses across time, looking at entrepreneurs who achieved success against incredible odds.

- Provide case studies of young innovative African Americans, such as Sean Combs, Master P, Russell Simmons, Will Smith, FUBU, etc. Be sure to include athletes.

- Make education relevant by connecting curriculum to capitalism. Include Haptic experiences, such as class stock clubs, school stores, and clothing design/graphic design. Understanding the business model should be the status quo for each component.

- Implement job shadowing with local businesses and vocational education that includes carpentry and automotive shop, as well as technology and multimedia.

- Facilitate monthly youth business seminars that emphasize a particular component of owning a business. Invite parents to attend.

- Make entrepreneurship a class elective (something different from business administration).

- Utilize a business mentoring program to connect one youth with a mentor from a business.

- Use business and entrepreneurship models to teach writing, reading, and math. This might include writing about personal and financial goals or mock business plans, along with short and long-term business prediction models.

- Incorporate lessons about the power and importance of giving and altruism in all discussions about the economy, business, and entrepreneurship.

Helping Black males and the other students in your classes get a handle on finance doesn't have to take up a big chunk of your school year, especially if you have the right lessons at your fingertips. Whether you teach third-grade math, fourth-grade social studies, seventh-grade math, or high school economics, chances are you can begin online to plan a money management class. In addition, if you are bold enough, you can include a section where students are encouraged to develop a business.

From downloadable lesson plans that take up one class period to online games that teach key concepts, the Web is an invaluable resource for locating everything you will need to integrate lessons about economics, personal finance, and entrepreneurship into your curriculum. Here are a few other sources that are broken down by grade level.

Elementary School

On the Federal Reserve Bank of New York's Education page (www. newyorkfed.org/education), you'll find the Econ Explorers Journal, a workbook designed to help elementary school math students understand money. In one activity, students visit a local bank to collect savings account and checking account deposit slips and a car loan application. Then they create characters that deposit and withdraw money, pay bills, and take out a car loan, all while drawing pictures to illustrate what happens at each step. The lesson teaches the basics of bank accounts, interest rates, and budgets.

The NCEE offers the EconEdLink Web site (www.econedlink.org/lessons), which includes dozens of free, downloadable lesson plans for K-12 students. For elementary school students, check out "A Perfect Pet," which teaches children about making choices when they have limited resources. It uses a downloadable story about a trip to the pet store, as well as a puzzle and other activities, to reinforce the point.

The Jump$tart Coalition for Personal Financial Literacy (www. jumpstart.org/mdb) offers links to hundreds of other Web sites that offer lesson plans geared toward every grade level, especially elementary school grades. Check out, for example, the lesson on borrowing and lending from Take Charge America. It's a natural for social studies teachers covering a unit on the Revolutionary War. It teaches lending using a book about Benjamin Franklin and facts about how the American colonies borrowed money from France for the war effort.

Middle School

Middle school math teachers can teach basic financial literacy using a downloadable, four-lesson math curriculum supplement called Money Math (www.treasurydirect.gov/indiv/tools). Students use math concepts to learn about budgets, expenses, interest, and taxes. For instance, a lesson called Wallpaper Woes asks students to figure out the area of a room that needs to be wallpapered and calculate how much it will cost.

For lesson plans that prepare students to be entrepreneurs, check out those from NCEE, such as All in Business (www.econedlink.org/lessons). You'll find activities that teach business plan essentials, including how to figure out a business' costs and benefits. It also offers links to other Web sites that can supplement the lesson, such as the Real Planet (www. missouribusiness.net/irs/taxai/realplanet), which uses funky characters to teach teenagers about entrepreneurship. Other lessons on the topic for elementary school, middle school, and high school students can be found at These Kids Mean Busines$ (www.thesekidsmeanbusiness.org).

The Web site Rich Kid, Smart Kid (www.richkidsmartkid.com) has a number of financial lesson plans for all grade levels, including some interactive games. To help teach your middle school students about debt, this game uses a story about a boy who wants to buy a video player but lacks the cash. The activities include writing a creative story about a similar dilemma and making a collage. The complete plan also comes with a rubric.

High School

Teach your students how to budget with a lesson from the Federal Reserve Bank of San Francisco (www.frbsf.org/publications/education) that also prepares them for the financial realities of different jobs. Students learn about budgeting, saving, and investing, and they can play a game to help illustrate how one's education, job, and spending habits make a difference in their financial security.

To prepare your students for the barrage of credit card offers they'll encounter, go to Consumer Jungle (http://consumerjungle.org/). The site requires registration, but the materials on it are free. Choose the section on credit, and you'll get a complete unit, including an outline, the standards it meets, vocabulary, and lessons that range from how to choose a card to the meaning of credit scores. You can also download Microsoft PowerPoint presentations.

For detailed lesson plans on entrepreneurship and personal finance, go to Merrill Lynch's Investing Pays Off (http://philanthrophy.ml.com), which offers teaching guides for elementary school, middle school, and high school students. The high school guide includes questions to test your students' financial knowledge and worksheets to accompany short lessons on budget planning, time management, choosing a career, and recognizing financial opportunities. Each of the fifteen lessons includes group discussion points and a question designed to tap critical thinking skills.

Hands on Banking®

Another great source of information for educators and parents is an innovative financial literacy program, Hands on Banking, developed by Well Fargo as a free community service. Hands on Banking is an interactive financial literacy curriculum for students' grades 4-12 and adults. This teacher's guide is designed for the Children/Teens (grades 6 to 8) curriculum of the program. Hands on Banking was developed to teach both the basics of good money management and the skills needed to create a brighter financial future. The lessons examine financial concepts and decision-making through illustration, real-life problems, and mathematical computation. The curriculum is relevant to students' lives and is designed to support their financial success.[28]

Hands on Banking is intended for educational purposes only and contains no commercial content. The educational material is available free of charge in both English and Spanish, both on the Web (at www.handsonbanking.org and www.elfuturoentusmanos.org) and on CD-ROM. The curriculum is designed for both self-paced, individual learning or for classroom use. The teacher's guide is designed to be used alone or as an adjunct to the online/CD-ROM program. The online Children/Teens curriculum is divided into five units, plus an assessment. Each unit contains multiple lessons. The teacher's guide condenses each online unit's lessons into a smaller number of sections. The lessons in this guide contain activity worksheets for you to use with your students. This curriculum is designed to be presented in the given lesson sequence. Depending on, however, what is appropriate for your students, you may wish to establish your own sequence. Problem solving is woven into all of the program's units. Students apply both their understanding of basic banking concepts, as well as strategies to solve challenging problems in different contexts.

The lessons in this program adhere to the following mathematics and financial literacy and standards:

• National Council of Teachers of Mathematics (Principles and Standards for School Mathematics, 2000)

• National Council of Economic Education and the National Association of Economics Educators and the Foundation for Teaching Economics, Voluntary National Content Standards in Economics (1997)
• JumpStart Coalition for Personal Financial Literacy, National Standards in Personal Finance.

Teachers are encouraged to integrate the content into other lesson plans and use the curriculum as a springboard to address real-life situations. Please refer to your own state, local, district, or school standards to determine the appropriateness of the lessons for your students.

The No Child Left Behind Act is a federal law designed to improve the academic achievement of all students, particularly those who are minorities, disabled, economically disadvantaged, or have limited English proficiency. The Act requires teachers of mathematics to provide all students with equal opportunities to excel and the mathematical skills and knowledge they need to actively participate in American society. Consistent with the objectives of the No Child Left Behind Act, the Hands on Banking/El futuro en tus manos curriculum and supplemental materials for grade levels 4-12 are aligned with both state and national educational standards for mathematics, reading, and economics. The materials are flexible enough so that educators can make the materials relevant to their students' lives and address real-life financial situations.

Do You Have What It Takes To Be a Successful Entrepreneur?

There is no question about it: times are challenging for everyone. Dealing with the changing economic problems we are facing will require new businesses and effective ways for managing these businesses. It's estimated that small businesses, many created by entrepreneurs, will play a vital role in rebuilding the workforce and the economy in America and around the world. If you believe you have what it takes to build a successful business or to teach young people how to do the same, then take a look at the 25 common characteristics that are shared by successful entrepreneurs and business people. Place a check besides each characteristic that you feel that you possess. This way, you can see how you stack up.[28]

Like any activity you pursue, there are certain requirements for success in a chosen activity. For students to do well in school, they have to study and develop effective test taking skills; to excel in sports, one must train and practice; to retire comfortably, one must become a informed, wise, and active investor. If your goal is success in business, then the formula is no different. There are certain things that have to be fully developed, implemented, and managed to have a successful business. This list contains what James Stephenson—an experienced home based business consultant with over 15 years of business and marketing experience—believes to be twenty-five of the more important requirements to start, operate, and grow a successful and profitable home business.

A detailed description of these characteristics can be found in the book, *Ultimate Home Based Business Handbook*, by James Stephenson, available from Entrepreneur Press. Take a few moments to read thru this abbreviated list of just a few items from his list to determine whether you have what it takes to get a home-based business through hard times.[29]

1. Do what you enjoy and remember to take time off.
2. Plan everything and stay organized.
3. Manage money wisely.
4. Remember it's all about knowing your customers.
5. Become a shameless self-promoter (without becoming obnoxious).
6. Project a positive business image and limit the number of hats you wear.
7. Level the playing field with technology.
8. Become known as an expert in your field.
9. Invest in yourself and build a rock-solid reputation.
10. Grab attention everywhere you can.
11. Master the art of negotiations.
12. Follow-up constantly.

How well did you do with the characteristics? Even if you don't have all of these characteristics, don't fret. Most can be learned with practice and by developing a winning attitude, especially if you set goals and commit through strategic planning, to reach those goals in incremental and measurable stages. Being a successful entrepreneur takes hard work, but the rewards of creating your own business and teaching young people to do the same are fantastic. To some extent, the characteristics of successful entrepreneurs are very similar to the characteristics of successful teachers and parents.

Summary and Conclusions

As you think about the downfall of some of the major industries around the world, keep in mind that the creation of jobs in small and moderate size companies are primarily due to entrepreneurial activities. Even so, it seems that every day, headlines bring us troubling news of our increasingly fragile and faltering economy. The largest collapse of financial institutions since the Great Depression ricochets across the globe, as investors, politicians, and homeowners scramble to make ends meet over expanding chasms of debt. When the economy rides and stumbles on $700 billion promises—and pocket money vanishes with a few clicks of a mouse—it becomes increasingly urgent to teach young people the basic skills of personal finance. It is today's students who will pay for yesterday's poor choices. Their journey through a slowing economy will be greatly enhanced by learning how to spend wisely, maintain good credit, develop an entrepreneurial mindset, and take out safe, reasonable loans.

While there are several financial gurus you should learn about, the advise of Suze Orman—a New York Times mega bestselling author and undeniably America's most recognized expert on personal finance—seems solid.

If following the financial advice of Suze Orman is not your thing, then at least start reading about personal finance. If you are like us, you will soon discover that Orman, a Certified Financial Planner has written seven consecutive New York Times bestsellers: *Suze Orman's 2009 Action Plan*; *Women & Money*; *The Money Book for the Young, Fabulous & Broke*; *The Laws of Money, The Lessons of Life*; *The Road to Wealth*; *The Courage to Be Rich*; and *The 9 Steps to Financial Freedom*, as well as the national bestsellers, *Suze Orman's Financial Guidebook and You've Earned It, Don't Lose It*. While these books don't directly speak to the need for developing financial literacy in Black males, the information is useful for educators and parents who are interested in motivating Black males to become financially literate entrepreneurs.

The creative potential of most Black males far exceeds their academic performance. Outside of school, many are creating multimedia projects, web pages, lyrics and rhythms for songs, poetry, and a number of other products that can be easily transformed into a small business. It's so easy to believe that a high school senior who is an excellent student could be paid for tutoring younger children, while it's difficult to believe that a star athlete can get paid for teaching younger children how to excel in sports. But what's great is that we have seen examples where both have developed very successful businesses. One young man, age 16, hired his mother to work for him because his Internet business was producing too much work for him to handle by himself. By the way, the star athlete was a straight A student from an impoverished home. He created his business to provide some financial relief for his mother, a single parent, who was working two jobs to keep a roof over his head and that of his younger sister.

One of the most peculiar things about education in our country is that students attend school for only nine months. There was a time when we needed the low cost labor that teenagers provided to farmers and road work crews during the summer months, but those jobs and times are long gone. The need for young adults to take on summer employment continues to exist for many families, but most young adults find jobs in fast restaurants or retail stores. Few students attend school or even read books during the summer months, and much of what they learned during the academic year is lost. Nowhere is this loss more apparent than reading and mathematics, areas in which our high school seniors lag far behind their peers in other countries. We have clearly entered a period where we've got to shift our attention to the educational and work experiences we are providing students during the summer months. If you are a parent reading this, then encourage your son to seek out summer work at banks and other financial institutions. The jobs for students are rare, but the chances of landing a summertime job at a financial institution improves for students who do volunteer work at these institutions throughout the academic year. If you are a teacher, then consider developing internships for students to have placements in banks, financial institutions, and other businesses where students can learn about the ethical practices of doing business. One program I'm familiar with in New York teaches inner city children to think like Wall Street executives over the course of a year internship where students are provided jobs during the summer months.

Our role as educators and parents should never be to block the path to financial inquiry. Every idea a young Black male has about developing a business and making money is a good idea for a particular time and place. Our role should be to help young people develop their ideas and to teach them how to make sound financial decisions about their ideas. If we can teach them to make sound financial decisions while they are teenagers, then we can feel assured that they will continue to make sound financial decisions as adults. It is necessary for Black males in school today to acquire a great financial education, including global economics. Unlike many of us, they will have to make major financial decisions earlier in life, and making bad decisions will have long-term consequences on their ability to purchase a home, secure credit, and develop an adequate retire plan.

Few people could have imagined the impact of Amazon, Google, YouTube, Yahoo or any of the other Web-based business ventures, but the market for Internet-related businesses is full of young people, some of whom—but not enough—are Black males. It will take a special effort to invest your time and talent in helping Black males and all of your other students to learn about economics, personal finance, and entrepreneurship. If you don't, then who will?

12

Holla If You Hear Me: Giving Voice to Black Male Youth Through Hip hop

By Danya Perry, Mervin "Spectac" Jenkins,
Patrick "9ᵗʰ Wonder" Douthit, and
Chris "Dasan Ahanu" Massenburg

Did you hear that new Fifty Cent song? He was talking about "putting in work!" Isn't that gang related? Does he intend on killing someone? This is not what I want my youth to be exposed to. They are eating this rap up, and I don't know how to counteract the negative messages. This is a conversation many parents and educators have heard. Hip hop has only been around for approximately 30 years but has achieved a status that most genre's cannot boast. Hip hop has been blamed for the corruption of young minds, for being the purveyor of a lost generation, and lastly (my favorite), the reason why children have "lost their minds." I cannot help but utter the gentle poetic words of Maya Angelou, "and still I rise," which has been the mantra of Hip hop since its inception. The true essences of Hip hop will continue to rise above all of the pitfalls of its development. Commercialism will not define what Hip hop has meant to my generation and so many others. Selling out Hip hop to make a dollar has turned the genre to a grossly misunderstood mechanism. Not to worry, Hip hop will rise out of the current status—as we grow up, so will Hip hop.

Let's just assume that Hip hop is here to stay, regardless of the countless attempts to censor and ban this genre. Although violence, sex, and drugs seem to be very common themes in contemporary Hip hop, Hip hop purists would argue that the modern day genre isn't even Hip hop, but a complex version of rap. Confused? Good. We will analyze why this is an important point to understand if the art form is to be used to empower black male youth. We may have been tricked into thinking that Hip hop is one-dimensional and we should understand the history before we condemn it completely. This chapter will focus on the history, ability, and opportunities, and strategies of Hip hop to empower young black males with the genre.

The Backdrop of Hip hop

Everything starts as words that are strung together to help us clarify our thoughts about what we want to create, what we wish to become, and how we feel about ourselves. Words help provide a mental picture of what we are creating for society and ourselves. As our people suffered through the emotional and physical pains and brutality of slavery, it seems that one aspect of our African culture that was not suppressed was our ability to use words through songs, poetry, and storytelling to rekindle memories of life in our homeland and capture our reflections about life in this new land.[1,2] Long before Hip hop and rap, our people used words imbedded in spiritual songs to convey messages about the safe passageways to freedom so that slaves on the run could locate safe places to rest and hide. And long before the so called "negro spirituals," our people (slaves) used the rhythms and beats of the drum and berimbau as a means of communicate without their bosses understanding what was being communicated. Hip hop, gospel, blues and many of the musical forms we appreciate today have deep roots in African culture.[3,4,5,6,7]

To understand the importance of Hip hop for today's youth, we can draw some connections from an earlier form of art that imitated life. Jazz has served as a predecessor to Hip hop, or better yet, Hip hop's play cousin. In other words, they are so close, you may want to claim them as family. There are so many undeniable similarities that it warrants a discussion regarding the intent and importance of the genre for the people. From the beat of ragtime and driving brass bands to soaring gospel choirs mixed with field hollers and the deep down growl of the blues, jazz's many roots are celebrated almost everywhere in the United States. The realization of this link will assist in bridging our understanding of the importance of Hip hop to the youth that we serve, especially our black boys. We can start to lay the groundwork by stating that jazz is indigenous to American and spoke to and about the unheard populations. Jazz birthed many styles and had various interpretations, but the soul of jazz created a backdrop that examined life and was a sign of the times. Similar to Hip hop, jazz held the distinction of being rebellious and outspoken. Jazz created an unbridled opportunity to address political discourse, social toxicity, and down-right disgust. Jazz migrated from the South and landed in an area that changed the landscape of music and even provided mortar for the concrete that was necessary to build the foundation for Hip hop. Where? Harlem.[3,6]

Interestingly enough, rappers today have recognized poetry and jazz pioneers such as Langston Hughes as the "original master rapper." As Brooklyn-raised rapper Talib Kweli states, "Hughes was the first black poet to keep it real—he represented his hood, just like the rappers."[8] So, in drawing the comparisons, one has to introduce Hughes, who in 1925, published one of his most famous poems, *The Weary Blues*.[9] The poem is a combination of blues and jazz with personal experiences. It embodies blues as a metaphor and form. Throughout the poem, music is not only seen as a form of art and entertainment, but also as a way of life; people living the blues. Hughes' ability to incorporate poetry with music and history with art has given him the reputation as one of the leading black artists of the twentieth century. "The Weary Blues" allows the reader to seek to unlock the mystery of the blues, for both the musician and themselves.

The Weary Blues expressed the sentiments of the jazz and blues and expressed the wide range of black America's experience from grief and sadness to hope and determination. He strongly believed that music and poetry worked together. These tenets are what set off what is termed as the Harlem Renaissance. This period allowed for the out-front and public celebration of our culture.[2] Hughes and other pioneers helped to provide a sense that there was something special about African Americans. Jazz, poetry, art, drums all provided reminders of who we were and expressed our collective outrage for being uprooted from Africa, remixed with others, then provided second-class citizenship. This rhythm had not been on earth before but undeniably laid the tracks for what we are experiencing today. The art forms that reflected the Harlem Renaissance are mirrored in Hip hop today; the language and the times are the only things that have changed.

Thinking about one of Hughes' more popular poems, provides an interesting backdrop to the need for the encouragement of expression through words and music. Mother to Son[10]paints a picture of the challenges that blacks were facing ("Well, son, I'll tell you: Life for me ain't been no crystal stair . . . And places with no carpet on the floor.") during this period, from poverty to lack of voice to the subtle nuisance of fatherless homes. Still, at the same time, I see hope within the lines ("So, boy, don't you turn back . . . Don't you fall now.") and I observe hints of resilience and perseverance, along with a touch of dogged determination. Who better to explain the experience? One who was known for walking the streets of Harlem to observe and listen to the inner workings of the community? Hughes spoke to us and for us.

Who speaks to the youth now? Who has been given the honor of sharing with the world and leading a new generation? Please identify the individual who will use their words to inspire change and celebrate blackness. Oddly enough, there will never be another Harlem Renaissance, but Hip hop stands securely on the shoulders of greats such as Langston Hughes. Hip hop has not forgotten the pillar of great pieces of work and the struggle. Hip hop will continue to carry the legacy of passing down from generation to generation the daily struggles through oral tradition.[1,11]

What Is Hip hop?

From a historical perspective, Hip hop is a form of expression that has roots imbedded deep within ancient African culture and oral tradition. Modern day rap music finds its more immediate roots in the subculture of Reggae music. In the 1970s, a Jamaican DJ pioneer, Kool Herc, moved from Kingston to the West Bronx, New York and became a rap trendsetter. Herc was known for chanting over the instrumental or percussion sections of popular songs. At this time, the lyrics or rapping was called "emceeing." Herc also popularized the usage of an audio mixer and two turntables, which are the staple set-up for any current rap group.[12]

This fast rising fad became extremely popular to young urban New Yorkers because of its raw nature. In terms of economic feasibility of starting a music group, Hip hop was probably the most inexpensive. All one needed was a beat and lyrics . . . no guitar, drums, or singing lessons. Rapping was a verbal skill that could be practiced and honed to perfection at anytime. There were no governing rules. All that was important was the originality and ability to rhyme on time to the beat of the music. As time passed, the emcee became a highly regarded position in neighborhoods, similar to those of sport stars, tough guys, and comedians.

Four Elements of Hip hop
(1) Emceeing
(2) DeeJaying
(3) Graffiti Art
(4) Break Dancing

Hip hop is the culture from which rap emerged. The four elements of Hip hop include graffiti art, break dancing, dee-jaying, and emceeing (rapping).[7,12] Hip hop is a lifestyle with its own language, style of dress, music and mind set that is continuously evolving. Currently, break dancing and graffiti aren't as prominent as the dee-jaying and emceeing. It is also important to note that the words 'rap' and 'Hip hop' have been used interchangeably. It should be noted, however, that while all aspects of Hip hop culture still exist, they have evolved.

To date, Hip hop's existence is due to an older generation's rejection of the values and needs of young people. In the beginning, Hip hop's driving force was self-expression and the desire to be seen and heard.[1,4,7]

Because of some major format changes that took place within black radio in the early 1970s, Hip hop became what it is today. Before Hip hop, the black radio stations played an integral part in the community as a musical and cultural storyteller. Hip hop reflected the values and customs of the day in particular communities. "It set the tone and created the climate for which people governed their lives as this was a primary source of information and enjoyment," responds Davey D, a renowned Hip hop historian. This fact was particularly true for the youth.

Hip hop continues to be popular for today's youth, especially boys. Because it is an accessible form of self-expression, the rap profession became popular because of the false illusion of its profitability. Ask any young black boy, and they will more than likely mention a career-goal surrounding athletics and/or music entertainment (and sometimes both). Hip hop is big business and motivates poor children to escape their situation. There are many children that believe all they need to do is write some good rhymes and they can achieve the "good life." This "good-life" takes the shape of jobs and opportunities to create a stream of revenue for many ambitious youth. Capitalizing on Hip hop does not always has to be in the form of rapper or DJ, but can extend to artist management, sound engineer, marketing, publishing, choreographer, music video director, record label owner or employee. Careers have been made and educators must highlight the notion that the "good-life" does not always have to be accomplished by being on stage. But perhaps being a stage director (or a teacher or principal who is also a performer) could be just as fulfilling.

One of the fundamental elements of Hip hop is that everything is interconnected. Most tunes you hear on a CD are written by one person, produced by another person, sung by another person, and an entirely different team of people are contracted to create and produce and choreograph the music video for MTV or BET. In a similar way, this chapter, while being primarily written by the first author, was dependent on the cooperative work and insight from the other three authors that you will learn about later in the chapter. I am blessed to have each of them in my corner to nurture my intellect and to bring about a fuller understanding of the role that Hip hop plays in education and society as a whole.

Life Through Music

Enter Mervin Jenkins—an educator who has worked for and with people, especially the youth, of all ages for over a decade. Mervin also leads a dual life as the Hip hop artist known as "Spectac." As an educator, Mervin student-taught at the elementary level, taught middle school art, worked as a high school assistant principal, central office administrator, middle school principal, and most recently Assistant Director for the Eastern Division of AVID (a National program designed to put students in the middle on a path for a four year college or university). In the same breath, "Spectac" managed to tour most of the East Coast and perform at some of its biggest music venues. His career as a Hip hop artist soared in 2003 when his single titled "Lessons from Da Ghetto" made its mark by gaining a spot on the billboard as one of the top 100 songs on the Hip hop and R&B charts. Either way, Mervin and "Spectac" had a voice that focused on building the spirits of youth. Mervin explains that it is critical to "speak" to the youth in a voice that is recognizable. "As a Hip hop artist, I know the vernacular and I know what they listen to."

As an administrator and a life-long educator, Mervin uses this to his advantage. He encourages all of his teachers to become innovators in the classroom and to build the bridges toward youth by embracing the culture that made "Spectac" who he is today. "Use Hip hop to connect with young black males, if not then you are at a severe disadvantage," responds Mervin. This disadvantage primarily centers around missed opportunities to encourage learning, reduce and dispel beliefs of inferiority, and most importantly show them that you care. Does integrating Hip hop into the pedagogy work? Well, Mervin was honored at his school district as the 2007-08 "Principal of the Year." "From my days as a middle school student until I was close to graduating from college I honestly had no idea how it all connected. You need to get a good education, is basically what everybody said. From the homeless folks on the corner, to the drug dealers, to the professionals with their Ph.D.'s, they all said it. How ironic, because now as an educator, I say it too. But interestingly enough, I realized through me being a child of Hip hop, it isn't always about what you say, but it's how you say it." Mervin is speaking to the next generation of youth and giving them hope for a future. While at the same time, "Spectac" is speaking for Hip hop and giving educators relief in the fact that it can be used as a tool. Either way, the question both identities seek to make a difference whether in rhyme or arithmetic.

Many critics of the day do not regard Hip hop in the same light as jazz, but jazz went through the same wringer. Whether opponents of derogatory language or misogynistic views, jazz and Hip hop had their detractors. Understanding what Hip hop can do to empower our black boys is not about accepting profanity or encouraging gang membership. Utilizing Hip hop to create voice and correct wrongs is by no means supporting misogyny. The world is filled with physical and emotional vulgarity and Hip hop is recognizing it all. These few lines of the Prayer[13] ("Lord why is it that, I go through so much pain." "So if it takes for me to suffer, for my brother to see the light." "Give me pain till I die, but please Lord treat him right.") by Baltimore-born, New York-bred rapper, DMX's, shares the introspective side of Hip hop and the obvious need for change, externally and more importantly, internally. Just as jazz heard everything (the cries, the hurt, the joy, aspirations, the whispers, the rhythms, the people and history) Hip hop is listening, as well.

I'd Rather be a Professor, than a Producer

Enter 9th Wonder, Grammy-Award winning producer who has worked with the likes of Jay-Z, Mary J. Blige, Destiny's Child, Erykah Badu, and Ludacris. Not to diminish his acclaimed career as a soulful Hip hop producer, but 9th would claim that his greatest accomplishment was teaching college-aged youth about the culture that has given so much to him personally. 9th Wonder is a professor at North Carolina Central University and Duke University and instructs youth from the ages of 18-21 about Hip hop history. 9th explains that "this class is significant because in a university, the goal is to become free-thinkers."

In the role of motivating free-thinkers, 9th is challenged with opening these students eyes to the world of Hip hop prior to Tupac and the Notorious B.I.G., as well as give them a global perspective and how Hip hop is cross sectional. Hip hop is known for talking about the struggles of the time, Grand Master Flash gave us "The Message," which explained the heroin epidemic. Hip hop and music in general has always been the backdrop of a revolution or movement. James Brown chants "I'm Black and I'm Proud," during a time where African-Americans struggled with equality. What was going on in 1968, the year that signaled the end of the Kennedy-Johnson presidencies, the nexus of the Civil Rights movement, and mounting anti-war sentiments regarding Vietnam. But the defining moment was the loss of Dr. Martin Luther King as a purveyor of what the world "could" look like. The music captured and explained the pain, loss, and inspired a generation. Just like James Brown, N.W.A. provided the background music to inner-city violence, rising unemployment, and continued plights of the impoverished and minorities. 9th touts, "either way, Hip hop almost signal handedly globalizes what was going on in the world from the perspective of children who's parents lived through the Civil Rights era."

As a professor, 9th takes the role serious as he speaks to students about his life as a music producer. "They [students] listen to me because I am a producer and work with famous artists, but I cherish the role as professor, because I can teach students to think about the world around them and to provide a critical analysis of what they see on a day-to-day basis." In this capacity, 9th talks to his students to give them a global perspective of Hip hop and focuses on the timeline. "There is a log going on between those 'dashes' in the world . . . socially, economically, and politically," responds

9th. It is important to give the youth all of these perspectives and show them that Hip hop provides a mode to explain the mood. Universities are starting to recognize the cross-disciplinary properties of Hip hop. From music class to social studies, Hip hop provides a universal view and can enhance the teacher-student relationship so that learning can be facilitated. "Adults need to understand that music controls the younger generation and we need more educators to recognize the potential of Hip hop and its positive influence."

What Can I Do With These Words in My Head

Enter Chris Massenburg, a Durham, NC-based spoken-word artist, poet, emcee, activist, playwright, and educator better known as Dasan Ahanu. Dasan considers Hip hop to be the foundation of everything that he does. He sees the culture as not only a way of life, but also as a way of understanding and interacting with the world. "When I think about the 4 elements of Hip hop, I see an all encompassing cultural phenomenon." Dasan offers. "The way you walk, talk, move, think, and see is represented. How do you not consider that when you think about educating today's young people?" It is this belief that has guided Dasan in his work as a teaching artist. "Performing gave me an opportunity to meet people who were innovative in thinking about how to reach young people. I wanted to share my ideas and they wanted someone that the children would see as being interesting and engaging." He accepted every offer to conduct a workshop, talk to a group of children, help plan curriculum, develop programming, or teach writing. "Each opportunity was a way to develop, not only as an educator, but as a thinker and an artist. I wasn't operating in a vacuum. I was able to get practical application of my theories. Good or bad, I was growing. I was also seeing a positive outcome with the children. They were showing me the possibilities."

Dasan has shared his love for Hip hop and his belief that it can be used in the classroom with as many educators as he can reach. He has worked with University of North Carolina Chapel Hill's Student Coalition for Action in Literacy Education on Hip hop and literacy. He has also worked with teaching fellows at UNC-Chapel Hill, teachers in Duke University's Literacy Through Photography Program, and with public school teachers in Durham, Orange, and Wake County Schools.

Dasan feels that his diverse experiences as an artist and child of Hip hop are his greatest benefit in working with teachers. Dasan wants educators to think about how they can help children to see the power of the culture. "It's not just about beats and rhymes. There are so many other facets. When you understand this is about a culture, then you can see so many possible outlets." For Dasan its not rhetoric, he practices what he preaches.

As a Spoken-word artist, Dasan has toured the country sharing his own special brand of poetry. He also advocates its place in Hip hop culture. "Every kid that grows up impacted by Hip hop culture finds their own place within it. When it comes to emcees, not all of them rap. Some choose Spoken-word as their expression of choice; especially young women." It is within Spoken-word that Dasan found his outlet and his voice. "I always wrote rhymes, freestyled with my friends, but it was at a poetry open mic that I first touched the stage. The Spoken-word community took me in. They showed me what I could really do with these words in my head." Dasan was a founding member of the poetry slam team in Charlotte, NC that became regional champions and national champions on two occasions. He went on to start the Jambalaya Soul Slam in Durham, NC and found the Bull City Slam Team.

Dasan continues, "Spoken-word has always been expected to be the grassroots voice of Hip hop. That's where people expect to hear the social commentary, the political commentary, the historical references, struggles, and the stories that touch, uplift, and inspire us. Spoken-word is where you get all that with the edge, flavor, and rebelliousness of Hip hop." That's why poetry has become a valuable resource in the classroom. It allows for an exchange. Teachers feed children information to fuel their writing. In return, the children can share their thoughts, ideas, and observations with teachers. It's a way for Hip hop and learning to share the same space without anxiety or concern.

As a playwright, he helped found Black Poetry Theatre, a theatre company creating and producing original productions centered on poetry, spoken-word, soul, and Hip hop. "I take Hip hop with me into whatever I do. I feel a responsibility to do so." As a creative consultant and event planner, Dasan has worked with a number of organizations and institutions developing cultural arts events, festivals, and shows. "If you use Hip hop as a way of reinforcing critical thinking and analysis you empower young people to innovate within their culture. We are seeing it more and more.

Where there are doctors, politicians, lawyers, psychologists, and other professionals who don't feel like they have to let go of Hip hop. They can impact their culture from within rather than leave it behind."

Currently, Dasan is the artist in residence in the English Department at Saint Augustine's College. It is there that he tries to guide future artists. He also seeks to learn from them how to continue to use the culture he loves as a way to impact learning. "They teach me something new everyday. I then try to pass that on to every educator that I meet." Dasan is working on delving deeper into curriculum and instruction while developing new pedagological approaches that can be passed on. "Teaching at the college level has challenged me to arm myself with the necessary tools to soldier the place of Hip hop in pedagogy." In addition to his work as an educator, Dasan continues to create and record music. He can be found on stage performing poetry, competing in slams, and hosting events. He is currently developing new productions for Black Poetry Theatre and working on new works of urban fiction. "The more I try, the more experience I gain. That means that I have more to share. As adults who grew up with Hip hop, we have to be stewards of the culture. We can't just be historians and supporters. We also have to be educators and innovators. We have that responsibility to carry our culture forward."

Embracing Generation "Y"

Educators, youth-serving professionals, and educators need to understand that the current youth culture is media driven. Ultimately, most youth are influenced by music and other forms of media. One can look at influence in regards to voice. There are many contributors to youth influences, but some segments of a child's life have a louder voice than others. For the youth of the 1950s, the family voice was louder than that of music and media. This is not to say that there was not negative music in the 50s, but they were not more influential than the family, school, and church. For youth in the 2000s, it is clear that music and media have a louder voice than all of the aforementioned, with family and school having the least influence. One may assume that this media influence focuses primarily on fashion, technology, and an occasional dance craze. Alongside these trendy items, one will find that values, morals, and character are being shaped and formed based upon media icons. This cannot be trivialized, because we are working with youth who have a completely different set of values than most educators and parents. This generational gap, however, that we are recognizing has been a source of conflict and confusion between parents and children since the 1950's.

Baby-boomers' outlook on the work-life balance is completely different than Generation Y'ers. With today's youth, the values placed on what is important or popular are driven by the music and media. The influence of music and media is vastly different from the family values that were the main influence on young people in the 1950's.

Educators and parents alike should prepare themselves to bridge the cultural and musical gap. Being multicultural and competent in the nuances of the current youth culture and specifically to the needs of young black males, is paramount.[14,15] This competence is one of the first steps in empowerment and, most importantly, resiliency building. Providing these young black boys with the ability to stay focused on their goals while coping with difficulties is the goal at hand. The preparation process should include the following components: conducting a self-assessment of the styles of leaning; establishing a welcoming and supportive learning environment at home and in the classroom; increasing relationship-building opportunities through cooperative learning strategies; and the realization that children today have been multi-processing large bits of information from the day they were conceived. This last point is important because it emphasizes that today's youth are far more capable of multi-tasking than their parents. I've heard many stories about parents purchasing electronic gadgets (VCR, DVD, cell phone, etc.) and being frustrated for days because of their inability to get it to function properly once they get it home. But when they become overwhelmed, one of their children figures out all of the functions within a matter of minutes. There is no doubt that one of the consequences of being exposed to more information is that different kinds of competencies and intelligences emerge. It is my belief that Hip hop can be an avenue for enhancing the kinds of intelligence that black males need to thrive in this multimedia drive world

Enhancing Multiple Intelligences With Hip hop

Viewing the black male learner as an active participant, educators are reexamining ways to activate appropriate learning strategies during the instructional process. While there has been considerable focus on cooperative learning strategies and the shift from behavioral to cognitive learning theories, I will examine the theory of multiple intelligence and explore how Hip hop in the classroom can be used to enhance multiple intelligences.

Several researchers have developed theories of multiple intelligence, the most notable being Howard Gardner's Theory of Multiple Intelligence.[16,17,18] In his book, "Intelligence Reframed: Multiple Intelligences for the 21st Century," Gardner reviews the seven intelligences he introduced in his first book, "Fames of the Mind: The Theory of Multiple Intelligence," and adds another—the naturalist intelligence. Gardner defines intelligence as "a biopsychosocial potential to process information that can be activated in a cultural setting to solve problems or create products that are of value in a culture."[18] He suggests that intelligence are neural conditions that will or will not be activated by opportunities, personal decisions, or values. He also states that everyone possesses these intelligences, noting that people acquire and represent knowledge in different ways. Gardner's proposed eight areas of intelligence, including the following:

- Linguistic Intelligence: the ability to use words effectively, whether orally or in writing
- Logical-Mathematical Intelligence: the capacity to use numbers effectively and to reason well
- Spatial Intelligence: the ability to perceive the visual-spatial world accurately and to perform transformations on those perceptions
- Bodily-Kinesthetic Intelligence: expertise in using one's body to express ideas and feelings and facility in using one's hands to produce or transform things
- Musical Intelligence: the ability to perceive, discriminate, transform, and express musical form
- Interpersonal Intelligence: the ability to perceive and make distinctions in the moods, intentions, motivations, and feelings of other people
- Intrapersonal Intelligence: self-knowledge and the ability to act on the basis of that knowledge
- Naturalist Intelligence: expertise in recognizing and classifying living and nonliving forms within one's environment. Gardner (pg. 49)[18] notes, "The young child who can readily discriminate among plant or birds or dinosaurs is drawing on the same skills

(or intelligence) when she classifies sneakers, cars, sound systems, or marbles."

In thinking about Gardner's Theory of Multiple Intelligence, it is important to remember that each person possesses all eight intelligences and that most people can develop each intelligence to an adequate level of competency. To this extent, educators have successfully implemented Gardner's Theory into their classrooms and have discovered that all learners can benefit, including students from diverse cultural backgrounds.[19,20]

Applying The Theory of Multiple Intelligence to Hip hop

One of the many benefits of using Hip hop in the classroom to enhance learning is that it allows students to construct and communicate knowledge in various ways. Hip hop classroom projects also encourage group work and social interaction, but they do not require a uniform experience for all students.[12,21,22] For example, when assigning students to work on classroom Hip hop projects, students should be placed in groups that provide them with the opportunity to take advantage of their strengths, as well as to nurture their weaknesses. For example, students who are identified as spatially intelligent might be responsible for the graphic content, layout, and visual media of the Hip hop project. Students who are identified as musically intelligent might be responsible for inputting audio/sound effects and creating the musical score for the project, while students who excel in bodily-kinesthetic intelligence could be responsible for creating dance and movement for the Hip hop project. Students who are linguistically intelligent might create the lyrics for the rap songs.

It is important to note that all students have all intelligences, although one or more may be stronger than others. Placing students in classroom teams that capture the diversity of their intellectual profiles can provide them with the motivation, skill, and support necessary for them to learn. Working in diverse groups allows students to nurture their weaknesses and capitalize on their strengths. Students are able to make valuable contributions to group projects as well as argument their intellectual profiles. Given the ongoing evolution of Hip hop, teachers are confronted with the possibility of combining Hip hop and multimedia projects.

Over the last decade, advances in technology have made it possible for teachers and students to develop elaborate multimedia programs in the classroom. Computer-based multimedia uses computers to present multiple media formats that convey information in a linear or nonlinear format. Creating a supportive atmosphere for students to create projects combining Hip hop and multimedia reinforces students' technology skills and invites them to work cooperatively and use a variety of media to express their understanding of what they are learning. This approach to learning encourages students to think differently about how they organize and present information. Consequently, multimedia projects using Hip hop might provide students with opportunities to show greater descriptive detail, unique perspectives, and diverse interest and skills. Opportunities to explore concepts and express understanding through Hip hop and multimedia may create a positive turning point in the academic motivation, the development of a student's intelligence, and the desire that black males have for learning. In essence, producing Hip hop/multimedia projects might encourage black males to feel more confident as producers of knowledge rather than passive consumers.

Now that we have more clarity in regards to the evolution, perception, themes and the interface of Hip hop with multiple intelligences, Hip hop will be used as the backdrop to our discussion of strategies to empower black males. These are the top five strategies to empower black male youth through Hip hop:

1. Hip hop Can Assist in Cultivating Creativity

Music composition refers to the structuring of a piece of music. In Hip hop terms, this is writing lyrics for a specific beat or instrumental and the arrangement. This can be a great and easily translatable activity to explore creativity in a music class, chorus, or band. The connection between the status quo and Hip hop is where you gain interest from most black males. My experience in schools across the nation supports that most music related classes do not attract the black male youth population. In the South, however, you will see more black males involved in bands and choruses because of the long-standing tradition. One Southern school band director in Georgia said, "The best mechanism to recruit black males for the band is playing popular Hip hop songs at sporting events." He also explained, "Most of these black boys want the recognition of doing something great in the eyes of their peers, and entertainment/athletics seem to be the most viable way to do so."

Assisting youth who are interested in musical arts are not as challenging as working with youth who may not have the opportunity or resource to become involved. Integrating Hip hop in school can be done innovatively. Some examples include the following:

- Remixing the current school song or athletic fight song
- Creating musical public service announcements for special events (i.e., anti-drinking initiatives for the prom or graduation)
- Developing song composition contests on specialized topics (i.e., anti-bullying initiatives)

The byproduct of inspiring creativity through music is school-connectedness. Black males statistically lead the school-to-prison pipeline, and most experts believe that one of the early warning signs that a child will drop out of school is the failure of the child to connect with their school.

Imagine with me, if you will. Little Jamal has only been recognized for bad behavior. Now he's being heralded as a local hero as he provides his lyrics to the backdrop of Pomp and Circumstance at the high school graduation. So let's analyze what is right with this picture. With the assistance of an innovative educator, Jamal was given an opportunity to have some meaningful involvement in his school. This opportunity was meaningful because it recognized one of his talents, while continuing to engage Jamal in the school. This could have easily been another story of a dropout who had all the potential in the world, but could never realize it. But instead, it has now given Jamal a new trajectory that can carry him to the next level. Is this a stretch? Maybe? Let's ask Jamal after graduation. True story.

2. Examining Current Events, Social Issues, and the Human Condition

As alluded to earlier, Hip hop is a purveyor of the current state of affairs. One could say that Hip hop is a microcosm of what's going on in the world. The basis of Hip hop is that you speak what you live. "If you don't live, how are you going to speak it," states Public Enemy's own Chuck D. Public Enemy.

Integrating Hip hop into courses surrounding politics, health, language, and economics could be easily implemented. Having youth report on current events as stated by their favorite Hip hop act would provide the listener with a new perspective. Young Bloodz, Young Jeezy, Young Joc, and other artists provided their own insight on the tragic events surrounding of 9/11. I recall in my high school social studies class having to tediously cut out newspaper clippings each week and write a few sentences about that particular event. There was an obvious disconnect (at least for me) from the lesson to how I applied it to my life. If I can be completely honest, I had no interest in the Ronald Regan administration until N.W.A. made it being acceptable to talk politics on the streets.

Educators must allow students, in some capacity, to connect with global, national, state, and local events in a manner that makes sense to them. They will begin to listen to their beloved music in a different light, almost measuring music based on its ability to actually say something of importance. Some examples of opportunities to integrate this lesson include:

- Utilizing a "Viewpoint of Week" activity, which asks students to highlight a specific viewpoint of one of their favorite Hip hop acts and connect it to current events
- Starting a mock Hip hop record label business or analyzing a current record label, which would employ lessons of economics
- Starting a debate club and/or engaging in debates over topics highlighted by rappers or topics of criticisms over Hip hop (i.e., censorship)
- Encouraging students to determine whether there are differences in the social, political, and economic issues that are being addressed by Hip hop artists around the world

This strategy should provide educators with numerous opportunities to empower young black males. In the past, educators' knowledge of what the rappers are actually saying, mainly because they don't listen to the music, has been minimal. What will often happen is the students will (excuse the terminology) "police themselves" or "call each other out" on misinterpreted lyrics or misquoted song intentions. It is also important to understand that some youth feel very passionately about their Hip hop heroes, so it is critical to not disrespect each other's opinions when engaging in activities.

3. Creating Conducive Learning Environments

School violence prevention is at the forefront of planning and strategies to ensure a safe and conducive learning environment. Most violence prevention experts explain that this is achieved by assessing the physical plant and layout of the school. Parking lot lighting, accessible entrances from the outside, and other blueprint concerns are critical in such efforts. But more important is ensuring that practices, policies, and programs address the population and student needs. For instance, character education at the school is a sure way of emphasizing traits for success. Honesty, respect, perseverance, determination and others can be integrated in various capacities. Discussions about respect at the classroom level can prove to be telling on how the current youth culture view this term. Current rappers view respect on levels that may not align with how educators view it. This is a critical discussion because youth are, what I like to call, LUI (Listening Under the Influence). In other words, youth tend to give credence to the rappers' definition and are influenced more by the "bling-bling." Therefore, what occurs is that as popularity or wealth grows, the validity of one's philosophical beliefs soars. Youth have to decide which definition of respect to follow.

Understanding that teachers have an uphill battle in this regard, there are opportunities to assist in this challenge. Along with issues related to character education, there are other strategies to create welcoming learning environments, which include the following:

- Utilizing the "Bad Meaning Good" activity, which calls for youth to analyze character traits of their favorite rapper versus those in school character education initiatives.
- Playing popular Hip hop instrumentals in the background during class assignments. This can be used as positive reinforcement for achieving classroom milestones (e.g., a month with no discipline referrals allows for youth to bring their favorite instrumental / or "clean" song to be played).

Creating conducive learning environments should not be limited to cameras and metal detectors. The way youth relate and respect each other and authority figures are just as important in school safety efforts. This is an opportunity to re-address social competencies that we want our youth to uphold, versus those of celebrities.

4.   Employing Opportunities to Discuss Real World Issues

School is a good litmus test of real world operation. You have lunchroom politics, parent-teacher U.N. meetings, and fashion "dos and don'ts" every morning on the bus. There are many challenges that our youth face on a daily basis yet very limited opportunities to provide their input in a structured environment. I recall having serious conversations with classmates on the opposite sex while walking from class to class. How was I to know that my friends were getting their expert information from Slick Rick. They didn't provide any disclaimers and I didn't ask for any references. I'm sure my parents, wife, and past girlfriends would have advocated for a good "straightening out" of my ideals regarding sex and relationships at that time. But, my peers, media, and music all had "louder voices" that seemed more acceptable to me at every level of my schooling. Educators have to become louder.

Rappers offer some very damaging views on women, and, sadly, our boys find value in them. This, along with other misinformation, allows our black boys to walk into situations with inaccurate perceptions of life and limitless counts of misplaced values. This provides educators with yet another opportunity to divert these ideals. Some opportunities include:

- Employing facilitated and structured round-table discussions or study circles on pervasive themes of Hip hop themes. Themes can include, but are not limited to:
    1) Understanding the opposite sex.
    2) Understanding hidden rules for success.
    3) Utilization of violence as effective means to resolve conflict.
- Empowering youth to host a "town-hall" meeting or forum for parents and community members on "The Current Youth Culture" or "What's Right and Wrong with Hip hop."
- Allowing youth to design and disseminate newsletters, brochures, and/or other literature on "The State of Hip hop," along with other related topics.

These opportunities to discuss what's important to youth are few and far between. Educators must understand that the voice of youth will be heard, whether in a structured manner or a violent outburst. My father once told me that "my" generation was not taught how to "effectively and efficiently protest." He blamed himself and other adults in becoming passive in efforts to encourage constructive demonstration. Without this outlet, black boys will continue to be unheard, which unfortunately results in under-achievement. Learned hopelessness, low self-esteem, and inferiority complexes can all be linked to the muffling of a voice.[23]

5.   Developing Opportunities for Meaningful Involvement

School connectedness has been alluded to in many of the aforementioned strategies. To ensure such a connectedness, educators most make a concerted effort to develop opportunities for all students to be meaningfully involved. Oftentimes, black males are given such opportunities in the capacity of sports. Not saying that the honor society and student government are out of the realm of possibility, but we have to become cognizant of those youth who may be at higher risk of academic failure and do not receive encouragement to be involved on other levels at the school. In the same breath, we have to recognize the unattractiveness of school involvement to young black males. The perception, needless to say, is not congruent to the messages persistent in rappers lyrics. One must remember that rappers do grow up and begin to look at life differently. Let's look at one of the most notorious rappers from the south; Master P. The drug-dealer turned rapper turned record label owner turned entrepreneur turned civil rights activist? The transition from living the street life to trying to save youth from the street is Master P's evolution. Although many have not witnessed, but Master P has been a huge proponent to the anti-violence movements since that day in Baton Rouge when a young man was killed and three children were wounded in the gunfight at the 1998 annual parade to celebrate the life and accomplishments of Dr. Martin L. King, Jr. Master P responded immediately by working with the staff of a radio show to organize a conference for peace and a weekly program where young people could voice their opinions about the violence problem in Baton Rouge.

In 2008, Master P released a song and video entitled "Black History," which describes the struggles of African-Americans during the 1960's and not forgetting "who died for the rights of many." Master P while accompanied by his son, in a prophetic way, is passing down vital history in a manner that can be interpreted by the youth. Not a history book, but in rhyme (with a catchy beat). This lesson by Master P is an example that many of our youth can learn from and should give educators some perspective of Hip hop's potency. Check the video out on YouTube, you will be pleasantly surprised. So once again, let's discuss options for the integration of Hip hop into academic programming.[24]

- Utilizing "Teacher for a Day" activities for students, which allows for the development of lessons plans surrounding Hip hop and life, alongside lecturing skills.
- Encouraging Hip hop parent symposiums/seminars completely facilitated by youth on related topics.
- Allowing youth to develop a "Slanguistics" staff development for educators, emphasizing the current youth culture and opportunities to build relationships.

Measuring the impact of meaningful involvement is difficult. Anecdotally, you will impact attendance, discipline referrals, and youth's overall desire to be in school.

I recall having the opportunity to provide musical direction for an assembly for Black History Month. My science teacher asked me to find a song that was appropriate for the occasion. This simple task opened my eyes in terms of what I could provide to "my" school. I not only ended up choosing a song from my own personal collection, U.N.I.T.Y." by Queen Latifah, but also serving as the head greeter for school board members and "go-to-guy" for anything that needed lifting. These simple tasks helped me become an invested member in my school community. If you've never heard the song, go download it (legally) and you will see why I was entrusted to be the song selector for the following year's assembly.

These strategies can prove to be a powerful tool in efforts to empower and enrich the classroom experience. These strategies are suggested in a manner that allows the educator some flexibility in the application in the lesson. Another great resource that educators should know about is "The Hip hop Education Guidebook: A Sourcebook of Inspiration and Practical Application."[21] This guidebook provides more traditional lesson plans that have Hip hop themes interwoven. Some of the lessons topics that are provided include Leadership, Peer Mediation, Social Justice,

Tolerance, and Diversity. The guidebook also shows how to integrate Hip hop into language arts, math, and science class. Interestingly enough, in North Carolina, we use the guidebook to provide educators with a weeklong seminar to help them create lesson plans for using Hip hop in the classroom. Resources such as these are readily available, but you have to look and be open to a different approach to reach youth.

Summary and Conclusions

Hip hop is here to stay and will be an important facet of our youth and their development for years to come. The approach to empower through Hip hop is an innovative process yet one that requires one to engage in self-assessment. This assessment will examine your perspective on life and how it was shaped by art. The empowerment of black male youth through Hip hop is important, but we all need to become cognizant of the messages that are being expressed (misery, suffering, anger, and hopelessness, love, hope, and perseverance) and fully understand that the messages warrant a second glance. If art imitates life, then let's focus on the life that our youth are living as several well known recording stars have done.[25,26,27,28,29,30,31,32]

Educators, I recommend that you continue down the path of motivating youth to become involved at the school-building level. Peaking and revitalizing education in our youth is critical regardless of their situation. I understand that we "teach the way that we were taught," but our youth are learning from what we learned. And if we learned that there is only one way to teach, then we are at a disadvantage. Step out of the box. Create a conducive learning environment that supports pro-social behaviors and allows for input from the key stakeholders; our youth. The social competencies that are being fostered through the Hip hop strategies are what's important. The true empowerment occurs when the educator bridges the gap from a generational and cultural perspective. Educators and youth-serving professionals should stand strong in the fact that there are aspects of Hip hop that are not for children. Perpetual conversations about some of the inappropriate messages are necessary. But in the same breath, Hip hop can be a strong ally in sparking creativity, encouragement, and expression. Take Flocabulary, for example, which took root in the mind of the founder and lyricist Blake Harrison while he was still in high school. He was a good student, but he still struggled to memorize facts for tests; he wondered why it was so easy to remember lines to his favorite rap songs but so difficult to memorize academic information. Blake realized that if a rapper released an album that defined SAT vocabulary words, students would have a fun and effective way to study for the SAT.[22]

After studying English at the University of Pennsylvania and working on his rapping at parties, Blake moved to San Francisco where he met Alex Rappaport, a talented musician and producer. Alex had studied music at Tufts University and was writing music for indie films and TV commercials. He also produced ring tones for cell phones. Both he and Blake found jobs at a local Italian restaurant to help pay the bills.

During a game of basketball one day, Blake mentioned his old high school idea of vocabulary rap to Alex. Alex said, "That's a great idea. Let's do it." A month later, the duo had a demo recorded, which they sent around to various educational publishers. When Sparknotes, the world's largest educational web site, commissioned two songs, Blake and Alex realized they had created something real. The name practically invented itself: Flocabulary.

In November 2004, they launched Flocabulary.com. By April 2005, they had completed their first full length album, featuring 12 songs that define 500 SAT vocabulary words. By the summer of 2005, Flocabulary had appeared in the Boston Globe, Chicago Tribune, New York Times, Fitness Magazine, and in numerous blogs on the Internet. In the fall of 2005, Flocabulary began their "Shakespeare is Hip hop" school tour, performing shows up and down the East Coast. In November of 2005, Flocabulary was featured on MTV News. In April of 2006, Flocabulary's SAT Vocabulary CD + book hit bookshelves worldwide, thanks to a deal with Cider Mill Press and Sterling Publishing. By September, ABC News reported that Flocabulary helped raise average SAT scores at one high school by 50 points. Soon after, Flocabulary was featured on CNN, Fox News, NBC Today, and Geraldo At-Large. That same spring, Flocabulary was awarded first prize in Columbia Business School's Outrageous Business Plan competition in the social value category.

Flocabulary followed up the success of their SAT book with Hip hop U.S. History in December 2006. That project, which aims to teach students American history through fact-filled narrative raps, was praised by Cornel West and Howard Zinn as "extraordinary" and "necessary." To complete the project, the duo teamed up with some of New York City's most talented underground rappers and artists, including April Hill, Akir, and Grey. The album's single, "Let Freedom Ring" which features the voice of Martin Luther King Jr., became a podcast hit. As news of Flocabulary's mission spread, various artists and academics began to throw their weight behind the movement. In March 2007, Flocabulary got a chance to work with Grammy Award-Winning artist 9th Wonder on their newest album: Shakespeare is Hip hop. The album seeks to bring Shakespeare to life for today's students through a combination of original Shakespeare rapped over beats, modern day verse translations, and dramatic readings. The album features a host of new artists including Spectac, Median, Netty, 9th Wonder, and Christopher "Play" Martin.

In 2008, Flocabulary expanded their line of educational programs to include products for math and science. They also completed a multi-leveled vocabulary program called The Word Up Project. With ten products in all, Flocabulary relies on the insight and experience of educators, like Mervin Jenkins (Spectac) and 9th Wonder, to ensure that their products are effective and aligned to today's educational standards. But, please remember how the idea started!

For parents, I have the following recommendations: Bridge the gap with your children by understanding what Hip hop means to them. The genre itself creates an outlet for expression and can be used to also create a wider gap if not approached amicably. Disregarding Hip hop will, in essence, hurt any attempt to increase opportunities in relationship building. Allow your youth to "lean wit it and rock wit it," and at the same time speak about how there was a time you danced the "twist." Use opportunities presented by Hip hop to converse with youth. Remember that Hip hop assists in the explanation of the daily experiences of our youth. To understand your youth is to understand what they deem important and how they measure success. Rap with them, then when the music stops, continue to rap (talk) some more.

13

Breaking Through the Barriers to Excellence

By Kenston J. Griffin and Christopher Land

Introduction

It is no secret that, in the 21st century, educators continue to struggle motivating African American students, especially males, to take a proactive approach to their education in and outside of the classroom. Statistics from across the US indicate that African American males typically lag behind children from all other ethnic/minority groups and have been labeled "at risk" for academic failure and becoming a burden to society. From our standpoint, however, African American males are at-risk for being great champions. Chris and I, as well as the other African American male educators who have contributed chapters to this book, know that African American males are creative and powerful beyond all means. The one factor that will ultimately determine whether Black males will become successful is whether teachers provide them with the techniques and procedures for training their minds.[1,2,3,4]

If you really want to transform your relationship with African American males, then you must be fully committed to the advice that will be shared. In doing so, not only will transformation occur, but you will explore some secrets that are applicable, powerful, and necessary to reach and teach African American males. These same procedures will also assist your work with students, regardless of their ethnicity or gender. Ask yourself if you really want to transform how you work with African American males to motivate them to achieve academically and in life. If you decide not to embark upon this transformation process, then your fear has just overcome your faith. We caution you to evaluate your thought process as soon as possible, as your fear may influence how you deal with African American males in other arenas. Nevertheless, our purpose is to let you in on a secret: you already have everything you need to overcome your fear and the challenges you have motivating and educating African American males.

This chapter promises to not only inspire and motivate you to make changes in your own personal life, but it also provides you with ways to successfully educate/work with African American males. This chapter will also provide different activities that will inspire African American males to excel in the classroom.

Just imagine for a moment that it is your first day in class and you're excited about starting the year off right. You were informed that the composition of your class would be a little different. A large number of your students would be poor African Americans males whose parents don't place much value on education. In response, you've filled several bags, suitcases, and a couple of trunks with everything you would need to help teach your students. You have packed heavy for the adventure and you're carrying a lot of baggage. When you enter your classroom, you've got bags in each arm, a duffle bag hanging off of both shoulders, and you're pushing a trunk. Somehow, you've even managed to pull another behind you.

Somewhere between your decision to be a teacher (or school counselor, mentor, or to work with Black males), you stepped over to the baggage carousel and loaded up to prepare for your journey. Chances are you don't remember doing so because you did it without thinking. You probably didn't see a baggage terminal either because the carousel is not the one in the airport; it's the one in your mind. And not all that luggage you grabbed is made of leather; they are made of burdens and habits you acquired over the course of your career as a teacher.

There is a suitcase of doubt about your ability to connect to Black males and a sack of anxiety loaded with discontent about having to teach Black children. You have a duffle bag of low expectations on one shoulder and a hanging bag of cultural incompetence and lack of respect for Black males on the other. Add another duffle bag full of shame about having to work in a low performing school in a poor part of town on your shoulder. A suitcase of guilt about giving up time with your family to prepare for school is tightly gripped in one hand, while another one full of disrespect sits in front of you. Add a backpack of frustration, an overnight bag of confusion about how to motivate Black males, a trunk of fear, and another full of anger. Soon you're exhausted from lugging more baggage than a skycap. And it is just the first day of school.

Imagine for a moment that the Black males in your class are also prone to pack heavy. Much like you, they enter the classroom with duffle bags, suitcases, and overstuffed trunks filled with doubt about their academic abilities, shame, suspicion, poor academic habits, and fear about whether they are valued at school. Like yourself, Black males are exhausted from lugging all that baggage around, and they are ready to set all that stuff down.

What is a barrier? And how do you break through it to excellence?

As we prepare to take this journey, it is important to evaluate some previous trainings, thoughts, and philosophies. Remember, change is a process that occurs only after identifying and submitting to something or someone. The great poet Robert Frost stated, "To think is to put it in ink," I believe that everything we will ever do starts first in our minds. When we begin to talk about motivating and educating African American males, think about the barriers that come to mind. Take out a pen and some paper and don't stop writing until you've written down everything you think might be a barrier to your work with African American males.

We've used this activity to capture the thoughts of hundreds of educators and parents. What we've discovered is that there is a lot of denial and a tendency to blame parents, society, other teachers, poverty, Hip hop, rap music, television, and the lack of positive role models for academic excellence. In other words, educators across the nation point the finger of blame at everyone for the difficulties they have working with Black males. Rarely do they point the finger at themselves. They believe that teachers know their content, so the problem they have reaching Black males must be elsewhere. The big problem with their attribution of blame is that the chances of changing any of these things is about as weak as Chris and me changing sand into water. Denial of responsibility for the problem means they don't believe their expectations and relationship (or lack thereof) with Black males impact their academic performance. In essence, they have erected some huge barriers as a way to insulate themselves from dealing with the burden of responsibility for motivating, educating, and lifting the spirit of Black males.

What Are Barriers To Excellence?

According to Webster Dictionary, a barrier is "an obstruction: a fence or anything that blocks or hinders." Clearly, Black males are engaging in several social practices that block their engagement in academics pursuits. In our work with 40 school systems across the United States, however, we have found teachers to be primary barriers to Black male achievement in the classroom. We have also found that barriers to excellence for African American males extend well beyond the classroom. And more importantly, we believe that reducing these barriers will require more than a back-to-school kick-off talk, a mid-year push, or an end of the year grade extravaganza, which seems intended to make the students and staff feel good than with providing practical strategies for motivating Black males. The real question is whether after these trainings concluded, educators implemented the strategies and methods. In the case of our company, Dream Builders Communication, Inc. (DBC), barriers were reduced. In a school we have been working with for three years, for example, we have increased reading scores by 88 percent and math scores by 58 percent.

The school's success was greatly enhanced by the fact that the superintendent, principal, and staff recognized the need for assistance in reaching minority students, especially African American males. Part of the program's success can also be attributed to positive and supportive relationships we established between the principal, staff, students, parents, and the community. We have achieved similar results with other schools that have resulted in DBC becoming one of the nations' fastest growing training and development firms.

So, before we get into the suggestions for breaking barriers, let's take a few moments to examine some of the barriers that can hinder your work with African American males. As you read the list, keep a mental tally of the items that are true for you.

Some of the barriers we have discovered include:
1. Being afraid of African American males.

2. Limited or rigid interactions with Black males and Black people in general.
3. Unwillingness to consider the learning styles of students in developing lessons.
4. Lack of awareness of your own teaching style and its impact on students.
5. Not knowing what steps to take to make a difference.
6. Discomfort in teaching students who come from a culture of poverty.
7. Fear of failing.
8. Limited qualification to teach in your content area.
9. Feeling to proud to admit you need help reaching African American males.
10. Lack of understanding the culture dynamics of race and culture.
11. Lack of interest in understanding the culture of Black males.
12. Worry about what others might say about you working closely with Black males.
13. Feelings of indifference about working with African American males.
14. Fear of negative feedback from coworkers.
15. Concerns about the extra time and attention it will take to work with Black males.
16. Concerns about your non-Black students complaining about the time you give to Black males.
17. The use of punishment as your disciplinary and classroom management strategy.
18. Anxiety about what your own family will think about your work with Black males.
19. Pessimism about the outcome.
20. Fear that parents of Black males might accuse you of stereotyping their son.

How well did you score? If you answered true to four or less of the statements, then you have relatively few barriers in your work with African American males. Our advice is for you to take a close look at the few items and deal with them using the same skills you've used to avoid the other barriers. If you answered true to five or more of the statements, then seek out additional training, find a mentor who is successful with Black males, and carefully read the chapters in the book that apply to the statements. Whatever you do, take some actions to reduce your score. Consider the increased taxes we will absorb to deal with increased suspension rates, drop out rates, truancy, and crime because you were unwilling to break through the barrier to motivate and educate Black males.

False Evidence Appearing Real (FEAR)

A professional thief by profession, he terrorized banks and the Wells Fargo stage line for nearly a decade. His name became synonymous with the dangers of frontier life. And he did it all without firing a shot or taking a hostage because his presence was enough to paralyze the strongest man. His weapon was his reputation and his ammunition was intimidation. Black Bart, a hooded bandit armed with a deadly weapon is credited with stealing the goods of dozens of stagecoaches during his reign of terror between 1875 and 1883. No victim ever saw him, and no sheriff could ever track his trail.

Bart reminds us of another thief who is still around today. You've never seen his face either, but you know him. His name is fear, but unlike Bart, he doesn't care about your money or your jewelry. He wants something more precious. He wants your courage, and his task is to leave you feeling timid and confused about your willingness to break through the barrier to educate Black males.

Of all the barriers we have identified, fear of making changes is perhaps the strongest barrier hindering the process for educating Black males. Fear is the emotion you experience when you are in danger or you expect something bad to happen. Fear is a signal that something is going to happen that you need to be prepared to cope with or change. The tragedy for most people is that either they try to deny their fear, or they wallow in it. You don't want to surrender to fear or amplify it by thinking of the worst that could happen, nor do you want to pretend it's not there. The best approach for dealing with fear is to prepare yourself mentally and figure out what actions you need to take to deal with the situation.

Our goal in this chapter is not to analyze your fears or barriers, but to offer you some practical and effective ways to leave the baggage hindering your work with Black males outside of the classroom. In doing so, you'll learn how to help Black males free themselves from being prisoners of their own intellect. As the responsible adult, educator, and parents, you'll have to make the major adjustments. You have to break through the barriers that are holding you back from being a great teacher, parent, mentor or counselor.

How do you break the barriers? The first thing that you must do is understand that sometimes it is better to be liked than it is to be right. Being liked in the beginning will provide you much success down the road. Remember the movie *Freedom Writers*? [5] In the movie, Hilary Swank, plays the role of Erin Gruwell, a new, excited schoolteacher who leaves the safety of her white-middle-class hometown to teach at a formerly high achieving high school that has recently put an integration plan in place. Her enthusiasm is rapidly challenged when she realizes that her class is comprised of "at-risk" minority students, also known as "unteachables", and not the eager college bound white students she was expecting. The high school students assimilate into racial groups in the classroom, fights break out, and eventually most of the high school students stop attending class.

Not only does Gruwell meet opposition from her high school students, but she also has a difficult time with her department head, who refuses to let her teach her high school students with new books in case they get damaged and lost, and instead tells her to focus on training them discipline and obedience. She gradually begins to earn the trust of her students and much of her fears and those of the students dissipates when they start recording their diaries, in which they talk about their experiences of being abused, seeing their friends die, and being evicted. Rather than judge, Gruwell listened, observed, related, shared, and then, she was accepted and appreciated by the students. Notice she never talked, instructed, or behaved inflexibly. By contrast, we see educators and parents making the mistake of not building strong relationships with young people, and sometimes they act as if they are working by themselves rather than with other teachers. Some methods to assist you in breaking the barriers with some of your students/children can take place in non-traditional classroom and home settings, such as the cafeteria, hallways, designated bus location, living rooms, etc. Just realize that teachable moments can happen anytime and anywhere.

Create Opportunity for Student to Share Their Ideas

Let your students/children "share freely." This is the opportunity for you to become the student. This interaction will enhance your listening and social skills, and you'll gain insights about what they find interesting and how they perceive and solve some of their tough problems. Just remember, manage your facial expressions. Young people are facing today what many adults have never experienced. Your verbal expressions are powerful, but the non-verbal expressions are even more powerful. To be liked, give them your undivided attention. Then you will not have to work so hard to be right. In chapter nine, a section entitled "Creativity and Life in the 21st Century" indicated that the ability to capture and preserve new ideas is the most important competency students need for developing their creativity. Allowing students to share thoughts and ideas they have captured in a journal is a great way to enhance creativity and strengthen your relationship with Black males. Encouraging your students (or sons) to keep a journal about whatever pops into their heads validates for them that you care about them.

Nurturing Black Males' Respect for Self and Others

Another barrier that may need to be broken is the lack of respect. Some young people today appear not to have a clue as to what respect is. I remember sitting in my aunt's house, and Aretha Franklin was on the radio singing a song called R-E-S-P-E-C-T. The song states, "All I need is a little bit of respect." But how can young people really give you respect if they are never taught how to give it appropriately.

This barrier is one that must be carefully modeled and taught. One false move and you can lose it all, as it relates to this word. I have asked thousands of students across the country what their definition of respect is, and my research shows that they know it means to hold someone or something in high regards. Many African American males respect Lebron James or Kobe Bryant's ability to play the game of basketball; however, the work ethic required to reach this type of success is misunderstood. Many also respect P Diddy and Jay Z's bling, but are not aware of the reading and writing skills one must acquire to reach the level of professionalism and success as a Hip hop artist icon.

Respect can be an easy adjustment as long as we know what respect is to the students. So, whether it's Kobe on the basketball court, or Jay Z on stage, it doesn't really matter. Just be open to where the student is coming from and hear what they are saying about respect. In doing so, you may discover many do have it; they just need our assistance in shaping and developing it. Giving and receiving respect begins with an open conversation about respect and ends when Black males enthusiastically get involved with classroom and extracurricular projects where they learn about self-respect and discipline.

We've got to teach Black males the value of assisting others without expecting something in return. It is also important that they learn how to view challenges as just obstacles trying to get in their way. For example, Earl, a student 10th grade student, got involved with a project where he adopted a family during the holiday season. His role was to collect food, clothing, and household items. Because of the immense sense of respect he feels, he gained the confidence to try out for the chess club at his school. With his help last year, his high school chess club placed second in the state championship.

Mary teaches at a Title I school, and she has been able to accomplish a great deal. At the beginning of every school year since our training four years ago, Mary has been using music to help students comply with classroom rules. First, Mary plays Aretha Franklin's "Respect" for the first 30 days of school. Second, she talks about respect from her point of view, providing the students with visuals and writing this information on the board to be displayed all year long as a constant reminder. And third, every 30 days, she asks the students to develop a top 10 list of ways to have respect in the classroom. Mary says, "short term goals work better and it keeps students engaged the entire year." Mary has been promoted from math teacher to an assistant principal. The discipline referrals have decreased by 47 percent, and the entire school now listens to this song at the beginning of the year, too. This technique has created so much success that the school district is considering implementing a similar strategy in multiple schools.

Mary's steps were simple but essential. She began implementing her steps on day one by using music relative to the desired objective, role modeling, engaging the students, and making change periodically to keep it interesting. By making sure, everyone is consistent and accountable to the rules and having fun, the students will speak highly of you, and parents eventually, will get engaged, too.

After reviewing the word respect, you now must also identify your niche. The word niche is defined as a place, employment, status, or activity for which a person or thing is best fitted. In a nutshell, your niche is something you are good or gifted at doing. I would highly suggest that if you want to be accomplished at breaking barriers in working with African American males, you must know your niche.

Knowing Your Niche

Many educators assume that by virtue of a high level of education or simply being Black, they are experts at working with Black males. It should be noted that effective educators do not always stay on task with the lesson plan but typically plan there lessons around the students. All of these things are great, but until you operate in your niche, you are really just spinning your wheels. So let's talk about ways to operate in your niche and some best practices in reaching African American males. Begin by taking a few minutes to identify your areas of strength.[6,7,8] Again, take out a pen and some paper and don't stop until you've written down everything you think are the strengths in your work with African American males. If it's difficult for you to identify your strengths, consider asking Black males in your classroom to help you with this exercise. But once you've identified your strengths, it is important for you to consider ways that you have used your strengths to break through the barriers to excellence. Determine what socio-economic, emotional, or psychological structures may have influenced your work with Black males. After you evaluate these potential external (and even internal) influences, determine if any them can be altered inside of your classroom to provide students with increased levels of awareness, security, and desire to incorporate change.

Statistics continue to show that students' success is truly impacted by their environment, peer association, and support systems or the lack thereof. Educators must perform all facets of the profession and accept responsibility for influencing the student's growth. But before undertaking this task, you must be willing to grow.

Your Circle of Influence

Identify the people you spend time with on most days. Consider their gender, ethnicity, age, and personal status, amount of time you spend with them, and their role in your life. Many people quickly identify the people they work with on a daily basis. Interestingly enough, most people seek the comfort of people who are more like themselves in their beliefs and values. In addition, although most of the workplaces are fairly "integrated" as far as ethnicity/race is concerned, most people tend to spend the majority of their time with people who are members of their own ethnic and racial group. This does not mean that the person is a racist or dislikes working with people from different ethnic/racial groups. However, it does mean that their experiences with understanding the cultures and customs of people outside of their personal circle/race are limited. Similarly, this does not mean that you are not gifted in working with students outside of your circle. It does suggest that additional work may be required to reach this goal. A very detailed biography of who you are could be derived from a list of your closest daily contacts. Birds of a feather flock together.

We must begin to evaluate the individuals we allow to influence and impact our lives and deposit into our core being. Therefore, the first step you've got to undertake in working with African American males is to have them identify five or so close friends who influence their lives. Ask questions about whether their friends attend all of their classes, what they do after school, and whether their friends always turn in their homework. In other words, you've got to ask questions to make sure you understand the real influence of their friends. The first stage of transformation begins when we assist African American males to evaluate who they are and who they could become. Start with the end in mind, this will provide direction for this process.

The second stage begins with our taking an honest assessment of our lives and the goals we have established or the lack thereof. Did we set ourselves up for failure by not planning for success? Educators, parents, and friends, establishing goals for your life is a good thing, but a plan of action is even better. This allows for accountability, which is nothing more than being responsible and establishing a check and balance system that will keep us on the path to acquiring those goals. To a certain extent, the stages are very similar to those of several well known life coaches and self-empowerment experts, simply suggesting that educators apply the principles to the empowerment of African American males.[9,10,11,12,13,14,15,16,17,18,19]

If you operate in your niche, all things are possible. For example, John, a 15-year educator/parent/coach, attended a conference where I (Kenston J. Griffin) gave a keynote address and conducted a workshop. The title of the keynote was "It Only Takes Everything You've Got." During this address, I shared some methods to work inside of your niche. First, I asked the audience for their definition of the word niche, and then I shared my definition. This process was to ensure we had a common defining point. I asked a few preliminary questions, then I asked someone to volunteer to share his or her niche. Although I am not a hunter, the man who volunteered talked about hunting, and I could not only feel his excitement, but I could see and hear it. During the session, the attendees where encouraged to conduct the same activity with their students.

Weeks later, we received a letter from John, who wrote, "Mr. Griffin your presentation was outstanding, and you kept my attention the entire time. And, yes, I did do the niche activity with my students and the football team. First, I asked them to share what non-school related activities they loved to do. Second, I shared that I love to spend time with my wife and grandchildren. Third, I asked my students to explain how we could accomplish doing the things we loved and do them well. Fourth, I asked them how we could share at least one example per week. Lastly, we came up with ideas and strategies. Now, because my students look forward to sharing, I am three chapters ahead of all the other teachers as it relates to English. And because my students, especially my African American males, write about our stories/niches, I understand what they are facing and how I need to respond or not respond to situations. The greatest reward is that 90% of my students passed their end of course test; yes, that includes my African American males. This technique is incredible. God bless and keep changing the minds to ultimately change lives."

Another way to operate in or identify your niche is by identifying areas that you operate in without difficulty. We call this passion. When you work in your passion, you may tend to feel free and full of joy. To better understand passion, let's look at some individuals most would identify as being passionate.

- Dr. Martin Luther King, Jr: He was not just passionate about African American people; he was passionate about people.

- Oprah Winfrey: She is not just passionate about African American children; she is passionate about all children.
- Forrest Whitaker: He is a passionate producer, director, and Oscar award winning actor who cares about all people.
- Dr. Ernest H. Johnson: A teacher's teacher! He is not only saying it, but he's doing it—reaching, teaching, and training. He is the GLUE (Giver of Lover Unconditionally to Everyone) that the other authors and myself needed to complete our work for this book and to take on other projects to de-condition Black males from seeing themselves as failures and not worthy of success.
- Tom Joyner: He is not just enthusiastic about his radio programs; he is passionate about helping Black students complete their college education.
- Denzel Washington: An award-wining actor who is passionate about being a father and role model for all males.
- Thurgood Marshall: He was passionate about the civil rights of African Americans and equal justice for everyone.
- Hill Harper: He is not just passionate about his acting roles; he is passionate about being a writer and his desire to motivate young people to take an active role in local, state, and national politics.
- Robin Roberts: She is an enthusiastic morning news television host and crusader for the prevention of breast cancer.
- Dr. Bill Cosby: He is a passionate entertainer, educator, and author who is passionate about the need to truthfully address social, economic, and educational problems Black Americans face today.

The list goes on and on. You can select names of passionate people in your world to fill in the blanks, but to really win, and win big, your name must be in one of the blanks. So how do you get passionate about a group of students that appear to have so many problems? Answer: One student at a time.

Personally, I read and re-read and have students to read with me before our day together even starts. Some ask how to get non-reading students engaged? I start and conclude every day with two positive affirmations. Positive affirmations are defined as the act of affirming or the state of being affirmed; assertion; something declared to be true; a positive statement or judgment. I model this process daily. I ask my students to read affirmations independently and to write them down. Initially, some chose not to write them down, but when a student expresses the desire not to read, I provide an index card with these words; "I do not know your current situation, but I know that you can control it. Help me help you, please!" This has proven to be effective and even enjoyable, especially after students begin to respond positively.

Another strategy I use to assist students in engaging in the daily affirmation process is to allow them the opportunity to create their own positive affirmations incorporating the use of music and dance. Provided below are just a few for you to use and adopt.[20,21]

- The mediocre teacher tells. The good teacher explains. The superior teacher demonstrates. The great teacher inspires.
- A man who does not read good books has no advantage over a man who can't read them.
- If better is possible, good is no longer an option.
- The tragedy of life doesn't lie in not reaching your goals. The tragedy lies in not having any goals to reach.
- Fear is temporary, but regret is permanent.
- The anger you have for your enemy will often burn you up first.

Affirmation can have a powerful impact on students because of how the messages reach the subconscious mind. An iceberg serves as a useful metaphor to understand the unconscious mind, its relationship to the conscious mind, and how the two parts of our mind can better work together. But, just like an iceberg, the real power resides deep beneath the surface. As an iceberg floats in the water, the huge mass of it remains below the surface. In this way, the iceberg is like the mind. The conscious mind is what we notice above the surface, while the unconscious mind, the largest and most powerful part, remains unseen.

The unconscious mind holds all awareness that is not presently in the conscious mind. All memories, feelings, conditioned habits, and thoughts that are out of conscious awareness are by definition "unconscious." It is also called the subconscious and is known as the dreaming mind, deep mind, or sleeping mind.

Knowledgeable and powerful in a different way than the conscious mind, the unconscious mind handles the responsibility of keeping the body running well. It has memory of every event we've ever experienced;

it is the source and storehouse of our emotions, and it is often considered our connection with Spirit and with each other.

No model of how the mind works disputes the tremendous power that is in constant action below the tip of the iceberg. The conscious mind is constantly supported by unconscious resources. Just think of all the things you know how to do without conscious awareness. Do you remember learning how to drive a car? Learning with an automatic transmission was one thing, but trying to remember all of those extra steps you had to make to drive a manual shift may have appeared to be unachievable and unbelievable. When you consider all of those steps, it is remarkable that any of us learned how to master the task. Today, as you got into your car, did you give any thought to the hundreds of steps that were necessary for you to drive from home to work? Everything we do starts as words that are programmed into our conscious mind. Once we understand the power of our words, they transform into habits that propel us to perform by rote. These are skills, not facts; they are processes, requiring intelligence, decision-making and training.

Besides these learned resources that operate below the surface of consciousness, there are important natural resources. For instance, the unconscious mind regulates all the systems of the body and keeps them in harmony with each other. It controls heart rate, blood pressure, digestion, the endocrine system and the nervous system, just to name a few of its functions.

The conscious mind, like the part of the iceberg above the surface, is a small portion of the whole being. The conscious mind is what we ordinarily think of when we say "my mind." It's associated with thinking, analyzing and making judgments and decisions. The conscious mind is actively sorting and filtering its perceptions because only so much information can reside in consciousness at once. Everything else falls back into unconsciousness.

If an affirmation is repeated often, the words eventually become part of the subconscious and, just like driving a car, you'll find yourself acting in ways reflective of the affirmation (e.g., I am somebody and I am a great student) without being consciously aware. In time, these actions or skills will become powerful habits, the kinds of habits that result in Black males becoming successful.

The less you associate with some people, the more your life will improve. Any time you tolerate mediocrity in others, it increases your mediocrity. An important attribute in successful people is their impatience with negative thinking and negative acting people. As you grow, your associates will change. Some of your friends will not want you to go on. They will want you to stay where they are. Friends that don't help you climb will want you to crawl. Your friends will stretch your vision or choke your dream. Those that don't increase you will eventually decrease you. Consider this:

- Never receive counsel from unproductive people.
- Never discuss your problems with someone incapable of contributing to the solution, because those who never succeed themselves are always first to tell you how. Not everyone has a right to speak into your life. You are certain to get the worst of the bargain when you exchange ideas with the wrong person.
- Don't follow anyone who's not going anywhere. With some people, you spend an evening; with others, you invest it.
- Be careful where you stop to inquire for directions along the road of life.
- Wise is the person who fortifies his life with the right friendships. So, in being wise always evaluate the company you keep.

After reviewing and reading the passage, our students discuss the benefits of making the ideas in the poem a part of their lives. We encourage you to have your students read this poem and make it a part of your classroom motto. This is a great tool to show your students the power of the right and wrong type of company to keep. These words can positively affect you and the company you keep as an adult, but they can have a tremendous impact on our African American males.

Susan, a seventh grade teacher in Florida, has worked with DBC for the past 4 years. One of her favorite classroom training models is effectively using positive affirmations. Notice the key work effectively. Susan starts and ends every class with a positive affirmation. If a student appears to get off task, she asks the entire class to repeat the affirmation of the day twice. This concept is so powerful that each block has an affirmation, and the students are so excited that they want to know the other blocks' affirmations. DBC has found that there is proof in the pudding, but one must be willing to taste it. Finally, Susan reports that this has grown so much that students put their favorite affirmation on their desk during their end of grade test (EOG) because they believe the words and they have put in prior work.

Pointing African American Males Toward Their Goals

Black males understand about learning for passion rather than just for grades. They have often experienced this phenomenon when they spend countless hours learning the complex lyrics and rhymes of every song on an album only to show off their accomplishment to their peers. They have similar experiences when they see an article while surfing the Web. They read the article and look up additional information if it's interesting, even if it has nothing to do with what they are researching. But many Black males tell us that it's hard for them to think of a time when they really enjoyed learning in the classroom.

James, a high school senior, for example, believes that most of what we gained from school has little value to his life. "Let's face it, high school is just a means to an end; it's a stepping stone to get many brothers like me out of the system and into the streets. All I every wanted to do is become a firefighter, but school never allowed me to be in charge of my learning experience. My teachers never listened to me and never tried to point me toward my goals," he said. While his goals are different from the student who wants to become a doctor or lawyer, the one universal truth is that how hard a Black male works in schools depends on whether the work is related to his goals in life.

Black males who have no dreams tend to slack off and many eventually dropout of school altogether. The big problem, however, is not the lack of dreams, but that many of these young Black males have dreams that don't involve going to college. They see no connection between what they are learning and their dreams. As a result, they never learn in school purely for the enjoyment of learning. They are told, unconvincingly, like many other students that enjoyment will come later when they attend college and find a fulfilling job.

Goals must be personally meaningful in order to spend time each day working on them. That's why it's crucial for you to establish goals that are relevant to you. Your goals must excite you and drive you even when you aren't in "the right frame of mind." Black males sitting in your classrooms are no different, except they don't have a clue about how to set goals and monitor their progress. So, how do we point African American males toward their goals and keep them on target to reaching them? The answer is simple; we have to introduce them to a process whereby they can explore their own thinking about what they want to accomplish in their lives. And while there are many great programs about goal setting, nothing seems to be more powerful than having Black males generate a list of 101 things they want to accomplish things that will bring them great joy, happiness and a sense of fulfillment. It might see like a simple task, but most adults, like Black boys, have a hard time initially dreaming up the list. But what's so magical about generating the list is that after working on it for a while, most Black boys begin to realize that they are making a list of their personal goals.

Once the list is completed, it will be easy to organize the items into these classic categories: fun/outrageous goals, money goals, family goals, career/job goals, health goals, personal development goals, and spiritual goals. Once this is accomplished, the hard work is to determine the top goal in each category. We've had some boys generate the list in a couple of days then spend a week discussing with us the reasons for choosing their top goals. And somewhere in their discussions, it happens: they begin to see the connections between their top goals, and they understand that they are thinking about their own thinking.

Making the list of 101 things helps to teach Black boys to find inspiration in themselves. Once they understand that we (parents, educators, mentors, and counselors) value their thinking and support them, they will often make their learning experience into whatever it needs to be to accomplish their goals. The real secret is to point them in the direction of their joy and happiness. Because just like us adult, once a Black boy feels good about himself and what he's doing, then he will work harder to fulfill his dreams.

Create An Environment Where Black Males Feel Important

"I feel like an alien, like I don't belong, and sometimes I wish that I could get my teachers to just change places with me so they can feel what I'm going through," said Tyron, a bright ninth grader. This sentiment is similar to many of the Black males we have encountered in our work. They don't feel connected and believe that their teachers see them as anonymous rather than people with a real need to be relational. As long as Black males feel like they are standing on the outside looking in, they will never be interested in learning. You've got to make each and everyone of them feel important and valuable. And forget about encouraging them to go out for the football or basketball teams; there simply aren't enough space on the team for all of the Black males in the your classroom.

Look inside of the classroom and you'll find many opportunities to assign Black males to important leadership roles. Outside of your classroom, there are younger students who might need help with homework or reading. Encourage back males to get involved with these programs in your school and community. John, for example, is a tenth grader who volunteers to read the newspaper to senior citizens on Saturday mornings. "At first, I wanted to quit. I thought about everything I could be doing on Saturday mornings, but after I had been reading for a few weeks, I realized how much the people were looking forward to me being there with them. I would never have thought in a million years that I would feel so important or that reading to old people was something special. And to believe that one man had his life insurance policy changed so that I am the beneficiary so that when he passed on I will have some money for college . . . Helping out like this has changed my life," says John.

Black boys like John, if given a chance, can make a big difference in the lives of students at your school. Tim, for example, is a tenth grader you want around when you are having problems with your computers and other multimedia equipment. The boy is a genius when it comes to producing movies, but he is just getting by, making Cs, in his courses. Although he has never made a movie, he has studied every movie made by his role models, Spike Lee and Clint Eastwood. The opportunity presented itself for Tim to work with two other boys, both exceptional students, to develop a script and direct, film, and produce a short movie. Initially, Tim took a backseat role in the project because he thought he wasn't as smart as the two other boys. The movie seemed like it was going nowhere fast until Tim's teacher encouraged him to assume the leadership role on the project "All I needed to hear was those encouraging words from my teacher and we were on our way. My teammates started to believe in me and we worked together to produce our video. I can honestly say that the satisfaction I got from seeing the video and the feedback from my teacher and classmates was better than making As in all of my courses."

Tapping Into African American Males' Creativity

The Webster's Dictionary defines the word "tap" as to strike lightly. It also defines the word "creativity" as inventive or stimulating the imagination. According to 100 African American males ages 13 to 17 served by our company across the southern part of the county, tap means to move and creativity means to be original. Now when asked that question in an educational context, over 80% of these same African American males stated that most teachers neither want to hear what they have to say nor the context in which they wish to say it. African American males also stated that drumming on a desk, beat boxing, or rapping/humming a song is their way of being creative. What they want is some downtime to just think about their thinking and to get lost in their thoughts. It's similar to what happens to us when we are reading a good book or listening to our favorite music.

Our task is not to debate whether what Black males are saying to us is right or wrong, but to encourage them to think about their thinking. The good teacher explains. The superior teacher demonstrates. The great teacher inspires. So, the question is how can you tap into the creativity of Black males or any of your students?

You've got to consider the rules you have established for how and why learning in accomplished in your classroom. If you have established strict guidelines about the work you expect from homework and classroom assignments, then you have closed the door to creativity. Loosen up a bit and give them some freedom to grasp what you are teaching; you'll discover that they will feel a great sense of accomplishment. Don't get us wrong, having a highly structured classroom with concrete and sequential lessons plans is essential. This approach will be very effective for many students, but some students (and not just back males) learn better if the strategy used to teach allows for more random and abstract thought.

When Black boys feel more in charge of their learning, you will find it easier to teach them the step-by-step approached required to master certain materials. And something as simple as letting students know they will be tested using an open-ended essay as opposed to a closed-ended multiple choice test can make a difference. If you followed every single guideline, chances are you would not be reading this book. Regardless of the subjects you teach, you've got to remember that the students in your classroom are not miniature versions of yourself. They have their own unique ways for seeing the world and learning information. Every now and then, you will get lucky and you'll find yourself feeling blissful teaching a classroom of students with learning styles that are similar to your own, but if you want better results all the time, you have to structure how you are teaching to tap into the creativity of Black males. And one of the most effective ways to accomplish this is to challenge Black males to think.

Challenge Black Males To Think

The customary approach to teaching is to use strict guidelines and, essentially, to spoon-feed students the information they need to ace tests. Students need structure and guidelines, but it's OK to focus on the big picture of topics and allow students to appreciate the lessons they can derive from them. For example, Samuel, an 11th grader, told us about one of the best teachers he has ever had. "We read two letters, one written by W.E.B. DuBois and the other written by Booker T. Washington, which showed how their ways of thinking differed and sometimes split African Americans apart. What was cool about the teacher is that she allows us to discover these differences ourselves rather than just tell us about them during a lecture. We worked in small learning teams where each team member was required to learn different things about DuBois and Washington. We debate each other and other teams. And our teacher made room for us to debate current topics like Barack Obama's speech on Reverend Wright," explained Samuel.

If you want to motivate Black males to excel in school, then help them find their own voice and their own self-respect. Provide them teaching materials that portray several sides of an argument and opened their mind to information that most text books fail to mention. Loosen up, keep your guidelines, and engage Black males and all your students in ways that evoke deeper thinking about what you are teaching.

Bring Out The Best Self of Black Males

The best way to bring out the best in African American males is to expect the best. Today, as you read these words, America is still celebrating the election of its first African American president, Barack H. Obama. His story, like many Black males, involves a father who was not active in raising him and a grandmother who stepped into when his mother passed away. And being the son of a white woman and Black man, from Kenya caused some anguish about his ethnic identity. Despite these challenges and others, he did not stray from his dream, which was to be the best at whatever he made up his mind to do. And all of the authors of this book are thankful that he became a Harvard educated lawyer, a United States Senator, and a tech savvy president.

At this moment in history, one of the best models for Black boys to mimic is President Obama. But there is a catch; he's not our first and only Black male role model of greatness. Our history is full of great examples of Black men who have overcome insurmountable odds to achieve success. The problems is not the lack of examples. The problem lies with a lethargic teaching force that is either uninterested in helping Black boys to become great or they are uninformed about how to bring out the best in Black males. How can teachers bring out the best in African American males? Dr. Martin Luther King, Jr., in a sermon titled "The Three Dimensions of a Complete Life," delivered at the New Covenant Baptist Church in Chicago on April 9, 1967, points out that "Too many Negroes are ashamed of themselves, ashamed of being Black. To love yourself, you've got to rise up and say from the bottom of your soul . . . I am somebody. I have a rich, noble, and proud heritage. However exploited and however painful my history has been, I'm Black, but I'm Black and beautiful." What Dr. King was speaking about was the need for Black people to accept themselves regardless of their talents and limitations.[22]

Few Black males sitting in your classrooms will rise up to become a United States senator or president of the United States. Statistics say that less than fifty percent will graduate from high school, and very few will rise to the heights of genius in the arts and sciences. But each of them has a special gift, a talent that connects them to their purpose for being on this planet. Your role as a parent or educator is to help cultivate those talents so that Black males see and understand the dignity of work associated with their gifts. Brining out the best means that you will help Black males accept and appreciate themselves and their talents. Dr. King said to the congregation that morning, "What I'm saying to you this morning, my friends, even if it falls your lot to be a street sweeper, go on out and sweep streets like Michelangelo painted pictures; sweep streets like Handel and Beethoven composed music; sweep streets like Shakespeare wrote poetry; sweep streets so well that all the hosts of heaven and earth will have to pause and say, 'Here lived a great street sweeper who did his job well'."[23]

And if you can instill within them this sense of dignity while they are still young, you might look back one day and realize that you helped a Black boy stay in school. He might have not gone to college, but because of you, he cultivated his talents and became a productive member of society.

You might ask yourself, "What will happen if I stop to help the Black males in my classroom?" But the real questions should be "What will happen to Black males in my classroom if I don't put forth the effort to help them bring out their best?"

Consistency

All of us can change our actions for a moment and produce a desirable result. Beginning teachers who seeks out a mentor to help them learn how to use discipline, compassion, and love to keep their classroom focused prove that everyday. But to be truly successful, they must be consistent in their actions. Their classroom falls apart if they return to the same classroom with management techniques they had before applying the lessons from their mentor. It works the same way in other areas of your life. You need to develop consistency in your daily actions with Black males to produce long-lasting results.

Being consistent in your actions will help you to continually perform at a high level. Develop the mindset that looks at success as a long-term proposition. Commit yourself to sustaining your performance for as long as it takes to win. And even after you reach your objective, you'll reach for an even higher goal because you've developed the habit of winning. You have become someone others can depend on to get the job done, and you'll be richly rewarded for your efforts.

By consistently utilizing your abilities to accomplish your goals, you will continue to improve. It has been said that repetition is the mother of skill. By repeatedly performing a task, you'll develop a skill that others rely on, and you'll be in demand. Your ability to get things done will elicit confidence and trust from others. Moreover, you will find it easier to get the help you need to complete a task that's important to you. You will become a person others admire because of your sustained performance and never-ending desire for improvement. Mastering the art of consistency will set you apart from those who work when they feel like it. Being consistent means that the life you want five years from now depends on what you are saying today. Being consist will enable you to fully understand that words can either bless or curse your future work with Black males.

Your words have creative power. Too many teachers go around saying, "I'll never reach Black males. I'll never understand how to motivate Black male. It's too late for me to change how I feel about teaching Black boys. I'll keep doing what I'm doing and retire. Our schools' test scores are never going to improve." Then they wonder why they don't see things turn around. It's because they're calling defeat into their future. They're calling in mediocrity. Don't let that be you!

When you get up in the morning, no matter how you feel, no matter what things look like, instead of using your words to describe your situation, use your words to change your situation. Teachers who are successful in reaching and motivating Black males make a declaration of faith by saying, "This is going to be a great day, and I'm going to motivate all my students to learn."

When you do that, you are choosing to bless your future. You are calling in favor, increase, and opportunities. You are opening the door for great blessings to occur. If you aren't reaching and motivating Black males, then examine what you are consistently focusing on in your interactions with Black males. Black males who thrive and achieve academic excellence consistently engage in routines that produce excellent results. And what make this possible is the consistent advice and guidance they receive from their teachers.

Consistency is a winning habit that requires focused work. Every successful teacher (parent, counselor or mentor) has developed the capacity to work relentlessly on his or her goals. After deciding on a worthwhile endeavor, successful teachers place all of their efforts behind their goals. They consistently take the steps necessary to reach their goals. Realize the importance of developing the habit of consistency and you'll be firmly on the road to what you seek. Winners expect to win because they know that by doing certain things everyday they will eventually reach their goals. Sir Isaac Newton said, "A body in motion tends to remain in motion . . ." So start your "success snowball." It will pick up momentum with each passing day. You will get better at performing the tasks necessary to obtain your goals. You can win big if you move towards your dreams with consistency.

Attitude

Attitude is more important than facts. It is more important than the past, education, money, circumstances, failures, success, and what other people think or say or do. It is more important than appearance, giftedness or skill. It will make or break a company . . . a church . . . a home. Attitude will make your work with Black boys a peaceful experience or turn it into a nightmare. The remarkable thing is we have a choice every day regarding the attitude we will embrace for that day. We cannot change our past . . . we cannot change the fact that people will act in a certain way. We cannot change the inevitable. The only thing we can do is play on the string we have, and that is our attitude. I am convinced that life is 10% of what happens to me and 90% of how I react to it. And so it is with you. We are in charge of our attitudes. Look at attitude as a must.

Attitude is the center of a Black boy's motivational life. If the fruit of a tree is bad, you don't try to fix the fruit; you treat the roots of the tree. And if the actions of Black males are out of line with their academic goals, it's not enough to help them change habits; you have to go deeper. You have to go to the heart of the problem: attitude. It is important for you to model the attitude and behavioral routines you want Black males to learn.

When a Black male gives you a difficult time in class, do you quickly reprimand or reflect on the real meaning of his behavior? What you do depends on your attitude. When your schedule is too tight or your to-do list too long, do you lose your cool or keep it? What you do depends on your attitude. When you have the opportunity to make jokes and unflattering comments about Black males, do you turn and walk away or do you memorize every word and pass it on? What you do depends on your attitude. Do you see Black boys who are doing poorly in school as a burden or as an opportunity to make sure they receive a quality education? That, too, depends on the state of your attitude.

You attitude dictates whether you harbor a grudge or give grace, indulge in self-pity or seek peaceful solutions to break through the barriers that are holding you back from reaching Black males.

If you address external challenges while ignoring the inside—your attitudes—the issue will persist. For example, Jackie, second-year teacher, found herself feeling at a loss about how to handle the angry thoughts she experienced when Black boys acted out in her classes. A well-meaning co-worker suggested sending the boys to detention. Another teacher can't seem to get Black boys to take out the earphones and stop listening to music on their IPods in her classroom. The solution? Confiscate the IPods and lock them away until the end of the academic year. Jean, a third-year math teacher has tried everything she knows to motivate Black males to embrace math. She knows the students are capable, but she decided to solve the problem by having the students moved to a lower level math class.

Case after case of failing to treat the root of the problem has resulted in short-term solutions. One thing is clear: These solutions don't get at the root of the problem—attitude. The key to getting Black males to change their attitude is for you (the teacher, parent, counselor, mentor) to check your own attitude about teaching Black males. Maybe the advice to young people from Malcolm X is being applied by Black males sitting in your classrooms, "See for yourself, and listen for yourself and think for yourself. Then you can come to an intelligent decision for yourself." Most want to learn, and they are looking for you to show them the way. They want you to build on their interests, not all the time, but enough so that they feel like valuable members of the learning community you are creating within your classrooms.

We advised Jackie, the second-year teacher having problems with Black boys acting out in classes, to communicate eye-to-eye with the boy and let him know in concise terms that she would not tolerate any more acting out from him because she has higher expectation for him. "It was a bit of a challenge at first, but I was the problem. I had to change my thinking about the problem and communicate what I wanted from a standpoint of respect rather than fear." In the end, Jackie didn't have to threaten the boys with sending them to the office or say any of that sort of thing. The classroom management problems that were not solved using this approach vanished when she built into her curriculum regular times for students to talk and interact with each other.

"I have to admit I was amazed how many student problems disappeared after I started allowing children to spend a few minutes talking with each other. They want to do the same things we do when we come to meetings and lectures; they want to talk now and then," said Jackie.

Advice to Parents and Educators

To effectively use the information in this chapter, you must spend time, quality time, working with the young African American males in your life. The sooner you decide to address the problems that are hindering your work with Black males, the better you and your students will be. Even if the process is painful and the problems are difficult to manage, the sooner you intervene, the more likely it is that Black males can be steered back on track.

Take the case of a woman who has discovered a lump in her breast. The initial response is anxiety, fear and worry about the worst possible outcome; breast cancer that has to be treated with chemotherapy or a mastectomy. If the lump is ignored, there is a good chance that the condition will get worse, but moving forward to deal with the initial lump might reveal that it's just a harmless cyst or some other problem that can be easily managed. But if the woman continues to deny the potential seriousness of the problem, then the situation can easily escalate to the point where it's life threatening.

Denial is what has contributed to many of the academic challenges we currently have with Black males, particularly those in middle and high school. As incredible as it may seem, the main reason that a Black male in middle or high school can't read is that he is the product of some type of social promotion rather than a sincere attempt for educators to provide him with a foundation for learning. Rather than deal with the difficulties of motivating and educating Black males, we have created an environment at school and society that contributes to Black males feeling uncomfortable, unloved, and not valued. In essence, we have denied the seriousness of early symptoms and denied Black males the right to the same quality of education as their white counterparts. The end result is that many don't seem to care about the value of an education or they disengage altogether and drop out.

This chapter, as do the others in this book, contains several suggestions for motivating and educating Black males. To use the information in this chapter requires you to take a honest look at your own behavior. Let's take a few moments to examine the extent to which you are currently using the procedures outlined in this chapter to enhance your work with African American males. As you read the list, keep a mental tally of the items that are true for you.

The barrier breakers that are reviewed in this chapter:

1. Have I identified my barriers to motivating and educating Black males?
2. Do I create opportunities for Black males to share their experiences?
3. Have I nurtured Black males' so that they respect themselves and others?
4. Do I know my own niche—those areas of strength I already possess?
5. How well do I understand the power of my circle of influence?
6. Have I pointed and steered African American males toward their goals?
7. Do I create an environment where Black males feel important and respected?
8. How well do I tap into the creativity of Black males?
9. Do I consistently challenge African American males to think critically?
10. Do I help Black males to bring out their best self?
11. Do I teach African American males about the power of consistency?
12. Do I have a positive attitude about my work with Black males?

How well are you doing? Few teachers, Black or white, are fully engaging Black males in their classrooms. Regardless of how many of these questions that you answered in the affirmative, you've got some work to do. Our advice is for you to take each questions and spend a day contemplating your compelling reasons for making it a part of your educational practices with Black males. Just like setting other goals for your life, if you are going to be successful in making these practices a part of your work with Black males, then you've got to examine your compelling reasons for the goals. Regardless of how important you believe the items on the list are, they will remain nothing more than wishful ideas unless you devote some quality time developing your reasons for making them part of your life. Making either of the items on the list an important part of you teaching practices is an ambitious undertaking. We have worked with many teachers who say they are interested in improving their work with Black male students, but they simply refuse to engage themselves in the process to turn their belief into a reality. There are 12 questions on the list, and we want you to make a commitment to spend time (10-15 minutes) each day, before starting your workday, for twelve consecutive days. You will need a pen and a notebook to keep a record of your work. To turn either of the items on the list into a reality takes work. But the work is easy and exciting if you follow these seven steps:

Step 1: Re-read the section of the chapter where the item is discussed.

Step 2: You've got to picture in graphic detail how much failure to make this item a part of your work will negatively impact your life. Your main objective is to make the pain of not working on this item feel so real, so intense, so immediate that you can't put off changing how you are dealing with Black males in your classroom. Take a few moments to picture in graphic detail how your failure not to make this item part of your work with Black males will negatively affect you and the people who are most important to you. Picture in detail how your life (and your Black male students) will be five, ten and twenty years from now if you continue not to make this item an important part of your work with Black males. Think about all of the messy personal, family, and financial problems that could happen to yourself (and your Black male students) because you failed to make this item a part of your educational practices with Black males. Now take out your notebook and record your thoughts.

Step 3: Now that you have linked some emotional pain to not working on the items, the next step is for you to link positive sensations to working on the items. Take each item and picture in graphic detail how great you will feel after adopting the attitudes, values, and beliefs reflected by the item. Think about how your relationships with my Black students and important people in my life will be because you made this item part of my life. Think about what you and your students will gain mentally, emotionally, physically, financially, and spiritually by making this item part of your teaching routine. Working on the items this way will ignite your intrinsic need to be relentless in making the item a part of your work with Black males. Your mastery of this technique resides with your willingness to associate an almost unbelievable amount of discomfort with not making the item a part of your work routine. The pain has to be sufficient so that not making the item a part of your work is incredibly painful, while adopting the item is perceived as being attractive, fun, positive, and pleasurable.

Although you might like to deny it, the fact remains that what drives your work routine with Black male students is an instinctive reaction to pain (frustration) and pleasure (accomplishments), not your intellectual calculations. Just like the Black boys in your classrooms, you have to look deep within yourself to learn which of your buttons to push to adopt new routines or to change bad habits (See Chapter 6 for example of how this process is used to turn academic excellence into a habit).

Step 4: Select a different Black male student every two days or to be the recipient of this hand written note from you: "Dear (Name of Student), I have been thinking about ways to help you improve your grades and to become a better student. I've got some ideas, but I want to know your thoughts. Let's talk in a few days.

Step 5: Read your responses to the negative and positive power questions during your lunch time. Then answer the question, "What action can I take now, at this very moment and before the day is over, to make this item a part of my life?"

Step 6: At the end of your day or before retiring for bed, repeat the process that you engaged in at the start of your day. Record your responses to the questions in your notebook.

Step 7: If you find yourself feeling troubled and disturbed about your work with Black males, it means you've just got to dig a little deeper and focus on the reasons for making the item a part of your routine work with Black males. Your progress depends on your willingness to change and your level of motivation (or compelling reasons) to change. If you are not driven to make working on the item a regular part of your teaching routine, then you haven't discovered enough motivation. All this means is that you need to spend some additional time examining what you (and the Black males you teach) will lose out on if you don't make the item a part of your life.

It takes time and effort to develop the routines for successfully motivating Black males. Changing your routines can happen in a moment or a few days, but if you are looking to change, you must have the ability to persevere. When you think of perseverance, one sure way to reach your goal is to start with the end in mind. One person that refused to stop moving forward until he reached his goal is President Barack H. Obama. This son of a Kenyan father and a American white woman found a way to earn a law degree from Harvard and win a Senate seat in Illinois before winning the hearts of millions of Americans on his journey to become the first African American president of the country. President Obama knew what we wanted, and his vision was so vivid that young voters—probably the largest number of young voters in history-flocked to the polls to turn his vision into a reality.

Persevering means you've got to have goals that compel you to focus on them as though you have already achieved them. Realize that your goals and dreams will not die if you persevere beyond the barriers placed in your path. You don't have to be a Black man, or a man at all, to have a lasting and positive impact on Black boys, but you've got to be willing to step outside of your comfort zone and consistently take actions that move you in the direction of your goals. Something as simple as surrounding yourself with poems, like the one below, can provide inspiration for those times when you have doubts about your work with Black males.

With the right attitude and your ability to help young people win, you can use the lessons in this chapter to close the achievement gap for African American males. African American males are not lost. In many cases, they are simply misunderstood or not guided in the right directions. So be firm but fair, and use the resources in this chapter and all other chapters in this book to assist you in reaching all students.

Like many of the boys in your classroom, the childhoods of the contributors of this book were not the all American story—two parents and a white picket fence. We didn't go through school with a 4.0 grade point average and no behavioral problems. But we made it. It took parents, grandparents, aunts, uncles, cousins, and many great teachers to shape our success.

A teacher, a master teacher, does not judge a student based on the previous years and write him off. A master teacher understands that Black boys do not think creatively about their own education. But they know once they show Black males how to free their minds, they will always be free. Their minds, just like ours, will either enslave them or offer them endless possibilities for examining their concerns and managing whatever challenges may arise in their lives.

14

What Society Gains by Ignoring the Sexual Development Of Black Boys

By Morris Gary III

Introduction

Throughout my life, I have made many fatuous mistakes, oversights, errors in judgment and have downright messed up real bad on many occasions. Most of my profound errors were a direct result of my ignorance about people, relationships and most of all, sex. I learned about sex from my mother's anatomy books, my brother's girlie magazines, dirty jokes in the barber's chair, pseudo-knowledgeable classmates, an unfortunate opening of a door in what was a de facto brothel located across the road in the community liquor house, and observing reproductive efforts of an array of farm animals. The farm animals' sexual antics were by far the most sexually accurate but so profoundly lacking in the emotional aspects of the human sexual encounter. For me, these encounters would come later in settings as diverse as plum tree thickets, hilltop campsites, creek alcoves, barns, and homes of some of my girlfriends before their parents got home. These clumsy, mystical experiments were carried out with the daughters of my neighbors. They were acts of prepubescent, mutually ignorant sexual mimicry. No one explained to me that with each sexual encounter, I would want to keep, I say own, that female's body parts that had brought me so much pleasure in their myriad ways. The mystery of womanhood was about me, and I had the desire to know more about women than I knew about myself. No clothes line containing women's clothes was safe from my stare; the lingerie section of the Sears catalog accompanied me to the outhouse but was rarely crushed and made utilitarian.

Experiential learning is hard and, at times, unforgiving. My sexual ignorance grew faster than I did, and by 10th grade, I had persuaded a girl to allow me to be her clumsy and inept lover. Almost every Friday, five minutes after her mother went to sleep, we'd be on each other like rabbits returning from a year long abstinence retreat. Neither snow nor rain nor heat nor gloom of night stayed me from the swift, and I do mean swift, completion of my appointed task. We had sex, much of it unprotected, for over a year. Only the bubbles of Koromex foam stood between me and procreation, and bubbles have been known to burst.

Three days after my 18th birthday, I learned what it was to be a teen father. Twenty months later, I became a father again. My second child came because I didn't really know how I got my first child; barnyard observations, girlie magazines, anatomy books, brothel voyeurism and "know less than nothing" friends did little to abate these outcomes. Good grades, athleticism, becoming an Eagle Scout at 14, being a faithful member of that little AME church and a good citizen was as ineffective as birth control for me as it has been for thousands if not millions of other Black boys who aren't socially and emotionally ready to be parents. Being a good child will not save our sons from premature fatherhood, sexually transmitted disease, or destructive relationships. But in this chapter, I will share with you a number of actions that, when judiciously applied, will.

I readily confess that I know little if anything about women and girls other than what I have academically studied, heard women speak about, read in their writings, and been allowed to experience when attempting to communicate with women. I don't know what women do, what women think and I cannot testify to the moral turpitude of women and girls, as far too many women and girls, because of ineffective community support have to endure abusive survival situations (in some communities the animal shelter gets more donations than the battered women's shelter). Many single mothers sacrifice their own physical and emotional wellbeing in exchange for groceries and diapers provided by an abusive father.

As a Black man, I have been given deference for being born male. Black women have historically and consistently taken care of me and other Black men. I often think that I could strangle the Pope in Times Square and have that act captured on video and there would be some Black women who would proclaim my innocence before I could be booked at the local jail. These women are cut from the same cloth as their ancestors who lied to the night riders and hid escapees from the white babies they had wet nursed who are now lynch mob leaders. Support is a wonderful thing, but support of egregious acts teaches irresponsibility to Black boys.

Today, Black boys experience all that I have experienced. As a young male, I learned through trial and error that my chances of fully understanding a problem increased when I suspended and adopted an attitude of honesty, positive regard and true respect for the issue. I learned that seeking to understand rather than being understood and embracing ideas through analysis significantly increased my understanding and stimulated further study. In this chapter, I offer a brief biological, psychological, economic, sociological, cultural and historical analysis to illustrate some of the variables affecting Black boys' sexuality and what society has gained from ignoring their sexual development.

A way to understand a society is to observe who is safe, who is validated, and who has genuine status. In the United States, many Black boys are far from safe, mainly validated by sports, entertainment or underground economic activities, and have a dubious socioeconomic status that is dependent upon many factors not under their control.[1] Many Black boys are marginally enfranchised, have limited wise support, and can't afford to make life mistakes and still have a reasonable hope of recovery. There are Black boys who have never, for the most part, had a break in life or experienced the caring, compassionate, and supportive embrace of a father.

Each reader of this chapter probably knows of at least one Black boy who is economically deprived, emotionally and nutritionally undernourished, under educated, never valued, and without successful role models. Epigenetics supports the notion that Black boys like the one described above will experience a disproportionately high incidence of social maladies and health challenges. And the cycle seems to repeat with subsequent generations. In this way, the disenfranchised continue to suffer and perpetuate a lesser quality of life for successive generations. This explains the tendencies of families and in fact whole groups of people being affected disproportionately by certain diseases, for Blacks; diabetes, asthma, high blood pressure and cardiovascular disease.

The Black Youth Project notes that 55% of Black youth receive their primary health care from community health clinics or hospital emergency rooms; only 32% of White youth share this experience. A 2000 California State University study reveals that 13% of the African American mothers in the study never received any prenatal care and received care that was considered to be inadequate. The generational ramifications of this are obvious and the effects of a poor biological start in life can be almost insurmountable.[1,2]

Humans under stress seek forms of escape. For Black people, the use of psychoactive substances is prevalent. We sleep too much, eat too much, drink too much and use sex as a psychobiological palliative. Epigenetics predicts that the effects of these practices also generationally accumulate, with these tendencies being passed on to children and grandchildren of the Black race. Black boys from better situation fall prey, too. Black boys do what they see men do to become men.

The fact is there is no gene for race. Much of what we call race is a social construct based on generations of environmental adaptations that lead to physical differences in appearance. Socio-cultural conditioning provides the individual labels and the human concepts of prejudice. Stereotyping provides the racial group label. Neither prejudice nor stereotyping is based on sound scientific methods, yet people who rely on this fallacious reasoning label Black boys as being sexually promiscuous and slow academically.

There appears to be a mistrust of scientific investigation, research and application in the Black community. Far too many rely on conjecture when it comes to the sexual development of Black boys. Our society has made violence sexy, but marrying society's mode of procreation with destruction is frightening, dangerous and never beneficial. Wishing that Black boys would be respectful, nonviolent, non-abusive to women and girls is not an effective deferent to violence against women and girls. The same can be said about homicide rates, teen pregnancy, the "baby's daddy disconnect," drug use and commerce, and incarceration rates. If we are to have an effect on these problems, then we've got to adopt a cultural world view that does not glorify sexual dysfunction. The price paid by all of us is far too high and seems to buy more of the same. Some of the readers will be quick to point out that girls share accountability in this culture of sexual underdevelopment, exploitation and self destruction.

In the Beginning, There Was Sex

Sex is the most overused, misunderstood and under-instructed subject for Black boys. Misinformation, deception, marketing propaganda and outright lies, both gender specific and otherwise, cloud their environment. The level of sexual knowledge among many Black boys is atrocious, and in an area where ignorance can kill you as well as those who associate with you, this is unacceptable. Not knowing the biological basic mechanics of procreation is not just a problem for our youth, as many adults who are charged with enculturation also lack this knowledge.

As a species, humans are hardwired for sex. Through sex we get here and through sex far too many of us leave this planet. The sexual process is the mode of our existence, but limited knowledge, denial, mystery and downright ignorance prevails. The end result is that is that young people today might know more about sexual positions and how to please a mate, but they seem reluctant to practice safe sex.

The limbic system of our brain is evolutionarily ancient, powerful and designed to promote among other things, sexual procreation without much regard for social graces, mores, or customs. It is connected to the prefrontal lobe and contains the "pleasure center." This center is so powerful that in experiments involving surgically modified mice, the mice will choose death by starvation rather than avoid continuous stimulation of the pleasure center. Interestingly enough, the pleasure centers in our brains are also wired in ways that make it very tough to avoid engaging in behaviors that are pleasurable.

Truly successful societies design ways to train and guide their boys in preparation for manhood and the inherent leadership that usually accompanies this status. A major part of this preparation is to help boys delay the gratification of temporary pleasures so that they can achieve long-term goals. Given the current mating patterns in the Black community and the lack of sufficient and effective positive enculturation, the outlook is less than promising for many young Black males.

How Black Boy's Sexual Development Got Ignored

Black folk in America assimilated European ideas about sexuality, along with the historical loss of African identity. Much of the Black experience is linked in some way to slavery and slave owners were very aware of the sociology of captivity. They went to great extents to separate and dominate by dividing Africans on the basis of tribe (many of whom were historical enemies), language and affiliation.[3] The success of these practices led to higher productivity for the slave owners and greater distrust among Blacks, especially between males and females. Granted that concepts of "menstrual pollution" and male superiority were present before the slave trade, it was the intentional creation of distrust between genders that remains a lynchpin of Black male misogyny. These enforced social mores were in contrast and conflict with traditional African sexuality, while much of the European sexual knowledge was a product of Queen Victoria's well documented "don't ask, don't tell generational ignorance model." In this model, women and men were kept ignorant about each other's bodies. There is at least one case of a man refusing to consummate his marriage because his spouse had pubic hair. Even doctors were only allowed to examine the parts of a woman's body that were commonly publicly exposed.

During Victoria's reign, the sun never set on the British Empire and this repressive pseudo-moralistic system was disseminated around the world, disrupting healthy indigenous sexually functioning cultures en masse. This Victorian model encouraged the further sexual subrogation of women's rights to control their bodies and sexual pleasure. At the time, the belief that only women of low social status enjoyed sex. It also afforded men the right to have as many consorts as affordable, including arranged training dalliances with women of lower social status, such as maids, and sometimes sex workers. By far, the Victorian model did not encourage males or females to learn about sex. In contrast, the West African culture, from which the ancestors of the majority of Black boys emerge, provided for the complete education of Black boys and girls in the sexual aspects of life. Around 12 or 13 (the age of ascension) boys and girls went through rites of passage. Not all these rituals were alike, but the common thread was the thorough and complete transfer of socio-sexual knowledge by elders (proven wise men and women) that were entrusted with this responsibility.

Social

Many Black boys are sexually socialized via commercial media, word of mouth, observation, experimentation, the Internet and direct inspection. For most, there is no council of elders, mentors, or wise persons armed with reliable knowledge delivered in an acceptable manner. The commercial media was designed to sell products, not raise children. Still, too many Black families allow almost unfettered access to our children by any or all marketers. Much of the word of mouth information is based on sketchy facts and shaky logic. This misinformation is passed from one person to another and accepted as fact by younger boys.

Black boys' sexual observations are colored by commercialism and entertainment. Few have been exposed to an efficacious treatment of the subject, and given the amount of soft and hard pornography, shallow erotica, and sexually provocative material they consume, an unrealistic mindset is expected. Because of survival living arrangements, many have seen or heard various sex acts being performed with their mothers, sisters, or others and received no explanation or education as to what was really taking place. Left to their own uninformed devices, they developed a confused, often false matrix of sexual knowledge where as little as 31% of Black youth had sex education in high school.[1] The reader can only question how many received adequate sex education at home.

Black boys learn sex through experimentation, some of which includes same sex activities. "You show me yours, and I'll show you mine" includes boys comparing their penis sizes and the prestige that comes with extended girth and length. The historical myth of Black male physical and stamina-related hyper-sexuality continues to be promulgated. But, most males learn about their penises through touching themselves, and at times, other males, as the magic of erectile tissue are alluring. Small boys look at older boys and wonder why their penises are not the same size, color, etc. Many participate in this learning exercise, but in our society, homophobia prevents this from being discussed among males. This can lead to confusion, self—doubt and an information vacuum.

Many males will confess to playing "doctor" and "spin the bottle," but few will identify the gender of the actual patients. It is to be noted that in warrior societies, male children were removed from their mothers (usually around the age of eight) to begin training in an all male environment. Depending on the culture, this move was based on the belief in "menstrual pollution" (males would avoid even walking the paths of women who were menstruating). In others, it was a way to remove the feminine influence that is perceived to be non-warrior-like. The Sambia of New Guinea believed that boys must avoid all things feminine as they were taken under the mentorship of older warrior males. During this time, the boys served the older warriors with absolute loyalty. When the boy had grown and demonstrated the necessary skills, he was allowed to marry. The Spartans, Greeks, Romans, and a number of other cultures ascribed to these and similar activities in the production of male warriors. Black boys receive a lot of quasi-military training (street soldiers), but is should be remembered that armies have traditionally been misogynistic; in fact, the process of "sacking the city" consisted of killing all males older than the age of about eight and raping and killing all women except those who were valued as slaves for sex and work.

Black boy's sexual socialization reflects the socialization of Black folks in America. When the social history of the United States is viewed objectively, it is difficult to dispute that it is one of cultural conflict, domination, slavery, and genocide. These seminal national foundations are passed from generation to generation and explain the way we treat each other as groups and individuals. Our ability to dehumanize whole groups and individuals allows the subtle and most brutal atrocities to occur. Atrocious actions often result from group membership. Group members first comply with group rules, then identify with the group norms, and finally internalize the group beliefs. Internalized beliefs are further solidified by awarding status and displacing internal hostilities onto target groups. Black boys learn to use their maleness to advantage, as they are keen observers of who has power in our society. Black boys can figure very quickly that white men have power. Though they openly claim to be in conflict with these white men, many mimic the same methodology and activities to control women, girls, and others of lesser status, such as were used during slavery. A more thorough treatment of this can be found in Dr. Joy Degruy Leary's work Post Traumatic Slave Syndrome, which addresses the generational effects of social conditioning on Black folks.[4]

Black boys teach me more than I ever teach them. I ask more questions than I answer and listen more than I speak. Over time for me, this has been a very powerful communication process. Parents, teachers, and other adults will often ask me to make a snap judgment on the nature and cause of some child's misbehavior, misdeed or societal transgression. This question invariably leads to others, many of them repetitive, the chief complaint being expressed as frustration over the lack of progress, change if you will, in their children and children in general. If you are getting the same unsatisfactory answer, then ask a different question. The questions that are most neglected are those most asked by Black boys: questions about girls and male sexual development. In my work with Black boys, I have found it useful to explain that we males have no experience being girls and never will. By focusing on men and boys, blaming, scapegoating and sexual putdowns are removed from the discussion and replaced with self-inspection, social responsibility and respect for others.

Homophobia

Few social issues are more unnerving to Black boys than homosexuality. The reasons for this overreaction are not as obvious as they appear on the surface. Other than the leftover Victorian sensibilities about sexuality, much of the homophobia in Black boys is rooted in sexism. To illustrate this, I will cite the University of Georgia 1996 study by Lohr in which self-identified homophobic men and self identified non-homophobic men were exposed to visual scenes of heterosexual and homosexual sex.[5] A plethysmograph (a pressure sensitive device for measuring penile erection) was used to record the men's reactions to these stimuli. The results revealed that men who self identified as homophobic showed a significant arousal when viewing the homosexual sex scenes. Some of this could be due to anxiety and some to the interest of the homophobic men perhaps wanting to have sex with men. Irrespective of amount of the anxiety experienced, how do you fake an erection? Are these results bi-curiosity, socio-sexual dissonance or latent homosexual desires? Whatever conclusion you reach, the one thing that is certain is that men experience some level of physiological and possibility psychological arousal when they view erotic scenes of men.

Another line of reasoning is based on deep questions in a modified Socratic form. When homophobic men are asked why they dislike homosexuals, the reply is inevitably, "Because that act like women and do things (including sexual things) that women do." For some, "acting like women encompasses showing emotions, empathy, sympathy, fear and being able to cry "out of grief" and not just when they lose the big football game. If a man hates another man because he acts or does things that women do, then who does he really hate?

In dealing with homophobia, Black boys (including the homosexual, bi-curious ones) are bombarded by messages of intolerance and hate from gangster rap, religious leaders, and social constellations. This is even more pronounced in middle school where boys are struggling to move into manhood, in most cases without effective and efficacious models. An alternate way to question these homophobic beliefs is to offer support from organizations that are also homophobic. By pointing out to these boys that they share beliefs with organizations such as the Ku Klux Klan, Nazi Party, Aryan Nation, Aryan Brotherhood and Al Qaeda, then ask them how acceptable they would be in those organizations. This exercise usually brings a quick awareness to the true issues of bigotry and prejudice.

Homophobia is intensely damaging to Black boys because it suppresses appropriate affect in males and puts down women when males use the sex organs of women to verbally putdown men they don't like. Some of the young males I work with are quick to point out their belief that homosexuality is a choice. This I counter with the following question: Who would choose to live a life of denigration, physical danger, and possible rejection by family and friends? Who would choose to have their civil rights denied and always be concerned about validation, acceptance, and safety?

Psychological

Many of the psychosexual issues experienced by Black boys are a direct and indirect result of the cognitive distortions derived from the environments and family constellations they experience. Black boys who obtain much of their sexual world view from entertainment suffer more than other groups as a four minute video usually does not explain the difference between women acting sexually accessible and really being that way. Many of our boys receive an abundance of miseducation and witness any number of activities that are sexually violent, abusive, and controlling. They witness these acts without competent explanations or seeing negative consequences for the perpetrators, most of whom are men. Some of these boys are further confused when their mothers and these men become sexual. Given the mode of Black boys' psychosexual education, it is no wonder that this segment of our society has a spectrum of beliefs that are mostly built on myths. The more dangerous consequences occur when vital aspects of their lives are threatened and questionable issue arise about their manhood, which leads to behaviors that distort their thinking to the point that the naturally occurring, nurturing feelings about women are replaced with outward sexual objectification.

Sex sells and Black boys are fed a steady diet of ideas and information that paints women as entities designed for their sexual gratification without a relationship as the basis.[6] These boys have great difficulty in becoming aware of any aspects of human sexual interaction except their own. Therefore, when interacting with girls, they often resort to verbal and other forms of violence when they don't get their way. They have a distorted view of what girls think and want; they have a kind of "sexual tunnel vision." In addition, Black boys will often use labels to categorize the social worth of women. Any number of negative words like bitch, whore, trick, chicken head, skank, shorty, rip, etc. are in their vocabulary to describe women and girls. The majority of these terms have sexual overtones and suggest that how much or with whom a female has sex determines her worth.

Cultural

One of the reasons older Black people are so upset by Hip hop music is that it exposes how Black boys really feel about women and girls and our miseducation of them. Hip hop's sexual, and at times misogynistic, content reminds us of the many poor examples we have directly and indirectly set for our boys. Embarrassment is often a precursor of anger, and this anger we generationally project on our boys via lack of formal enculturation, creates distance between generations. The arts have historically and culturally been a way for disenfranchised people to express true feelings about unpopular views. In some ways, what Hip hop says about Black boys and sex is a gift and wake up call to older and assumed wiser generations. This is illustrated in a letter gleaned from the writings of my students who participated in a support group exercise.

Dear Grown Folks:

We can't talk to you directly because you don't want to hear what we have to say. So we'll get your attention the same way you get ours—with negativity you have conditioned within us by hitting, yelling, screaming, intimidation, blowing us off, and not talking with us but at us. I curse you out cause you curse me out; I come in late just like you do; I don't keep my word because you never keep yours; and I have sex because to be a Black man, I need to have a woman. If I have two women, I am a player; three women make me a gangster, four or more makes me a pimp. It must be true because I see it in all parts of society. I see it in athletes, musicians, artists, business people, performers, parents, preachers, teachers and self described leaders. The comedians tell jokes about using violence to solve every problem, and everybody laughs—and all of those folks laughing look just like me.

We are rewarded for being violent, controlling and even being abusive to women, girls or anyone with less power, and we become irresponsible because you were irresponsible when you brought us here without a plan for our safety. In many cases, you left us to fend for ourselves. We don't need you to be our best friends; we just need you to be our best parents. You call my boys thugs, nothings, scrubs, busters and worse, but they only do what they see the big companies do. They only want to get paid and get laid.

It is your first job to create a safe environment in which we can live, survive, and thrive. We need to be consistently safe, especially from you and the many other bad models that we are exposed to. The first bullies we met were our big brothers, and at times, you too terrorized me. Much of this danger comes from sexual abuse, misuse and misinformation, a lot of which comes from relatives and the folks you get high with. We learned what we learned from what we see men do. Like you, we also need to belong to something or someone and, most of all, we really need to be respected and valued for all that we do. If you can't give this to us, then we know who can.

Sincerely,
Your Son

Important Message to Parents and Caregivers

To sexually educate Black boys, parents or caregivers need to have an open mind concerning the current research about sexual behavior. If you are ambivalent about talking about sex, it will be better to find someone who is more objective to provide the sexual education to Black boys. Our society has allowed popular media to hijack this responsibility and popular media is designed to use sex to sell products, not educate.

Secondly, a parent or caregiver needs to be knowledgeable of the biological, psychological, social, cultural, historical and economic aspects of sex. Emphasis should be placed on teaching Black boys that sex involves the deepest emotions. They should be informed that both instinctual and learned emotions will hover around ownership and possession of their sex partner(s). Ample time should be spent explaining and illustrating the power and effects of sexual bonding, romantic love and that all important non-sexual, unconditional love.

Information on masturbation (self-love) and sexual gratification techniques are topics that are difficult to discuss without the shame based ignorance that is so contributory to knowledge deficits that lead to bad outcomes. You will need to be cautious about being cavalier or dismissive about these powerful feelings. You don't have to be an expert, but continuing education is most helpful. An internal honesty and approachable demeanor benefits Black boys, as some are well aware of their lack of accurate knowledge about sex. This is not the time for guessing. If you don't know something, admit it, find out, and then get this information to the boys as soon as possible. Black boys will often ask questions based on recent and/or anticipated experiences. Your information could be pivotal in their sexual decision making so don't delay. Available are self-administered inventories that will help the reader to determine both comfort and knowledge about sex.

A third factor in sexually educating Black boys is quality myth busting. I have found that a large numbers of Black boys believed that:

1. Girls who are sexually assaulted by former boyfriends "had it coming." Some even believe that females who are attacked in or around certain venues were "asking for it."
2. Females who dress in revealing clothing are no more than whores and what happens to them is of little importance.

3. If you have sex with a pregnant girl, the baby will be marked by you.

Many of the previously illustrated beliefs and activities have combined to produce some of the following statistical conditions among Black boys.

Based on the 2007 results from the Black Youth Project, an exhaustive survey of 1590 Black, Hispanic and white youth, our Black boys are in deeper trouble than postulated.[1] For our purpose, we will consider the survey sample demographic; youth ages 15 to 25, our target market. It is to be considered that a number of Black boys begin there sexual experiences well before the lower range of 15. In fact, the 2005 Youth Risk Behavior Sexual Survey reports that 26.8% of male Black youth surveyed had had intercourse before the age of thirteen.[7]

A big issue for boys is that they are about three and a half years less mature than girls throughout adolescence. If you consider the socialization of Black boys and the relative lack of effective systematic social emotional learning, then the age maturity gap between boys and girls could be wider. Some of the findings of this study will be illustrated here to help you fully understand what society gains by ignoring the sexual development of Black boys.

Premarital Sex Experiences

- 70% of the Black boys reported engaging in vaginal intercourse, with 77% of Black youth reporting that they or their partner used some form of protection every or almost every time.
- 50% of the Black males believed that it is okay for teenagers to engage in sex if they are in a serious relationship.
- 60% of Black boys believe its okay to have sex if you use protection. Yet only 26% believe that fathering or giving birth to a child without being married would be embarrassing to their families.
- 62% of Black males report engaging in oral sex, with 50% reporting that they or their partner used condoms or dental dams every time or almost every time they had oral sex.
- 38.7% of Black males and 18.6% of Black female youth had had sex with multiple partners (four or more partners).
- 51.3% of males and 43.8% of females had sex within one month of the survey date.

Attitudes about Family and Children

- Only 27% of Black youth believe that having a baby requires them to stay with the baby's mother or father.
- 69% of Black youth surveyed see having a baby as an impediment to them fulfilling their goals, with 66% believing that the government should promote marriage via tax breaks and special benefits for married couples.
- 50% of Black youth believe it is better if a man is the main financial breadwinner of the family.
- 38% of Black female youth agree that a single mother can raise a child as well as a married couple.

Condom Usage

- 91% of Black youth feel that they could persuade a partner to use a condom, yet only 23% strongly agree with the statement "When I have sex, I feel in control," while 82% agreed with the statement "When I have sex I feel good about myself.
- Among the 33.9% of currently sexually active students nationwide, 62.8% reported that either they or their partner had used a condom during last sexual intercourse.
- 76% of Black youth believe that condoms should be available in high schools, with 20% of the Black boys agreeing.

Views On Abortion

- 47% of Black youth feel that abortion is always wrong, yet 37% know someone personally who has had an abortion, while 58% disagree with the government making abortion illegal under any circumstances.

Sex Education

- 31% of Black youth have had no formal sex education, while the majority of youth (75%) who received sex education had the course work as part on another class.
- 93% of Black youth believe that sex education should be mandatory, with 76% of Black youth believing abstinence only education to be inadequate.

AIDS Risk

- 38% of Black youth reported personally knowing someone with AIDS, yet only 11% of Black boys report their risk of infection to be high.

Impact of Hip hop Music on Sex

- 58% of Black youth listen to rap music daily, with 48% watching rap programming several days per week. 72% view rap as having too many references to sex, while 59% of Black boys believe that rap has too many references to violence.
- 44% of Black boys feel that rap music does not portray Black men in a negative or offensive way.
- 57% of Black boys agree that rap music "portray Black women and girls in a negative of offensive way," 43% did not.

The Black Youth Project (http://Blackyouthproject.com) is a most laudable and much needed study that probably due to political consideration, was not as comprehensive as it could have been. Given the myriad living conditions that some Black boys are forced to adjust to, some current research would be most helpful. Current in-depth research on Black boys (some of whom are sex workers) and the "unmentionable" sexual practices of anal sex is most needed. Going back to 1993, there is some evidence that there is a significant increase in anal intercourse between men who have sex with men and heterosexual, bisexual and/or bi-curious Black boys and men who have sex with females.

The concept of the down low brother (DLB) is replete with fallacious reasoning, numerous concepts of causality. A concept such DLB causing

HIV/AIDS or any disease plays well as popular talking points, but its unprotected sex that causes sexually transmitted diseases. Vaginal, oral, anal or any combination thereof can be a mode of transmission, not a cause of a STD. Hence if young people are empowered with sexual honesty and the capacity to consistently and correctly practice safer sex, then so-called brothers on the "DL" or sisters who were "burning' would be a lesser factor in the spread of disease. I am amazed at all this talk about the "DL" when there is so little discussion about young Black men incarcerated in the United States. Men entering prison are often HIV positive, and some have consensual, commerce or forced sex. These same men will eventually return to society and "reclaim their manhood' with the girls and women they left behind. Few of these girls and women have the capacity to negotiate with a man or boy who was probably violent, abusive and controlling in the first place.

Sexual expression among humans exists on a spectrum. Anal, group sex, and sexual assault should be studied more closely. Anal intercourse is an increasingly popular form of sex among youth. My students tell me it's being greedy and wanting to fill every hole just like they do on the videos. Black boys are exposed to an array of erotic and pornographic movies depicting, in many cases, a dominate male being "serviced" by any number of females without relationship, concern or consequences of any kind. Anal penetration is increasingly shown as the highlight movies that culminate with the "money shot" with ejaculate being sprayed over the face and into the mouth of the allegedly grateful and most willing female. Anal sex goes back to Greek, Roman, and other cultures. For Romans, the penetrator (modern day slang "topman") kept his manhood status while the recipient (bottom man) was viewed as a receptacle and of lesser status. Genarlo Wilson, convicted at age 17 in Douglas County Georgia of statutory rape and sentenced for 10 years, apparently believed that a fifteen-year-old girl could give consent while being videotaped and listening to rap music. His sexual miseducation was extreme, and he has a permanent record to show for it. His actions imitate the recurring theme in many rap songs "getting head" and non-relational detached sex.

Though most are based on some historical factoid (a fact-like conclusion) they are in essence irrational beliefs. Irrational beliefs are based on fallacious reasoning, skewed or selective evidence. Selective evidence is often based on fear, and unaddressed fear in stress producing.

Effective sexual education begins early, and most authorities cite 3 to 4 years of age as a time to begin educating children about clear-cut issues, such as gender differences and explanations of observed sexual activities in the environment (including humans). Watching media like Animal Planet, The Discover channel and other such shows are very helpful in illustrating to children (as well as adults) the basic sexual biological functions. Explaining the underlying emotional aspects is another matter requiring a level of knowledge, communication skills and in depth social emotional learning (SEL). In order to educate or reeducate, a systematic debunking of myths must take place.

Sexual myth busting with Black boys is difficult and resistant to change due to the environment of abuse, violence and misogyny many Black boys inhabit. The men of Batterer's Intervention Program (BIP) organizations such as Emerge, The Oakland Men's Project, and Men Stopping Violence, among others, have done much to expose men and boys worldwide to a way of living and being non-violent, non-abusive, and non-controlling to women, girls and others of lesser power in society. Their approach is to deconstruct the intersecting oppressions of sexism, classism, racism and homophobia. The process begins with each boy's awareness of his effects upon women and girls and others, followed by an acknowledgement of his worst treatment of a woman or girl and other social transgressions. After this boys are required to take a number of actions that require self inspections and non-violent confrontation of self and other males concerning the treatment of women and girls. For males to begin to shed the misogyny of our society they must embrace women's reality first then proceed to deconstruct the well conditioned prejudices and gender based power of being born male in a society that gives lip service to, but does not truly value females as much as males. Much of what Black boys learn about females is based on historical (and I do mean historical beliefs) since many females have been written out of much of the story of humankind.

For me, manhood is a process. Each time I think I have it mastered, I learn something else I should know, do, say or improve upon. By focusing on my effects on others rather than their effects on me, I control what I can learn to control—me. Given that boys (we hope) grow to enter the process of manhood after reading the preceding, it is no wonder the following recent historical statistics exist and this information is based only on incidents and cases that were reported. This sexual miseducation of Black boys manifests itself in many of the social maladies that are profoundly apparent. The following is a listing of some of the statistics that are directly and indirectly linked to the ignored sexual development of all boys, including Black boys. The existing milieu of developmental socio-sexual ignorance, male dominance, misogyny, power-control issues, and the resultant abuse takes a dramatic toll on our society. Consider that boys are displaying power-control issues as early as pre-school, with documented data for middle school. Black boys were included or were a factor in all of the cited studies.

Dating Violence

- In one study of eight and ninth graders 25% indicated that they had been the victims of dating violence, with 8% reporting sexual abuse.
- Women 16-24 have the highest per capita rate of intimate partner violence.
- Teens are at higher risk for abuse than adult women with 21.7% experiencing abuse as opposed to 15.9% for adults.
- Younger girls, ages 11-15, experience more severe violence—62%.
- The experience of rapid repeat pregnancy (RRP) correlates well with intimate violence. These women are also at a substantially higher risk to miscarry.
- Girls who have been physically or sexually abused are 16% more likely to smoke, 10% more likely to drink, 17% more likely to use illegal drugs, and 20% more likely to practice bingeing and purging. Suicide ideation and actual attempts were 6 to 9 times more prevalent.
- Battered shelter-dwelling young women, ages 12-20, attended school 22.4% less and made good grades 15.9% less that non-battered women.

Intimate Partner Violence (IPV) during Pregnancy

- High school girls who are pregnant are four to six times more likely to be abused.
- 12.5% of mothers ages 12 to 18 reported being physically assaulted by the father of their babies. Of these, 40 percent

report experiencing violence at the hands of family members or relatives.

- IPV among teen mothers was highest at three months postpartum. IPV increased from 40 to 62 percent during this period.
- Seventy-five percent of mothers reporting IPV during pregnancy also reported it within 24 months after delivery.
- Seventy-eight percent of mothers who experienced IPV during the first three months postpartum had not reported IPV before delivery.
- Women with a history IPV have more difficulty with obesity and tobacco use.
- Adolescent girls who witness IPV are two to three times more likely to use tobacco and marijuana.

Adolescent dating violence over time progress to adult intimate partner violence. Sex and social, emotional immaturity is a volatile mixture, with violence being a highly prevalent outcome.[8] Black boys with unaddressed sexual developmental needs contribute significantly to this milieu. This impact of this is illustrated in the following from the National Coalition against Domestic Violence (NCADV):[9]

- Of the 1.5 million women raped or physically assaulted by intimate partners in the United States in the year 2000, 324,000 were pregnant when the violence occurred.
- Women with unintended pregnancies are four times more likely to experience violence than women with planned pregnancies.
- Pregnant women who are victims of IPV are more likely to experience depression and suicide, alcohol, tobacco, and drug use, delay prenatal care, have pregnancy complications and deliver low birth weight babies.
- In 2002, 76 percent of IPV homicide victims were female; 24 percent were male.
- Murder is the second most common cause of death for pregnant women (31%) 56 percent were shot, while the rest were stabbed or strangled.
- 77 percent of pregnant homicide victims are killed in the first trimester of pregnancy. This doesn't include the questionable and

undetected deaths or deaths where pregnancy was not noted on the death certificate.

Conclusions and Recommendation

What I've tried to do with this chapter is present details about what society will lose if we avoid teaching Black boys how to have responsible sexual relationships. The damage in terms of unwanted pregnancies, sexually transmitted diseases, HIV/AIDS, jail terms for nonpayment of child support, and abusive relationships are horrible and grossly underrepresented. So, what do we gain from ignoring the sexual development of Black boys? There is no simple answer, but I hope that we all understand that ignoring the sexual development of Black boys or any other group of teenage boys is not acceptable.

Whereas there is no easy way to measure the burden on society resulting from the ignorance that Black youth have about sexual responsibility, but the cost in tremendous.[10,11] For example, in the United States for the year 2005, a staggering 69.3% of the Black live births were to unmarried mothers.[12] Setting any moral judgment aside, the economic implications of this statistic are staggering and it is safe to conclude that the vast majority of the fathers of these children are also Black with many of them lacking the resources or sexual responsibility to avoid repeating the same act.

Males and Chew in a California study surmised that for girl's age 17 at time of their babies' birth 71% of the fathers were post-school adult men. For 15-year-old girls 52% had post-school adult men as their babies' fathers. For the very young mothers, 11-14 years old, the peer fathers (boys in the same age group) were 2.2 years older, for older fathers the gap was 7.3 years with 62.2% of the non-marital births having post-school fathers.[13]

The 2007 National Urban League Equality Index list Black men as having 73.3% of the overall status of whites in the United States. Black men experience 57% of the economic status, 78% of the health expectations, 79% of the educational status, 66% of the social justice and 105% of the civic engagement of whites. Obtaining civil positive status while burdened with child support, relationship drama, educational and economic deficits is at best an uphill battle and loaded with risk for the fathers, children and the females involved.

Black men are more than twice as likely to be unemployed as white males and make only 75% as much a year. They are nearly seven times more likely to be incarcerated, and their average jail sentences are 10 months longer than white men. In addition young Black males between the ages of 15 and 34 are nine times more likely to die of homicide their white counterparts and nearly seven times more likely to suffer from AIDS. The AIDS threat is further highlighted by the fact that Black women are 24 times more likely to become afflicted with HIV/AIDS than white women.[10,11]

Linking the preceding data to the sexual development deficits of Black boys is obvious and bolsters the answer to our original question: What do we gain from ignoring the sexual development of Black boys? We've already gained the derived maladies and continue to do so at an alarming rate across the socio-economic spectrum and ever deeper into the Black American subculture. We will continue to reap the bitter fruit from the under cultivated and often neglected tree of Black boyhood until the disparities of inequality consumes the resources that the whole culture accumulates.

You may be a parent, teacher, administrator or some other stakeholder who works with or cares about the fate of Black boys. Some of what you have read only goes to corroborate what you already know, and some validates your conclusions from life experiences. If you are working with Black teenage boys (or any teenage boys), then the chances are quite high that they are having unprotected intercourse, which coupled with the use of alcohol and illegal drugs increases their tendency for high-risk sexual behaviors and violence. As parents of daughters, you must be concerned because many of your daughters, Black and white, are having sex with boys who are also having unprotected sex with other partners. If you ignore their sexual development, the problems will continue to have a ripple effect, resulting in sexually transmitted diseases, including HIV/AIDS, teenage pregnancy, intimate violence, and further economic and social problems for Black males and all of society.

The following is a list of recommendations that could go far to augment the outlook for Black boys and our culture:

1. Examine your personal life to determine if you have the current scientific knowledge about adolescent age-appropriate sexual development. Don't balk at the levels of sexual activity of your

students. Share information, as you may be the only adult who gives accurate information to your Black male students, and get information to educate yourself about what you don't know.

2. Have a working knowledge of the sexual bio-functions of males and females, as this allows you to speak authoritatively about the subject on various levels. This will also give you an advantage when being questioned by other adults, many of whom will be less knowledgeable than you.

3. Understand the psychological history of Blacks in general and how sex is interwoven into the milieu of Black boys' persona.

4. Respectfully confront irrational thoughts with truthful information that will serve to promote rational thoughts, behaviors, and attitudes.

5. Become a respectful sexual myth buster by staying aware of the current media depictions of sex, including the activities on the Internet and in music videos. Use these sources as reference points in discussions so that you can incorporate age-appropriate concepts into the quality core curriculum of your state.

6. Teach peace constantly by adopting non-violent communications patterns within your classroom and daily life. Model this, especially in times of stress.

7. Develop a zero tolerance for violence, abuse, bullying and oppression.

8. Stress the sexual knowledge gap to the Parent Teacher and Student Associations and use these meetings as a springboard for knowledge sharing. This will allow parents to participate and increase their knowledge about sex.

9. Develop ways to socio-sexually educate parents, stakeholders, and caregivers without them knowing they are being educated.

10. Work to bring about changes in school board policy that will train all school staff and develop active interventions designed to abate sexual ignorance. With Black boys disengaging from school as early as fourth grade, it is imperative that this education begin as early as possible.

11. Work to build coalitions that will get comprehensive, effective "real life" sex education into our schools, beginning in elementary school and continuing throughout. This is the best chance to deprogram Black boys who have sexual developmental deficits.

12. Use community stakeholders to bring in active effective programs on sexually transmitted diseases (STDs), healthy relationships, abuse and battering, and the fallacy of male superiority.
13. Teach Black boys how to say no to the status quo so as not to participate in misogyny and sexist activities. Show them how to question the existing social beliefs.

15

The Role of Resiliency in Achieving Against the Odds

By Winston Sharpe

Introduction

African American males have waded through the trenches of racism, poverty, and discrimination of all kinds and have continued to stand tall despite the numerous obstacles and attacks that society has launched against them. The mistreatment and negative portrayal of African American males is an ongoing saga that began with slavery nearly 400 hundred years ago and has continued to the present day educational apartheid and technological divide in America. At the moment Africans set foot on American soil, the very essence of the African culture was forever changed. African slaves in America lost functions, social power, and authority over their own destiny and self-governance.[1,2,3] Slavery forcibly altered the traditional family structure, traditional marital roles, and the values of Black children. This assault has continued with the high incarceration of African American men and women, welfare and school segregation laws and policies, social work, disenfranchisement, urbanization, and lack of employment and medical benefits that undermine the strength of the family. Yet, African Americans

381

males have found creative ways to endure and retain some African values and structures, while contributing to our country and our world.

Although many political, social, and economical ills exist in the African American community, there tends to be resistance for acquiring a broader, truer understanding of life for African American males. Sadly, Eurocentric paradigms tend to depict Black males as being welfare recipients, violent convicts, drug addicts, and academic failures. Though not always acknowledged, over the years, African American males have responded with amazing resiliency; this is the good news. The survival of African Americans keeps hope alive for all Americans, and I have no doubt that social scientists and education scholars have overlooked research about the endurance, fortitude, and resilience of African Americans males. In fact, some of the same literature that has been written about pathology and problems among African American males can actually be useful for the ills plaguing American families and communities in general. Because of their strength, resiliency, and refusal to fall down, African American males, as a people, are a real testimony that negatives can be turned into positives. Accordingly, it is the responsibility of educators and researchers, specifically those who are African American, to investigate and to teach children how African American males have developed the fortitude and resilience to endure the hardships of life in America.[4,5,6,7,8,9]

What is Resilience?

Resilience, for most people, refers to the psychological strength and capacity of a person to withstand stress and frustration and not allow stressful life events (e.g., death of a loved one, chronic illness, unemployment, etc.) to cause emotional, physical or spiritual problems, while the individual thrives to fulfill their potential despite, or perhaps because of, the stress and frustration they experienced. This is the mainstream psychological view of resilience.

The central process involved in building resilience is the training and development of adaptive coping skills. I have come to live by a basic model of stress and coping. A stressor (i.e. a potential source of personal and emotional difficulties) occurs, and I go through a cognitive appraisal to decide whether the stressor represents something that can be readily dealt with or is a problem that may be beyond my coping resources. If the source of stress is considered a danger to myself or the people closest to me, coping responses are triggered. My coping strategies are generally focused on solving the problem, managing my emotions, or seeking emotional support from others, typically family members or my closest friends. I've also found that when I'm in that resilient mode, I'm more inclined to see problems as opportunities for growth. I seem not only to cope well with unusual strains and stressors but to experience such challenges as learning and development opportunities, as well.

Resilience is what shapes a young Black boy into a great Black man. One of the challenges facing parents, teachers, and educators is the dilemma of how to instill and teach resiliency to young Black boys. It seems difficult because resiliency is not a subject like gym or social studies that can be formally taught. It is a state of mind that can be adopted through living life and learning from the examples of others, as well as from taking life's invaluable experiences and using them for the benefit of others and yourself. There are several factors that interfere with us being able to teach our children to be resilient as well as factors that allow us to enhance resiliency in our children. The question is how to identify it. In my case, I take a hard and close look at what events occurred in my life and how I came through them. I also look at what fundamental changes occurred with my perspective on life as I continue to face even more obstacles. The things I faced in the street are much more different than I face as a leader in corporate America, the community, my business, and at home, but all require me to practice resiliency.

While much has been written about resiliency, very little attention has been given to understand resiliency for Black males and how it related to academic success. Therefore, the purpose of this chapter is to discuss resiliency as it pertains to Black males, examine how resiliency contributes to academic success, determine both the factors that hinder and enhance resiliency for Black males, and, finally, to suggest ways that parents and educators can enhance resiliency among Black males.[6,9,10,11,12,13,14]

Beginning With The End In Mind

I don't know about you, but it would be highly unlikely for me to do business with a building contractor who insists that he does his best work without having a blue—print or plan for building homes. He then claims that sometimes he starts with the roof while other homes he had put the walls up first before putting in the plumbing. For some, he starts with cinderblocks and then uses clay to put on the finishing touch, while he uses a combination of straw and a special mud for the foundation in some of his projects. And then there is the exciting story about how he waited until the entire house was built before he decided where to put in windows. I'm sure you get the picture, and I'm certain that neither you nor I would do business with this contractor. Regardless of how good the deal the contractor is willing to provide, it just does not seem good enough without a plan for exactly how the home will be built or what it will eventually look like. We might be interested in looking at some of the homes he has built, but I know we would not do business with him because of his failure to give us an idea of how our home will look in the end. We would not do business with this contractor because it doesn't seem like he would produce the results we desire.

The Bible describes the process by which God created the heavens and earth (Genesis, Chapter 1). Verse 26 says, "And God said, Let us make man in our image, after our likeliness: and let them have dominion over the fish of the sea, and over the fowl of the air, and over the cattle, and over all the earth, and over every creeping thing that creepeth upon the earth. Verse 27 describes God's creation; So God created man in his own image, in the image of God created he him; male and female created he them. Many of the modern-day motivational experts, such as Steven Covey, author of the world renowned book, "The Seven Habits of Effective People," have claimed that success of all forms is directly linked to the ability of a person to have a clear and vivid picture of the outcome they desire from their actions.[15] With this as a background, I want you to understand my story and what it offers you as a way to understand resiliency. Rather than take you back to the start, I will begin, where I am now, and we will move back a bit so that you can have a vivid picture of the important role that resiliency played in shaping me into be the man that I am today.

As a part of my executive leadership training, I had to take a test to identify my strengths. It was very interesting to me that resilience was not one of the strengths listed. As I looked around the room and saw the MBAs and senior leaders that took the straight and narrow path through life, I realized that I was abundantly blessed. Being one of the few Black males permitted to ascend to a position of leadership, I realized that being resilient got me to where I am.

Corporate America Is Eating Me Alive!

At times, the politics, secret alliances, and drama that goes along with making your way up the corporate ladder tends to be stressful and taxing on the mind, body, and soul. Pair that with managing rental properties remotely, and you have a recipe for a meltdown. Then I think of where I have come from and realize that I am in a world away from where I was. I take myself back to the times where I struggled to make ends meet and the worries I had about taking care of my sons.

It has taken me so long to write this chapter. I look at myself in the mirror and ask myself if I am taking personal accountability for all my actions. I know that taking accountability has been one of the things that made me resilient. To honestly look at myself and own my actions continues to help me grow spiritually and professionally. You may think that you are seeking accountability by saying "I did that" or "I apologize for that." But real accountability is about taking a daily inventory of yourself and your actions and making day-to-day adjustments and changes to ensure that you harm no one. It is my intention to make sure that all of the people that come in contact with on a daily basis have something good to remember me by.

Resilience can only be achieved by our children if we (parents, mentors and educators) teach them to take personal accountability of all their actions. There were people in my path that did just that! They called me on my bullshit, so to speak. Early on, I experienced the harsh consequences of my actions and the type of tough love that contributed to my development and understanding how to be resilient. I harnessed the health of all my experiences, which made me grow; it also made me responsible for my actions and taught me how to take responsibility for the actions of others who work under my supervision. Today, I am responsible for my children and the children of the parents I supervise and mentor. It is my God-given responsibility to ensure that every child that I come in contact with leaves me with a better understanding of the world and know that the strength to have a better life is already within them.

Can we ever really pinpoint the times where we stopped acting helpless and started exercising our learned resilience and independence? I really cannot pinpoint the times in my life when everything was clear about how what I was learning would contribute to my growth. Whether we recognize them totally depends on the people in our lives who have taken an interest in teaching us how to be resilient and deal with any situation. You get the tool, but you really don't know what it's for until you need it. Remember when your grandmother or mother used old sayings that didn't make sense until twenty years? When it made the difference between winning or losing or breaking down mentally or making it through whatever dilemma you were facing at that time? That is a part of the resilience that was instilled in us. There are so many people, events and situations that go into what makes us and our children resilient, but the questions I want to answer in this chapter are, How can we make sure that our children are resilient? How can we teach them to be resilient? What tools can teachers, mentors, and educators provide Black boys to make them resilient?" I hope that I can share with you what contributed to my personal development and how I became resilient. The fact that I'm still here, living on this planet, is a testament to my resilience. But what is resilience? How does resilience contribute to academic success for Black males?

The Dynamic Power Of Resiliency

Whereas some individuals seem to be more resilient than others, it should be recognized that resilience is a dynamic quality, not a permanent capacity. Resilient individuals demonstrate dynamic self-renewal, whereas less resilient individuals find themselves worn down, emotionally drained, and physically exhausted from having to cope with life. Ultimately it seems to me resilience is some kind of dynamic quality that is very private. If rooted firmly in the inner sanctum, resilience can hibernate but remain alive during times of difficulty and oppression, then flower when circumstances become nearly unbearable. It is the inner voice that is most prevalent in the human psyche; the inner voice is constantly chattering away.

Human psychological experience is fundamentally shaped by what happens in the inner sanctum, or core beliefs. When events become overwhelming, when adrenalin surges, when things go wrong, resilience emerges as the capacity to still find the wherewithal to cope with situations despite all odds. Living by will alone, though, is not enough. It takes a lifelong and daily commitment to concentrate and exercise one's deepest capacities in order to genuinely consider oneself resilient to a wide variety of challenges. For example, I went through a period where I was promoted to a better paying leadership position, but it would require me to relocate from Charlotte, North Carolina to Milwaukee, Wisconsin. The new position would also require me to supervise approximately 120 people and be responsible for ensuring their training to deal with their duties at work. Relocating and coping with the prospect of supervising all of those people was stressful enough, but I am the landlord for 17 properties that are homes for seventeen families that depend on me for a decent place to live. All of my properties are in Charlotte, along with my fiancée. To say that I am constantly stressed-out about all of this is an understatement. But, life goes on for me and other Black men who are coping with similar circumstances. Rather than sit around and have a pity-party and feel overwhelmed, I'm doing many of those things that I have learned from my previous experiences. I feel that I can handle what is happening because of how I've learned to cope. I know that most people would cope better if they did at least some of the things that are listed below.

Try these actions to cope with stress and develop your resilience.

- Develop a network of supportive people.
- Develop a greater sense of empathy and compassion for others. Take responsibility for the wellbeing of family members, co-workers, etc.
- Read and educate yourself.
- Attend seminars and lectures about self-development.
- Go back to school to further your education.
- Reach out to family members and friends.
- Talk to mentors on a regular basis.
- Think about the future of your children and what legacy you wish to leave them.
- Think about how you can give to others instead just thinking about your circumstances.
- Join a gym or find a regular way to work out.
- Join civic organizations so that you can give to the community.
- Network with other successful people. In my case, I looked for other successful Black males who were working in corporate settings.

It should be noted that resilience does not guarantee one's survival because we all die sooner or later. And many of the most resilient people in the world are being cut down in the midst of what seems like a productive life. In the process of living and dying, we get to ride the waves of life, and having resilience just makes it easier to cope with whatever life throws your way. As I have thought more about what resilience means and why it's so important to the survival of Black males, I've thought more about the general characteristics of resilient people. Below are my thoughts about the characteristics of resilient people.

Resilient People:

- Bounce back from almost anything
- Have a "where there's a will, there's a way" attitude
- Tend to see problems and change as an opportunity for growth rather than a threat
- "Hang tough" when things are difficult
- Seeing small windows of opportunity and make the most of them
- Have deep-rooted faith in a system of self-transformation
- Have a healthy social support network
- Have the wherewithal to competently handle many different kinds of situations and people
- Have a wide comfort zone
- Recover from experiences of a traumatic nature
- Have mental fortitude
- Stay physically fit, particularly when things get tough
- Have coping mechanism in place to deal with stress
- Faith—Have a relationship with God

Examples of Resilient People

While there are many examples of famous people, including Black males, who exhibit these characteristics of resilience, most resilient people, however, are not famous. Their lives, nevertheless, characterize by actions, events, and experiences that taught them to overcome what could be viewed as disastrous, but to utilize such experiences to ride higher than ever. You are probably aware of people such as Anne Frank, the Jewish girl who kept famous a diary and notes while hiding from Nazis or Helen Keller, blind and deaf from birth, who demonstrated remarkable resilience in learning how to communicate and live with passion. You are probably also comfortable looking at Black males such as Nelson Mandela (jailed for decades in South Africa during apartheid, he later became leader of the country) and Dr. Martin Luther King, Jr. (murdered civil right leader) as examples of resilient people because they are famous, but there are many others.

Resilient people are not necessarily "good" people. Resilient people can be found in all walks of life, the good, the bad and the ugly. The concept of resilience has no direct relationship with morality. The notion of resilience in this sense is value-free. A controversial example of a resilient person is Rubin Carter. Carter was a famous African American boxer who demonstrated considerable resilience in getting himself released from jail after being convicted of a triple murder. Carter attracted considerable publicity through his book, media, and then an inspirational movie ("Hurricane") about his life, time in jail, and court proceedings, etc. However, if you look through various Web pages on Rubin Carter, you will find considerable claims and evidence suggesting Rubin is not as innocent as he or the movie wished to portray.

Another controversial example of a resilient person is the flamboyant boxing promoter Don King, who has made his mark in the courtroom as well as by promoting boxers, such as Muhammad Ali, Mike Tyson, and Evander Holyfield, to name a few. Prior to entering the world of boxing, King lived in Cleveland, Ohio. After dropping out of Kent State University, he ran an illegal bookmaking operation and was charged for killing two men (two separate incidents 13 years apart). The first was determined to be justifiable homicide despite the fact that King had shot the man in the back. King was convicted of second degree murder of an employee who owed him money. In an ex parte meeting with King's attorney, the judge reduced King's conviction to manslaughter for which King served just under four years in prison. Don King has been a lightning rod for controversy throughout his career. He has been the subject of several lawsuits by boxers he managed who alleged that they were forced to hire King's relatives and cronies. He has faced charges of tax evasion by the IRS. Rumors of jury-tampering have swirled around him. King has been investigated for possible connections with organized crime. During a 1992 Senate investigation King took the Fifth Amendment when questioned about his connection to mobster John Gotti.

To be able to grow up in a home riddled with alcoholism, violence, love and to become a responsible citizen in my community, a reliable, trustworthy, and successful employee in the corporate world, and to live with minimal resentments is resilient. Resilience to me means that, in spite of the most severe types of prejudices and racism, I can reach up to, into a God of love that asks me to love rather than be loved, to understand rather than be understood. It means the ability to form bonds with people that do not look like me, to sit through countless numbers of interviews only to be rejected because of past indiscretions.

It is my belief that most of us are resilient people, some to a more or lesser degree. I believe those of us do not become hateful, bitter, and give up on whatever hopes and dreams we once had. Without an attitude of resilience and learning to trust at least one other person, I would either be dead or incarcerated for life. I don't believe resilience is a stand-alone product. Someone along the road helped me find faith that the darkness in life's passageways doesn't last forever. I needed and got a mentor that showed me the light at the end of the tunnel. Being resilient means I don't stop learning and growing.

Growing up young, Black, and male in America will either teach you to hang in there and persevere, no matter what, or it will teach you what it means to be a repeat offender. It will teach you what it means to be unable to get up in the middle of the night and walk in to the kitchen for a late night snack. I strongly believe that if I were not resilient, I would know in intimate detail how my forefathers felt when they went, hat in hand, to the back door of the bosses' homes asking for some of the leftovers to feed and clothe their families.

Being resilient as a Black male is to spring back from and successfully adapt to adverse social, emotional, and economic circumstances. The dictionary provides this definition of resilience: an ability to recover from or adjust easily to misfortune or change. To a great extent, resilience depends on the ability of Black males to intelligently think about their circumstances rather than to become a prisoner of their emotions. As you are well aware, emotions, particularly anger, are often the catalyst for many of the poor decisions that Black males make when they are faced with adverse circumstances or pressures from peers. An increasing body of research from the fields of psychology, psychiatry, and sociology is showing that most people—including young people—can bounce back from risks, stress, crises, trauma, and experience life success.

There are many successful Black male entrepreneurs who have struggled throughout history to overcome extreme prejudice and the unavailability of economic resources. They had a strong work ethic, trust in their fellow man, and tenacity, and they sharpened their minds to take advantage of opportunities. They took responsibility and ownership for there own actions and destinies. Our children have to be taught to do the same. We must ensure that our children are given heroes to emulate, as well. One of my heroes is Chris Gardner who was once homeless and jobless and faced what some would call overwhelming odds. He raised his toddler son while struggling with homelessness and became a self-made millionaire, entrepreneur, motivational speaker, philanthropist and one of the top Black stock brokers in the industry.[16]

As of 2006, Chris Gardner is CEO of his own stock brokerage firm, Gardner Rich & Co, based in Chicago, Illinois, where he resides when he is not living in New York City. Gardner credits his tenacity and success to the "spiritual genetics" handed down to him by his mother, Bettye Jean Triplett, née Gardner, and to the high expectations placed on him by his children, Chris Jr. (born 1981), and his daughter, Jacintha (born 1985). Gardner's personal struggle to establish himself as a stockbroker while managing fatherhood and homelessness is portrayed in the 2006 motion picture The Pursuit of Happyness, starring actor Will Smith.

In my case, there are times when I find it hard to believe that I've had the opportunity to work for Wells Fargo in Milwaukee, Wisconsin, which is where Chris Gardner was born. My childhood was problematic. My parents went through a divorce when I was at a young age and I witnessed, firsthand, how my mother coped with the stress of divorce by becoming an alcoholic. Looking back, I now realize how tough it was for her to raise me without any support from my father, a Jamaican immigrant, who was deported from the country. I had to deal with all of this and more, such as taking care of my younger brother, going to school, avoiding gangs and the brothers with the drugs, and figuring out how to fit in with the right crowd. As I look back on all of this, I realize that I had no one to depend on except me. Life was tough for me as a young boy.

Forced to depend on myself to endure the emotional hardships I was experiencing, I quickly learned how to put my emotions in check; I simply had no time for pity parties. I was angry, upset, confused, and feeling out of control. The situation was bad, but I always felt loved, even by my father who was often thousands of miles way because of his immigrant status. I realized, however, that if I was going to become somebody, I had to take care of how I was feeling. Today, I know that emotional reactions to life can be as destructive as walking through a minefield. You can blow yourself up if you aren't careful about where you step.

Handling Emotions and Resilience

To understand resilience, you've got to understand the central role that emotions play in the lives of Black males. It is one thing to know all of the statistics about how bad life is for Black males, but it is sometimes overwhelming to consider that bad circumstances have literally drained the emotional life out of Black males. Yet, despite the tremendous levels of shame, disgust, frustration, depression, anger, and general uncertainty, there are some Black males who have come to understand how handling their emotions can enhance their ability to cope with life. To do so has required them to understand four valuable lessons about emotions.

First, they have mastered their ability to perceive emotions, which has to do with the nonverbal reception and expression of emotion. Facial expressions, such as happiness, sadness, anger, and fear, are universally recognizable, but the capacity of Black males to accurately perceive emotions in the face or voice of others provides a crucial starting point for more advanced understanding of emotions.

Second, to handle emotions successfully, Black males have to use emotions to facilitate their thinking and to prioritize their thinking about the circumstances they are facing in their lives. It is important for them to direct their thinking toward matters that are truly important or to help carry out creative thought.

Third, to handle emotions, you must come to understand that each emotion conveys possible messages and actions associated with those messages. Happiness usually indicates a desire to join with other people; anger indicates a desire to attack or harm others; fear indicates a desire to escape, and so forth. A message of anger, for example, may mean that the individual feels he or she has been treated unfairly. The anger, in turn, might be associated with specific sets of possible actions: peacemaking, attacking, retribution and revenge-seeking, or withdrawal to seek calmness.

Understanding emotional messages and the actions associated with them is one important aspect of this area of skill. Once a person can identify such messages and potential actions, the capacity to reason with and about those emotional messages and actions becomes of importance as well. Fully understanding emotions, in other words, involves the comprehension of the meaning of emotions, coupled with the capacity to reason about those meanings. Finally, Black males have to understand that, regardless of their circumstances, the emotions they are experiencing can be managed. Whereas the means and methods for emotional self-regulation are the topic for other chapters in this book (See Chapters 6 and 13), it is important for you to examine the power of emotions in the lives of Black males in order to understand why some develop the resilience to cope with life and excel, while others do not.

Factors That Interfere With Resilience

Not having a way to deflect and cope with anger is probably the major interference with the development of resilience among Black males. Black males are constantly made to feel that we are not as good as others are; people fear us, they challenge our authority, they act as if we don't belong, and we are treated like second class citizens in a nation that we helped to build. Anger is a misunderstood emotion for Black males who have been taught to suppress or curb their anger, regardless of how justified it may be, because Black male anger frightens white America.

Today, slavery and legal segregation are over, yet the evidence of institutional racism radiates throughout the land. Black males receive the blunt force of racism in America, but they must keep their cool in order to survive in America, particularly corporate America. Just because these angry feelings are not verbally expressed, however, does not mean that they don't find expression in the homes or workplace of Black men. The cost of keeping so many bad feeling to themselves has been great, and it's hard for a Black male to feel proud about being Black and male if the fear of punishment is always looming overhead. Unlike the days of the past, when punishment was a physical beating, today many lack males live in fear of losing their jobs, not receiving favorable evaluations at work, being stopped by police officers for no apparent reason, and not having the resources (e.g., adequate housing, health care, etc.) to support themselves or their family.[17]

A second factor that hinders the development of resilience among Black men is the inability to cultivate a strong set of social communication skills. To a certain extent, social communication skills go hand-in-hand with coping with anger, as the ability to assert oneself without violating others is the basis of conflict resolution. For Black males who are members of the non-dominant culture in America, the ability to move back and forth between their primary culture and the dominate culture without assimilating into it means learning the "codes of power" while retaining their own cultural and self identities.

It takes some know-how for Black males to be comfortable developing relationships and positive attachments to other people outside of their race and ethnicity, particularly if that person is a white male. Just think about it for a moment: White males, more so than any other group in America, represent the image of who has been responsible for much of the pain, anguish, and humiliation that Black males have received since they were enslaved and brought to America. I would image that you would have a difficulty being a friend to someone who has been the source of pain for your family. It would be difficult for you to develop certain other traits, such as empathy, caring, compassion, altruism and forgiveness that are the hallmarks of resilience. In the case of empathy, it helps facilitate relationship development because it helps form the basis of morality, forgiveness, and compassion and caring for others. Empathy is the fundamental "people skill" Black males need to develop. It enables him to read feelings from nonverbal cues so that he will be better adjusted emotionally, more popular, more outgoing, and more sensitive.

If a Black males attempts to survive without getting over his anger toward white people and developing the empathy necessary to sustain positive relationships, he will be seen as an angry psychopath. Even if he is highly educated, having attended the finest schools in America, if he lacks empathy, then his chances for success are slim. Empathy, the ability to know how another feels and understand another's perspective, is the hallmark of resilience.

The third factor that slows and hinders the development of resilience among Black males is not having been taught a process for making skillful decisions. Like strenuous exercise, skillful thinking is hard work. And as with athletes, Black boys need practice, reflection, and coaching to think well. With proper instruction, the thought process of Black boys can become precisely focused. Something as simple as a game of chess can be used to teach Black boys to analyze their thinking and the consequences of their actions. For most of us, learning how to make skillful decisions boils down to developing the habit of using self-reflective questions like these:

- What do I already know about the problem, and what resources do I have or need to handle the problem?

- How can I draw on my past successes to solve this new problem?
- What questions do I need to ask to learn more about this problem?
- How might I look at the problem from a fresh perspective?
- How can I make the problem clearer, more precise, and more detailed?
- Can this problem be broken down into smaller parts so that I can have a way to deal with each part?

Learning to think begins with recognizing how we are thinking, listening to ourselves, observing our own reactions, and realizing that our thoughts either compel or repel us to make certain actions. Most of our thinking is automatic and embedded in habits that don't allow us to examine our emotions and bodily reactions to our decisions. However, the good news is that Black boys can be taught to slow the process down and to consider the consequences of their actions before making decisions. A simple and very effective tool I learned from one of my mentors is the "One-Minute Problem Solving Routine." It's an easy critical thinking skill exercise and it work like this: For any problem that you have identified, take one minute to create a list of the different possibilities, regardless of how outrageous they appear, for solving the problem. Next, examine all of the possibilities and then make a decisions about the first, second, and third best choices. The next step is to make a list of the great and wonderful changes (the pleasures you will experience) that could occur as a result of using the solutions generated for solving the problem. Next, describe everything you will sacrifice if you avoid using the solutions you generated. Finally, evaluate the two lists and determine whether your reasons for solving the problem compel you to use the solutions.

When you teach Black boys to think about their thinking, you are teaching them skills they will use throughout their lives. You are teaching them to generate questions about their options, the consequences of these options, and to seek out the best options in light of the consequences. Unfortunately, most Black boys in school today aren't exposed to teachers who teach them to discipline their minds by learning to think. They cover mandated teaching material and superficial instruction that favors teaching Black boys the correct response to multiple choice questions over thinking. Clearly, there is much to admire in students who know a great deal of information and who can easily pass the numerous mandated tests. But for many students, this approach to teaching leads to boredom among students, particularly Black males. If all students were bound for college that would be a different story, but the present practice of forcing all students into academic courses so that they can simply pass mandated tests is not working well. If we focused on teaching all students to think well, regardless of their courses, we might find that this causes them to be more interested in the subject. And if a Black boys decides early on that college is not for him, we should be open to helping him design an excellent career through technical education courses where he can choose his own course of study.

The final factor that hinders the development of resilience is the failure to acknowledge that thoughts are things. Your thoughts are not just wispy little clouds drifting through your head. Your thoughts are things. They are actually measurable units of energy. Thoughts are biochemical electrical impulses. They are waves of energy that, as far as we can tell, penetrate all time and space. Your thoughts are powerful. They are real, they are measurable, and they are energy. Every single thought you have is a statement of your desires to the universe. Every single thought you have generates a physiological change in your body. You are a product of all of the thoughts you have thought, feelings you have felt, and actions you have taken up until now. And the thoughts you think today, feelings you feel today, and actions you take today will determine your experiences tomorrow.

We know from polygraph, or lie detector tests that your body reacts to your thoughts. They change your temperature, heart rate, blood pressure, breathing rate, muscle tension, and how much your hands may sweat. These kinds of physiological reactions occur not only when you are lying, but in reaction to every thought you have. Every single cell in your body is affected by every single thought you have!

So, you can see the importance of learning to think as positively as possible. Negative thoughts are toxic, and they affect your body and relationships in a negative way. They weaken you, make you perspire, create muscular tension and a more acidic environment within your body. They increase the likelihood of cancer (cancer cells thrive in an acidic environment) and other disease. They also send out a negative energy vibration and attract more experiences of the same vibration. Positive thoughts, on the other hand, will affect your body in a positive way. They will make you feel more relaxed, more centered, and alert. They stimulate the release of endorphins in your brain, reducing pain and increasing pleasure. In addition to this, your positive thoughts send out a positive energy vibration that will attract more positive experiences back into your life.

Most of us are fairly aware of our conscious thoughts, but it is important to become aware of our subconscious thoughts, as well. Our subconscious mind is pretty much running the show, and since most of us have a constant negative tape playing in our heads, we are continually sending out negative messages. You must learn to reprogram your subconscious mind and transform your negative internal thoughts into healthy positive ones.

By looking closely at your beliefs and self image, you can work on eliminating any limiting or negative ideas. This negative self talk is like static, or interference, on a phone call: it will interfere with, distort, and even block the frequencies of your positive intentions. If not removed, it will reduce your ability to create and manifest the future you desire. Sometimes you've got to let everything go—purge yourself. If you are unhappy with anything, whatever is bringing you down, get rid of it. Because you'll find that when you're free, your true creativity, your true self comes out. Unfortunately, many of us have a fairly stubborn tendency to hold on to our old negative thoughts and self images. It's our comfort zone (our familiar concepts of reality) that we have become accustomed that tends to get stuck in our subconscious where we grow beliefs of inadequacy, fear, and doubt. Most of these limiting thoughts and feelings stem from past incidents, beliefs, and experiences that we've internalized over the years and turned into our personal truths. These negative concepts can sabotage us and keep us from realizing our fullest growth and potential unless we make a conscious decision to address them, release them, and let them go.

Think about trying to drive a car with the parking brake on. No matter how much you try to accelerate, the parking brake will keep slowing you down. But as soon as you release it, you will automatically and effortlessly go faster. Your limiting thoughts, feelings, and behaviors are psychological parking brakes. They will slow you down unless you make a committed effort to let them go and replace them with more positive thoughts and beliefs. You must be willing to release your negative mental programming and step out of your comfort zone in order to make room for a positive, healthy self image and belief system. Doing so will allow you to more easily and effectively attract the positive energy and experiences that you desire in your life.

Beliefs are just your habitual thoughts, and they can be changed through affirmations, positive self-talk, behavioral changes, and visualization techniques. These are extremely effective tools in releasing old negative thought patterns. But if your negative programming is so deeply rooted that you are experiencing great difficulty in letting go, then you may want to try another approach. The real secret is to keep taking actions until you find something that works for you. There are many great books, audio courses, and seminars that will help you learn how to quickly and powerfully release your negative mental programming and return to a place of pure peace.

Enhancing Psychological Resilience: Can We Teach Resilience?

For Black males to enhance their resilience, they have to become comfortable knowing their own psychology and understanding the power of their subconscious mind. The conscious mind is the part of you that thinks and reasons; it's the part of your mind that you use to make everyday decisions. Your free will resides here, and with your conscious mind, you can decide just what you want to create in your life. With this part of your mind, you can accept or reject any idea. No person or circumstance can force you to think consciously about thoughts or ideas you do not choose. The thoughts you do choose, of course, will eventually determine the course of your life. With practice, and a little bit of disciplined effort, you can learn to direct your thoughts to only those that will support the manifestation of your chosen dreams and goals. Your conscious mind is powerful, but it is the more limited part of your mind. According to Emmanuel Donchin, director of the Laboratory for Cognitive Psychophysiology at the University of South Florida, "As much as 99 percent of cognitive activity may be non-conscious." The fact is, as adults, we spend most of our time subconsciously reacting to life rather than consciously creating it.[18]

The Conscious Mind has:

- Limited processing capacity
- Short term memory (about 20 seconds)
- The ability to manage 1 to 3 events at a time
- Impulses that travel at 120 to 140 mph
- The ability to process an average of 2,000 bits of information per second

Your subconscious mind is actually much more spectacular. It is frequently referred to as your spiritual or universal mind, and it knows no limits except for those that you consciously choose. Your self-image and your habits live in your subconscious mind. It functions in every single cell of your body. It is your connection to God, your connection to source and universal infinite intelligence. Your subconscious mind is habitual and timeless, and it works in the present tense only. It stores your past learning experiences and memories, and it monitors all of your bodily operations, motor functions, heart rate, digestion, etc. Your subconscious mind thinks literally, and it will accept every thought that your conscious mind chooses to think. It has no ability to reject concepts or ideas. What that means is that we can choose to use our conscious mind to deliberately reprogram our subconscious beliefs, and the subconscious mind has to accept the new ideas and beliefs; it can't reject them. We can actually make a conscious decision to change the content of our subconscious mind.

The Subconscious Mind has:

- Expanded processing capacity
- Long term memory (past experiences, attitudes, values, and beliefs)
- The ability to manage thousands of events at a time
- Impulses that travel at over 100,000 mph
- The ability to process an average of 4,000,000,000 bits of information per second

As you can see, the subconscious mind is far more powerful than the conscious mind. Think of your mind as an iceberg. The part of the iceberg you see, the part above water, is your conscious mind. It represents only about one sixth of your actual mental capacity, and the part below water (the other five sixths) is your subconscious mind. When we operate primarily from the conscious mind (as we typically do), we are only using a fraction of our true potential. The conscious mind is a much slower and more cumbersome vehicle than the subconscious mind. So, the goal here is to learn to tap into the vast power of our subconscious mind in order to use it to our advantage.

We must create room in each day to "check in" with our subconscious spiritual mind. Daily time spent quietly without any external distractions will strengthen our connection to who we really are. We can connect with our subconscious mind through the use of several techniques, including affirmations, visualization, prayer, contemplation and meditation, gratitude and appreciation, and the use of positive focus techniques. In my case, I've used all of these techniques, and I would not be the man I am today if they were not a constant part of my life. I struggled to learn that my conscious thoughts were getting me in deeper trouble with myself. Many of these thoughts reinforced the problems I was experiencing in my life, but using my subconscious mind (through affirmations and visualizations), I quickly learned that my subconscious mind could take me where I want to go and help me reach my goals in life much faster and easier than my conscious mind ever could. So, by teaching Black boys to connect with and utilize the amazing speed, power, and agility of their subconscious minds, we can show them how to effectively attract and create the results they desire.

Resilience is not a fluke; it generally emerges in people who understand the power of their subconscious mind, train hard, and have particular attitudes, cognitive and emotional skills, and a deep determination to overcome serious challenges. Building the psychological resilience of at-risk populations has become an increasingly popular target of community intervention, youth work, social work, and personal development programs. Community efforts to enhance resilience of Black males through intervention programs have been increasingly seen as proactive, preventative, potentially cost-saving in the short and long-run, and positive approaches to minimizing psychological dysfunction. Enhancing psychological resilience seems to be an underlying theme in psychological work as well as in challenge-based personal development programs, such as Outward Bound. A simple formula for fostering someone's growth and development of resilience is: Growth = Challenge + Support.[11,19,20,21,22,23,24]

Black males can endure any level of challenge if they receive the training and support necessary to cope with the challenge. On the other hand, even a small challenge caused by negative life circumstances may be too much and lead to traumatic experience if the person isn't well supported. In my case, I could have never coped with the new responsibilities of being promoted, relocated to a new city, managing my landlord responsibilities, staying connected to my son, and plans for my life with my fiancée if I had no support.

As I look back over my life and the way I was forced to learn to cope, I realize how fortunate I was in to be resilient. I'm not saying that I don't continue to feel overwhelmed by life, because I routinely go tough my ups and downs, like everyone. But, today, I go through my routines to cope with these circumstances as if I was commanded to so my some unseen power.

Advice To Parents and Educators

You've read the chapter and learned a lot about me and how I see the concept of resilience. While little academic research exists about the relationship between resilience and academic success among Black males, there are countless stories about how Black males have overcome insurmountable odds in pursuit of their dreams. The big question is: How can you teach Black boys to be the master of themselves? My advice to you is as follows:

- Parents and teachers have to believe that Black boys can be resilient. If you don't believe they can become successful, then they will take your cues and do as you believe.
- Parents have to provide positive reinforcement and use language that projects a positive future.
- Look for positive role models; they do exist. If you can't find living Black male role models, then have the boys read about famous Black men from the past or celebrate the accomplishments of one of their friends who consistently does positive deeds.

- Expose Black boys to tasks that are very challenging and difficult but require much mental effort and concentration to be completed. This will help to build their self-confidence.
- Encourage Black boys to develop their relationships within the church to enable them to be exposed to different social structures. For example, some of the boys will be musically inclined but probably have never considered singing in the church choir or playing an instrument in a Hip hop church band.
- Expose Black boys to real problems that will allow them to develop real solutions so they can learn how to develop their problem solving skills.
- Anger management is a necessary part of your discussion with Black boys. Tell them that being angry is a natural response to unjust and unfair treatment. Let them know that being angry is not a problem and that the only problem with anger comes when it is negatively expressed.
- Teach Black boys how to set goals for today, tomorrow, and the future. Help them begin the journey toward their goals with the end in mind.
- Reading has to become a fundamental part of all of your interactions with Black boys. This will enable them to become lifelong learners.
- Teach Black boys to become action-oriented people who strive to reach their goals.
- Encourage Black boys to develop their real gifts and talents. This will help them maintain a confident and positive self-image.
- As parents, ensure that the school systems are hiring emotionally competent counselors and teachers who are committee to resolving the emotional problems of Black boys.
- Take a course or class to learn how to communicate with your sons. We must learn to talk to our children instead of putting in a DVD and leaving them on their own for hours at a time.
- Take away some of the video games and replace them with trips to the library.
- Teach Black boys that they have to practice emotional resilience, as well.

A Special Message to Parents

The most important life skill you can teach a Black boy is resilience. His gift for bouncing back will be useful in college, in the workplace, as a parent, and when relationships fail. If I had to choose one trait for my children, resilience, would be my pick. Scrappers who can shake off the stiff jabs and keep coming often get the split decisions. Some young brothers have everything—the family background and great role models—it takes to build a strong foundation for success. Don't despair just because some of the boys you teach or your own son have inherited some of that indifference and lethargy concerning the pursuit of the American Dream. If you can conjure up a family culture that exalts resilience, nurture can trump nature and make your children tough. Regardless of the circumstances, you have to embody the traits you would like to pass on. Experts say "actually being a role model" continues to be more effective than even the most well-honed homilies about resourcefulness. So when that landmark deal, the one you've been working on for two years, goes south, don't let your children see you hiding in the garage, sucking down cans of beer and crying over the premature death of your career. Remember the traditional image of a parent being the steady hand on the tiller. Make these thoughts the background music in your home and the Black boys you have been entrusted to educate and care for will grow up good and feisty. They'll be looking for defeats from which they can come roaring back.

1) There are many ways to look at a problem. Always celebrate the art of adjusting, refiguring, dealing with changing conditions. If you're putting in a patio, make a point of mentioning how you navigated around some obstacle. When tinkering in the garage, think out loud. Let your son in on the process: You just need something to hold this 2-by-4 in place while you drill a pilot hole. Let's see . . . aha! Make sure they know you admire people—athletes, parents, children—who can adapt and improvise.

2) Create opportunities to praise their good work. A fundamental sense of self-worth helps children pop up after a blow. But by now, lots of parents have so overdone building self-esteem ("You are such a wonderful child!") that millions of odious little twits feel really good about themselves. Resist the current vogue of constant kid-stroking. Instead, commend the children on their own efficacy, their usefulness in the world. How? The old-fashioned way: lawn-mowing, leaf-raking, garbage duty, table-setting, dishwashing, pet care—all of the time-honored obligations children just

hate. The sight of a mown lawn tells a boy that he can polish up the world. Remember, your goal is to raise a resilient adult, not to be the most popular guy in the house.

3) Find ways to honor their opinions. Just as children need a belief in the utility of their efforts, they also need to feel that their personalities send ripples out into the pond. So when your kids try to make a joke, be sure to chuckle at the effort. No, don't crack up at lame attempts at humor—that messes with reality—but just enjoy the effort. Find a way to credit your children with changing your mind about something—a TV show, a political issue. Don't wait until they're actually right, as that might not happen for years. But the idea that something they said made Dad rethink helps them feel influential in their way. Incidentally, this trait, allowing others to convert you, is the single best way to become popular everywhere—in the office, at home, wherever you roam. There is nothing more charming than honoring the other guy.

4) Use affirmations and catchy phrases often. The best fathers accept an obligation to repeat annoying aphorisms endlessly and endure the mockery that comes with the job. Resilience-promoting bromides, which are so vexing to 12-year-old ears, will, years from now, inspire your grown children through tough times. Any adage featuring the phrase "the measure of a man is his character" is good and should be used often. Consider favorites like "the willow bends, but never breaks" and "anybody can fall down, but it takes a man to get up."

5) Respect failure for what it truly represents. In your house, there are two kinds of failure—the bad kind that springs from sloth or carelessness and the good kind that shows you were stretching, not content to play it safe, and determined to do something with your days. If people are going to turn out resilient, they'll need to fail now and then. So let them. Think of it as practice. Teach children that life can be strong, productive, and it will keep moving ahead. And urge them to watch the ball roll past the hole. Some golfers jack a 15-footer six feet past the hole and turn away in disgust, horrified by their ham-handedness. But the successful ones take their medicine and watch the ball roll past the hole, and know exactly how the comebacker for bogey breaks. Mental-health pros argue that self-esteem shortfalls often stem from so-called attribution issues. Simply put, children with low self-esteem tend to attribute their successes to something external and their failures to some intrinsic shortcoming. So if they do well on a test, they believe the test was easy, but conversely,

if they do poorly, it's proof of their stupidity. This is especially common among Black boys. The most resilient among us attribute things properly, understanding that most often achievements are traceable to skill and/or effort and that sometimes failures are just bad luck. Use your trademark subtlety to link success to their efforts and to make it clear that sometimes we'll fail for no good reason.

6) Admit your mistakes. Don't hesitate to let your children see you've had a setback and that you make mistakes. If even a titan like you can screw up, they'll come to see failures as an inevitable part of life. And when you're wrong and you know you're wrong, say you're sorry. Mistakes aren't fatal; they're just mistakes. Fresh starts are what America is all about. If a Black boy is to flourish, he needs a charismatic adult in his life, and that adult has to be conscious of the charisma of the child and complement the child. Exactly how the adult salutes the child does not matter, as long as it is clear that that the boy understood the spark that produced the complement. This isn't to say that the grown-up is a pushover, but just that even if there is static between the adult and child, a positive complement is message number one. The rest is details. The adult knows the great truth about a Black boy who often doubts he's much of anything. This charismatic adult doesn't have to be a parent. He or she can be a teacher, a coach, a grandparent, or a neighbor.

Epilogue

The Covenant For Motivating and Educating African American Males

By The Champions for Peace Mastermind Institute

Racism is a commonplace experience for Black males in America, even in the system of education. But there are many Black males who have transcended the ill effects of racism and have productive lives in an unjust society. To a certain extent, each of the Black male contributors to this book have distinguished themselves as successful in their fields, in spite of tremendous obstacles. The driving force for most of us was the powerful commitment and promise made by our parents and grandparents that we would have opportunities that exceed their wildest dreams.

Many of us were the first generation to graduate from high school and attend college. We wanted to learn all that we could with the intent of using our knowledge to further the advancement of our people and provide for our families. Although our parents and grandparents' covenant was tacit, the essence of the agreement was communicated to us at every phase of our lives. Much like the African tradition of oral storytelling, stories about the importance of education and the denial of literacy were passed down from generation to generation.

Our grandparents, uncles, and aunts had talks with us about the hard times they endured because they didn't have the necessary education to get a better job. We were told countless stories about slaves who were hanged because they were discovered reading and Black people who were cheated out of their land or other highly valued goods because they couldn't read. They told us stories about the reading and writing classes secretly held before and after Sunday church services. They shared stories about Black students going to school in one-room shacks that had no desks or chairs. Students sat on long wooden benches and did their work on their laps, writing on single sheets of paper the teacher would tear from a tablet. Our elders told us stories about how literacy laws were enacted to keep Black folk from voting and how African American teachers were paid substantially less than white teachers who also had better schools, books and other supplies. Above all else, they made sure we understood that the pursuit of education for Black people was the way for us to frame a new and empowering identity.

Our mothers, fathers, and neighbors took us aside to remind us about the importance of doing well in school and to help us understand the links between having a good life and doing well in school. Our families celebrated when we graduated from high school, and members of the community often provided some of the monetary resources we needed in order to attend college. In all of these conversations, the message was clear: There is a predictable relationship between education and socioeconomic development. We were encouraged to pursue education to assert ourselves as a Black man. We pursued learning because it uplifted us and prepared us for leadership. Most of us grew up poor, but the people in our lives had a covenant about how they were going to help us get an education, something they were denied.

For many of us, the continuous articulations about the value of education created within us a belief system, like a force field, that filtered out messages about our intellectual capabilities and other stereotypes about our behavior that were grounded in racism. The stories told to us about our parents, grandparents, and other elders in our communities showed us who we could become. Today, the problems Black boys face in school and society, although seemingly more complex and intense, are basically the same as those we and our parents faced. What seems to have changed is the rich tradition of family and community members instilling in Black males the intense and persistent belief that they can have academic success, regardless of constraints and impoverished conditions. Another change is the notable lack of African American teachers, particularly males, that Black students interact with on a daily basis at school and in their communities.

Given the current conversations about the underachievement of African American males and the problems they continually face because of their lack of education, we hope and pray that you (teachers, parents, school counselors, grandparents, and guardians) have found some answers within our book to help curb this crisis. But the words are just words until you make a commitment to help African American males engage in or refrain from specific actions. The building blocks for all of our habits are the words we use to express our beliefs, our values, and our attitudes. Strung together, our habits reflect our knowledge, skills, and our character. Our habits are powerful and consistent factors that unconsciously exert control over our daily actions and ultimately produce effective or ineffective results in our work with Black males. With this as a backdrop, we ask you to re-examine your behavioral routines (your habits) and commitment to working with Black males under your care. The twelve principles outlined in the covenant can serve as an invaluable roadmap to success.

1) Begin with the end in mind. Have a definite purpose about your work with African American males. Know what your goals are, know what you want from Black males, and know what skills, attitudes, and beliefs you want to help them acquire. Having a definite purpose also means that in addition to having clear goals, you are willing to make a commitment to teach Black boys how to set, monitor, and move toward their own academic, personal, family, economic, spiritual, and career goals. Just like each of us, having goals provides direction, purpose, and meaning to this journey called life. If teachers, parents, and counselors like you had made this commitment a decade or so ago, perhaps the dropout rate among Black males would not be 58 percent and 33 percent of Black males between the ages of 20 and 39 might not be incarcerated or under some correctional supervision. We do not know what a commitment to Black males will mean in terms of unemployment, but anything less than a figure double that of whites in this country would be a reasonable goal. With more Black males gainfully employed, there is likely to be an impact on the 70-plus percent of Black babies born out of wedlock and the percentage of Blacks living at or under the poverty level. Your commitment can make a difference!

2) Make a commitment to enter into a mastermind alliance—a working and supportive relationship—with at least one other person who maintains a covenant about his or her work with Black males. There is real power in the coordinated efforts between two or more people working in harmony to attain specific goals. Keep in mind that it is important to adopt a definite purpose and plan for the mastermind alliance. This will help each member determine the benefits they will receive in return for their cooperation. In doing so, harmony will prevail in the group. Much like the alliances you form with other supportive adults, encourage Black males to seek out at least one of their peers (or a younger sibling) who is committed to becoming a better student.

3) Regardless of your ethnicity or gender, make a commitment to become knowledgeable about how the identity of Black males is shaped by African American cultural beliefs and the lack of truthful information about the contribution of Black males to the fabric of life on this planet. When you address the different learning styles, build on student strengths, and use culturally inclusive curricula, you are doing the right things to generate a sense of belonging in your students. The main reason many Black males aren't psychologically engaged in learning is that they have never been welcomed in the classroom or school community. Rather than emphasizing academics and the type of classroom performance we want from Black males, schools have created a positive culture around athletics and have made a priority of attracting Black males into athletics rather than scholarly activities. If the only positive images Black boys see and know about are athletes and entertainers, then it should not be a surprise that most Black boys want to become professional athletes or entertainers. Regardless of the courses you teach, there are ways to find links between the course content and some aspect of African American culture, as well as the culture of other ethnic minority students. African Americans have contributed to the fabric of knowledge in every field of study from math, science, medicine, and technology to the creative arts like sculpture and photography. Unfortunately, the textbooks used in our public schools don't reflect the rich contributions of African Americans, particularly males, to the fabric of life in our country or the world. Just imagine what it would be like tomorrow morning, if all over the world, as people brought their automobiles to a stop at a red light, a small sign flashed "Be Thankful for Garrett Morgan—The Black Man and Son of Former Slaves Who Developed the Traffic Signal."

4) Make a commitment to showing Black males how to embrace everything and everyone with an attitude of love. Whether you believe it or not, the simple act of greeting everyone with love (sub-vocally and mentally saying, "I love you") will impact them and yourself. It's terribly difficult to be upset with someone you have greeted with love, and it's almost impossible to not greet them with a smile, even if their behavior is not in line with your expectations. Of all the actions you can teach Black males, this simple act can open the hearts of people in their lives and doorways to opportunities. Just as love is the best weapon to open the hearts of people in your life, love can also be a shield to repel the arrows of hate and spears of anger Black males are likely to experience throughout their lives. If you help them to cultivate the habit of greeting everyone and every situation with love, then you will instill in them a habit that will enable them to walk unencumbered among all manners of people and situations. In this book, we have consistently talked about the power of your relationship with Black males. More than anything else, it is the quality of your relationship that matters most to the wellbeing and success of Black males.

5) Instruct Black males how to take actions daily to move toward goals. Without having this inner power, there won't be any energy to complete those goals that you have set. To successful teach students of color, Black males in particular, you must answer this question right now: What actions can I take today, right now, to move toward the goals I've set for working with Black males? One of the powerful things about setting goals is that we tend to share our ideas with people in our lives. For you, teachers and parents, it's important for you to share your goals with the Black males you are teaching. Outline your plan toward your goals. Through observing your actions, they will learn about the power of taking daily actions to accomplish their goals. Black males, just as all other students, are motivated by their feelings about what they believe will happen in the classroom. If Black males have been made to feel incompetent (you can't learn based on your performance), alienated (you and your culture are not important to anything we are learning), useless (there is nothing about you or your people that adds value to the class), and helpless (there is nothing you can do to improve you academic performance), then its unlikely that they will be motivated to learn or stay in school. Helping Black males learn that daily steps they take to achieve an education are important will help

them feel important. When they feel important, they will feel invested in attending school and participating in their own educational experience.

6) Help Black males go beyond the call of duty to produce a quality outcome. Most teachers render more services than they are paid to render. The key, however, is to render the service all the time without having a negative attitude. It's amazing what information children, Black males included, have about the personal and professional problems that teachers are experiencing at their schools. It is equally amazing how unaware teachers are about the impact that their attitude and ill feelings have on the temperament of the classroom. As indicated in several chapters throughout the book, most of our behavior is subconscious. Most of us are not conscious of how we allow our personal mishaps to lessen the quality of the services we are rendering. Many teachers and parents are willing to "go the extra mile" when everything is going well, but when things are going badly, they render poor service. Black boys, more so than all of the other students in your classes, are likely to mimic your behavior. So make sure they see you consistently going beyond the call of duty and rendering your services with a positive attitude. If you want them to put that extra effort into a paper or class project or reading assignment, then let then see you operating the same way!

7) Teach Black males to focus on goals and to be resilient in the face of adversity and hardships. This might be one of the highest forms of self-discipline since it requires a person to coordinate all of their mental faculties and direct them to accomplishing goals. Regardless of what you say to Black males about their academic performance, expectations, or their motivations, they are more likely to believe in your behaviors. They are more likely to believe and emulate how you behave when faced with difficulties than what you say about how they should behave. When your students witness you seeking peaceful resolutions to conflicts, they are more likely to do the same when conflict and adversity threaten to interfere with their goals and dreams.

8) Teach Black males how to visualize themselves performing at the highest level. You've got to ask yourself whether your expectations and interactions with Black males are different than other students. Chances are there are differences in your visualization of the academic performance of Black males and those students for whom you have the highest expectations. If you can't see Black males performing at the higher levels, the chances are good that you are engaging in some differential

treatment of Black males that reflects your lower expectations about their performance. Can you change your biased thinking? Yes, you can. It is hard, but we hope you will use the information in this book to help you become aware of the different ways you treat Black males and consciously alter your behavior, that impacts the performance of Black males. It is always important to use verbal and nonverbal messages that convey value and worth to Black males. Interacting with Black males in this manner will often contribute to a vision of them that helps you gain their cooperation and inspires them to draw upon your enthusiasm.

9) Teach Black males to take care of themselves physically and emotionally. Considering the typical diet of Black adolescent males, it should be a surprise that they have very little psychological or intellectual energy available to carry out the multitude of complex tasks associated with reading, writing, and arithmetic. If what they are consuming lacks life and energy sustaining nutrients the brain and body needs for optimal performance, the mental output and academic performance is likely to be a reflection of their lethargy. If you want Black males to have the psychological and intellectual energy to be successful in the classroom and in life, then you've got to encourage them to take care of themselves and to learn about the connections between their brain, their body, and what they eat and drink. There is a good chance that some of them have parents or family members whose lives were cut way too short because they filled their bodies with junk foods that rotted out their bodies and minds. Many educators navigate around the health and hygiene issues of the students in their classes simply because they don't understand the relationships between academic performance and health behavior or they simply don't know how to the address the problem or they feel like they are intruding into an area that should be reserved for the parents. Take it from me, most parents are at a loss about how to deal with the epidemic levels of obesity, diabetes, and sexually transmitted diseases among children. My bet is that most parents would eagerly accept any advice you offer to help them curb these and other problem their children are facing. And just like you, they have heard all of their lives that breakfast is the most important meal that a child needs, but unlike you, they might not fully understand the reasons and they might not know what constitutes a healthy breakfast. You have access to information, and you don't have to be a health expert to provide Black parents and their sons with truthful information and tips about healthy living.

10) Help Black males understand that their creativity is valued and needed. If Black boys fully understood the real meaningful contributions of Black people to the planet earth, they would feel a level of unselfish pride and happiness that would never be shattered by the day-to-day struggles they are experiencing. As a teacher (or school counselor), have you used the history of Black people to make Black males feel good about themselves or to make them aware of their roles and responsibilities toward themselves, their families, and their communities? What do you know about the history of your Black male students? What I have learned is that many educators, including those who are themselves Black, lack knowledge of Black history. Just as one cannot teach a subject one does not know, one cannot effectively teach students one does not know. When you know your students' history, you know your students. Regardless of the reasons why history books have failed to reflect the accomplishments and scientific discoveries of Black people, the fact is that Black boys lack easy access to truthful information about the creative accomplishments of their people, except for sports and entertainment. If you really want to see Black males performing at a higher level in your classes, you've got to develop ways to make them feel wanted, appreciated, and valuable to your classroom and curriculum. Your students' history is their collective past, of which they are both product and reflection. By familiarizing yourself with the history and culture of Black males, you will be in a much better position to teach your students their story. Here are a few books that I would recommend to get you started on learning the history and culture of your Black male students:

- Introduction to African Civilizations, by John G. Jackson
- The African Origins of Civilization, by Cheik Anta Diop
- Stolen Legacy, by George G.M. James
- The Miseducation of the Negro, by Carter G. Woodson
- Before the Mayflower, by Lerone Bennett Jr.
- From Slavery to Freedom, by John Hope Franklin
- Introduction to Black Studies, by Maulana Karenga
- Blacks in Science, by Ivan Van Sertima
- Black Inventors in America, by McKinley Burt Jr.
- King: A Biography, by David Lewis
- The Autobiography of Malcolm X, by Alex Haley
- The Immortal Life of Henrietta Lacks, by Rebecca Skloot

- At The Dark End of the Street: Black Women, Rape, and Resistance—A New History of the Civil Rights Movement from Rosa Parks to the Rise of Black Power, by Danielle L. McGuire
- Slavery by Another Name: The Re-Enslavement of Black American From the Civil War to World War II, By Douglas Blackmon
- The New Jim Crow: Mass Incarceration in the Age of Colorblindness, by Michelle Alexander

11) Make a commitment to prepare Black males with skills for the 21st century. Defining the skills necessary for success in the next generation is often an elusive task. What skills will be needed for Black males to be competitive in the global marketplace? How can we equip Black males for success in a world we can only envision? The gap between what children are learning in school and what they need to be successful in work and life has become more noticeable. Black males have consistently complained that one reason they are not engaged in the classroom is that the information they are receiving has nothing to do with life and the skills they need to be successful. Educators have often interpreted this message to mean that Black males were uncomfortable with the cultural context (e.g., white middle class values) in which learning occurs rather than an objection to the outdated ways (e.g., text books and in-classroom rather than multimedia and service or problem based approach) in which children are required to learn. But one thing is true, regardless of how you look at the gap between what students are being taught and what they need for life in the 21st century: Black males will need to master far more than reading, writing, and arithmetic. In a recent article by the Association for Supervision and Curriculum Development (ASCD), the Partnerships for 21st Century Success (a collaboration of educators, business and community leaders, and policy makers working to define the skills needed for the next generation of workers) identified four skill areas that all students will need to master.[1]

- Core Content Subjects: English, world language, math, economics, financial literacy, entrepreneurial literacy, science, geography, history, government and civics, global awareness, art, and personal health care skills.

- Creative Thinking and Learning Skills: Critical thinking and problem solving skills, social and emotional intelligence, communication, and collaboration.
- Information, Media and Technology Skills: Information literacy, media literacy, and information and communication literacy.
- Life and Career Skills: Flexibility, adaptability, self-direction, social and cross-cultural skills, productivity, leadership, responsibility, and accountability.

The bottom line is that for Black males to be engaged in today's classroom, we must teach them with tools that are relevant to their lives and their futures. If teachers are to equip Black males to be successful in a globally competitive workforce, teachers must infuse 21st century skills into the classroom environment. This is likely to be a tremendous challenge for teachers in the US, given their already strong tendency toward providing Black males with a far less rigorous education.

12) Make a commitment to convince Black males that reading is the key to success. Of all of the basic academic skills, reading is the one skill that is fundamental to every kind of success, whether academic, social, physical, spiritual, family, or financial. Without the ability to read with speed and comprehension it will be difficult for any person to master the four skills areas that people will need to be successful in the 21st century. To succeed in school and life, African American males need ongoing opportunities to learn and practice essential skills. This is especially true during the summer months. Many African Americans males have a wonderful image of summer as a carefree, happy time when they can sleep until noon, play basketball all day, watch movies until well past midnight, and never consider (because of the lack of affordability or access) the prospect of enriching experiences such as summer camps and trips to museums, parks, and libraries. When the school doors close, many Black males struggle to access educational opportunities, as well as basic needs such as healthy meals and adequate adult supervision.

Did You Know?

- All young people experience learning losses when they do not engage in educational activities during the summer. Research spanning 100 years shows that students typically score lower on standardized tests at the end of summer vacation than they do on the same tests at the beginning of the summer.[2,3,4,5,6,7,8]

- Most students lose about two months of grade level equivalency in mathematical computation skills over the summer months. Low-income students also lose more than two months in reading achievement, despite the fact that their middle-class peers make slight gains.

- More than half of the achievement gap between lower-and higher-income youth, including African American males, can be explained by unequal access to summer learning opportunities. As a result, low-income youth are less likely to graduate from high school or enter college.

- Children lose more than academic knowledge over the summer. Most children—particularly children at high risk of obesity—gain weight more rapidly when they are out of school during summer break.

- Parents consistently cite summer as the most difficult time to ensure that their children have productive things to do.

If you want to maximize the great strides you make during the academic year with Black males, you've got to become an advocate for providing children with summer activities that boost their academic abilities. At this defining moment in our history, America faces few more urgent challenges than preparing our children to compete in a global economy. The decisions our leaders make about education in the coming years will shape our future for generations to come. President Obama's vision for a 21st century education begins with demanding more reform and accountability, coupled with the resources needed to carry out that reform; asking parents to take responsibility for their children's success; and recruiting, retaining, and rewarding an army of new teachers to fill new successful schools that prepare our children for success in college and the workforce. Ultimately, though, this vision ends in classrooms, homes, or mentoring and counseling sessions where teachers, parents, and counselors have to wrestle with their own commitment to teaching Black boys. We need your help, and we encourage you to consider seriously, what a promise like the one below can mean to Black males living in America.

From this day forth, I promise to become consciously aware of my habits and to work to adopt habits that help Black males learn that they can achieve whatever their minds can conceive and believe. From this day forth, I promise to:

1. Begin with the end in mind—black males are successful students—and to have a definite purpose about my work with African American males.
2. Make a commitment to enter into a mastermind alliance, a working and supportive relationship, with at least one other person who maintains a covenant about his or her work with Black males.
3. Make a commitment to become knowledgeable about how the identity of Black males is shaped by African American cultural beliefs and the lack of truthful information about the contribution of Black males to the fabric of life on this planet.
4. Make a commitment to show Black males how to embrace everything and everyone with an attitude of love.
5. Instruct Black males how to take actions daily, including the summertime, to move toward their goals.
6. Help Black males go beyond the call of duty to produce a quality outcome in their academic and personal work.
7. Teach Black males to focus on goals and how to be resilient in the face of adversity and hardships.
8. Teach Black males how to visualize themselves performing at the highest level.
9. Teach Black males to take care of themselves physically and emotionally.
10. Help Black males understand that their creativity is valued and needed at school and in the community.
11. Make a commitment to prepare Black males with skills for the 21st century.
12. Make a commitment to convince Black males that, regardless of the goals they have established for themselves, reading is the key to success.

If you still have some lingering doubts about the importance of your role in educating Black males, we ask you to engage in a compelling reasons exercise. This is an exercise where you examine the consequences of your promises to motivate, educate, and lift the spirit of African American males. Read each question below and take a few moments to imagine how failing to keep your promise will negatively affect you, Black boys, and the families these boys will have one day. Picture in detail how your life (and those of your Black male students or your son) will be five, 10 and 20 years from now if you don't keep your promise.

- How will I feel about myself knowing that I failed to keep my promises?
- What will it cost me (and my Black male students or my son) emotionally and spiritually if I do not keep my promises?
- What impact will my failure to keep my promises have on the families and future children of my Black male students (or my son)?
- How will my failure to keep my promises impact the future employment of my Black male students (or my son)?
- What are the long-term consequences to me (and my Black male students or my son) if I don't keep my promises?

Don't worry if you shed a few tears; we all have. The consequence to Black males, society, and yourself are grim if you don't assume an active role in the education of Black males. It's difficult to imagine what could happen to someone's life if you fail to fulfill your promises to show them how to become successful. On the other hand, it's relatively easy to imagine the positive consequences of your choice to make a difference.

Like the unquenched thirst of many educators, school counselors, and parents who are seeking relevant ways to motivate, educate and lift the spirit of African American males, we were also thirsty to provide some solutions. If you are acquainted with physical thirst, then you know that your body is made of 80 percent water. Your body and brain needs water to stay alive. Your mouth needs moisture to swallow; your glands need sweat to keep your body cool; your cells need blood to carry them; your brain needs fluid to transit messages throughout your body; your joints need fluid to lubricate them. Your body needs water to function smoothly the same way plants need sunshine to grow. If you let your fluid level get low and deprive your body of necessary fluid, your body will tell you. Mental confusion. Dry mouth. Muscle cramps. Thick tongue. Headaches. Weak knees. Irritability and diminished ability to concentrate.

We deprived African American males of the best and most exciting ways to motivate and educate them, but they had no direct way to tell us. We have taken their disinterest in school to mean something other than their attempt to tell us that they were thirsty for exciting ways to be engaged and to learn. We deprived them of their civil rights to a quality education, and they told us through their misbehavior, lack of attention in class, and their unwillingness to regurgitate facts and information that had no relevance to them or their cultural background. Just like you are thirsty for ways to reach African American males, they too are thirsty for enticing ways to be recognized as scholars who are more than capable of producing outstanding work.

We pray that this book provided some ways to quench your thirst!

The Contributors to the Secrets for Motivating, Educating, and Lifting the Spirit of African American Males

Obakunle Akinlana is a professional storyteller, musician, a published writer, and he is the founder and president of Ife Cultural Arts Center, Inc., producer of the Igunnuk African Heritage Festival and a practicing Babalowo. Akinlana resides in Atlanta, Georgia. He enjoys reading, art, farming, Gung fu, fishing, herbs, and billiards. Akinlana regularly presents his stories about Africa and its people at school conferences and cultural festivals. He travels regularly to Africa to share his craft.

Chike Akua is an award-winning educator, author, and consultant with over fourteen years experience as a classroom teacher. A former "Teacher of the Year," He is best known for his books "A Treasure Within" and "Reading Revolution" (co-authored with Tavares Stephens). Akua specializes in developing quality, culturally conscious, innovative curriculum resources to meet the diverse needs of today's students. He has been featured in Ebony magazine and served as a facilitator for the Tavis Smiley Foundation's Youth To Leaders Conference. Brother Akua is currently pursuing a doctorate in education as he continues to travel nationally and internationally as an educational consultant and ordained Minster.

Pryce Baldwin, Jr., is a resident of Garner, North Carolina and a retired educator from the Wake County School System. Pryce began his career in Brooklyn, NY, teaching in elementary grades for 10 years. It was during this time that he married Yvonne Stallings and became the father of Pryce Alexander, III and Yvette Narcicily. He is a graduate of North Carolina A & T State University and has done further study at North Carolina Central University, Fordham University, and Long Island University. His work history includes teacher, administrator, and teacher trainer. While working in Wake County, Pryce served as director of the Helping Hands mentoring program, which provided mentoring, academic enrichment and counseling services to nearly 1,000 African American males. His community involvement is in the area of prison ministry, mentoring and missionary outreach. He serves as a deacon at St. Matthew Baptist Church in Raleigh, NC.

Jerold Marcellus Bryant, a graduate of North Carolina State University, is an author, poet, and spoken-word artist who resides in the metro Atlanta area. Single Man Screaming, his first novel was 2001 Ebony Magazine read for the summer. Jerold travels nationally performing and speaking to young adults and colleagues about defeating racism and promoting values that improve education for all students. Jerold has worked for several education companies dealing with early-childhood, elementary and higher education. As a consultant, he has trained and assisted students and parents about getting into college, publishing books and starting businesses. Currently, Jerold is working on his next novel, Invisible Fathers, and his first book of poetry, Feel These Words.

Phillip "Professor Pitt" Colas is an African American rapper, Hip hop artist, martial arts practitioner, teacher, filmmaker, and accomplished Harpist who has produced two films of a trilogy around the theme of Kung Fu Meets Hip hop. He is also a television journalist and music producer. His most recent album, The Organic Equation, touches on themes such as ancestral roots, meditation and social change. His goal in working with youth is to provide an alternative Hip hop that focuses on youth development and community building without the influence of the mainstream corporate image that exploits the medium. He is working with Matthew Fox to present an intergenerational and interracial after-hours wisdom school called YELLAWE (Youth and Elders Learning

Laboratory for Ancestral Wisdom Education). The pedagogy is based on Fox's new book, The A.W.E. Project, which emphasizes the arts, youth development, social and ecological justice, while also developing inner disciplines ranging from martial arts to chanting/meditation and other contemplative practices.

Patrick "9th Wonder" Douthit is a native of North Carolina who was drawn to music at an early age. As a youth, 9th Wonder spent his days playing one of several instruments he was proficient in for the school band, and the afternoons listening to Afrika Bambataa, Soul Sonic Force, Biz Markie and Slick Rick. In the tradition of producers DJ Premier, Pete Rock, Hi-Tek and Kanye West, 9th Wonder has built a bridge that spans the underground and commercial hip-hop world. Like the jazz greats Miles Davis and Thelonious Monk, 9th "feels" his music, and because of that intimate connection, he creates a sound that transcends hip-hop, and becomes one with soul, jazz and R&B. 9th Wonder has produced for a wide array of artists ; including Jay-Z, Destiny's Child, Erykah Badu, Mary J. Blige, The Game, Lloyd Banks, Memphis Bleek, De La Soul, Murs, and others. Recently, 9th Wonder, along with Christopher "Play" Martin from the Hip hop group Kid-n-Play, were appointed Artist-In-Residence by the Chancellor of North Carolina Central University to create a Hip hop history class in the music department. His background in classical music and music theory give his music a sonic breath and maturity that surpasses his years.

Morris Gary III is currently works as a prevention intervention specialist at the Dekalb Alternative School in Stone Mountain Georgia. Many of the children he serves are in trouble because they have violated the students' code of conduct. Educated at Morehouse College, Georgia State University and Clark Atlanta University in community counseling, Morris eclectic professional interest include psycho-social-cultural correlates and there use in the therapeutic process with children. Morris has worked in batterer's intervention programs for youths and adults, court mandated violence reeducation programs, mental health agencies, rape crisis centers, and has been a volunteer lecturer with AID Atlanta for 18 years. As a father of three boys and four girls, he has had the personal experience of being a single custodial parent. Morris enjoys coaching community recreational sports and he is currently preparing for his first 100-mile bicycle race.

William "Bill" Greene was born and raised in New York and is a product of the New York City public school system. He attended Morehouse College in Atlanta and received a B.A. in Psychology before returning to New York to pursue a graduate degree, Masters of Arts in Social Studies, at Columbia University's Teachers College. He also holds certification in educational leadership from Troy State University and a specialist degree from Argosy University. He recently finished his last class in his doctoral program in curriculum and instruction, also from Argosy University. Bill taught in New York for two years before returning to Atlanta as a teacher at North Clayton High School. During his five years at North Clayton High School he severed as co-department chair and taught World Geography, Ethnic Studies, and Psychology. Along with his many responsibilities in the classroom, Bill found time to serve as a wrestling and football coach. Additionally; he coached two high school state Chess championship teams that were nationally ranked. During his last year at North Clayton High School, he was voted Teacher of the Year before leaving the classroom to become a school administrator. Bill has served as an assistant principal of two schools, Executive Director for the Department of Teaching and Learning, and first principal of the Open Campus High School before being named the Executive Director of the Perry Learning Center.

Anthony (Tony) Goldston was born and raised in North Carolina. He attended high school in Randolph County, which is in the central part of the state where about 15 percent of the students were African American. Tony attended college at University of North Carolina at Greensborough and North Carolina A & T University. He has been a certified Art Education teacher for 20 years and over that time, he has mentored a countless number of African American males and established several mentoring program. His art interests include photography, watercolor, stain glass, and he has a passion for weaving African American history, particularly the study of the Harlem Renaissance, into the study of art. In addition to his work as an arts educator, Tony works as a substance abuse counselors with his father.

Kenston J. Griffin is a native of Statesville, North Carolina and currently resides in Charlotte. He received his Bachelor's Degree from Livingstone College, and Master's Degree, in just one year, from the University of South Carolina in the fields of Social Work and Psychology. Mr. Griffin, recognized as a nationally known motivational speaker and trainer, is the author of three highly successful books: New Days, New Ideas; If Better is Possible, Good Is No Longer an Option; Your Turning Point Starts Now. Mr. Griffin founded and currently presides as Chief Executive Officer of Dream Builders Communication, Inc., a consulting firm that teaches individuals and organizations how to rejuvenate one's spirit and amplify one's ability to succeed, both personally and professionally, by ensuring measurable results.

Mervin A. Jenkins is an educator who leads a dual life as the Hip hop artist known as Spectac. As an educator, Mervin taught middle school art, worked as a high school assistant principal, central office administrator, middle school principal, and most recently accepted a position as the Assistant Director for AVID (Advancement Via Individual Determination) Eastern Division—a non-profit organization dedicated to getting students on track for a four-year college education. Mervin was honored as the Chatham County School District's 2007-2008 "Principal of the Year." Over the years, many organizations have had the pleasure of working with Mervin to help motivate and inspire both youth and adults. Mervin earned his B.A. degree from Benedict College in Columbia, SC, and his M.Ed. in secondary education administration from Charleston Southern University in Charleston, SC. Under his Hip hop alias "Spectac," Mervin engages youth by presenting life lessons using the technique of storytelling combined with a touch of Hip hop music. As a result, Life Through Music was founded and in May 2007 Mervin performed at the Kennedy Center in Washington, DC, where he collaborated with several artists on the 'Shakespeare is Hip hop' project.

Stephon Hall is a 2004 graduate of Western Carolina University where he majored in Business Administration and Law. Stephon is currently working as a personal banker for Well Fargo in Charlotte, North Carolina and plans to attend law school in the near future.

Stephen Hall graduated Cum laude from Western Carolina in 2004 while focused on Training and Developing with a major in Communications and Elementary School Education. Stephen is currently working as a Program Assistant with the Charlotte Mecklenburg School System in Charlotte, North Carolina.

Vandorn Hinnant studied visual art at NC A&T State University, and at UNC-Greensboro, and then lived in NYC as an intaglio printer for the Czechoslovakian born German artist Josef Werner. His original works of art are in numerous public and private collections across the USA, and some works are in private collections in Africa and Europe. He has guest curated art exhibitions, served as a curator at NC A&T State University's African Heritage Center, taught studio art courses at Winston-Salem State University in the mid 1990's, and has guest lectured at colleges and universities in the Southeastern USA. Along with being a studio artist, Vandorn serves as an educational consultant working with youth and adult learners, and is currently teaching a at Duke University's Osher Life Long Learning Institute through the Department of Continuing Education.

Ernest H. Johnson, a Psychologist with a focus on health and human performance, is the president of The Champions for Peace Leadership and Mastermind Institute, which sponsors literacy development workshop, wellness and health seminars, entrepreneurship programs for youth, and operates as a think-tank and incubator for over twenty-five African American male entrepreneurs. Dr. Johnson is a former professor and director of Behavioral Medicine Research at Morehouse School of Medicine and Assistant Professor at the University of Michigan Medical Center. Dr. Johnson is an expert on the role that emotional intelligence plays in the achievement needs of African Americans and a highly sought out professional/motivational speaker and consultant. Dr. Johnson is currently a faculty member of The North Carolina Center for the Advancement of Teaching, where he designs multidisciplinary professional development programs for educators, many of them focused on the challenges educators have reaching and motivating African American males. He earned his Ph.D. is psychology at the University of South Florida. His current work at Champions for Peace focuses on rediscovering the best ways to motivate African American children that were loss when schools across America integrated and over 30,000 African American teachers were persuaded to leave the teaching profession.

Christopher Land was raised in Charlotte, NC, and then pursued his Computer Information Systems degree at DeVry University—Atlanta, GA. After pursuing his degree in Computer Information Systems, he worked with Hewlett Packard as a Computer Engineer and Engineering

Trainer. With one of the most uniquely blended backgrounds in technology and education, Christopher has become one of the nations most sought trainers. Through his involvement in the community, his wit, and uncanny sense of humor, coupled with the ability to deliver a positive message to youth and adults, he was recognized as "A Gem in the Crown of the Queen City." Presiding as the Chief Operations Officer of Dream Builders Communication Inc., Christopher designs and develops engaging educational sessions for faculty/staff and students. His participation in multiple national diversity and inclusion councils, school improvement planning, and corporate sales/strategy sessions has heightened his awareness, sensitivity, and understanding of the needs of African American males and their teachers.

Ray Mapp earned a B.S. degree in computer science and history from Johnson C. Smith University and he is currently the president of Black Miracles, a company that publishes both art and literature highlighting African American contributions. He has devoted more than 25 years to studying the scientific, cultural, and other contributions of African American men and women. Based on researching more than 200 contributions, Mapp co-authored the Black Miracles Book-On-A-Poster which is the only known quick reference guide to inventions by African Americans. Ray believes that a public school curriculum that includes African American intellectual contributions will improve America and provide African American males with many undiscovered role models. Ray has presented workshop about the Black Miracles Book-On-A-Poster project at various national conferences for educators and engineers. He is pursuing a Masters in Educational Design with a focus on developing classroom materials for K-8 grade classrooms that encourages African American to consider careers in science, technology, engineering, and mathematics (STEM).

Chris "Dasan Ahanu" Massenburg is a public speaker, organizer, workshop facilitator, poet, spoken-word performer, songwriter, writer, emcee, and loyal Hip hop head born and raised in Raleigh, North Carolina. In addition to performing across the country, Dasan has hosted many poetry, jazz, Hip hop, and cultural arts events across the state. He is one of the founders of Black Poetry Theatre (BPT) and has been a writer, director, producer, and cast member of six productions. Also an active participant in poetry slam, Dasan has competed regionally and nationally for six years as a founding member of Durham, NC's own Bull City Slam Team. As a recording artist, Dasan has collaborated with many of North Carolina's most notable emcees, vocalists, and musicians. In 2007 he collaborated with producer Scott Warren, known also as Picasso, to form The Jim Crow Jackson Experiment. Their self titled debut album was released domestically by local indie record label Amp Truth Records and internationally by Australian indie Grindin Records. He is currently a creative consultant and resident artist at the Hayti Heritage Center in Durham, NC and an artist-in-residence in the English Department at Saint Augustine's College in Raleigh, NC.

Danya Perry works for Communities In Schools (CIS) of North Carolina as the Director of Program and Youth Development. Prior to CIS, Danya worked for the Center for the Prevention of School Violence where he was a research associate prior to becoming the Youth Out of the Education Mainstream (YOEM) Coordinator, which focused on alternative learning programs and building resiliency in at-risk youth. In 2000, Danya began work in the capacity of Youth Development Specialist with the Department of Juvenile Justice and Delinquency Prevention. As a Youth Development Specialist, Danya worked to close the minority achievement gap, build conducive learning environments, decreasing the disproportionate suspension and expulsion rate of minority youth, preventing gang activity and eliminating youth suicide. Danya completed his first book on youth violence, "Preventing Violence & Crime in America's Schools: From Put Downs to Lock Downs" and is currently working on a project that focuses on integrating Hip hop into the classroom and teacher pedagogy.

Winston Sharpe is the cofounder of the Champions for Peace Leadership and Mastermind Institute. Winston is an experienced financial advisory who has held various leadership positions at Wells Fargo for a decade. While working in financial services, Winston created community-based programs for mentoring at-risk youth and established an entrepreneurship program for African American males that allows members to focus on mathematics, marine sciences, critical thinking skills, and leadership development while experiencing the underwater world of scuba diving. Winston is a certified National Geographic Diver, entrepreneur, and he often speaks to youth, parenting, and community groups about financial management as well as the importance of being a good steward of aquatic resources. Despite hardships and disappointments while growing up, he often acknowledges the importance of the people in his life that contributed to the development of his resilience to receive a BA degree from Queen University in Charlotte, North Carolina and an MA from Cardinal Stritch University in Milwaukee, Wisconsin.

Tavares Stephens works as an educator, writer, and performance poet. He is author of Soulfood Cafe and Reading Revolution. He has worked as classroom teacher, instructional coach, and educational consultant, focusing on the areas of mentoring and best practices in instruction. Many of the African American males he has mentored, some of whom come from impoverished backgrounds, have successfully graduated from high schools and are currently enrolled in some of the top universities in the nation. The focus of his poetry are his students and the audience is typically left in awe after listening to his poetry. Tavares currently lives in Stockbridge, Georgia, with his wife Nicole. He is pursuing a Masters in Fine Arts while continuing his work utilizing interdisciplinary and multiple intelligence techniques to facilitate self-inquiry, character development, and academic performance.

Madafo Lloyd Wilson is a professional storyteller, musician, author, and community activist. For fifteen years, Madafo coordinated an award winning mentoring program for African American boys within the New Hanover County School System of Wilmington, NC. A storyteller and musician, he has traveled extensively, collaborating with artists throughout the world. Madafo is co-producer, writer and host of a syndicated storytelling program, Public Radio International a Season's Griot, and has self-published his first storybook entitled, "The Greedy Hyena." Madafo currently resides in Miami Beach, Florida.

Mychal Wynn was born in rural Pike County, Alabama, attended the Chicago Public Schools, is an honors cum laude graduate of Northeastern University, and currently resides in Marietta, Georgia. An internationally recognized expert in school improvement planning, closing the achievement gap, and college planning, he currently serves as the CEO of the Foundation for Ensuring Access and Equity, a nonprofit educational foundation committed to widening the college pathway for students from underserved and underrepresented groups. His 26 published works include: Empowering African-American Males to Succeed: A Guide to Increasing Black Male Achievement, Increasing Student Achievement: A Guide to School Improvement Planning, Ten Steps to Helping Your Child Succeed in School, Don't Quit: Inspirational Poetry, Follow Your Dreams: Lessons That I Learned in School, and the college planning series for middle school and high school students.

-NOTES-

Preface

[1] Woodson, C.G. (1992). *The Mis-edication of the Negro*. Hampton, VA:UB. & U.S. Communication System. (Original published 1933).

[2] Toldson, I.A., Fry Brown, R.L., and Sutton, R. M. (2009). "Commentary: 75 Years after the Mis-edication of the Negro: New Imperatives for the Education of Black Males." *The Journal of Negro Education*, 78, 3, 195-203.

[3] Special Issue of The Journal of Negro Education: Academic Success for School-age Black Males (2009). Volume 78(3). Howard University, Washington, DC.

[4] Burrell, T. (2010). *Brainwashed: Challenging the Myth of Black Inferiority*. Carson, CA: Smiley Books.

[5] Black doll test by Kenneth Clark and Mamie Phipps Clark. *With an Even Hand: Brown Vs Board of Education at Fifty*. http://www.loc.gov/exhibits/brown/ brown-brown.html; http://abagond.wordpress.com/2009/05/29/the-clark-doll-experiment/; http://en.wikipedia.org/wiki/Kenneth_and_Mamie_Clark.

[6] New doll test by Kiri Davis: http://www.finalcall.com/artman/publish/ National_News_2/New_doll_test_produces_ugly_results_2919.shtml; Black or White something to think about http://www.youtube.com/ watch?v=MqSFqnUFOns; *A Girl Like Me*, http://www.youtube.com/w atch?v=17fEy0q6yqc&feature=related.

[7] The case of *Brown vs. Board of Education*: http://www.streetlaw.org/en/ Case.6.aspx;

http://en.wikipedia.org/wiki/Brown_v._Board_of_Education; http://www.pbs.org/jefferson/enlight/brown.htm.

Editor's Introduction: Answering the Call for Help

1. Jackson, J.H. (2010). *The Schott 50 State Report on Black Males and Education*. Cambridge, MA: The Schott Foundation for Public Education. Available at: http://blackboysreport.org/bbreport.pdf.

2. Diploma Count 2008 (June 2008). "School to College: Can State P-16 Councils Ease the Transition?" *Education Week* Vol. 27, Issue 40. Available at: http://www.edweek.org/media/ew/dc/2008/DC08_Press_FULL_FINAL.pdf.

3. Diploma Count 2010 (June 2010). "Graduation by the Numbers". *Education Week*, Vol. 27, Issue 34. Available at: http://www.edweek.org/media/ew/dc/2010/DC10_PressKit_FINAL.pdf.

4. Kunjufu, J. (2010). *Reducing the Black Male Dropout Rates*. Chicago, ILL: African American Images.

5. Alexander, M. (2010). *The New Jim Crow: Mass Incarceration in the Age of Colorblindness*. New York, NY: New Press.

6. "Black Students College Graduation Rates Inch Higher But a Large Racial Gap Persist." The *Journal of Blacks in Higher Education* (2007). Available at: https://www.jbhe.com/preview/winter2007.

7. Wong, H. et at (2005). The North Carolina Center for the Advancement of Teaching Impact Study. Prepared by the NCCAT Program Evaluation and Research Committee. 276 NCCAT Drive, Cullowhee, NC.

Chapter 1

1. Edelman, M. W. (2001). "What Can We Do?" Quoted from: *How to Make Black America Better: Leading African American Speak Out* (p. 122). New York, NY: Anchor Books.

2. Wynn, M. (1992): *Empowering African-American Males to Succeed: A Ten-Step Approach for Parents and Teachers*. Marietta GA: Rising Sun Publishing.

3. National Center for Education Statistics (1999). "The Condition of Education." Washington, DC: *NCES* June 1999.

4. National Center for Education Statistics. "Educational Achievement and Black-White Inequality." Washington, DC: *NCES* July 2001.

5. Bernstein, J. (1995). *Where's the Payoff? The Gap Between Black Academic Progress and Economic Gains.* Washington, DC: Economic Policy Institute.

6. Heckman, J.J. and LaFontaine, P.A. (2007). *The American High School Graduation Rate: Trends and Levels.* Discussion Paper No. 3216, *Institute for the Study of Labor.*

7. Jackson, J.H. (2010). *The Schott 50 State Report on Black Males and Education.* Cambridge, MA: The Schott Foundation for Public Education. Available at: http://blackboysreport.org/bbreport.pdf.

8. Diploma Count (June 2008). "School to College: Can State P-16 Councils Ease the Transition?" *Education Week* Vol. 27, Issue 40. Available at: http://www.edweek.org/media/ew/dc/2008/DC08_Press_FULL_FINAL.pdf.

9. Toldson, I.A., Fry Brown, R.L., and Sutton, R. M. (2009). "Commentary: 75 Years after the Mis-edication of the Negro: New Imperatives for the Education of Black Males." *The Journal of Negro Education*, 78, 3, 195-203.

10. Special Issue of The Journal of Negro Education: Academic Success for School-age Black Males (2009). Volume 78(3). Howard University, Washington, DC.

11. The Employment Situation (June 2010). Available at: http://www.bls.gov/news.release/pdf.

12. Prison Inmates at Midyear—2009. Available at: http://bjs.ojp.usdoj.gov/content/pub/pdf/plm09st.pdf.

13. *The Nation's Report Card: Reading 2009.* Grade 8 Reading. Available at: http://nationsreportcard.gov/reading_2009/; http://nces.ed.gov/nationsreportcard/.

14. Ford, D.Y. and Harris, J.J. (1991). "Meeting the Socio-psychological Needs of Gifted Black Students." *Journal of Counseling and Development* 69, 577-580.

15. Hrabowski, F.A., Maton, K.I., and Greif, G.L. (1998). *Beating the Odds: Raising Academically Successful African American Males.* New York, New York: Oxford University Press.

16. Ellison, R (1952) *Invisible Man.* New York, NY: Signet Pub.

17. Guerra, P.L. and Nelson, S.W. (2010). "What Culturally Responsive Educators Can Do To Prepare High School Students and Parents For College." *JSP* October Vol. 35, Pages 61-62. Available at: www.learningforward.org

18. Wynn, M. (2000). *Follow Your Dreams: Lessons That I Learned in School.* Marietta GA: Rising Sun Publishing.

19. Wynn, M. (2005): *Empowering African-American Males: A Guide to Increasing Black Male Achievement.* Marietta, GA: Rising Sun Publishing.

20. Wynn, M. (2007). *Teaching, Parenting, and Mentoring Successful Black Males: A Quick Guide.* Marietta, GA: Rising Sun Publishing.

21. Johnson, E.H. (1998): *Brothers on The Mend: Understanding and Healing Anger for African American Men and Women.* New York, New York: Pocket Books.

22. Les Brown. Information available at: http://www.lesbrown.com/lesbrown. com/english/meet_lesbrown.html.

23. Ben Carson. Information available at: http://carsonscholars.org/; http:// en.wikipedia.org/wiki/Ben_Carson.

24. Goleman, D. (2000). *Working With Emotional Intelligence.* New York, NY: Bantam Books.

25. Goleman, D. (2006a). *Emotional Intelligence: 10th Anniversary Edition; Why It Can Matter More Than IQ—10th Anniversary Edition.* New York, NY: Bantam Books.

26. Goleman, D. (2006b) Social Intelligence: The New Science of Human Relationships. New York, NY: Random House.

27. Bender, D.R. (1967). "A Refinement of the Concept of Household: Families, Co—residence, and Domestic Function." *American Anthropologist* 69, 493-504.

28. Leichter, H.J. (1974). *The Family as Educator.* New York: Teachers College Press.

29. Leichter, H.J. (1978). "Families and Communities as Educators. Some Concepts of Relationships." *Teachers College Record* 79, 567-658.

30. Gadsden, V. (1999). "Black Families in Intergenerational and Cultural Perspective." In M. Lamb (Ed.), *Parenting and Child Development in Nontraditional Families.* Mahwah, NJ: Lawrence Erlbaum.

31. Gadsden, V. (2000). "Intergenerational Literacy Within Families". In M.L. Kamil, P.B. Mosenthal, P.D. Pearson, and R. Barr (Eds.), *Handbook of Reading Research*, vol. III (pp. 871-888). Mahwah, NJ: Lawrence Erlbaum.

32. Gadsden, V. (1998). "Family Culture and Literacy Learning." In J. Osborn and F. Lehr (Eds.), *Literacy For All: Issues in Teaching and Learning* (pp. 32-50). New York: The Guilford Press.

33. McAdoo, H.P. (2007). *Black Families*. Thousand Oaks, CA: Sage Publication.

34. Powell, C. and Powell, A. (September 28, 2010). *Education Nation Summit*. Videos about the causes, consequences, and prevention of the dropout problem in America. Available at: http://www.americaspromise. org/Our-Work/Dropout-Prevention.aspx'; http://www.educationnation. com/index.cfm?objectid=52551750-6149-11E0-BB14000C296BA163 &categoryid=62085970-C589-11DF-8243000C296BA163.

Chapter 2

1. Wolter, R. (1984). *The Burden of Brown: Thirty Years of School Desegregation*. Knoxville, TN: University of Tennessee Press.

2. Hancock, S. (2006). "White Women's Work: On the Front Lines in Urban Education." In Landsman, J. and Lewis, C.W. (Ed), *White Teachers and Diverse Classrooms: A Guide to Building Inclusive Schools*, Promoting High Expectations, and Eliminating Racism, Stylus Publishing, Sterling, VA.

3. Milner, H.R. and Howard, T.T. (2004). "Black Teachers, Black Students, Black Communities, and Brown: Perspectives and Insights From Experts." *The Journal of Negro Education*, 73(3), 285-297.

4. Tillman, L.C. (2004). "Unintended Consequences? The Impact of the Brown v. Board of Education Decision on the Employment Status of Black Educators." *Education and Urban Society*, 36(3), 280-303.

5. Hudson, M.J. & Holmes, B.J. (1994). "Missing Teachers, Impaired Communities: The Unanticipated Consequences of Brown v. Board of Education on the African American Teaching Force at the Pre-collegiate Level." *Journal of Negro Education*, 63(10), 388-393.

6. Epps, E. (1999). *Race and School Desegregation: Contemporary Legal and Educational Issues*. Available: www.urbanjournal.org/articles/article0003.pdf.

7. Anderson, J., and Byrne (2004). *The Unfinished Agenda of Brown v. Board of Education*. New Jersey: John Wiley & Sons.

8. Haney, J. (1978). "The Effects of the Brown Decision on Black Educators." *The Journal of Negro Education*, 47, 88-95.

9. Ladson-Billings, G. (2004). "Landing on the Wrong Note: The Price We Paid for Brown." *Educational Researcher*, 33(7), 3-13.

10. Hawkins, B.D. (1994). "Casualties: Losses Among Black Educators Were High After Brown." *Black Issues in Higher Education*, 10(23), 26-31.

11. Ethridge, S.B. (1979). "Impact of the 1954 Brown v. Topeka Board of Education Decision on Black Educators." *Negro Educational Review*, 30(4), 217-232.

12. Holmes, B.J. (1990). *New Strategies Are Needed to Produce Minority Teachers*. Elmhurst, IL: North Central Regional Education Laboratory.

13. Landsman, J., and Lewis C.W. (2006). *White Teachers/Diverse Classrooms*. Stylus Publishing, Sterling, VA.

14. Howard, G. (1999). *We Can't Teach What We Don't Know: White Teachers, Multicultural Schools*. New York: Teachers College Press.

15. US Census Bureau Reports. *Educational Attainment in the United States*, 2003, 2007, 2010. Available at: http://www.census.gov/prod/2004pubs/p20-550.pdf; http://www.census.gov/prod/2004pubs/p20-550.pdf; http://www.census.gov/hhes/socdemo/education/.

16. Mobley, P. and Holcolmb, S. (2008). NEA, *A Report of the Status of Blacks in Education*. Available at: http://hin.nea.org/assets/docs/mf_blackstatus08.pdf.

17. National Center for Education Information. (2007. *Teacher Quality and Alternative Certification Programs*. Available at: www.ncei.com/testimony051399.htm

18. National Center for Education Information.(2007). *Profile of Alternate Route Teachers*. Available at: www.ncei.com/part.html.

19. Burnim, M.V. and Maultsby, P.K., eds. (2006). *African American Music: An Introduction*. Routledge, New York, NY.

20. Goldschmidt, H. and McAlister, E. (2004). *Race, Nation, and Religion in the Americas*. New York: Oxford University Press.

21. Lincoln, C. E. and L. H., Mamiya. (1990). *The Black Church in the African American Experience*. Durham: Duke University Press.

22. Sernett, M. C., eds. (1999) *African American Religious History: A Documentary Witness* (Second Edition). Durham and London: Duke University Press.

23. West, C. and Glaude, E. (2003). *African American Religious Thought: An Anthology*. Louisville, KY.: Westminster John Knox Press.

24. Zuckerman, Phil, eds. (2000*). Du Bois on Religion*. Walnut Creek, CA: AltaMira Press, 2000.

25. Baldwin, J. (1962). *The Fire Next Time*. New York, NY: Vintage Books Inc.

26. Thompson, G.L. (2004). Through Ebony Eyes. San Francisco, CA: John Wiley and Sons, Inc.

27. Perry, T., Steele, C., and Hilliard, A. (2003). *Young, Gifted and Black: Promoting High Achievement Among African American Students.* Boston, MA: Beacon Press.

28. Hrabowski, F.A., Maton, K.I., and Greif, G.L. (1998). *Beating the Odds: Raising Academically Successful African American Males.* New York, NY: Oxford University Press.

29. National Urban League (April 2007). *The State of Black America: Portrait of the Black Male* (Statistics, pg 52). Silver Spring, MD: Beckham Publications Group.

Chapter 3

1. Brown, O.L, and Millner, C. (2005). *The Promise: How One Woman Made Good On Her Extraordinary Pact to Send A Classroom of first-Graders To College.* Doubleday, New York, NY

2. *No Child Left Behind Act.* The Elementary and Secondary Education Act as reauthorized by the No Child Left Behind Act of 2001. www2.ed.gov/nclb/landing.jhtml.

3. Perry, T., Steele, C., and Hilliard, A. (2003). *Young, Gifted and Black: Promoting High Achievement Among African American Students.* Beacon Press, Boston, MA.

4. Zeichner K.M., and Liston, D. (1996). *Reflective Teaching: An Introduction.* Mahwah, NJ: Lawrence Erlbaum.

5. Rodgers, C. (2002). "Defining Reflection: Another Look at John Dewey and Reflective Thinking." *Teachers College Record.* 4(4), pp. 842-866.

6. Palmer, P.J. (1998). *The Courage to Teach: Exploring the Inner Landscape of a Teacher's Life.* San Francisco: Jossey-Bass.

7. Schön, D.A. (1990). *Educating the Reflective Practitioner: Toward a New design for Teaching and Learning in the Professions.* San Francisco: Jossey-Bass.

8. Farrell, T. (1998). "Reflective Teaching: The Principles and Practices." *Forum* 36(4), 10-17.

9. Goleman, D. (1995). *Emotional Intelligence.* New York, NY: Bantam Books.

10. Goleman, D. (2006).*Social Intelligence.* New York, NY: Bantam Books.

11. Gardner, H. (2006a). *The Development and Education of the Mind: The Collected Works of Howard Gardner.* London: Routledge.

12. Gardner, H. (2006b). "Howard Gardner Under Fire." In Jeffrey Schaler (Ed.). Illinois: Open Court Publishing.

13. Gardner, H. (2006c). *Multiple Intelligences:* New Horizons. New York: Basic Books.

14. Gardner, H. (2007). *Five Minds for the Future*. Boston: Harvard Business School Press.

15. Hilliard, A. (2001)." Race, Identity, Hegemony, and Education: What Do We Need To Know Now?" In *Race and Education: The Role of History and Society in Educating African American Students*, ed. William Watkins, James Lewis, and Victoria Chou, pp.7-33. Boston: Allyn and Bacon.

16. Hilliard, A., and Sizemore, eds. (1984). "Saving the African American Child: A Report of the National Alliance of Black School Educators." *Task Force on Black Academic and Cultural Excellence*. Washington, D.C.: National Alliance of Black School Educators.

17. Hilliard, A.(1990).*Ancient Africa's Contribution to Science and Technology*. NSBE: National Society of Black Engineers Magazine 1, No. 2: 72-75.

18. Hilliard, A. (1991b) *The Meaning of KMT (Ancient Egyptian) History for Contemporary African American Experience*. Part II Color 1, No. 2: 10-1319.

19. Hilliard, A. *A Selected Bibliography (Classified) and Outline on African American History from Ancient Times to the Present: A Resource Packet*. Rev. ed. Atlanta.

20. Hilliard, A. (1992). "The Meaning of KMT (Ancient Egyptian) History for Contemporary African American Experience." *Phylon*, 49, Nos. 1-2: 10-22.

21. Hilliard, A.(1993a). *Bringing Maat, Destroying Isfet: The African and African Diasporan Presence in the Study of Ancient Kmt*. Atlanta.

22. Hilliard, A.(1993b). Fifty Plus *Essential References on the History of African People*. Baltimore: Black Classic Press.

Chapter 4

1. Kunjufu, J. (2004). *Countering the Conspiracy to Destroy Black Boys, Vols*. Chicago, Ill: African American Images

2. Wynn, M. (2005): *Empowering African-American Males: A Guide to Increasing Black Male Achievement*. Marietta, GA: Rising Sun Publishing.

3. Wynn, M. (2000). *Follow Your Dreams: Lessons That I Learned in School*. Marietta GA: Rising Sun Publishing.

4. Wynn, M. (2007). Teaching, *Parenting, and Mentoring Successful Black Males: A Quick Guide*. Marietta, GA: Rising Sun Publishing.

5. Useni, E.P. (1987). *Harvesting New Generations: The Positive Development of Black Youth.* Chicago, IL: Third World Press.

6. Woodson, C.G. (2011). *The Mis-education of the Negro*, written in 1933 and reprinted by Tribeca Books.

7. Blackmon, D.A. (2008). Slavery By Another Name: The Re-Enslavement of Black Americans from the Civil War to World War II. New York, NY: Double Day.

8. Akbar, N. (1998*). Know Thyself.* Tallahassee, FL: Mind Productions & Associates.

9. Hilliard, A. G., Damali, N., and Obadele, W.L. (1987). The teachings of Ptahhotep: the in the world, Blackwood Press, Atlanta, Georgia.

10. Hilliard, A. G. (1997). SBA: The *Reawakening of the African Mind.* Gainesville, FL: Makare publishing.

11. Hilliard, A. G. (2002). *African Power.* Gainesville, FL: Makare Publishing.

12. Kafele, Baruti (2004). *A Handbook for Teachers of African American Children.* Jersey City, New Jersey.

13. Karenga, M. (1984). *Selections From the Husia.* Los Angeles, CA: University of Sankore Press.

14. Imhotep. Information available at: http://en.wikipedia.org/wiki/Imhotep; http://www.touregypt.net/featurestories/imhotep.htm; Mostafa Shehata, MD (2004), "The Father of Medicine: A Historical Reconsideration", *J Med Ethics* 12, p. 171-176 [176].

15. Ptahhotep. Information available at: http://www.fordham.edu/halsall/ancient/ptahhotep.html; http://en.wikipedia.org/wiki/The_Maxims_of_Ptahhotep; Jacq., C (1999). *The Living Wisdom of Ancient Egypt.* New York, NY:Simon and Schuster.

16. Dr. Mar Dean—computer scientist. Information available about his inventions at: http://www.black-inventor.com/Dr-Mark-Dean.asp; http://www.math.buffalo.edu/mad/computer-science/dean_mark.html 'http://blackhistorypages.net/pages/mdean.php; http://en.wikipedia.org/wiki/Mark_Dean_(computer_scientist).

17. Dr. Thomas Mensah, a native of Ghana. Information available at: http://www.ghanaweb.com/GhanaHomePage/people/person.php?ID=165; http://biography.jrank.org/pages/2422/Mensah-Thomas.html.

18. Ani, M. (1980). *Let the Circle Be Unbroken: The implications of African Spirituality in the Diaspora.* New York, NY: Nkonimfo Publications.

19. Akua, C. (2001). *A Treasure Within: Stories of Remembrance & Rediscovery.* Conyers, GA: Imani Enterprisers.

20. Akua, C. and Stephens, T. (2006). *Reading Revolution: Reconnecting the Roots*. Conyers, GA: Imani Enterprisers.

Chapter 5

1. Hale, T. A. (1998). *Griots and Griottes: Masters of Words and Music*. Bloomington, Indiana: Indiana University Press.
2. Hoffman, B. G. (2001). *Griots at War: Conflict, Conciliation and Caste in Mande*. Bloomington, Indiana: Indiana University Press.
3. Goss, L. and Barnes, M.E. (1989). *Talk That Talk: An Anthology of African-American Storytelling*. New York, New York: Simon and Schuster/ Touchstone.
4. Mapp, R. *Black Miracles—Book-on-a-Poster* presents the scientific contributions and discoveries of African Americans. Available at: ʰttp:// www.blackmiracles.com/index.shtml.
5. Pennebaker, J.W. (1997). *The Healing Power of Expressing Emotion*. New York, NY: The Guilford Press.
6. Pennebaker, J.W. (2004). *Writing to Heal: A Guided Journal for Recovering from Trauma and Emotional Upheaval*. Oakland, CA: New Harbinger Publications.
7. Elias, M.J. (2008). "How to Foster Children's Resilience While They Wait for Schools to Improve." *Edweek.org*. December 8, 2008.
8. Elias, M.J Ogburn-Thompson, G., Lewis, C., and Neft, D. (2008). *Urban Dreams: Stories of Hope, Resilience, and Character*. New York, NY: Hamilton.
9. Princeville hit hard by Hurricane Floyd, opens African American museum. Available at: http:www.wral.com/news/local/story/6037817/.
10. Barnes, J. (2004). *Faces from the Flood: Hurricane Floyd Remembered*. Chapel Hill: Univ. Of North Carolina Press.
11. Ricket, Ellenwood, ed. (2000). *Eye of the Storm: Essays in the Aftermath*. Wilmington, NC: Coastal Carolina Press.
12. North Carolina Language of Life Project (NCLLP). Information Available at: http://ncsu.edu/linguistics/ncllp/
13. Fluker, W.E. (2009). Ethical Leadership: The Quest for Character, Civility, and Community. Minneapolis, MN: Augsburg Fortress Press.
14. Laws of Life Essay Contest. Available at: www.lawsoflife.org/contest.
15. Templeton, J. (2000). *Discovering the Laws of Life*. West Conshohocken, PA: Templeton Press.

16. Ashe, A. and Rampersad, A. (1994). *Days of Grace*. New York, NY: Ballantine Books.

17. West, K. (2009). *Glow in the Dark*. New York, NY: Rizzoli Publishers.

Chapter 6

1. Thompson, G.L. (2004). *Through Ebony Eyes*. San Francisco, CA: John Wiley and Sons, Inc.

2. Landsman, J., and Lewis C.W. (2006). *White Teachers/Diverse Classrooms*. Sterling, VA: Stylus Publishing.

3. Perry, T., Steele, C., and Hilliard, A. (2003). *Young, Gifted and Black: Promoting High Achievement Among African American Students*. Boston, MA: Beacon Press.

4. Burrell, T. (2010). *Brainwashed: Challenging the Myth of Black Inferiority*. Carson, CA: Smiley Books.

5. Baptiste, D. A. (1986). "The image of the Black Family Portrayed by Television: A Critical Comment." *Marriage and Family Review*, 10(1), 41-65.

6. Bibliography of Minorities and Racism and the Press. Available at: http://www.racismos.org/recursos/bibliografias/Medios%20y%20racismo%202007.pdf.

7. Kunjufu, J. (2004). *Countering the Conspiracy to Destroy Black Boys, Vols*. Chicago, Ill: African American Images

8. Wynn, M. (2005): *Empowering African-American Males: A Guide to Increasing Black Male Achievement*. Marietta, GA: Rising Sun Publishing.

9. Kunjufu, J. (2006). *An African Centered Response to Ruby Payne's Poverty Theory."* Chicago,Ill: *African American Images*.

10. Robbins, A. (1997). *Unlimited Power*. New York, NY: Free Press/Simon and Schuster.

11. Robbins, A. (2003). *Awakening The Giant Within: How to Take Immediate Control Of Your Mental, Emotional, Physical and Financial Destiny*. New York, NY: Free Press/Simon and Schuster.

12. Covey, S.R. (2004). *The Seven Habits of Highly Effective People*. New York, NY: Free Press.

13. Tracy, B. (1995). *Maximum Achievement: Strategies and Skills That Will Unlock Your Hidden Powers to Succeed*. New York, NY: Fireside edition/Simon and Schuster.

14. Andreas, S. and Faulkner, C. (1994). NLP: *The New Technology of Achievement*. New York, NY: William Morrow and Company.

15. U.S. Department of Education, National Center for Education Statistics. Status and *Trends in the Education of Racial and Ethnic Minorities*. Available at: http://nces.ed.gov/pubs2010/2010015/chapter4.asp; http://nces.ed.gov/pubs2010/2010015/tables/table_17b.asp; http://www.blackamericaweb.com/?q=articles/news/moving_america_news/20769.

16. U.S. Department of Education, National Center for Education Statistics. *The Condition of Education in 2011*. Available at: http://nces.ed.gov/programs/coe/.

Chapter 7

1. Haley, A. (1976). *Roots: The Saga of an American Family*. New York, NY: Double Day and Company, Inc.

2. Blackmon, D.A. (2008). *Slavery by Another Name*. New York, NY: Anchor Books.

3. Allen, R. (2008). "Reading First: Sustaining Success in Difficult Times." *Association for Supervision and Curriculum: Education Update*, Volume 50, Number 12, December 2008. Available at: http://www2.ed.gov/programs/readingfirst/index.html.

4. 2000 National Reading Panel: Available at: *http:nationalreadingpanel.org*

5. Tatum, A. W. (2005). *Teaching Reading to Black Adolescent Males: Closing the Achievement Gap*. Portland, ME: Stenhouse Publishers.

6. Tatum, A.W. (2007a). "Literacy Development of African American Adolescent Males." In A. Berger, L. Rush, and J. Eakle (Eds.). *Secondary School Reading and Writing: What Research Reveals*. Urbana, IL: NCTE.

7. Tatum, A.W. (2007b). "Building the Textual Lineages of African American adolescent males." In K. Beers, R. Probst, and L. Reif (Eds.). *Adolescent Literacy: Turning Promise into Practice*. Portsmouth, NH: Heinemann.

8. Tatum, A.W. (2008). "African American Males at Risk: A Researcher Study of Endangered Males and Literature That Works." In S. Lehr (Ed.). *Shattering the Looking Glass: Issues, Controversy, and Trends in Children's Literature*. Norwood, MA: Christopher Gordon.

9. Collins, M. (1990). *Marva Collins Way*. New York: Putnam, Inc.

10. Haley, A. (1966). *The Autobiography of Malcolm X*. New York, NY: Penguin Books.

11. Upchurch, C. (1996). *Convicted in the Womb: One Man's Journey From Prisoner to Peacemaker*. New York: Bantam Books.

12. Populations of African American Males. Available at: www.blackdemographics.com

13. Boyd, C. (1991). *Plain Teaching*, Chicago, Ill:Westport Publishers.
14. Fashola, O.S. (2005). *Educating African American Males*. Thousand Oaks, CA: Corwin Press, an affiliate of SAGE Publications.
15. My Baby Can Read. Available at: http://www.yourbabycan.com/.
16. *The Partnership for Reading* is a collaborative effort by three federal agencies—the National Institute for Literacy (NIFL), the National Institute of Child Health and Human Development (NICHD), and the U.D. Department of Education—to bring the findings of evidence-based reading research to the educational community, families and others with an interest in helping people learn to read. First established by congress in 2000, The Partnership was authorized by the No Child Left Behind Act of 2000 (P.L. 107-110). Information about the research is available at: http//:lincs.ed.gov/publications/publications.html; http://lincs.ed.gov/publications/pdf/ERF_FINAL_REPORT_July_2010pdf; http:// lincs.ed.gov/publications/pdf/ECL_Recomendations09.pdf.
17. Manley, D. and Friend, T. (1992). *Educating Dexter*. Nashville, TN: Thomas Nelson, Inc.
18. Carson, B. (2011).*Gifted Hands 20th Anniversary Edition*. Grand Rapids, MI: Zondervan Publishing.
19. Carson, B. (2006). *Think Big*. Grand Rapids, MI: Zondervan Publishing.
20. Jenkins,G., Davis, S. and Hunt, R. (2002). The *Pact: Three Young Men Make a Promise and Fulfill a Dream*. New York: Riverhead Books.
21. Wynn. M. (2005). *Follow Your Dreams*. Marietta, GA: Rising Sun Publishing.
22. Alexander, K.L., Entwisle, D.R., and Olson, L.S. (2007). "Lasting Consequences of the Summer Learning Gap." *American Sociological Review* 72(2), 167-180.
23. Kim, J. (2004). "Summer Reading and the Ethnic Achievement Gap." *Journal of Education of Students at Risk* 9(2). 169-189.
24. Kim, J.S. (2006). "Effects of Voluntary Summer Reading Intervention on Reading Achievement. Results From a Randomized Field Trial." *Educational Evaluation and Policy Analysis* 28(4), 335-355.
25. McQuillan, J., and Au, J. (2001). "The Effect of Print Access on Reading Frequency." *Reading Psychology* 22(3), 225-248.
26. Heyns, D.P., and Grether, J. (1983). "The School Year and Vacations: When Do Students Learn?" *Cornell Journal of Social Relations* 17(1), 56-71.
27. Arlington, R.L., McGill-Franzen, A.M., Camilli, G., Williams, L., Graff, J., Zeig, J., et al. (2007, April). "Ameliorating Summer Reading Setback

Among Economically Disadvantaged Elementary Students." Paper presented at the American Educational Research Association Annual Meeting, Chicago.

28. Kunjufu, J. (2006). *An African Centered Response to Ruby Payne's Poverty Theory.* Chicago, Ill: *African American Images.*

29. Tips for Summer Reading. Available at: www.pbs.org.

30. Payne, R. (2001). *A Framework for Understanding Poverty.* Highlands, TX: Aha! Process.

31. Wynn. M. (2005). *Follow Your Dreams.* Marietta, GA: Rising Sun Publishing.

32. Edelman, M.W. (1992). *The Measure of Our Success.* Boston, Mass: Beacon Press.

33. Brown Sugar and Spice Books: Located at: http://www.brownssbooks. com/.

Chapter 8

1. Poster Modern Art Movement: Information available at: http://www. spokenoak.com/genre/pomo.html.

2. History of Spoken-word: Available at: http://en.wikipedia.org/wiki/ Spoken_word.

3. Smith, M.K. and Kraynak, J. (2009). *Take the Mic: The Art of Performance Poetry, Slam, and the Spoken-word.* New York, NY: Sourcebooks MediaFusion

4. Eleveld, M. (2007). *The Spoken-word Revolution Redux.* New York, NY: Sourcebooks MediaFusion.

5. Aptowicz, C.(2007). *Words in Your Face: A Guided Tour Through Twenty Years of the New York City Poetry Slam.* New York City: Soft Skull Press.

6. SlamNation: *The Sport of Spoken-word* (1998). Mychele Dee (Actor), Craig muMs Grant (Actor), Paul Devlin (Director). New York, NY: New Video Group.Before Russell Simmons' highly acclaimed HBO series Def Poetry Jam, SLAMNATION captured the cutthroat world of spoken-word poetry with an "energy that pulses, snaps and crackles. Beginning in New York City at the Nuyorican Poets Café's Grand Slam tournament, the film follows slam champion Saul Williams and three other top poets—Beau Sia, Mums the Schemer, and Jessica Care Moore—as they journey to the annual National Poetry Slam, the Super Bowl of spoken-word poetry.

7. National Poetry Slam: Information available at: http://www.poetryslam.com.

8. Miazga, M. (1998). The *Spoken-word Movement of the 1990's*. Available at: https://www.msu.edu/~miazgama/spokenword.htm.

9. *Def Poetry*, also known as *Russell Simmons Presents Def Poetry* or *Def Poetry Jam*. Available at: http://www.answers.com/topic/def-poetry; http://www.answers.com/topic/def-poetry#ixzz1QbUOUqcz; http://en.wikipedia.org/wiki/Russell_Simmons_Presents_Def_Poetry.

10. *Def Comedy Jam*, also know as *Russell Simmons Presents Def Comedy Jam*. Available at: http://www.answers.com/topic/def-comedy-jam.

11. Desai, S. R. and Tyson, M. (2005). "Weaving Multiple Dialects in the Classroom Discourse: Poetry and Spoken-word as a Critical Teaching Tool." *Caddo Gap Press*.

12. Fox, M. (1995). *The Reinvention of Work: New Vision of Livelihood for Our Time*. New York, NY: HarperOne.

13. Fox, M. (2004). *Creativity*. New York, NY: Tarcher.

14. Fox, M. (2009). *The Hidden Spirituality of Men: Ten Metaphors to Awaken the Sacred Masculine*. New World Library.

15. Fox, M. (1983). *Meditations with Meister Eckhart*. Bear and Company

16. Fox, M. (2006). *The A.W.E. Project: Reinventing Education/Reinventing the Human*. Published by CopperHouse, Kelowna, BC, Canada.

17. Anglesey, Z (1999). *Listen Up: Spoken-word Poetry*; New York Ballentine.

18. Herndon & Weiss (2001) "We Speak in Streetlights: A Workshop in Spoken-word Poetry." *Teachers and Writers* 32(4) March April 2001, 1-10.

19. Scott-Heron, G. (1974). *The Revolution Will Not Be Televised*. Flying Dutchman Records.

20. Performer: Booth, A. and Robeson, P. Composer: Hughes, L, Spoken-word, Spiritual Traditional, Welsh Traditional, Beethoven, L. et al. (2004). Paul Roberson reciting of Freedom Train and his concert over the telephone from Wales. *Freedom Train and the Welsh Transatlantic Concert* (Live Audio CD), Folk Era Records.

21. Roberson, P. (2009). *The Best of Paul Roberson*. (Audio CD) 101 Distribution

22. Hughes, L. (1995) *Voice Of: Selected Poetry & Prose*. (Audio CD). Smithsonian Folkways Recordings.

23. Williams, S., Sohn, S., Bonz, M., Wilson, L. and Sia, B. (1998). *SLAM*, Lionsgate.

24. *Super Fun Show*: Information available at: http://superfunshow.com.

25. Books about the Super Fun show: Available at: http://www.amazon.com/Super-Fun-Show/dp/B001442R0C.

26. Amen, Ra UN Nefer (1990). *Metu Neter Vol. 1: The Great Oracle of Tehuti and the Egyptian System of Spiritual Cultivation.*

27. Amen, Ra Un Nefer (1996). *Tree of Life Meditation System (T.O.L.M.).* Khamit Media Trans Visions Inc.

28. Reyes, G. (2006). "Finding the Poetic High: Building a Spoken-word Poetry Community and Culture of Creative, Caring, and Critical Intellectuals." *Multicultural Education*, Winter 2006.

29. Kass, J. (2003). *My Words Consume Me.* San Francisco 826 Valencia.

30. Youth Speaks. Information available at: http://youthspeaks.org/voice/about/what-is-youth-speaks-history/.

31. Toni Morrison 1998 interview on the Charlie Rose Show. Available at: http://dealnay.com/809642/charlie-rose-toni-morrison-march-16-1998.html; www.charlierose.com/guests/toni-morrison.

32. Haley, A. (1965). *The Autobiography of Malcolm X.* New York, NY: Grove Press.

33. Rilke, R. (1934). *Letters To a Young Poet.* London, UK: W.W. Norton & Company.

34. *Wordspeak.* Information available at: http://www.knightarts.org/community/miami/wordspeak-heats-up-national-poetry-semi-finals.

35. Tigertail productions and Wordspeak. Information available at: http://www.tigertail.org/home.html.

36. Information about the PEACE reach project. Available at: http://www.thefreelibrary.com/Weaving+multiple+dialects+in+the+classroom+discourse %3A+poetry+and . . .-a0141753936.

37. *Gear Up Program.* The primary goal of GEAR UP is to ensure all students in are prepared to succeed in postsecondary education. The GEAR UP program is built on two broad college access components: scholarship funding and early intervention initiatives Information available at: http://www2.ed.gov/programs/gearup/index.html.

38. Kozol, J (1991). *Savage Inequalities.* New York: Vrown Publishers.

39. Freire, P. (1970). *Pedagogy of The Oppressed*: Continuum.

40. Dyson, M.E. (1993). *Reflecting Black: African-American Cultural Criticism.* Minneapolis MN: University of Minnesota Press.

41. Dryson, M.E. (2007). *Know What I Mean? Reflections on Hip hop.* Philadelphia, PA: Basic Civitas Books.

42. Gabriel Benn and the *Hip-Hop Educational Literacy Program (H.E.L.P.).* Available at: http://www.classroomearth.org/node/1358.

43. *H.E.L.P. Hip hop Educational Literacy Program.* Available at: http://edlyrics. com/; H.E.L.P. on www.edlyrics.com.

44. National Reading Panel in 2000. National Institute of Child Health and Human Development (2000). "Report of the National Reading Panel: Teaching Children to Read: An Evidence Based Assessment of the Scientific Research Literature on Reading and it's Implication for Reading Instructions." *NIH Publication. No 00-4769.* Washington, DC: US Government Printing Office.

45. Diaz, M. Runell, M.(2007). *The Hip hop Education Guidebook, Volume 1.* New York, NY: Hip hop Association.

46. *Flocabulary.* Information available at http://www.flocabulary.com/bios. html.

47. Wolff, B. (2006) *Innovative Course Helps Hip hop Into the Classroom.* Madison, WI: University Wisconsin-Madison news.

48. Durand, A. (2002). *Black, Blanc, Beur: Rap Music and Hip hop Culture in the Francophone World.* Lanham, MD: Scarecrow Press.

49. Common and West, L. (2006). *The Mirror and Me.* Chicago, Il: Hip hop Schoolhouse.

50. Cool J, LL and Jib Jab Media (2002). *And The Winner Is.* New York, NY: Cartwheel, Scholastic.

51. Fresh, D. E. and Buckingham, J. (2002). *Think Again.* New York, NY: Cartwheel, Scholastic.

52. Latifah, Q. and Morrison, F. (2006). *Queen of the Scene,* New York, NY: Harper Collins.

53. Smith, W. and Nelson, K. (2001). *Just The Two Of Us.* New York, NY: Scholastic Bookshelf.

54. Youth Speaks-Wisconsin at the Office of Multicultural Arts Initiatives (OMAI) in the School of Education. University of Wisconsin at Madison. Information available at: http://www.news.wisc.edu/12837.

55. *New York Times,* "Sekou Sundiata Dies at 58; Performer of Text and Sound" July 20 2007.

56. AP via Topix.net "Poet, Performer Sekou Sundiata Dies" July 20 2007.

57. Sekou Sundiata. Information about his life available at: http://en.wikipedia. org/wiki/Sekou_Sundiata.

Chapter 9

[1] *Kahil, G. (1973). The Prophet. published by* Alfred A. Knopf.

[2] *A Dream Deferred* in Selected Poems of Langston Hughes, 1990. Published by Vintage Press, New York.

[3] Branch, T. (1989). *Parting The Waters: America in the King Years 1954-63.* New York, NY: Simon and Schuster.

[4] Branch, T. (1999). *Pillar of Fire: America in the King Years 1963-65.* New York, NY: Simon and Schuster.

[5] Branch, T. (2007). *At Canaan's Edge: America in the King Years 1965-68.* New York, NY: Simon and Schuster.

[6] Deasy, R. J., eds. (2002). *Critical Links: Learning in the Arts and Student Achievement and Social Development.* Washington, DC:AEP. Education Commission of the States, State Policies Regarding Arts in Education, Denver, CO: ECS.

[7] Murfee, E. (1995). *Eloquent Evidence: Arts as the Core of Learning.* Washington, DC: National Assembly of State of Arts Agencies.

[8] Herbert, D. (2004). "Finding the Will and the Way to Make Arts a Core Subject: Thirty Years of Mixed Progress, The State of Education Standard." Vol. 4, Number 4, Washington, DC: National Association of State Board of Education.

[9] Arts Education Partnership (2005). *No Subject Left Behind: A Guide to Arts Education Opportunities in the 2001 NCLB Act.* Washington, DC: AEP.

[10] Ruppert, S.S. (2006). *Critical Evidence: How The ARTS Benefit Student Achievement.* The Washington, DC: National Assembly of State Arts Agencies.

[11] Catterall, J. S. (2002a). "Involvement of Arts and Success in Secondary School." In R. Deasy (Ed.), *Critical Links: Learning in the Arts and Student Achievement and Social Development.* Washington, DC: AEP.

[12] Catterall, J. S. (2002b). "The Arts and the Transfer of Learning." In R. Deaey (Ed.), *Critical Links: Learning in the Arts and Student Achievement and Social Development.* Washington, DC: AEP.

[13] Catterall, J. S., Chapleau, R. and Iwanga, J. (2002). "Involvement in the Arts and Human Development: Extending an Analysis of General Associations and Introducing the Special Case of Intensive Involvement in Music and Theatre Arts." In R. Deasy (Ed.), *Critical Links: Learning in the Arts and Student Achievement and Social Development.* Washington, DC: AEP.

14. Education Commission of the States: State of the State Addresses at https:// ecs.org/ The summaries include education related proposals.

15. Goodman, J. R. (2002). "A Naturalistic Study of the Relationship Between Literacy Development and Dramatic Play in five-Year-Old Children." In R. Deaey (Ed.), *Critical Links: Learning in the Arts and Student Achievement and Social Development*. Washington, DC: AEP.

16. Page, A. (2002). "Children's Story Comprehension As a Result of Storytelling and Story Dramatization: A Study of the Child As Spectator and Participant." In R. Deasy (Ed.), *Critical Links: Learning in the Arts and Student Achievement and Social Development*. Washington, DC: AEP.

17. Moore, B. H. and Caldwell, H. (2002). "Drama and Drawing for Narrative Writing in Primary Grades." In R. Deasy (Ed.), *Critical Links: Learning in the Arts and Student Achievement and Social Development*. Washington, DC: AEP.

18. Vaughn, K. (2002). "Music and Mathematics: Modest Support for the Often Claimed Relationship." In R. Deasy (Ed.), *Critical Links: Learning in the Arts and Student Achievement and Social Development*. Washington, DC: AEP.

19. Minton, S. (2002). "Assessment of High School Students' Creative Thinking Skills: A Comparison of the Effects of Dance and Non-dance Classes." In R. Deasy (Ed.), *Critical Links: Learning in the Arts and Student Achievement and Social Development*. Washington, DC: AEP.

20. Tisman, S., MacGillivray, D., and Palmer, P. (2002). "Investigating the Educational Impact and Potential of the Museum of Modern Art's Visual Thinking Curriculum: Final Report." In R. Deasy (Ed.), *Critical Links: Learning in the Arts and Student Achievement and Social Development*. Washington, DC: AEP.

21. Kennedy, J. R. (2002). "The Effects of Musical Performance, Rational Emotive Therapy and Vicarious Experience on the Self-Efficacy and Self-Esteem of Juvenile Delinquents and Disadvantaged Children." In R. Deasy (Ed.), *Critical Links: Learning in the Arts and Student Achievement and Social Development*. Washington, DC: AEP.

22. Ross, J. (2002). "Art and Community: Creating Knowledge Through Service in Dance." In R. Deasy (Ed.), *Critical Links: Learning in the Arts and Student Achievement and Social Development*. Washington, DC: AEP.

23. Barry, N.J., J. Taylor, and K. Walls (2002). "The Role of the Fine and Performing Arts in High School Dropout Prevention." In R. Deasy

(Ed.), *Critical Links: Learning in the Arts and Student Achievement and Social Development*. Washington, DC: AEP.

24. Henderson, J. (2008). "Developing Students' Creative Skills for 21st Century Success." *Association for Supervision and Curriculum Development, Education Update*, Volume 50, Number 12.

25. Epstein, R. (1995). *Creativity Games for Trainers*. New York, NY: McGraw Hill.

26. Epstein, R. (1996). *Cognition, Creativity, and Behavior*. Westport, CT: Praeger Publishing.

27. Epstein, R. (2000). *The Big Book of Creativity Games*. New York, NY: McGraw Hill.

28. Robert Epstein on creativity. Available at: http://MyCreativitySkills. com; www.uwsp.edu/education/wilson/creativ/index.htm; http:// mycreativityskills.com/managers.

Chapter 10

1. Hill, P. (1997). *Coming of Age: African American Male Rites-of-Passage*. Chicago, Il: African American Images.

2. Hall, H.R. (2006). *Mentoring Young Men of Color: Meeting The Needs of African American and Latino Students*. Lanham, MD: Scarecrow Education.

3. Powell, K. and Harper, H. (2008). *The Black Male Handbook: A Blueprint for Life*. New York, NY: Atria Books/Simon and Schuster.

4. Davis, A. and Jackson, J. (1998). *Yo, Little Brother: Basic Rules of Survival for Young African American Males*. Chicago, Il: African American Images.

5. Wynn, M. (1992). *Empowering African American Males to Succeed: A Ten Step Approach for Parents and Teachers*. Marietta, GA: Rising Sun Publishing.

6. Wynn, M. (2006). *Empowering African American Males: Teaching, Parenting, and Mentoring Successful Black Males: Workbook*. Marietta, GA: Rising Sun Publishing.

7. Wynn, M. (2007). *Teaching, Parenting, and Mentoring successful Black Males: A Quick Guide*. Marietta, GA: Rising Sun Publishing.

Chapter 11

1. Baumol, W.J., Litan, R. E., and Schramm, C. J. (2007). *Good Capitalism, Bad Capitalism*. New Haven, CT: Yale University Press.

2. Casson, M. (2003). *The Entrepreneur: An Economic Theory*. Northampton, MA: Edward Elgar Publishing.

3. Gold, S. K. (2005). *Entrepreneur's Notebook*. Learning Ventures Press.

4. Busenitz, L. and Barney, J. (1997). "Differences Between Entrepreneurs and Managers in Large Organizations." *Journal of Business Venturing* vol. 12, 1997.

5. Green Jobs Bill. Information available at: http://www.opencongress.org/ bill/110—h2847/show;http://www.huffingtonpost.com/van-jones/ greencollar-jobs-energy—b_b_77934.html; http://www.govtrack.us/ congress/bill.xpd?bill=h110-6.

6. National Service Plan Fact Sheet. Available at: http://www. thepowerhour.com/news4/NationalServicePlanFactSheet.pdf; http:// www.wnd.com/?pageId=92288;http://www.freerepublic.com/ focus/f-news/2210468/posts.

7. Drucker, P.F. (1970). "Entrepreneurship in Business Enterprise." *Journal of Business Policy* vol 1.

8. Drucker, P.F. (2006). *Innovation and Entrepreneurship—Collins Business Essentials*. New York, NY: Harper Collins.

9. Drucker, P.F. (2008). *The Essential Drucker: The Best Sixty Years of Peter Drucker's Essential Writing on* Management—Collins Business Essentials. New York, NY: Harper Collins.

10. Schramm, C. (2006*). The Entrepreneurial Imperative*. New York, NY: Harper Collins. 11. Budles, A.(2002*). On Her Own Ground: The Life and Times of Madam C.J. Walker.*New York, NY: Scribner Publishing.

12. Hebert, R.F. and Link, A.N. (1988). *The Entrepreneur: Mainstream Views and Radical Critiques*. New York: Praeger, 2nd edition.

13. Pinchot, G. (1985). *Intrapreneuring*. New York, NY: Harper and Row.

14. Bhldt, A, Sahlman, W., Stancil, J. Rock, A., Nevens, M., and Summe, G. (1999). *Harvard Business Review on Entrepreneurship* (Harvard Business Review Paperback Series), Cambridge, MA: Harvard Business School Press.

15. Jarvis, J. (2009). *What Would Google Do?, Collins Business Essentials*, New York, NY: HarperCollins.

16. Stephenson, J. (2004). *Ultimate Home Based Business Handbook (Ultimate Series): How To Start, Run and Grow Your Own Profitable Business*. Irvine, CA: Entrepreneur Press.

17. *Jump$tart Coalition Survey* of Personal Financial Literacy Among Students. Information available at: http://www.jumpstart.org/assets/ files/2008SurveyBook.pdf; http://www.jumpstart.org/survey.html.

18. *Financial Literacy program at Cleveland Central Catholic High School.* Information available at: http://www.ascd.org/publications/books/110058e4/chapters/Financial-Literacy@-An—Imperative-in-Economic-Hard-Times.aspx; http://www.centralcatholichs.org/index.php?option=com_alphacontent&ordering=8&limi tstart=60&limit=10.

19. Karenga, M. (2008). *Kwanzaa: A Celebration of Family, Community, and Culture, 2ⁿᵈ. Edition*, Los Angeles: University of Sanfore Press.

20. *Kwanzaa Stamp.* Information available at: http://www.africawithin.com/kwanzaa/kwanzaa_stamp.htm; http://www.usps.com/communications/news/stamps/2004/sr04_070.htm.

21. *The Black Candle*—a landmark, vibrant documentary film that uses Kwanzaa as a vehicle to explore and celebrate the African-American experience. Narrated by world renowned poet Maya Angelou and directed by award-winning author and filmmaker M.K. Asante, *The Black Candle* is an extraordinary, inspirational story about the struggle and triumph of family, community, and culture. Information available at: http://theblackcandle.com/.

22. *The Black Wall Streets.* Information available at: http://en.wikipedia.org/wiki/Jackson_Ward; http://en.wikipedia.org/wiki/The_Black_Wall_Street; http://en.wikipedia.org/wiki/Greenwood,_Tulsa,_Oklahoma#.22The_Black_Wall_Street

22. http://en.wikipedia.org/wiki/Durham,_North_Carolina#20th_century.

23. *Buying Power of African Americans.* Information available at: http://www.uga.edu/columns/000918/front2.html; http://www.magazine.org/ASSETS/2457647D5D0A45F7B1735B8ABCFA3C26/market_ profile.black.pdf.

24. *The Jamaican Partner or Capital Accumulation System.* Information available at: http://www.docin.com/p-52196499.html; http://www.gdrc.org/icm/partner-sys.html.

25. *Habitat for Humanity.* Information available at:
http://www.habitat.org/getinv/apply.aspx?tgs=Ny80LzIwMTEgNzo0MDozNyBQTQ%3 d%3d.

26. *National Council on Economic Education (NCEE).* Information available at: http://www.councilforeconed.org/; http://www.councilforeconed.org/resources/.

27. *Ewing Marion Kauffman Foundation and the U.S. Department of Commerce's International Trade Administration (ITA).* A new Web-based resource and a series of upcoming symposia are part of a public—private partnership designed to advance entrepreneurship and economic growth throughout

the world. Information available at: http://trade.gov/press/publications/newsletters/ita_1107/peg_1107.asp; http://www.nwbc.gov/idc/groups/public/documents/nwbc/press_release022004.pdf.

28. *Hands on Banking*. Information available at: http://www.handsonbanking.org/en/.

Chapter 12

1. Dryson, M.E. (2007). *Know What I Mean? Reflections on Hip hop.* Philadelphia, PA: Basic Civitas Books.

2. Lewis, David (1994). *The Portable Harlem Renaissance Reader.* New York, NY: Penguin Books.

3. Burnim, M.V. and Maultsby, P.K. (2006). *African American Music: An Introduction.* London—New York: Routledge.

4. Durand, A. (2002). *Black, Blanc, Beur: Rap Music and Hip hop Culture in the Francophone World.* Lanham, MD: Scarecrow Press.

5. Fricke, J, and Ahearn, C. (2002). *Yes Yes Y'all: The Experience Music Project Oral History of Hip hop's First Decade.* Cambridge, MA: Da Capo Press.

6. Guthrie, R.(2003). *Race Music: Black Cultures from Bebop to Hip hop.* University of California Press.

7. Gioia, T. (1997). *The History of Jazz.* Oxford, Oxon: Oxford University Press.

8. Hudson, D. (2002). *Hughes' Dream of Harlem.* San Francisco, CA: California Newsreel.

9. "The Weary Blues" is a poem written by American poet Langston Hughes. Written in 1925, it was first published in the *Urban League* magazine, Opportunity. It was awarded best poem of the year by the magazine. Founded in 1910, the *Urban League* is the nation's oldest and largest community—based movement devoted to empowering African Americans to enter the economic and social mainstream. Later published by Hughes, L. (1945). *The Weary Blues*, New York, NY: Knof.

10. Hughes, L. (1994). *Mother to Son from Collected Poems.* The Estate of Langston Hughes.

11. Keyes, C. (2002). *Rap Music and Street Consciousness.* University of Illinois Press.

12. Yanofsky, D. and Smith, K. (2005). *Flipping The Script: Critical Thinking in a Hip hop World.* San Francisco, CA: Just Think Foundation.

13. *The Prayer, DMX* (2003). Recorded on the Grand Champ Album released in 2003 by Def Jam Recordings. Lyrics available at: hhtp://www.elyrics. net/read/d/dMX-lyrics/the-prayer-Vlyrics.htm/.

14. Hale, J.E. (2001). *Learning While Black: Creating Educational Excellence for African American Children.* Baltimore, MD: The John Hopkins University Press.

15. Jones, E.P. and the Washing Post Staff (2007). *Being A Black Man: At The Corner of Progress and Peril.* New York, NY: Perseus Books.

16. Gardner, H. (1983). *Frames of Mind: The Theory of Multiple Intelligences.* New York: Basic Books.

17. Gardner, H. (1993). *Multiple Intelligences: The Theory Into Practice.* New York: Basic Books.

18. Gardner, H. (1999). *Intelligence Reframed: Multiple Intelligences for the 21st Century.* New York: Basic Books.

19. Vialle, W. (1999). "Identification of Gifted Children: The Effectiveness of Various Measures of Cognitive Ability." *Roper Review* Vol. 14, No. 2, 1991, pp. 63-64.).

20. Vialle, W. & Perry, J. (1995). "Identification of Giftedness in Culturally Diverse Groups." *Gifted Education International* 1999 Vol. 13, pp. 250-257. A B Academic Publishers.

21. Diaz, M. Runell, M.(2007). *The Hip hop Education Guidebook, Volume 1.* New York, NY: Hip hop Association.

22. *Flocabulary.* Information available at: http://www.flocabulary.com/bios. html.

23. Hutchinson, E.O. (1994). *The Assassination of the Black Male Image.* Los Angeles, CA: Middle Passage Press.

24. Black History—Master P and Romeo. Available at: http://www. youtube.com/watch?v=ANzUxL8qknY; http://www.youtube.com/ watch?v=NkKGRcU7J9g.

25. Common and West, L. (2006). *The Mirror and Me.* Chicago, Il: Hip hop Schoolhouse.

26. Common and West, L. (2006). *I Like You, But I Love Me.* Chicago, Il: Hip hop Schoolhouse.

27. Common and West, L.(2006*). Hug Me, It's Okay.* Chicago, Il: Hip hop Schoolhouse.

28. Common and West, L.(2006). *ME: Mixed Emotions.* Chicago, Il: Hip hop Schoolhouse.

29. Cool J, LL and Jib Jab Media (2002). *And The Winner Is.* New York, NY: Cartwheel, Scholastic.

30. Fresh, D. E. and Buckingham, J. (2002). *Think Again.* New York, NY: Cartwheel, Scholastic.

31. Latifah, Q. and Morrison, F. (2006). *Queen of the Scene,* New York, NY: Harper Collins.

32. Smith, W. and Nelson, K. (2001). *Just The Two Of Us.* New York, NY: Scholastic Bookshelf.

Chapter 13

1. National Urban League (2007). *The State of Black America in 2007.* National Urban League, New York, NY.

2. Jones, E.P. and the Washing Post Staff (2007). *Being A Black Man: At The Corner of Progress and Peril.* Perseus Books, New York, NY.

3. Hutchinson, E.O. (1994). *The Assassination of the Black Male Image.* Middle Passage Press. Los Angeles, CA.

4. Thernstrom, A. and Thernstrom, S. (2003). *No Excuses: Closing The Racial Gap In Learning.* Simon and Schuster, New York, NY.

5. Freedom Writers. Information about the movie and story is available at: http://www.freedomwritersfoundation.org/site/c.kqIXL2PFJtH/b.5183373/k.DD8B/FWF_Home.htm; http://en.wikipedia.org/wiki/Freedom_Writers.

6. Wynn, M. (1992). *Empowering African American Males to Succeed: A Ten Step Approach for Parents and Teachers.* Rising Sun Publishing, Marietta, GA.

7. Wynn, M. *(2006). Empowering African American Males: Teaching, Parenting, and Mentoring Successful Black Males: Workbook.* Rising Sun Publishing, Marietta, GA.

8. Wynn, M. (2007). *Teaching, Parenting, and Mentoring Successful Black Males: A Quick Guide,* Marietta, GA.

9. Hill, N. (2008a). *The Law of Success In Sixteen Lessons by Napoleon Hill—Complete,* Unabridged. BN Publishing.

10. Hill, N. (2008b). *Think and Grow Rich: 70th Anniversary Edition-Updated.* CreateSpace.

11. Maxwell, J. (2002). *Your Road Map for Success: You Can Get There from Here.* Thomas Nelson Press, Nashville, TN.

12. Maxwell, J. (2003). *Attitude 101,* Thomas Nelson, Nashville, TN.

13. Maxwell, J. (2008), *Success 101: What Every Leader Needs to Know.* ThomasNelson Press, Nashville, TN.

[14.] Robbins, A. (1986). *Unlimited Power: The New Science of Personal Achievement.* New York: Simon & Schuster.

[15.] Robbins, A. (1992). *Awaken the Giant Within.* New York: Simon & Schuster.

[16.] Robbins, A. (2006). *Inner Strength: Harnessing the Power of Your Six Primal Needs.* New York: Free Press.

[17.] Covey, S. (1989). *The Seven Habits of Highly Effective People,* Free Press, New York, NY.

[18.] Covey, S., Merrill, A.R., and R. R. Merrill. (1994). *First Things First: To Live, to Love, to Learn, to Leave a Legacy.* New York: Simon and Schuster.

[19.] Covey, S. (2005). *The 8th Habit: From Effectiveness to Greatness.* Free Press, New York, NY.

[20.] Griffin, K.J. (2006). *Your Turning Point Start Now.* Dream Builders Communications, Charlotte, NC.

[21.] Griffin, K.J. (2007). *New Days, New Ideas.* Dream Builders Communications, Charlotte, NC.

[22.] King, M.L., Carson, C., and Holloran, P. (1998). *A Knock at Midnight: Inspiration from the Great Sermons of Reverend Martin Luther King, Jr.* New York, NY: Hachette Digital, Inc.

[23.] King, M.L. (1959). *The Measure of Man.* Minneapolis, MN: Augsburg Fortress.

Chapter 14

[1.] Black Youth Project. (2007). *Black Youth and Empowerment, Sex, Politics and Culture.* Available at: http://Blackyouthproject.com.

[2.] California Department of Public Health. (2004). *Infant Whose Mothers Received Prenatal Care in the First Trimester of Pregnancy.* Retrieved January 20, 2008. Available at: http://www.applications.dhs.ca.gov/vsq/default.asp.

[3.] Lynch, W. (1712). *The Willie Lynch Letter: The Making of a Slave.* Available at: http://www.itsabouttimebpp.com/BPP_Books/pdf.

[4.] Leary, J.D. (2005). *Post Traumatic Slave Syndrome: America's Legacy of Enduring Injury and Healing.* Baltimore, MD: Uptone Press.

[5.] Adams, H. E., Wright, L. W. & Lohr, B. A. (1996). "Is Homophobia Associated With Homosexual Arousal?" *Journal of Abnormal Psychology* 105, 440-445.

[6.] Motivational Educational Entertainment (2004). *This is My reality: The Price of Sex: A Look at Black Urban Youth Sexuality and the Role of the*

Media. The National Campaign to Prevent Teen Pregnancy. Available at: http://www.meeproductions.com/reality.

7. CDC, Morbidity and Mortality Weekly Report. "Youth Risk Behavior Surveillance, United States, 2005." *Surveillance Summaries* June 9, 2006, volume 55.

8. Family Violence Prevention Fund (2005). *The Facts on Teenagers and Intimate Partner Violence.* Available at: http://www.endabuse.org.

9. National Coalition Against Domestic Violence (2008). National Fact Sheets. Available at: http://www.ncadv.org/files/NationalFacts.pdf.

10. Jones, S. and National Urban League, (2007). *State of Black America Portrait of the Black Male.* Silver Springs, Maryland: Beckham Publications Group.

11. Jones S., Malveaux, J. and National Urban League, (2008). *The State of Black America. In The Black Woman's Voice.* Ashland, OH: Atlas Books.

12. Health, United States, 2007. Centers for Disease Control, Atlanta, GA.

13. Males, M. & Chew, K. S. (1995). "Adult Fathers an School Age Childbearing." Presented at the Annual Meeting, *Population Association of America*, April 6-8, 1995. [2], 15p. San Francisco, CA.

Chapter 15

1. Rael, P. (2002). *Black Identity and Black Protest in the Antebellum North.* University North Carolina Press. Chapel Hill, NC.

2. Levy, PB (1992). *Let Freedom Ring: A Documentary History of the Modern Day Civil Movement.* Praeger, Westport, CT.

3. Kelley, R.D.G and Lewis, E. (2000). *To Make Our World Anew: A History of African Americans.* Oxford University Press. New York.

4. Fordham, S. and Ogbu, J. (1986). "Black Students' School Success: Coping with the Burden of Acting White." *Urban Review* 18, (3), 176-206.

5. Golden, M. (1995). *Saving Our Sons: Raising Black Children in a Turbulent World.* New York: Doubleday.

6. Hrabowski, F. A., Maton, K. I., & Greif, G. L. (1998). *Beating The Odds: Raising Academically Successful African American Males.* New York, NY: Oxford University Press.

7. Gibbs, J. T. (1988). *Young Black and Male in America: An Endangered Species.* Dover, Mass: Auburn House.

8. Lamb, Y.R. (2006). "The Vanishing Black Male: Educators Tackle Reading, 'Riting, Recruitment and Retention." *Howard Magazine* 14(2), 30-33.

9. Conchas, G. Q. (2006). *The Color of Success: Race and High-achieving Urban Youth*. New York, NY: Teachers College Press.

10. Benard, B. (1991). *Fostering Resiliency in Kids: Protective Factors in the Family, School, and Community*. Portland, OR: Northwest Regional Educational Laboratory.

11. Benard, B. (2004). *Resiliency: What We Have Learned*. WestEd, San Francisco, CA.

12. Lee, V., Winfield, L., Wilson, T. (1991). "Academic Behaviors Among High Achieving African American students." *Education and Urban Society* 24(1), 64-86.

13. Connell, J. P., Spencer, M. B., & Aber, J. L. (1994). "Educational Risk and Resilience in African American Youth: Context, Self, Action, and Outcomes in School." *Child Development* 65, 493-506.

14. Gayles, J. (2005). "Playing the Game and Paying the Price: Academic Resilience Among Three High Achieving African American Males." *Anthropology & Education Quarterly* 36(3), 250-264.

15. Covey, S. (1989). *The Seven Habits of Highly Effective People*. Free Press, New York, NY.

16. Gardner, C. and Troupe, Q. (2006). *The Pursuit of Happiness*. Amistad/Harper Collins, New York, NY.

17. Johnson, E.H. (1998). *Brothers On The Mend: Understanding and Healing Anger for African American Men and Women*. Simon and Schuster, New York, NY.

18. Emanuel Donchin Publications about the conscious and unconscious mind. Available at: http://psychology.usf.edu/faculty/data/edonchin/.

19. Werner, E. E. (1982). *Vulnerable But Invincible: A Longitudinal Study of Resilient Children and Youth*. New York: McGraw-HillNew York: McGraw-Hill.

20. Cicchetti, D., Rogosch, F. A., Lynch, M., & Holt, K. D. (1993). "Resilience in Maltreated Children: Processes Leading to Adaptive Outcome." *Development and Psychopathology* 5, 629-647.

21. Ong, A. D., Bergeman, C. S., Bisconti, T. L., & Wallace, K. A. (2006). "Psychological Resilience, Positive Emotions, and Successful Adaptation to Stress in Later Life." *Journal of Personality and Social Psychology* 91(4), 730-749.

22. Reivich, K., and Shatte, A. (2002). *The Resilience Factor: 7 Keys to Finding Your Inner Strength and Overcoming Life's Hurdles*. Broadway.

23. Luthar, S. S., Cicchetti, D., and Becker, B. (2000). "The Construct of Resilience: A Critical Evaluation and Guidelines for Future Work." *Child Development* 71(3), 543-562.

24. Siebert, Al (2005). *The Resiliency Advantage: Master Change, Thrive Under Pressure, and Bounce Back from Setbacks.* Berrett-Koehler Publishers, Inc.

Epilogue

1. *Association for Supervision and Curriculum Development:* Education Update. Volume 50, Number 7, July 2008.

2. Alexander, K.L., Entwisle, D.R., and Olson, L.S. (2007). "Lasting Consequences of the Summer Learning Gap." *American Sociological Review* 72(2), 167-280.

3. Cooper, H., Nye, B., Charlton, K., Lindsay, J., and Greathouse, S. (1996). "The Effects of Summer Vacation on Achievement Test Scores: A Narrative and Meta-analytic Review." *Review of Educational Research* 66(2), 227-268.

4. Hayes, D.P. and Grether, J. (1983). "The School Year and Vacations: When Do Students Learn?" *Cornell Journal of Social Relations* 17(1), 56-71.

5. Heyns, B. (1978). *Summer Learning and the Effects of Schooling.* New York: Academic Press.

6. Kim, J.S. (2004). "Summer Reading and the Ethnic Achievement Gap." *Journal of Education of Students at Risk* 9(2), 169-189.

7. Kim, J.S. (2006). "Effects of a Voluntary Summer Reading Intervention on Reading Achievement: Results From a Randomized Field Trial." *Educational Evaluation and Policy Analysis* 28(4), 335-355.

8. Neuman, S.B., Celano, D.C., Greco, A.N., and Shue, P. (2001). *Access for all: Closing the Book Gap for Children in Early Education.* Newark, DE: International Reading Association.

Index and References

Rather than add to the length of this book and to save a few trees, we will include the index and references on the website: www.championsforpeace.net